Manchester Medieval Sources Series

series advisers Rosemary Horrox and Simon MacLean

This series aims to meet a growing need amongst students and teachers of medieval history for translations of key sources that are directly usable in students' own work. It provides texts central to medieval studies courses and focuses upon the diverse cultural and social as well as political conditions that affected the functioning of all levels of medieval society. The basic premise of the new series is that translations must be accompanied by sufficient introductory and explanatory material and each volume therefore includes a comprehensive guide to the sources' interpretation, including discussion of critical linguistic problems and an assessment of the most recent research on the topics being covered.

also available in the series

Andrew Brown and Graeme Small *Court and civic society in the Burgundian Low Countries, c. 1420–1520*

John H. Arnold and Pete Biller *Heresy and inquisition in France, 1200–1300*

Martin Heale *Monasticism in late medieval England, c. 1300–1535*

David Jones *Friars' Tales: Thirteenth-century exempla from the British Isles*

Graham Loud *Roger II and the making of the Kingdom of Sicily*

T. J. H. McCarthy *Chronicles of the Investiture Contest: Frutolf of Michelsberg and his continuators*

A. K. McHardy *The reign of Richard II*

Simon MacLean *History and politics in late Carolingian and Ottonian Europe: The Chronicle of Regino of Prüm and Adalbert of Magdeburg*

Anthony Musson and Edward Powell *Crime, law and society in the later Middle Ages*

Andrew Rabin *The political writings of Archbishop Wulfstan of York*

I. S. Robinson *Eleventh-century Germany: The Swabian Chronicles*

I. S. Robinson *The Annals of Lampert of Hersfeld*

Craig Taylor *Joan of Arc: La Pucelle*

Diana Webb *Saints and cities in medieval Italy*

for a full list of titles available in this series, please see www.manchesteruniversitypress.co.uk

THE DIVORCE OF KING LOTHAR AND QUEEN THEUTBERGA

MANCHESTER 1824

Manchester University Press

Medieval Sources *online*

Complementing the printed editions of the Medieval Sources series, Manchester University Press has developed a web-based learning resource which is now available on a yearly subscription basis.

Medieval Sources *online* brings quality history source material to the desktops of students and teachers and allows them open and unrestricted access throughout the entire college or university campus. Designed to be fully integrated with academic courses, this is a one-stop answer for many medieval history students, academics and researchers keeping thousands of pages of source material 'in print' over the Internet for research and teaching.

titles available now at Medieval Sources *online include*

Trevor Dean *The towns of Italy in the later Middle Ages*

John Edwards *The Jews in Western Europe, 1400–1600*

Paul Fouracre and Richard A. Gerberding *Late Merovingian France: History and hagiography 640–720*

Chris Given-Wilson *Chronicles of the Revolution 1397–1400: The reign of Richard II*

P. J. P. Goldberg *Women in England, c. 1275–1525*

Janet Hamilton and Bernard Hamilton *Christian dualist heresies in the Byzantine world, c. 650–c. 1450*

Rosemary Horrox *The Black Death*

David Jones *Friars' Tales: Thirteenth-century exempla from the British Isles*

Graham A. Loud and Thomas Wiedemann *The history of the tyrants of Sicily by 'Hugo Falcandus', 1153–69*

A. K. McHardy *The reign of Richard II: From minority to tyranny 1377–97*

Simon MacLean *History and politics in late Carolingian and Ottonian Europe: The Chronicle of Regino of Prüm and Adalbert of Magdeburg*

Anthony Musson with Edward Powell *Crime, law and society in the later Middle Ages*

Janet L. Nelson *The Annals of St-Bertin: Ninth-century histories, volume I*

Timothy Reuter *The Annals of Fulda: Ninth-century histories, volume II*

R. N. Swanson *Catholic England: Faith, religion and observance before the Reformation*

Elisabeth van Houts *The Normans in Europe*

Jennifer Ward *Women of the English nobility and gentry 1066–1500*

Visit the site at www.manchesteruniversitypress.co.uk/mmso for further information and subscription prices.

THE DIVORCE OF KING LOTHAR AND QUEEN THEUTBERGA

Hincmar of Rheims's *De divortio*

translated and annotated
by Rachel Stone and Charles West

Manchester University Press

Published by Manchester University Press
Altrincham Street, Manchester M1 7JA
www.manchesteruniversitypress.co.uk

British Library Cataloguing-in-Publication Data
A catalogue record for this book is available from the British Library

Library of Congress Cataloging-in-Publication Data applied for

ISBN 978 0 7190 8295 5 hardback
978 0 7190 8296 2 paperback

First published 2016

Typeset by Out of House Publishing
Printed in Great Britain
by Bell & Bain Ltd, Glasgow

To Edward and Ellie, and in memory of Harry Moseley

CONTENTS

FIGURES

ABBREVIATIONS

AB	*Annales Bertiniani*
ACW	Ancient Christian writers
AF	*Annales Fuldensis*
ANF	Ante-Nicene Fathers (online at CCEL: www.ccel.org/fathers.html)
CCSL	Corpus Christianorum Series Latina
CSEL	Corpus Scriptorum Ecclesiasticorum Latinorum
FoC	Fathers of the Church, Catholic University of America
GCS	Griechischen christlichen Schriftsteller der ersten drei Jahrhunderte
J + no.	P. Jaffe *et al.*, *Regesta Pontificum romanorum ab condita ecclesia ad annum post Christum natum MCXCVIII*, 2nd edn (Leipzig, 1885)
MGH	Monumenta Germaniae Historica
Capit.	*Capitularia regum Francorum*
Capit. Episc.	*Capitula episcoporum*
Conc.	*Concilia*
Epp.	*Epistolae (in Quart.)*
Poet.	*Poetae Latini aevi Carolini*
SRM	*Scriptores rerum Merovingicarum*
SS	*Scriptores (in Folio)*
NPNF	Nicene and Post-Nicene Fathers (online at CCEL: www.ccel.org/fathers.html)
PG	*Patrologia Graeca*, ed. J.-P. Migne, 161 vols (Paris, 1857–66)
PL	*Patrologia Latina*, ed. J.-P. Migne, 221 vols (Paris, 1844–55)
Settimane	Settimane di studi del Centro italiano di Studi sull'alto medioevo

ACKNOWLEDGEMENTS

The book you have before you has its origin in a conversation after a paper at the IHR's Earlier Medieval Seminar in 2006, and was written, in Hincmar's words, 'in the few little hours which we have extorted rather than borrowed from our multiple and very varied occupations'. Over the years that followed, we incurred many debts. Riccardo Bof, Karl Heidecker, Conrad Leyser, Zubin Mistry, Jinty Nelson and Karl Ubl all kindly provided copies of their work, before or after publication. Sam Hayes, Karl Heidecker and Gisela Hillner commented on knotty passages in earlier drafts (though any errors that remain are certainly our own), Mary Young and several anonymous readers provided feedback on the introduction and Hannah Probert expertly produced the accompanying map. The Bibliothèque Muncipale of Rheims and the Bibliothèque Nationale de France both graciously permitted the use of images of manuscripts in their collection, while the team at Manchester University Press has been a paragon of efficiency and understanding. Many others have provided assistance of various kinds along the way: but we should especially like to thank Letha Böhringer for her encouragement and support. We hope that our translation will encourage more people to consult her edition, without which this book would not have been possible.

MAP

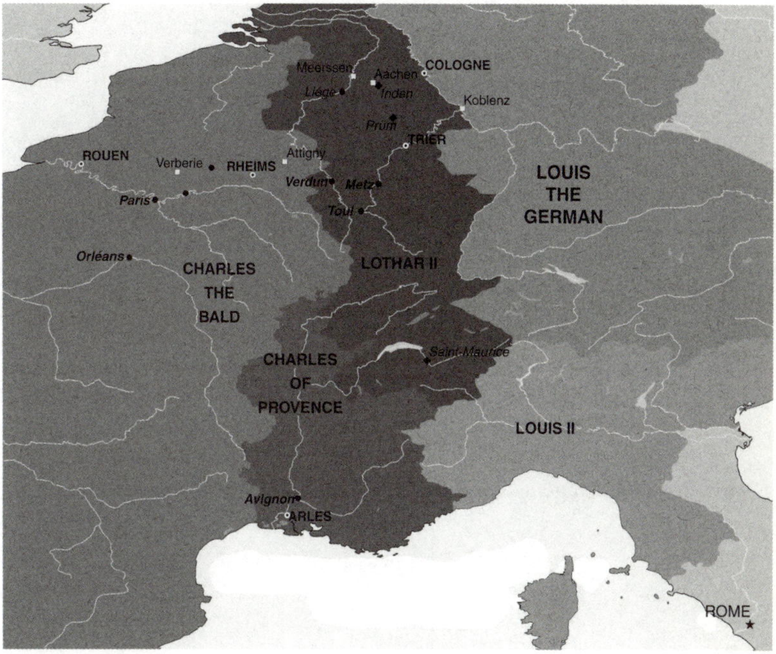

Figure 1 The Frankish kingdoms in 855 (the borders are indicative).

GENEALOGY

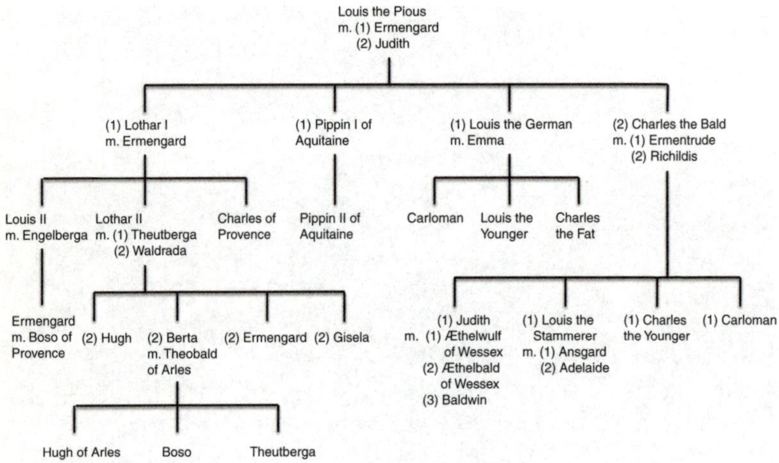

Figure 2 Simplified genealogy of Carolingian rulers.

BIOGRAPHICAL NOTES

Adventius, bishop of Metz

Adventius's family appears to have been relatively undistinguished, but he was an influential figure at Lothar II's court and became bishop of Metz in 858. Though he seems to have been consistently loyal to Lothar II, he nevertheless fostered connections to King Charles the Bald, and played an important role in Charles's coronation in Lotharingia after Lothar II's death in 869. The Treaty of Meerssen in 870 allocated the diocese of Metz to King Louis the German, but Adventius seems to have adapted well to that, too, and remained bishop of Metz till his death in 875.

Charles the Bald, king of West Francia

Born in 823, from Emperor Louis the Pious's second marriage to Judith, Charles was confirmed as king of West Francia by the Treaty of Verdun in 843. Charles took a keen interest in his nephew Lothar II's divorce case, and did not hesitate to interfere when it suited him, for instance by offering shelter to Theutberga. Charles rushed into Lotharingia as soon as he heard of Lothar II's unexpected death, and was crowned king in Metz in 869, though he was later compelled to concede some of Lothar's former kingdom to his brother, Louis the German. Charles died in 877.

Ebbo, archbishop of Rheims

An unusual example of social mobility in the Carolingian world, Ebbo was the son of Louis the Pious's wet-nurse, a connection which enabled him to pursue a very high-flying clerical career. Ordained as archbishop of Rheims in 816, he became caught up in the 833 rebellion against Louis the Pious. After Louis returned to power, Ebbo was publicly forced to give up his office at the Council of Thionville in 835. In 840, after Louis's death, Ebbo briefly returned to his see of Rheims, thanks to the support of Lothar I, but he was soon expelled by the forces of Charles the Bald. In 845, while Ebbo was still alive and attempting to return to his see (he died in 851), a new archbishop of Rheims was elected: Hincmar.

Engeltrude, wife of Boso

Engeltrude was a daughter of Count Matfrid, one of the pre-eminent figures during the reign of Louis the Pious, and was loosely related to Lothar II through his mother. She made an illustrious marriage to Boso, an Italian count who was part of an influential Frankish family group known to historians as the 'Bosonids', and probably Theutberga's brother. In the late 850s, Engeltrude left her husband, perhaps as part of a co-ordinated attempt to curtail the influence of the 'Bosonids'. Engeltrude fled to Lothar II for protection; she probably never returned to her husband, as several popes (and Hincmar) demanded.

Gunther, archbishop of Cologne

Ordained as archbishop of Cologne in the north of Lotharingia in the reign of Lothar I in 850, Gunther was one of the leading figures behind Lothar II's attempts to divorce Theutberga. When Gunther and Theutgaud took the report of the 863 Council of Metz to Pope Nicholas I in Rome, Nicholas rejected the council as invalid; in October 863 he deposed the two archbishops. Apparently abandoned by Lothar II, Gunther energetically contested the pope's decision, but without success. Gunther died in 873.

Hincmar, archbishop of Rheims

Hincmar was brought up in the prestigious monastery of St-Denis, near Paris, and served at the courts of both Louis the Pious and Charles the Bald. A tireless administrator, after his appointment as archbishop of Rheims in 845 Hincmar quickly became a dominant figure not just within the West Frankish kingdom, but in the Frankish Church as a whole, as demonstrated by the appeal made to him by unnamed Lotharingians, which resulted in the composition of *De divortio*. Hincmar made full use of his impressive familiarity with the legal texts of the time in his frequent quarrels with other leading figures, not least his own king, Charles the Bald. Hincmar died in 882 at Epernay, after he was forced to leave Rheims hurriedly in fear of imminent Viking attack.

Hubert, titular abbot of St-Maurice of Agaune

Hubert, brother of Theutberga, was a member of a powerful aristocratic group known to historians as the 'Bosonids'. He was influential in the lands immediately to the north of the Alps (and the titular abbot of St-Maurice of Agaune), and Lothar II's marriage to his sister in 855 was probably designed to ensure control of this region. When Lothar II abandoned the alliance and tried to rid himself of Theutberga, Hubert proved difficult to dislodge. He was eventually killed in 864 by a rival Frankish aristocrat, Conrad.

Lothar II, king of Lotharingia

Lothar II was the second son of Emperor Lothar I, and was probably in his later teens when his father died in 855. His kingdom covered a space later to be named after him: *Lotharii regnum* or Lotharingia, whence modern French 'Lorraine'. Much of his reign was taken up with efforts to replace his unwanted spouse, Theutberga, with his beloved Waldrada, with whom he had several children. By 869, Lothar II's perseverance seemed to be finally about to win out, as a new pope, Hadrian II, indicated that he might be more flexible than Nicholas I. However, on 8 August of that year, Lothar II fell ill as he travelled back from Rome. He died in the north Italian city of Piacenza, and his kingdom was eventually divided between his uncles.

Louis II, king of Italy and emperor

Louis II was allocated the kingdom of Italy by his father, Emperor Lothar I, even before the latter's death in 855. He was generally supportive of his younger brother Lothar II, despite a dispute over Provence early in their reigns; but these transalpine politics consumed only a small part of his energies, for Louis was most concerned with Italian matters. When Louis died in 875, Charles the Bald took over his kingdom.

Louis the German, king of East Francia

The Treaty of Verdun in 843 allocated the easternmost portion of Emperor Louis the Pious's kingdom to his son Louis, for this reason labelled in later centuries as 'Louis the German'. Louis was sympathetic to Lothar II during the early part of his reign, but his support was finely calculated, and Louis on occasion joined Charles the Bald in condemning the morals of their nephew. He later joined Charles in partitioning out Lothar's kingdom after his death, in a division confirmed by the Treaty of Meerssen of August 870.

Nicholas I, pope

The pontificate of Nicholas I (858–67) was eventful, largely as a consequence of Nicholas's own heightened consciousness of the power and responsibility of the papal office. His position on the divorce was consistent from the moment it came to his attention in 860: he saw no justification for the divorce to take place, and was clear that Lothar II could never marry Waldrada. His excommunication and deposition of archbishops Gunther and Theutgaud in 863, unprecedented in recent papal history, demonstrated his resolve and his confidence in his own authority. Only after Nicholas's death, with the accession of the less intransigent Hadrian II, did alternative possibilities briefly open up for the beleaguered king and his supporters.

Theutberga, queen and wife of Lothar II

As a member of an important Frankish family, Theutberga's marriage to Lothar II in 855 offered the king powerful and influential in-laws, notably her brother Hubert. Lothar II soon changed his opinion about this alliance, and began attempts to separate from her within just a few years. Fleeing to the court of Charles the Bald, Theutberga's subsequent reconciliation to Lothar II in 865 was a charade. Even before Lothar II's death, Theutberga became abbess of the rich monastery of St-Glossinde in Metz, and was also abbess of Avenay near Rheims. She was still alive in 876, when a relative bequeathed a medical book to her.

Theutgaud, archbishop of Trier

Theutgaud became archbishop in 847; he was the nephew of Hetti, the previous archbishop. He and Gunther were excommunicated and deposed by Pope Nicholas in 863. Unlike Gunther, Theutgaud seems to have accepted this sentence. He died in 868.

Waldrada, queen and wife of Lothar II

Waldrada was the mother of Lothar II's children, Hugh, Berta, Gisela and Ermengard, some of whom were possibly born before Lothar married Theutberga in 855. Waldrada came from a family that was aristocratic, but perhaps less important than Theutberga's. Crowned as queen in 863, Waldrada was excommunicated by Nicholas I in February 866. After Lothar II's death, she retreated like Theutberga to a convent, in her case Remiremont. Waldrada died on 9 April, but we do not know in which year.

INTRODUCTION

Between 858 and 869, an unprecedented scandal played out in Frankish Europe, becoming the subject of gossip not only in palaces and cathedrals, but even, as contemporary report had it, in the weaving sheds of peasant women.[1] For it was in these years that a Frankish king, Lothar II, made increasingly desperate efforts to divorce his wife, Queen Theutberga, and to marry instead a woman named Waldrada. Despite attempting every strategy at his disposal, including trial by ordeal, orchestrated public ceremony and formal written confession, Lothar II did not succeed; he died on 8 August 869, still married to Theutberga.

Lothar II thereby became the first European ruler to fail to rid himself of an unwanted spouse.[2] He would not be the last; but his failure was unusually weighty in its consequences, for as a result, his kingdom died with him. Today there survives only a shadowy memory of a realm that once straddled the modern border between France and Germany: Lotharingia, the Middle Kingdom.[3] This was a marriage dispute, then, on which rested the fate not just of just individual kings and queens but of whole kingdoms, and whose outcome durably shaped European history.

This book is a translation of the most significant source for this attempted divorce, a treatise known as *De divortio Lotharii regis et Theutbergae reginae*, written in 860 by Archbishop Hincmar of Rheims. In this introduction, we shall introduce the treatise and its author, and discuss some of its implications. It is not an easy work to follow, but it sheds much light on the Frankish world of its protagonists and on early medieval Europe in general. Our first task, however, is to understand the divorce case in its immediate political context, for these circumstances gave Lothar II, Theutberga and all the other participants their parameters of action.

1 Response 3: 122.

2 d'Avray 2015 surveys the royal marriage cases in which the medieval papacy became involved.

3 On the kingdom, see Airlie 2011 and MacLean 2013. The original kingdom, created in 843, comprised a long stretch of territory west of the Rhine, from the North Sea down to the Provençal coast, as well as northern Italy. After 855, it was subdivided into three kingdoms: Lotharingia, Provence and Italy.

1 The political background

Charlemagne's heirs

For a full understanding of the politics of Lothar II's attempted divorce, we should begin with the Franks' most famous king, Charlemagne (768–814).[4] After his brother Carloman's death and the subsequent disappearance of Carloman's wife and children, Charlemagne became the sole king of the Franks. Intensive campaigns of military conquest extended his rule from Catalonia to Hungary, while he also inaugurated a programme of religious and intellectual reform that stressed the need for kings and their subjects to please the Christian God who had helped the Franks to triumph over their enemies.[5] The scale of Charlemagne's subsequent achievement, and particularly his coronation as emperor in 800, set a powerful precedent for later Frankish kings who sought to model themselves on the man whom Hincmar and others already referred to as Charles 'the Great'.[6]

By chance, just one of Charlemagne's sons from legitimate marriage survived to adulthood, and thus to rule over the Franks.[7] This son, Louis the Pious, eliminated a potential rival, his nephew Bernard, with a ruthlessness belying his epithet.[8] But Louis the Pious was more, or perhaps less, fortunate than Charlemagne in the survival of his own children: from his first marriage, three sons (Lothar I, Pippin I and Louis the German) survived into adulthood. Louis conferred the imperial title upon the eldest, Lothar I, in 817; Lothar's younger brothers were also to be kings, but in subordination to him. The situation was complicated with the birth in 823 of a half-brother, Charles the Bald, from Louis's second marriage to Judith. Lothar I, Pippin and Louis the German all rebelled against their father in the 830s, and in 833 they even briefly deposed him, an event that shook the Frankish world.[9]

4 On Charlemagne, see Story 2005; Collins 2010: 280–99.

5 See Costambeys, Innes and MacLean 2011: 65–79 for the conquests and 142–53 for the programme of reform.

6 Nelson 1992: 13; see Response 6: 165.

7 On Louis the Pious, see de Jong 2009, especially 14–58.

8 Louis voluntarily did penance for his blinding of Bernard at an assembly at Attigny in 822: de Jong 2009: 35–6, 122–31. Response 5: 137 reveals Hincmar's presence at this assembly and his recollection of how the case of Northild was settled there.

9 On the rebellion, see de Jong 2009: 214–59. Ebbo, Hincmar's predecessor as archbishop of Rheims, played a prominent part in this rebellion: see 11.

Although Louis regained the throne in 834, conflict within the family continued, and Louis's death on 20 June 840 led to open war between the three surviving brothers, Lothar I, Louis the German and Charles the Bald. After two years of fighting, and Lothar I's long-remembered bloody defeat at Fontenoy (25 June 841), peace was eventually made at the Treaty of Verdun (843), which allocated approximately equal shares of the empire to all three parties. The 'vertical' division of western Europe it entailed (into West Francia, the Middle Kingdom and East Francia) would prove hugely influential in the long run, but at the time it was conceived as no more than provisional.[10] After 843, Lothar I's concerns were primarily with Italy, but both Louis the German and Charles the Bald harboured ambitions to reunite Charlemagne's heritage.[11] Despite several subsequent treaties between Lothar I, Charles the Bald and Louis the German, in which they pledged mutual co-operation, the kings continued in their attempts to undermine each other's position.[12]

When Lothar I died peacefully on 29 September 855, his kingdom was divided between his own sons, as he seems to have wished. The eldest, Louis II, was given Italy; Provence went to the youngest son, Charles; Lothar II, the key figure for this book, was allocated the Frankish heartlands north of the Alps.[13] Louis II felt unfairly treated by this allocation and was looking to challenge it; Charles seems to have been sickly and therefore vulnerable. Lothar II's immediate concern, therefore, was to protect himself against Louis II, while also attempting to take over the kingdom of his younger brother.[14] It was probably this conjuncture that led him, shortly after his father's death, to marry Theutberga, whose brother Hubert was abbot of St-Maurice d'Agaune in Switzerland and controlled the region around key Alpine passes.[15] Once Lothar II had made a peace treaty with his brothers in the second half of 856,

10 Nelson 1992: 132–4.

11 On Louis the German, see Goldberg 2006; on Charles the Bald, see Nelson 1992. Charlemagne's empire was briefly reconstituted under Charles the Fat: see MacLean 2003a: 123–9.

12 For the events of Charles's early reign, see Nelson 1992: 132–80. Response 12: 208–9 refers to a specific clause of the agreement made by the three kings at Meerssen in 851.

13 On Lothar II's activities before 857, see Heidecker 2010: 51–62.

14 Bauer 1994b: 42.

15 On Hubert see Biographical notes; Heidecker 2010: 59–62, 71–2. Response 12: 204 shows him as handing over Theutberga to be married, implying that their parents were dead by 855. Hubert is described relatively neutrally as a 'married cleric' by Hincmar in *AB* 862: 98, and so was probably only in minor orders. The claim by Heidecker 2010: 68 that he may have abused Theutberga must be compared with the statement of *AB* 860: 93 that she fled 'to her brother'.

however, the strategic significance of this region (and hence of the marriage) was greatly diminished.[16]

Though the tensions with his brothers were alleviated, it remained important for Lothar II to secure himself against his uncles. When Lothar I died, the magnates in Lothar II's portion of the kingdom sought support from Louis the German for their new king, and Louis probably formally adopted Lothar II.[17] In March 857, however, Lothar II chose to renew his father's alliance with Charles the Bald; Louis the German responded with an alliance with Lothar II's brother, Louis II.[18] Lothar II may have felt confident that he could play his uncles off against each other, and it was after his treaty with Charles the Bald that he made his first attempt to divorce his wife.

The chronology is somewhat uncertain, but it is likely that the initial charges against Theutberga were made in the second half of 857, and that Theutberga's champion undertook an ordeal in the early summer of 858.[19] As a result of this champion's success, Lothar was forced to take Theutberga back, though she may not have fully regained her position (the *Annals of St-Bertin* claim he kept her in custody).[20] The failure of this first attempt probably reflects political difficulties in Lothar II's court (as discussed below).

The political situation changed abruptly in August 858 when Louis the German, encouraged by West Frankish opponents of Charles the Bald, invaded his brother's kingdom. Initially it seemed that the invasion would oust Charles the Bald, and in November 858 Lothar II travelled to the palace of Attigny, deep in Charles's kingdom, to make an alliance with Louis the German.[21] Charles the Bald, however, was able to force his brother to retreat, and Lothar II then 'hastened' to reaffirm his previous alliance with the uncle on his western border.[22] Lothar II's support was valuable to both his uncles, and he now became a mediator in

16 The treaty was made at Orbe in Switzerland (*AB* 856: 83). Louis II later supported his brother in his divorce attempts, but his interventions were not significant until after 860: see Heidecker 2010: 141–2.

17 *AF* 855: 37; on the adoption, see Bauer 1994a: 20.

18 *AB* 857: 84.

19 Lothar was probably already attempting to rid himself of Theutberga before his unsuccessful expedition against Hubert in December 857. *AB* 857: 84 refers to Lothar 'putting [her] aside'. On ordeals, see below, 36–8.

20 *AB* 858: 87, dating her return to between the election of Nicholas I in April and Charles's siege of Oissel in July.

21 On this crisis, see Nelson 1992: 185–91.

22 *AB* 858–59: 89–90.

the long-drawn-out attempts to reconcile them. After a treaty made in 858, he also became the official heir to his brother Charles of Provence's kingdom.[23] Visiting his other brother Louis II in Italy in late 859, he handed over territory beyond the Jura mountains, both securing Louis's favour and ridding himself of a region dominated by Hubert.[24]

It was in these propitious circumstances that Lothar II began his second attempt to end his marriage with Theutberga, this time relying more directly on his bishops.[25] On 9 January 860 in the palace of Aachen, Theutberga allegedly confessed to one or more bishops certain sinful actions with her brother Hubert, actions that she claimed made her unworthy to be Lothar II's wife.[26] Lothar had reframed his marriage dispute as not simply concerning his role as husband and lord, but as the response of a Christian ruler to grave sins within his realm.[27] In order to support this procedure, bishops from beyond his own kingdom were invited to a council to be held at Aachen a few weeks later (the so-called Second Council of Aachen, held in February 860).

One of these bishops was Hincmar, archbishop of Rheims, who received a personal visit from Bishop Adventius of Metz on 25 January. Hincmar, however, was suspicious of the invitation and declined.[28] Others may have had similar reactions, since in the end only seven archbishops and bishops are mentioned as taking part in this February council. Three of these, however, came from outside Lotharingia, and the council was assembled in the names of Louis the German, Charles the Bald and Lothar II, so the council at least made a nod to representing the Frankish Church as a whole.[29] It was

23 *AB* 858: 87. In return Lothar II granted the counties of Belley and Tarentaise to Charles of Provence.

24 *AB* 859: 91. Schrörs 1884: 183 sees Lothar as hoping for Louis's help in gaining papal favour. Lothar later alleged (Response 1: 105, 109) that it was during the Italian trip that further rumours about Theutberga's conduct were made.

25 Response 3: 122 says that 'many bishops' had already been present at the ordeal in 858: those present included also some of those who wrote to Hincmar (Response 10: 178).

26 There are two slightly different accounts of this meeting: the so-called Booklet of Eight Chapters (Question 1: 96–8) and the Booklet of Seven Chapters (Response 1: 104–6); the latter gives the date. The events of 9 January are normally referred to as the First Council of Aachen, though they may have been merely preparations for the 'second' council in February. The suggestion by Firey 2009: 15–16 that there was only one 'council'/event seems implausible, given the dating of the documents.

27 Patzold 2010: 398–9.

28 Question 3: 120–1. On Adventius, see Staubach 1982: 153–214; Gaillard 1995.

29 Response 1: 107: the three bishops were Wenilo of Rouen, Hildegar of Meaux and Halduin/Hilduin of Avignon.

before the kings, bishops and secular magnates present at this council that Theutberga made a formal confession, and accepted a public penance.[30]

At first, Lothar II's manoeuvre seemed to have succeeded. There were still clerics and laymen within his kingdom who were hostile to his plans, and some of these contacted Hincmar and other bishops outside Lotharingia for advice; the fact that they asked for their names to be kept secret, however, suggests limits to their power.[31] Lothar II's relationship with his uncles also seemed secure; in June 860 at Koblenz, a peace treaty was concluded between Lothar II, Louis the German and Charles the Bald.[32] Yet by involving the Church more centrally in the divorce proceedings, the king had opened the way for a wide circle of participants to claim the right to become involved, and even to revisit the ordeal of 858.[33] Lothar's determination to be rid of Theutberga and his chosen strategy for doing so would prove very costly.

Lothar II's motivations

Three main suggestions have been made for why Lothar II was so resolute in his efforts to be rid of Theutberga. One focuses on his attraction to Waldrada, the woman he wished to marry, and with whom he had probably been in a relationship even before his marriage to Theutberga.[34] A second argues that his aim was to secure the succession, and that he divorced Theutberga because of her sterility.[35] A third view emphasises the changing political significance of Theutberga's family, specifically her brother Hubert.[36] Recently, many historians have preferred the latter two geopolitical explanations; yet these more 'realistic' interpretations are not necessarily easier to square with the evidence.

From the dynastic perspective, Lothar II and Theutberga had no children, and she herself asserted that she was sterile. However, that

30 Response 1: 109–10. Schrörs 1884: 185–6 suggests the involvement of lay magnates was to prevent their later resistance to the decision.

31 See below, 17.

32 *AB* 860: 93.

33 Bauer 1994b: 51; Patzold 2010: 397, 405. The significance of Theutberga's champion's success in the ordeal was debated: see below, 36–7.

34 See e.g. Schrörs 1884: 176–7; Airlie 1998: 3, 11–12. On the relationship, see Heidecker 2010: 52; Karras 2012: 38–42; *AB* 853: 77.

35 See e.g. Brühl 1964: 58–9; Staubach 1982: 119; Bauer 1994b: 45–6.

36 See e.g. Konecny 1976: 104–7; Böhringer 1992: 16–17; Heidecker 2010: 65.

assertion was only made late in the divorce process (867), while the initial allegations against her, which included the claim that she had aborted a child, implied that she was fertile.[37] Moreover, if the problem was the lack of an heir, it would be difficult to explain Lothar's determination to marry Waldrada in particular. Lothar had probably already had children with Waldrada before his marriage, but marriage to another young Frankish girl would also have offered him good prospects of children.[38]

It is also unlikely that Lothar II would have been preoccupied with his succession in 860. At that point, Lothar was only in his mid-twenties, while Charles the Bald (b. 823) was thirty-seven and Louis the German in his mid-forties. Although in fact Lothar II died before his uncles, had he lived to sixty as his father, grandfather and great-grandfather had all done, he would have outlived not only Charles and Louis but perhaps even their sons, and been in contention to inherit a substantial part of the Frankish empire.[39] In 860, Lothar's need for a legitimate son was real, but not urgent.

An alternative geopolitical explanation is to see Lothar II's policy as motivated by opposition to Hubert, whose political value had vanished with the Treaty of Orbe in late 856.[40] In this view, Theutberga was an unwanted legacy of an outdated alliance. Allegations that Hubert was committing 'homicides and innumerable adulteries and disgraceful fornication and illicit and intolerable plundering' in the St-Maurice area may have led Lothar to decide that the accusations of incest with his sister would seem plausible.[41] Yet by the start of 860, Hubert's position had been considerably weakened, and Lothar II had made territorial grants removing the areas under Hubert's control from his kingdom.[42]

37 Böhringer 1992: 13–15: explicit references to sterility first appear in the letters of Nicholas I from 867 (*Epistola* 45, 46, MGH *Epp.* 6: 320, 324). In particular, Adventius of Metz's account from 863 (*Epistolae ad divortium Lotharii regis pertinentes* 5, MGH *Epp.* 6: 215–17; Dutton 2003: 386–9) refers neither to sterility nor to non-consummation of the marriage.

38 On Waldrada's children, see Heidecker 2010: 52 n. 5. The names of Waldrada and three of her children (Hugh, Berta and Ermengard) are entered in the memorial book of the convent of Remiremont. Schmid 1968 dates this entry to the end of 861, but Gaillard 2006: 53 thinks it was written 863x865. Another daughter, Gisela, is mentioned in Regino, *Chronicle*, 882: 187. On the significance of these children's names, see below, 63, n. 404.

39 In 885, the only remaining legitimate adult male in the Carolingian line was Charles the Fat, who thus briefly controlled the whole of the empire.

40 See above, 4 n. 16.

41 Pope Benedict III, Letter to Hubert in 857 (MGH *Epp.* 5: 613).

42 See above, 5 n. 24.

Whereas Hubert and Theutberga had had sufficient political support for the ordeal to be decided in their favour in 858, there was no effective resistance to Lothar's actions at the Aachen councils in 860. By the time Hincmar wrote the first part of *De divortio*, Hubert had already fled to Charles the Bald (although he hung on to some of his alpine possessions).[43]

If Hubert was no longer a significant threat to Lothar II by 860, the latter's determination to achieve a divorce cannot be explained in this way, and makes even less sense after Hubert's death in 864.[44] If, instead, Lothar II's divorce was intended to replace a now politically insignificant Theutberga with a more advantageous marriage, why did Lothar insist on Waldrada as his second wife? Although she was probably noble, her family background is uncertain; if she had important political connections, it is difficult to explain why he put her aside in 855.[45]

These problems with Lothar II's alleged geopolitical motives mean that personal factors must be taken into account. They are certainly amply reported by the sources; Bishop Prudentius of Troyes in 860 talked of Lothar's 'irreconcilable loathing' for Theutberga, Hincmar described Lothar as 'ensnared in a blind passion by the wiles of his concubine Waldrada', Pope Nicholas warned Lothar about excessive passion for a woman, and the questions about love magic sent to Hincmar make clear that others saw emotional factors as key.[46] Such reports cannot simply be dismissed as naïve: Carolingian authors were perfectly able to recognise the political significance of marriages. In Lothar's long-lasting attempts to divorce Theutberga and marry Waldrada, the 'personal side' has to be taken seriously. It was precisely the way that royal bodies combined both personal and public concern that made kings and their consorts different from their subjects.[47]

43 *AB* 860: 93 and n. 7; Response 12: 207. *AB* 864: 121 describes Hubert as 'holding on to the abbacy of St-Maurice and other *honores* belonging to Emperor Louis of Italy against his [Louis's] will'.

44 Airlie 1998: 11–12.

45 Bauer 1994b: 45–6 summarises the debate on Waldrada's origins; see also Gaillard 2011: 305–6, suggesting possible links to the Welf family.

46 *AB* 860: 92; *AB* 862: 102; Nicholas I, *Epistola* 46 (MGH *Epp.* 6: 325): 'pro unius mulierculae passione et brevissimi temporis desiderio'; Question 15: 235.

47 Airlie 1998; Stone 2007b.

Charles the Bald and Louis the German

It has often been supposed that Lothar II's uncles deliberately attempted to sabotage his efforts to divorce Theutberga, by lobbying the pope, sponsoring opposition within Lotharingia, and not least by promoting Hincmar's intervention, all in the hope of inheriting Lothar's kingdom. As already suggested, however, it could hardly be foreseen in the early stages of the affair that Lothar would die prematurely and without legitimate heirs. Nor were Charles and Louis invariably hostile to their nephew. The council in February 860 that separated Lothar from Theutberga was summoned in the names of Lothar II, Louis and Charles, and though Hincmar was not present, two bishops from Charles's kingdom were.[48] The presence of Lotharingian bishops at the Council of Tusey in West Francia at the end of 860 also suggests that friendly relations were still possible between Charles and Lothar II; during the council Hincmar was even asked for advice on a separate marriage case by the Lotharingian archbishop, Gunther of Cologne.[49]

Relations between Lothar II and Charles had obviously deteriorated by 861, but this only brought Lothar II and his other uncle, Louis the German, closer together. At the end of the year, they jointly wrote to the pope to complain about Charles, and Louis may then have celebrated Christmas with Lothar II, and, perhaps, Waldrada.[50] Political possibilities remained fluid throughout the whole period: as late as 867 Nicholas I was writing to Charles the Bald to warn him against allying with Lothar and abandoning his support for Theutberga.[51]

Yet though it is unlikely that either Charles the Bald or Louis the German had a grand strategy, both kings were working in a political framework in which the reconstitution of Charlemagne's Frankish empire was always thinkable and desirable. No one could know what the outcome of the divorce attempts would be, but it would have become clear as soon as Lothar II hit difficulties that there was political capital

48 See above, 5.

49 Gunther asked for advice on the case of Engeltrude: see Hincmar, *De uxore Bosonis* (MGH *Epp.* 8: 81–2) and below, 50. On Gunther, see Biographical notes, and Georgi 1995. Hincmar made harsh comments about him at various points in *De divortio* (see e.g. Response 7: 168–9) but as well as their interaction at Tusey, in 865, after Gunther had been deposed by Nicolas I for his role in Lothar II's divorce, Hincmar helped circulate letters protesting at his treatment (Heidecker 2010: 167).

50 *Epistolae ad divortium Lotharii regis pertinentes* 3 (MGH *Epp.* 6: 212–14). See above, 7 n. 38 on the possible date of this meeting.

51 Nicholas I, *Epistola* 48 (MGH *Epp.* 6: 329–32).

to be made. At the very least, Charles and Louis could extort concessions in exchange for limited support or non-interference, as demonstrated by Lothar II's grants of lands and territories at different times to each uncle. Lothar II himself wrote in 864 that his uncles hoped to acquire his kingdom.[52]

Above all, particularly in Lothar II's darkest days – between 863 and 868 – the possibility that he might actually be deposed glittered on the horizon. Ruling Frankish kings had retired to monasteries before, and in the case of Louis the Pious in 833, had been coerced into doing so, partly on grounds of sexual misconduct within his own family.[53] His uncles watched as Lothar II became increasingly vulnerable to such charges. It is possible that suggestions he ought to do public penance had deposition as a sub-text: after all, Frankish bishops had not formally deposed Louis the Pious in 833, but they had achieved the same end by imposing a public penance on him, rendering him incapable of fulfilling the royal office.[54]

The very fact that Lothar II was unable to bring the divorce to a successful conclusion points to a tenacious opposition within his own kingdom, perhaps the same opponents who requested Hincmar's intervention. Charles the Bald and Louis the German were without doubt working hard behind the scenes to ensure that if the pope were to excommunicate the young king, they would have supporters within his kingdom who could promote them as more morally upright alternatives. By the mid-860s, both had a track record of opportunistic invasions of their relatives' kingdoms.[55] The divorce case promised them much if they played their cards right.

2 Hincmar of Rheims

Hincmar's appointment to Rheims

The author of our treatise, Hincmar, was of noble birth, and related to several counts; he was probably born in the first decade of the ninth

52 *Epistolae ad divortium Lotharii regis pertinentes* 7 (MGH *Epp.* 6: 218): 'in concupiscentia regni nobis'.

53 On the allegations about Louis's wife Judith, see Ward 1990; de Jong 2009: 185–205.

54 *AB* 833: 87–8: the assembly at Compiègne 'harassed him [Louis the Pious] for so long that they forced him to lay aside his weapons and change his garb to that of a penitent, driving him into the gates of Holy Church'. On penance, see below, 39–42.

55 *AB* 861: 96 gives Hincmar's hostile response to Charles the Bald's invasion of Provence.

century.[56] Brought up and educated in the rich monastery of St-Denis, he soon developed contacts with the imperial court of Louis the Pious. After Louis's death in 840, Hincmar supported Louis's youngest son, Charles the Bald, in his battles with his older brothers Lothar I and Louis the German. Hincmar's familiarity with the court and his intellectual talents together probably explain his appointment as archbishop of Rheims in April 845, where he would remain until his death in 882.[57] This was an important role, and shows the trust the young King Charles had in Hincmar. However, Hincmar's appointment to Rheims was not uncontested, since the position was at the time still claimed by his predecessor.

That predecessor was Ebbo, archbishop of Rheims since 816.[58] Ebbo had supported Lothar I against his father in the great rebellion of 833–34, and was singled out for punishment after Louis's restoration to the throne. Louis had previously deposed bishops for treason, but such a charge in Ebbo's case might have raised embarrassing questions about the many other rebels who had been pardoned.[59] Instead, at a council in Metz in early 835 Ebbo 'voluntarily' admitted that Louis had been unjustly deposed, and at the Council of Thionville soon afterwards confessed to having committed a 'capital crime' and resigned from his office because of his 'unworthiness'.[60]

Ebbo was sent to the monastery of Fulda to do penance, but he did not remain there for long. Declaring the 835 deposition an invalid show trial, and claiming that he had not been formally judged, he was able to regain his position in Rheims in 840–41 with the support of Lothar I. He was soon forced to flee by Charles the Bald's military successes, but not before he had ordained a number of clerics, some of whom would go on to become influential figures.[61] These men's ordinations rested on the invalidity of Ebbo's deposition in 835, while Hincmar's position as archbishop depended on that deposition's legitimacy: for Ebbo had still been alive – and claiming Rheims – when Hincmar was appointed

56 On Hincmar's career, see now Stone and West 2015, and in particular Stone 2015 and Nelson 2015: 44–7.

57 On bishops and archbishops, see below, 74–5.

58 On Ebbo's earlier distinguished career, see McKeon 1974.

59 On episcopal deposition, see e.g. *Annales regni Francorum* 818: 148 (Scholz 1970: 104); *AB* 863: 108. It is often not clear from such texts whether a deposed bishop is being removed only from his episcopal office or also from the priesthood.

60 *AB* 835: 32–3. On the events of Thionville, see de Jong 2009: 254–9. Hincmar had been present at this synod (Response 2: 114) and cites one of the contemporary texts discussing the deposition (Response 2: 119).

61 In particular, Wulfad, the future archbishop of Bourges: see Stone 2015: 15–16.

in his place in 845. As a result, the clerics ordained by Ebbo, along with opponents of Hincmar, continued to argue about Ebbo's deposition even after his death in 851, potentially threatening Hincmar's own status.[62] In 860 those supporting Lothar II's divorce were still able to discomfort Hincmar by drawing parallels between the trials of Ebbo and Theutberga; the matter was only finally settled in 868.[63]

Hincmar as archbishop

The archbishopric of Rheims was certainly a prize worth fighting for. Rheims itself was a resonant place for Frankish history: Clovis, the first king of a united Frankish kingdom, had been baptised by St Remigius, archbishop of Rheims, at the end of the fifth century, and Hincmar made much of this tradition.[64] The cathedral was also a wealthy institution, owning estates both in the surrounding region and in distant parts of the Frankish world.[65] Part of this wealth was channelled into supporting the cultural activities of the archbishops, and Hincmar in particular seems to have developed the archiepiscopal library, and to have fostered an active scriptorium, where manuscripts were copied by teams of scribes working under his command.[66]

The archbishop of Rheims also enjoyed leadership of an ecclesiastical archdiocese or province that was a core part of the Frankish world. The bishops of several nearby sees (including Soissons, Châlons-en-Champagne, Laon and Cambrai) were formally subordinated to Rheims, though the precise extent of Hincmar's power over them was uncertain and frequently contested.[67] Hincmar's province included many of the most influential and famous of Carolingian monasteries, in particular Corbie, linked to the production of the Pseudo-Isidore forgeries.[68] It was also the location for many royal palaces, where King Charles, and Hincmar with him, would spend a great deal of time. As such, it was absolutely central to Charles's kingdom;

62 Patzold 2008: 315–50; Booker 2009: 186–209 detail the continued struggles over Ebbo's deposition, including Ebbo's own arguments on the lack of judicial process at Thionville.

63 See below, 44.

64 See Isaïa 2015 on Hincmar's *Vita Remigii*.

65 Stratmann 1991: 45–53 discusses Hincmar's activities in protecting and regaining these estates.

66 Carey 1938; Dolbeau 2012.

67 On the geography and divisions of the province of Rheims, see Sot 1993: 17–42.

68 On Pseudo-Isidore, see below, 23.

through Cambrai, however, Hincmar's province also stretched into Lothar II's kingdom, which brought both problems and opportunities.[69]

Yet Hincmar's reputation did not rest solely on his institutional position, but also on his learning and forceful personality.[70] He was a prolific author.[71] From 848 onwards, he had been drawn into theological controversies about predestination, making a number of intellectual enemies in the process.[72] In 861, he took over writing the *Annals of St-Bertin* (*Annales Bertiniani*), one of our most important sources for West Frankish history.[73] Though not yet the dominant force that he would become, by 860 he had already won a name for himself as an expert in matters of Church tradition, having written substantial treatises on Church property and on the abduction of women.[74] It is therefore no surprise that his opinion was canvassed about King Lothar II's divorce; indeed, Lothar II's supporters claimed that Hincmar had already consented to the procedure that separated Lothar and Theutberga.[75]

Hincmar's motives for intervention

On the face of it, Hincmar's motives for writing *De divortio* are self-evident: he was one of a number of bishops whose opinion had been canvassed by a group from Lotharingia, including bishops and laymen.[76]

69 On Hincmar's difficult early relations with Lothar I, who attempted to remove him from his office, see Screen 2015.

70 Böhringer 2007: 268 thinks that Hincmar's diplomatic and negotiating skills may also explain why he was approached. Böhringer 2011: 148 points out Hincmar's skill at providing theological and canonical justifications for existing Frankish practices, such as the ordeal. On Hincmar's early career, see Devisse 1975–76: I, 115–279; Stone 2015: 7–10.

71 A list of Hincmar's extensive works can be found on the Repertorium 'Geschichtsquellen des deutschen Mittelalters' website, www.geschichtsquellen.de/repPers_118551280.html (accessed 12 February 2016). An increasing number are available in modern editions, but relatively few have been translated into English. Our *Collaborative Hincmar Project* blog, http://hincmar.blogspot.co.uk/ (accessed 12 February 2016), lists known translations and includes additional translations by us of works by Hincmar and his contemporaries.

72 On predestination (whether God had already decided who would go to heaven and hell), see Gillis 2015.

73 On the *Annales Bertiniani*, see Nelson's introduction to her translation. The annals are also important evidence for the early history of Lothar II's divorce; they were then written by Prudentius of Troyes, who was on bad terms with Hincmar.

74 On the *Collectio de ecclesiis et capellis*, see Wood 2006: 804–12; on *De raptu*, see Joye 2015.

75 Question 1: 96; Question 3: 120.

76 Preface: 92.

This group wanted their identity to be kept secret, but we may presume they were either unconvinced by the arguments for Lothar II's divorce and wanted a second opinion, or were flatly opposed to it and looking for ammunition.

Hincmar claimed that he was reluctant to become involved, and did so only because he had a duty to teach others.[77] That should perhaps be viewed with scepticism, but there is no doubt that his position was a delicate one. As we shall see, the rules about marriage were by no means fully established in 860. What is more, intervention in a case outside his ecclesiastical province left Hincmar open to the charge of exceeding his authority.[78] Moreover, there was the potential for papal involvement in the case, since appeals to the pope by Franks were becoming increasingly common in the second half of the ninth century.[79] Hincmar may not have been aware that Theutberga had already appealed to Pope Nicholas before 860, but he did know that Lothar II's court was in contact with Rome.[80] He would have realised that the eventual outcome was very difficult to predict and that there was the risk that what he wrote could come back to haunt him later. It is this that explains why *De divortio* is in general so circumspect: Hincmar was covering his back.

That circumspection has allowed some historians to surmise that Hincmar wrote to support his own king's position by blocking Lothar II's divorce.[81] Yet this seems unwarranted. Hincmar is by no means consistently opposed to remarriage as an outcome in *De divortio*, especially in the part of his text he wrote first (see below, 16–20).[82] His opinion does seem to have hardened during 860, but some of his sharpened rhetoric may reflect his shock at the assumptions underlying new

77 Preface: 92–3.

78 See below, 45–54 and 74–5.

79 de Jong 2015; Hincmar had already had several bruising encounters with popes, including one concerning a marriage dispute: see Stone 2007a: 472. Question 3: 120 reports rumours that he had sent letters via Adventius to the papacy agreeing with Lothar's actions.

80 See Böhringer 1992: 12 on Theutberga's appeal. It is possible that Hincmar was aware of papal involvement by the time he wrote the second part of *De divortio*: see Appendix Response 7: 318. On the planned mission to Rome by Adventius, one of Lothar's supporters, see Response 3: 124–5; Flodoard, *Historia Remensis ecclesiae* 3, 23: 303. Although Adventius is not mentioned as taking part in the Second Council of Aachen (Response 1: 107), Böhringer 1992: 12 n. 72 thinks the trip never took place.

81 See e.g. Brühl 1964: 59; Staubach 1982: 128–31. Ubl 2008: 349, by contrast, sees Hincmar as actively trying to assist Lothar. Böhringer 2007: 286–8 warns against treating Hincmar's views as purely cynical.

82 As Böhringer 2011: 147–9 points out, against Heidecker 2010.

questions that were sent to him, not because he had changed his mind about the case itself. If his intention had been to support Charles the Bald, it would be difficult to explain why he did not shy away in *De divortio* from transparent criticism of Charles, notably for his role in supporting Theutberga's brother Hubert.[83]

More important in motivating Hincmar's response was probably his very strong sense of the duties of bishops towards those committed to their pastoral charge. Marriage, in particular, was a topic that interested him; he saw it as one of the building blocks of the social order.[84] There is no reason not to believe Hincmar when he writes of his concern about the enormity of the issues involved: this was not just an abstruse question about Church law, but also about King Lothar's and Queen Theutberga's souls, and, thought Hincmar, potentially about the souls of countless other Franks too, since kings inevitably set an example.[85]

However, Hincmar should not therefore be imagined as a disinterested fighter for legality; still less as the chivalrous protector of the vulnerable Theutberga (whose potential execution he conspicuously refused to rule out).[86] Some parts of the work reflect attempts to protect his own position as archbishop, for instance in discussions of Ebbo's deposition.[87] He was especially concerned to stop others from misrepresenting his opinions, as they seem to have been doing.[88] Moreover, by producing *De divortio*, he was cementing his reputation as one of Francia's leading Church figures, someone whose opinion needed to be canvassed in such situations.[89] The dossier also made intervention in future disputes easier. His preferred tendency in intellectual and theological arguments was to overwhelm opponents with the weight of his authorities: he now had further weapons in his armoury, conveniently arranged for later use.[90] If Hincmar was pursuing anyone's agenda in writing *De divortio*, it was his own.

83 Airlie 1998: 13, 'Hincmar was not merely a party hack'. See e.g. Response 12: 207–8, where he implicitly criticises Charles for refusing to hand over the fugitive Hubert. On the political implications for Charles of *De divortio*, see above, 9–10.

84 Joye 2015: 194–200.

85 See below, 70–1.

86 See below, 55–6. On Hincmar as a noble fighter for justice and Theutberga, see e.g. Schrörs 1884: 205; Devisse 1975–76: I, 396.

87 See above, 11–12.

88 See above, 13.

89 Böhringer 2007: 275 suggests that one of the reasons that Hincmar refused to attend the Second Council of Aachen was that he would not be in charges of proceedings there!

90 Schrörs 1884: 204.

3 De divortio

Date of composition and circulation

As mentioned above, Hincmar's original spur to writing was a commission: a booklet of questions sent to him and other bishops by a group of Lotharingian clerics and laymen.[91] His answers to these questions formed the first part of *De divortio*. Around six months later, he received a second set of seven questions (this time sent individually to him, as a reaction to his previous comments), to which he responded in the second part of *De divortio*.[92]

Internal evidence provides some clues about the date of composition. The first booklet of questions reported rumours of events from late January 860, when Hincmar was visited by Bishop Adventius of Metz, so must have been written after that date.[93] It was probably sent to Hincmar together with a copy of the Booklet of Eight Chapters, a report of the Council of Aachen of 9 January.[94] The second set of questions, which Hincmar tells us was sent six months later, refers to a meeting of the Frankish kings at Koblenz in June 860, and thus must have been sent in the second half of the year.[95]

It is possible to refine these dates further. At the Council of Tusey in November 860, Hincmar responded to a question from Archbishop Gunther of Cologne about another marriage dispute, that of Engeltrude and Boso (see below, 50), by stating that Gunther could read more about the treatment of those who have confessed in another work of his; he then gives what is almost certainly a reference to the completed two-part *De divortio*.[96] The second part must therefore have been completed before November 860, so given the six-month gap between the two parts, we can narrow down the windows of each part's composition to February–April and August–October 860, respectively.

91 Preface: 92. Question 1's reference (96) to 'all you remaining bishops' suggests that the questions were circulated to a number of bishops (see Böhringer 1992: 20). Question 10: 178: some of this group questioning Hincmar had been present at the ordeal taken by Theutberga's champion in 858.

92 Appendix Introduction: 281.

93 Question 1: 96.

94 Both this document and the first series of questions have eight parts, but they should not be confused. The manuscript of *De divortio* provides the only copy of the texts from these two Aachen councils.

95 Appendix Question 5: 295.

96 *De uxore Bosonis* (MGH *Epp.* 8: 87): Gunther can find more written by Hincmar 'in the 22nd and 28th solutions of the questions, about which I have been asked

Any closer dating relies on less conclusive evidence. It is unclear whether Hincmar received the initial set of questions before or after the mid-February Second Council of Aachen. These questions do not refer specifically to the events of this council, but then neither do they refer to the First Council of Aachen, which evidently had already taken place.[97] Hincmar did quote a record of the Second Council, a text he called the *Tomus prolixus*, in the first part of *De divortio*, but these pages of the manuscript, together with those quoting another version of the First Council, the Booklet in Seven Chapters, were later additions (see below, 20), and so do not help give a precise dating.[98]

The great Hincmar scholar Heinrich Schrörs thought the events of the Second Council would have made some of the first set of questions put to Hincmar implausible or redundant. For instance, the questioners say they do not know Theutberga's offence and imply that she might give a written confession in the future: surely they must have been writing before the February council, when her offence was made public and she provided a written confession?[99]

Letha Böhringer, however, argued that the first set of questions was written after this council.[100] She saw it as implausible that the rumours reported about Adventius's trip to Rheims on 25 January 860 in Question 1 would have had time to spread before the Second Council took place.[101] In her view, Hincmar's questioners may well have deliberately remained vague, to avoid direct criticism of the procedures at the two councils and perhaps also to protect their anonymity, confining their questions to events mentioned in the Booklet of Eight Chapters.[102] She also thought that one of the questions, about the validity of a possibly coerced written confession by Theutberga,

by others', i.e. in *De divortio* Response 22 and Appendix Response 5, both of which indeed deal with Engeltrude. Hincmar's letter is addressed to a synod and refers to Gunther raising the question at an earlier session; this is presumably the Synod of Tusey in October/November 860. Though Hincmar says (81) that the question was asked 'yesterday', the length of the letter makes it possible that it is a written-up version of an oral reply by Hincmar.

97 Böhringer 1992: 22.

98 On the events, see above, 5–6. On the Booklet of Seven Chapters, see Schrörs 1884: 182, who sees it as intended for a lay audience, and Böhringer 1992: 9–10, who thinks that it may have been intended for a non-Lotharingian audience summoned to the Second Council of Aachen.

99 Schrörs 1884: 188.

100 Böhringer 1992: 21–3.

101 Question 1: 96.

102 Böhringer 1992: 21–3.

might well reflect the production of such a confession at the February council.[103]

The strongest piece of evidence that the first set of questions date from before the Second Aachen Council is their reference to the marriage dispute of Boso and Engeltrude. The questioners refer to the discussion of this case at the Council of Toul in 859, but without mentioning that it was also discussed at the Second Council of Aachen.[104] This might indeed imply that they were writing before it had taken place. Without knowing who the questioners were, however, and thus how quickly they were informed about the two councils, it is impossible to be certain on the point.

It is equally difficult to be certain how much influence Hincmar's text exerted, although he claimed it was written 'generally to all'.[105] It has been suggested that he presented the first set of his answers in June 860 at the meeting of Charles, Louis and Lothar II at Koblenz, and the completed second set at the Council of Tusey in November 860.[106] Some historians have identified echoes of *De divortio* in the Council of Aachen of 862, but none of the texts produced in 862 can be definitely linked to Hincmar's work.[107] As discussed below, only one manuscript of the text survives. Yet the fact that the second set of questions were sent specifically to him implies that his position was known to his questioners at least, and Hincmar was also able to assume that Archbishop Gunther of Cologne could access a copy. In any case, wide circulation was not the only or even the main measure of impact: being read or discussed by the right people was more important. However, *De divortio* was a topical work, and it was soon overtaken by events: the intervention of the pope from late 862, and the escalation of the situation in 863, made the work obsolete.

103 Question 10: 178. Heidecker 2010: 46 similarly sees the questions as produced after the Second Council.

104 Question 22: 270. On the case, see below, 50. In Response 22: 276, Hincmar quotes from the *Tomus prolixus* (from the Second Council) on the case.

105 Preface, 93.

106 Böhringer 1992: 26. Felten 1996: 300 points out the appropriateness of Hincmar's themes of peace and unity for the meeting at Koblenz, which aimed to reconcile Louis the German and Charles the Bald. Hincmar clearly could not have read out the whole first part there, since it was not 'suited for reading out' (Preface: 93) and would have taken several hours. On Tusey, see above, 9 and 16.

107 For varying views on the impact of *De divortio* and its possible echoes in later texts, see Schrörs 1884: 205; Devisse 1975–76: I, 386; Konecny 1976: 108, 116; Staubach 1982: 149, 175–7, 183–7; Böhringer 1992: 26–7.

The manuscript

The text translated in this book is preserved in a single ninth-century parchment manuscript, 25cm by 19cm, now in the Bibliothèque Nationale in Paris with the shelfmark ms. lat. 2866.[108] As well as the two parts of *De divortio*, the codex also contains Hincmar's letter about Boso and Engeltrude composed during the Council of Tusey in late 860.[109] It has survived the past thousand years well, but not wholly unscathed. Four folios are missing at the beginning of the book, so the text starts abruptly half-way through an opening set of chapter summaries. This means that we do not know the work's original title, if there was one. The current title was invented by modern editors, and it is unlikely that Hincmar would have used the word *divortium* ('divorce'). This word appears in the treatise only on two occasions, both in patristic quotations, and Hincmar did not think that divorce, as opposed to annulment of a marriage or simple separation, was possible (see below, 51–4).[110] A better title would be 'On the marriage of King Lothar and Queen Theutberga', but the existing one is now too hallowed by tradition to change.

What makes this somewhat scruffy manuscript especially valuable is that it appears to have been Hincmar's own copy of the treatise. Though it was physically written out by half a dozen Rheims scribes and not by Hincmar himself, the manuscript nevertheless brings us very close to the author. Close investigation of its structure and composition therefore helps tease out details about the process of the text's creation that we would otherwise not know.[111]

The first part of the manuscript to be written was that containing Hincmar's response to the first set of questions, in other words Questions and Responses 1–23, together with a conclusion and a preface (written after the main text).[112] The neatness of the text's codicological structure and organisation suggests it was copied from another (now lost) manuscript, perhaps the one sent to the men who had contacted

108 Black and white images of the original manuscript can now be freely viewed online at http://gallica.bnf.fr/ark:/12148/btv1b9078140k (accessed 12 February 2016).

109 *De uxore Bosonis*. See above, 16 n. 96.

110 Response 5: 132; Response 21: 263.

111 Most of what follows is taken from the superb introduction by Böhringer 1992 to her edition. The interested reader is directed there for further details on the manuscript, the additions, the scribal hands and Hincmar's use of his sources. See also Heidecker forthcoming on Hincmar's working methods for *De divortio*.

112 Heidecker 2010: 46–7.

Hincmar at the start of 860: presumably Hincmar would have wanted to keep a copy in his own records for later reference.[113]

As discussed above, Hincmar received a second set of questions in the late summer or autumn of 860. The first stage of the manuscript had probably already been finished by this point, since Hincmar's responses to these second questions were simply spliced in, written on fresh sheets of parchment added to the original codex. To smooth over the integration of this new material, the concluding lines of the original treatise on folio 97v (at the end of Response 23) were erased and recopied out at the end of his second set of responses (after Appendix Response 7). This splicing presumably took place in 860. The preface remained unchanged.

In addition to integrating this second set of questions and responses into his manuscript, Hincmar continued to revise the text and add new material, connecting it to the main body by means of asterisks and reference marks.[114] Some of these additions are simply corrections of errors in copying or in transcription, added in the margins. However, sixty-five additions were more substantial in scale.[115] In some of these instances, the margins of the manuscript were not big enough to accommodate the new text, so the scribes were once again obliged to insert entirely new pages into the manuscript.

These revisions were probably added not long after the two-part text was completed. The fact that Hincmar continued to revise the text so carefully and thoroughly suggests he thought it might come in useful at some point, and it is difficult to imagine him doing this after 863, when the whole context of the dispute had changed. We have included these additions in our translation, marked up with arrows (→ ←). This translation therefore represents a work that was never disseminated in this precise form, but was instead the result of Hincmar's lengthy reflection, spurred on as new sources became available.

Hincmar's sources

Hincmar's working methods for *De divortio* (as with many of his other texts) revolved around his emphasis on authoritative sources. He

113 On Hincmar's archiving practices, see Devisse 1975–76: II, 940–50.

114 Heidecker forthcoming: 'Hincmar used his own specimen of *De divortio* as an assembly of files on different subjects.'

115 Böhringer 1992: 39–65 provides a detailed discussion of the additions.

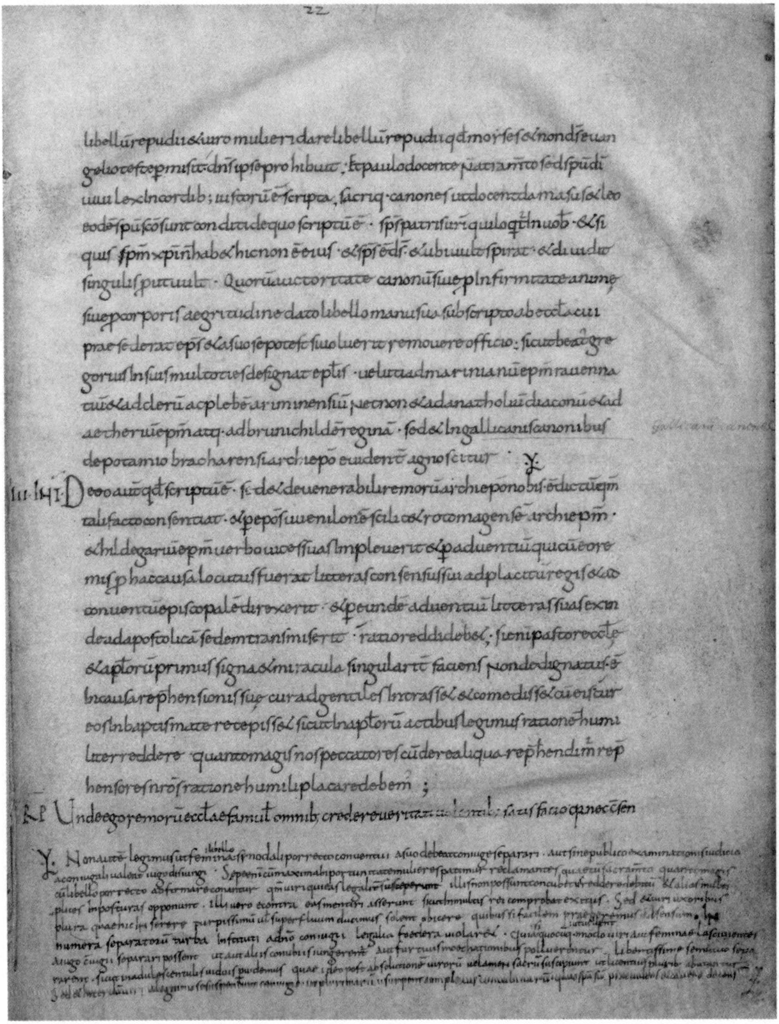

Figure 3 Manuscript of *De divortio*, Paris, BnF, ms. lat. 2866, f. 22r, showing the end of Response 2, Question 3 and the start of Response 3 (translation, 118–121). Note Hincmar's later additions in the lower margin.

stressed repeatedly that he was not replying to the questions on his own authority, but from 'scriptural authority and the doctrine of the Catholic Fathers', texts with which all new decisions must be compatible.[116] Hincmar was concerned that his contemporaries should not pass beyond the bounds of authority.[117] It is not surprising then that a large proportion of *De divortio* is composed of quotations, drawn from a remarkable range of sources. Historians are often inclined to categorise medieval texts into genres ('canon law', 'patristics', 'hagiography' and so on), and to some extent medieval manuscripts bear these categories out, but Hincmar was not trapped within these categories, and used whatever texts seemed to him authoritative and relevant.

That is not to say that he considered all his sources of equal standing.[118] The greatest authority of all was the Bible. In *De divortio*, Hincmar drew on both the Old and the New Testament very heavily. Sometimes he quoted the Bible explicitly ('As the apostle says'), but often he uses biblical wording without direct attribution.[119] Educated clerics like Hincmar had been brought up from childhood reading or hearing the Bible every day, so its phrasing would have come naturally to him. He could have expected his audience to recognise borrowings and allusions without needing to have them pointed out.

Hincmar used commentaries on sections of the Bible written by earlier churchmen such as Augustine of Hippo, Ambrose of Milan and Gregory the Great, and also Bede of Monkwearmouth-Jarrow.[120] He also relied on stand-alone treatises on particular topics, often by the same authors (for example, Augustine's *On the Good of Marriage*), and on their correspondence, notably the letters of Gregory the Great. Some of these works would have been well known to his audience, but others are more obscure, reflecting the growing wealth of Rheims's library under Hincmar. Some of this material he may have accessed through compilations, whether put together by himself or by someone else.

116 Preface: 92; Appendix Response 7: 318. In Response 3: 124 Hincmar quotes his own letter to Adventius of Metz, in which he states that he cannot reply to Adventius about the case until he has consulted the Scriptures and the Fathers, and closes the letter with a quotation from a letter of Pope Leo I. Response 7: 168 and Appendix Response 3: 290 refer to the 'loss of honour' (probably with its twin meaning of personal honour and office) of those going against canonical authority.

117 Response 5: 137.

118 Response 5: 139 refers to some canons as being of greater authority than others; see also below, 30–1 on the relative authority of councils.

119 Böhringer 1992: 265–72 lists all the biblical citations and parallels she has found.

120 See e.g. Response 6: 149–50, 153–4; Janet Nelson is currently working on an analysis of Hincmar's use of Bede.

Hincmar relied too on other kinds of authorities, notably decisions taken by previous Church councils, Roman legal material and, when he revised his text, contemporary or near-contemporary Frankish capitularies (royal edicts).[121] He also used a body of material he may have suspected was contemporary, the so-called Pseudo-Isidore forgeries: a label for a set of material that mixes genuine texts with forged letters supposedly issued by ancient popes and forged capitularies supposedly issued by Charlemagne and Louis the Pious.[122] In *De divortio*, Hincmar mainly used this body of material to support his own positions, though at time he criticises views expressed in it.[123] In order to make a particular point, Hincmar at times also quotes hagiographical texts, elements from royal diplomas and on one occasion even some poetry.[124]

Often Hincmar's quotation of this material does not correspond precisely to the modern printed editions of these texts.[125] This may be because the manuscripts on which he relied had different versions of the text than now survive, and occasionally it is because Hincmar has deliberately altered the text, in the interest of clarification or to strengthen his argument;[126] sometimes though it simply reflects the fact that he was working from memory.[127] Memory indeed should be included as one of Hincmar's sources, since he often brings his own recollections, both as a bishop and

121 Böhringer 1992: 273–5 lists the conciliar texts, papal decretals and secular law sources used. On Hincmar's use of secular law materials, see Devisse 1962; Corcoran 2015; Depreux 2015.

122 Fuhrmann 2001 provides a description of the Pseudo-Isidore collections (including the collection of capitularies supposedly produced by 'Benedict Levita'). Böhringer 1992: 274 lists the relevant passages used by Hincmar. There has been much recent controversy over the circumstances of the forgeries' composition, since Zechiel-Eckes 2001 demonstrated their use of a Corbie manuscript. Currently, suggested dates range from the early 830s to the 840s and 850s: de Jong 2014 provides an overview.

123 He criticises Pseudo-Isidore's prohibition on judging archbishops in Appendix Response 3: 287. Hincmar cites Benedict Levita negatively in Response 6: 163, but more approvingly in Response 10: 182.

124 Response 15: 243–7 includes a long extract from a *vita* of Basil the Great, while Response 12: 216 cites charter diplomatic; Response 6: 150 cites (although not by name) Theodulf of Orléans.

125 His citations can also be imprecise, perhaps deliberately, when he was not sure of his source: see e.g. Response 12: 193, where he simply refers to the 'laws of the Romans'.

126 In some cases the earlier text may itself have become garbled before he received it: see e.g. Appendix Response 7: 321. On changes to strengthen his argument, see e.g. Response 2: 116 from the Council of Carthage 418, and Response 17: 250, where he adapted a text on tracking down Manicheans to sorcerers.

127 As he says in the Preface: 93. See Böhringer 1992: 76 on his use of the Vetus Latina (pre-Vulgate translation of Bible) and Heidecker forthcoming on a key quotation in Response 5: 131.

as a youth, into the argument.[128] As in any age, not everything that was politically important was committed to writing. As a result, the text is scattered with references to hearsay and rumour.[129]

The amount of material deployed in *De divortio* is quite staggering, particularly when one remembers that writing treatises was not Hincmar's full-time occupation, and that it must have been completed within a matter of months, if not even weeks. After all, he was an active member of the royal court and a working bishop with all the responsibilities that entailed, so it is little wonder that he complained about the difficulties in finding time to write.[130] In a world without databases or key-word searching, gathering information on particular topics was no easy matter.[131]

Yet while there is no question that Hincmar was anything other than very knowledgeable – he could allegedly produce a treatise overnight if pushed – it should be remembered that he had a team of assistants working under him who could comb Rheims's extensive library for relevant citations.[132] The library doubtless had a catalogue, and many of its manuscripts were themselves arranged in ways that made reference easier: for instance, Hincmar drew heavily on one collection of Church traditions, the *Collectio Dacheriana*, that arranged its material thematically, rather than chronologically.[133] Moreover, Hincmar consciously and systematically made use of collections he had prepared earlier, ranging from lists of useful quotations to archived copies of completed letters and treatises, all of which were inserted where appropriate into this work.[134] By our standards, Hincmar was a ruthless self-plagiarist.

128 See e.g. recollections of the councils of Attigny 822 (Response 5: 137) and Thionville 835 (Response 2: 114–5).

129 See e.g. Response 1: 105 on the rumours about Theutberga's crime; Question 3: 120–1 on whether Hincmar had agreed to the actions of the Lotharingian bishops; Response 6: 165, where Hincmar reported what he had heard of Charlemagne's view of the ordeal; Appendix Response 1: 284 states that things said secretly must be brought to light.

130 In Appendix Introduction: 282, he complains about the many demands on his time; Schrörs 1884: 202 points out that he was writing a long treatise on predestination at the same time.

131 Response 3: 123–4: one of the reasons Hincmar cannot come to the synod in Aachen is that he needs time to read up on what the Scriptures say on such matters.

132 Hincmar claims that he wrote *De uxore Bosonis* (the only other text in the Paris manuscript) overnight: see above, 17 n. 96.

133 Heidecker forthcoming.

134 Böhringer 1992: 65–74, discusses in detail Hincmar's reuse of his earlier works in *De divortio*. We now accept her argument that Hincmar's treatise on *raptus* (abduction) preceded *De divortio*, contrary to Stone 2009: 437.

Structure and argument of the text

The first part of *De divortio* is divided into eight underlying sections, responding to the questions that Hincmar initially received. These sections were, however, further divided to make the twenty-three responses which appear in the manuscript. The aim was evidently to break up answers to complex questions for the sake of clarity, but problems in doing this mean that questions and answers do not always exactly match.[135] The original sections are as follows:

1 Question and Response 1–3: the procedure at the councils of Aachen
2 Question and Response 4–5: rules on marriage, divorce and remarriage
3 Question and Response 6–9: the validity of ordeals
4 Question and Response 10–11: the next steps in Theutberga's case
5 Question and Response 12: the sodomy charge
6 Question and Response 13–17: Lothar's relationship with Waldrada and sorcery
7 Question and Response 18–21: Lothar's possibilities of remarriage
8 Question and Response 22–23: the response of bishops towards appeals to them and the case of Engeltrude.[136]

The second part deals with seven further questions which Hincmar received six months after the first:

Appendix Question and Response 1–3, 6: who is able to judge the king?
Appendix Question and Response 4: can the king avoid further judgement in the case?
Appendix Question and Response 5: the case of Engeltrude
Appendix Question and Response 7: the effects of communion with the king.

Since the text's structure was determined by the questions put to him, Hincmar does not treat the problems in a systematic way. Moreover, as he develops certain points, material that is not strictly relevant to Theutberga's case is also worked in.[137] The fact that he wrote in some

135 Böhringer 1992: 37–8.

136 See 50.

137 As he himself admits in the Preface: 93 'things which perhaps do not pertain to this matter' and Response 14: 233 'although we were not asked about it [choosing between two evils]'. For example, see the discussion in Response 6: 152–6 of the ordeal by cold water, and Response 12: 209–17, on the king's responsibility to abide by written promises in charters.

haste, as he himself tells us, is doubtless responsible for the 'disordered order of responses';[138] he was also reluctant to offer hostages to fortune in the shape of definitive judgements (as discussed above, 14). All this makes the overall argument of the work difficult to grasp.

Hincmar's arguments are also sometimes difficult to follow because of how he used the many authorities he cited. Parts of *De divortio* are akin to *florilegia*, collections of passages from the Fathers with only a brief framework provided by the compiler himself. For example, Hincmar follows an extract dealing with confession, taken from the Booklet of Eight Chapters (one of the documents sent to him by his questioners), with quotations from the Psalms on the need to confess humbly, plus a sentence of exegesis from Gregory the Great on one of these texts.[139] None of this directly addresses the procedural validity of Lothar's case; the aim is more to demonstrate Hincmar's knowledge and orthodoxy. Similarly, in Response 4 he reused a substantial part of a dossier of citations he had collected on how marriage might be entered into.[140] This material is not relevant to Lothar and Theutberga's marriage, nor did Hincmar claim that it was. Hincmar's later additions to the text make this accumulation of sources of only tangential relevance even more noticeable, but it was already present at an earlier stage.[141]

In the urge to amass a weight of sources, texts describing slightly different situations are juxtaposed and taken as equivalent; only rarely does Hincmar explore the contradiction between his citations.[142] What is more, Hincmar exercised great freedom in how he interpreted these texts, sometimes without respecting the context of their original production. For instance, he applied papal letters dealing with a Late Antique society in which only slaves could be concubines to a Frankish world in which free woman could also have this status, and applied to kings rules developed

138 Preface: 93. Response 12: 192–5 cites passages on a variety of different sexual sins, without any obvious order.

139 Response 1: 100.

140 Response 4: 126–9. Böhringer 1990 and Böhringer 1992: 66–8 give detailed descriptions of the complex textual transmission of this collection; Heidecker forthcoming discusses its reworking in *De divortio*.

141 See Böhringer 1992: 71–2 on the 'perjury dossier' of citations added to Response 6: 146–50 despite their lack of relevance to the specific case. Hincmar subsequently reworked this collection of citations several times in other texts.

142 For example, Hincmar seems to refer to the Council of Worms 829 as authoritative in Response 5: 133 and as dubious in Response 6: 163. In Response 17, 252–3, Hincmar cites contradictory decisions on the *viaticum* and then implicitly ignores the decision he does not approve. But see Response 22: 274 for an attempt to reconcile two sources.

for bishops.[143] Hincmar was not always innovating here, for by his day, layers of interpretation of authoritative texts had developed, as successive authors cited and reworked earlier views over centuries.[144] Hincmar saw such reinterpretation of Scripture (and other texts) as acceptable, provided it remained compatible with Church tradition.[145] This caveat allowed him to maintain his own freedom of argument, while complaining about supposedly 'perverse' interpretations of texts by others.[146]

Nevertheless, although the text's overall effect may be weakened by its arrangement, Hincmar was quite capable of making a sharp logical argument, and he scored a number of points at the expense of Lothar and his episcopal supporters. For example, the Lotharingian presentation of Theutberga's offences as unheard of and novel was used by Hincmar to argue that therefore the whole Church was affected by them and so a general council was required.[147] A reference to laymen being aware of Theutberga's offences led Hincmar to demand that they should judge her case.[148] Hincmar also repeatedly pointed out inconsistencies in the procedures used. If Lothar had known Theutberga was not a virgin when he married her, why had he not complained at the time?[149] If Theutberga had confessed secretly to Gunther, why had he allowed the ordeal to take place?[150] Hincmar's text shows a man ready and able to take part in textual battles.

4 Law and justice

De divortio has traditionally been interpreted as a legal text, and Hincmar certainly has much to say about law and the procedure to be followed in settling disputes. Yet we must be careful not to overschematise. The Franks had at their disposal several overlapping methods

143 See below, 48. For bishops and kings, see Response 12: 209. Cf. Appendix Response 7: 306–7; and see below, 71–2.

144 In an extreme example, Response 15: 240 cites Bede quoting Augustine on a passage in Luke in which Jesus discusses the fate of Sodom.

145 Response 6: 156, 165.

146 See e.g. Response 1: 113 claiming that the *Tomus prolixus*'s citation of authorities does not support the synod's procedure; Response 7: 168 on Gunther using Leviticus to justify a breach of the confessional; Response 12: 196, 207–8, on abuse of biblical verses to claim that sexual sins outside the body are not sodomy and that sinners need not to be returned to a kingdom from which they have fled.

147 See below, 51.

148 See below, 50.

149 Response 12: 201: see below, 58.

150 Response 7: 168.

for dealing with wrongful activity, not all of which we would consider as 'legal': which of these was used in particular circumstances perhaps depended more on practicalities, in the context of the overarching importance of God's justice, than on strict categorisation.[151]

In broad terms, Hincmar distinguished between two routes for formal dispute resolution: secular or worldly law on the one hand, and ecclesiastical or Church law on the other.[152] In fact, one of his criticisms of the way Theutberga's accusation had been handled was that it had blurred the lines between them: Hincmar argued against bishops acting in a 'legal' capacity in Theutberga's case, and suggested a lay tribunal should summon her brother Hubert and investigate the alleged offences.[153] Yet such a neat procedural division between 'secular matters' and 'Church matters', and royal or secular law and canon or Church law, seldom held in practice, despite Hincmar and other Carolingian authors' insistence that it should. Nor was Hincmar necessarily consistent on which courts should hear different cases: in 868 he argued that a bishop (Hincmar of Laon) could not be subjected to secular courts, but although Hubert was a cleric and so theoretically specially subject to Church discipline, neither Hincmar nor anyone else ever mentioned this point in discussions of Theutberga's case.[154]

Recent studies of early medieval disputes have moved away from a tradition of legal history that presumed a coherent legal system and sought to uncover it through law codes and other normative sources.[155] Instead, emphasis has turned to law in practice: how disputes were settled flexibly, drawing on a variety of judicial and extrajudicial means of actions and influenced more by general norms than specific laws.[156] *De divortio* should be interpreted in a similar way: it is not a simple application of existing legal procedures to a case, but the creative discussion of a variety of legal and penitential concepts to ensure that justice (or at least Hincmar's idea of it) was done.

151 Cf. Firey 2009: 58–9.

152 See e.g. Response 19: 256: 'Christian laws, that is secular (*forenses*) and ecclesiastical ones'.

153 Response 2: 117; Response 12: 204–8.

154 On Hincmar's statements concerning Hincmar of Laon, see McKeon 1978: 24–8; on his arguments on the appropriate forum for marriage cases, see 50–1.

155 This traditional view of the 'official' structures and procedures of the Carolingian secular legal system is summarised in Ganshof 1965; Ganshof 1968: 71–97.

156 Davies and Fouracre 1986 is fundamental; see also Brown 2001 for an extended study of Carolingian disputes and Böhringer 2007, which shows similar principles at work in decisions by church councils.

Sources of secular and Church law

Hincmar accepted the general principle of 'secular' law courts, presided over by the king or his representatives.[157] Providing their judgements were compatible with Christian teaching, Hincmar thought they were binding, and argued that no one could simply evade their authority, not even by claiming sanctuary in a church.[158] He acknowledged the authority of Frankish and imperial Roman forms of secular law, even if they had been issued by pagan rulers;[159] he also accepted the existence of multiple laws for different ethnic groups.[160] The validity of all these laws, however, rested on their consonance with Christian teachings.[161] Such laws were authoritative because emperors and kings had been given authority by God to repress evildoers, as represented by their anointing.[162]

Clerics might demand that rulers promulgate laws on Church matters, but for the most part, formal disputes over Church order were dealt with separately.[163] From New Testament times, Church leaders had disciplined members of their congregations via household assemblies.[164] As the religion's institutional structures hardened, bishops became authoritative figures for dispute resolution, as embodied in the Late Antique idea of the *audientia episcopalis* (the bishop's tribunal).[165] The

157 Response 11: 189: 'Christian and fair judgements about secular matters are to be expected from secular men'; 190: 'questions of secular business are to be sorted out through legal trials – that is, just and Christian ones'. Appendix Response 7: 322: the existence of a 'people without law' (*populus sine lege*) is the fault of kings, not bishops.

158 Response 12: 207–9; Response 22: 271–3.

159 On Hincmar's knowledge of and attitudes to secular law, both Frankish and Roman, see above 23; On the association of kings specifically with Roman law, see e.g. Response 12: 209. Response 21: 268 refers to the 'natural' understanding of law by pagan rulers.

160 Response 5: 142, Response 12: 202. On the plurality of law in the Carolingian empire, see Faulkner 2016.

161 Response 5: 142: on Judgement Day people will be judged by 'divine laws', but 'public laws should be Christian'.

162 On anointing, see Response 12: 209; de Jong 2005: 106–8.

163 Response 5: 133.

164 Hincmar frequently discusses St Paul's judgement on a Corinthian man who had married his stepmother: see e.g. Response 10: 180; Response 13: 231; Appendix Response 3: 287; Appendix Response 7: 316. Such informal procedures needed to be reconciled with later more legalistic views of church discipline: see e.g. Response 10: 179.

165 On the Late Antique role of the *audientia episcopalis*, see the chapters by Harries, Lenski and Dossey in Mathisen 2001. Carolingian references to this tribunal are largely to the right of clerics to be judged by bishops.

Council of Nicaea in 325 for the first time brought together bishops from across the empire for the formal settlement of a number of disputes.[166] Councils continued to be important in the post-Roman world, whether limited to the bishops and clergy of one province or covering a wider area, and they issued collective judgements on contentious cases. In the course of issuing these judgements, these councils often produced texts known as canons, rules applicable not just to a singular case but more broadly within the Church. Hincmar drew on such canons very heavily in *De divortio*.[167]

The mass of material available, however, presented some problems, since there was no single authorised collection of conciliar canons, but rather a great many important works that circulated in various versions, with every manuscript offering a unique combination of texts, often reworded during copying.[168] Since there was no fixed set of authorities, Carolingian scholars could never be sure whether they had taken account of all relevant norms, which in any case sometimes contradicted each other.[169] As a way of negotiating this complexity, Hincmar, like others, applied a rough hierarchy.[170] The so-called ecumenical councils from Late Antiquity were unquestionably the most important, and the better attended the council, the more authoritative. Hincmar never, though, defined exactly what distinguished a 'general' from a 'provincial' council, and it is not clear, for example, why he did not consider the Second Council of Aachen to have been a general council.[171]

These criteria were not enough to remove all the contradictions and inconsistencies. Hincmar dealt with some of these by arguing that

166 Hincmar regarded this council's decisions as being unchangeable: see Appendix Response 7: 317; Sieben 1984: 99–100.

167 On Hincmar's attitudes to councils generally, see Sieben 1984: 75–112.

168 Kéry 1999 provides an overview of early medieval collections of canons, but her classification probably overstates their coherence. Böhringer 1992: 81–2, 85–90 provides details of Hincmar's use of such collections. On the rewording of canons, which might change their meaning, see Leyser 2016 and below, 62.

169 Patzold 2010: 405. Böhringer 2011: 150: the existence of contradictory canons meant that pre-Gratian authors had to pick and choose between them. Hincmar does this implicitly in Response 17: 252–3.

170 Explicitly in Response 22: 275: 'more councils or those of greater authority'; cf. Response 5: 139. Appendix Response 2: 286 sets out his theoretical hierarchy for appeals: provincial synods, general synods and then the papacy: see below, 74–5.

171 Schmitz 1979: 53–4 points out the lack of clarity in Hincmar's references to different type of councils, and sees this (27–8) as typical of most Carolingian thought on the topic.

some council decisions might be only applicable to particular times and situations, rather than universally.[172] The presumption that decisions were valid only if they were 'not against faith or religion', 'rationally approved' or 'reasonable and in accordance with the ecclesiastical rules', gave further leeway to pick and choose between texts.[173] Hincmar saw contemporary Church councils as able, indeed obliged, to make decisions on matters that existing canons did not cover; nevertheless if the resulting canons displeased him, such as the Booklet of Seven Chapters from the First Council of Aachen, they could simply be dismissed as unreasonable, or even potentially inauthentic.[174]

Moreover, Hincmar did not distinguish consistently between what we would call the theological (a category that only emerged in the twelfth century) and the legal. Canons and papal decretals (letters judging cases) were not the only relevant texts for resolving ecclesiastical disputes. His comments on appropriate procedure, for example, drew on a mix of Gregory the Great's letters, conciliar texts and biblical precedents such as Susanna and the woman taken in adultery.[175] We should not presuppose the existence of a neat ecclesiastical system; this did not emerge until the thirteenth century – if indeed even then.

Punishment and correction

In part thanks to their origin in separate traditions, secular and ecclesiastical fora varied in the punishment they imposed on guilty parties. Secular courts could impose corporal punishment, including capital punishment; Lothar II's original choice in 858 to deal with Theutberga in a royal court may have been with this in mind, for had she been found guilty, the death penalty would have been a possibility.[176] In these

172 Response 22: 274–5.

173 Response 22: 274; Appendix Response 3: 289, citing the Council of Nicaea, c. 5. Hincmar's views were firmly in the Late Antique tradition of denouncing 'robber councils', such as the Second Council of Ephesus, condemned by Pope Leo I (Appendix Response 2: 285).

174 Response 1: 107. On Carolingian councils making new norms, see Böhringer 2007: 276. The compilers of Carolingian concilar acts exercised considerable freedom in doing so: see Ubl 2014 on the different versions of the canons of the Council of Tribur in 895.

175 See e.g. Response 10: 178–80, 186–7; Response 11: 188; Response 21: 268–9. Hincmar frequently cited the biblical story of Susanna (Response 5: 143; Response 10 185; Response 11: 188; Response 21: 269); this is discussed by Devisse 1975–76: I, 402 and Firey 2009: 44–7.

176 See below, 54–64 on the offences and their penalties. Cf. *AB* 846: 63 on a man being executed for bestiality.

circumstances, Lothar II could have argued that to defend her or commute her punishment would itself be a dereliction of duty imperilling the realm. Several Carolingian bishops (including Hincmar) argued on other occasions that a king must severely punish any of his relatives found guilty of serious crimes, with death if necessary.[177]

In contrast, while ecclesiastical courts and councils could remove clerics from their office or degrade them, and could impose corporal punishment on those in religious life, they had relatively few sanctions for lay people. They could impose penance, but this was in principle only undertaken by the sinner voluntarily (though see below, 40). The only other option was one of the Church's oldest tools: excommunication, which had begun in the New Testament Church as social exclusion from the Christian community.[178] Augustine of Hippo regarded excommunication as the Church's equivalent of the death penalty, but in societies ruled by a Christian king, and where everyone was part of a single Church, excommunication took on new meanings.[179] Exclusion from the Church, now with society-wide effects, appeared increasingly as a temporary sanction, to force the contumacious into accepting penance, and in Francia from the sixth century became enmeshed with secular forms of power.[180]

For Hincmar, excommunication retained a 'medicinal' dimension, as a healing punishment imposed with the aim of leading the sinner back into reconciliation with the Church, for the sinner's own benefit.[181] Nevertheless, a sentence of excommunication was so severe as to be difficult to use in the ninth century. Hincmar argued that it could not be imposed simply on the basis of a secret confession, but needed either a public confession or conviction.[182] What is more, the 'contagious' effect of excommunication, by which those who refused to ostracise the excommunicated incurred the

177 On Hincmar's use of Augustine to justify executing royal relatives, see Stone 2012: 79–80; Stone 2015: 5.

178 On the anathema, a theoretically distinct and more severe penalty that meant 'eternal death' for those penalised, and which is occasionally mentioned in *De divortio* (Response 5: 161; Response 12: 205, 217, 219; Response 17: 251), see Vodola 1986: 14–16.

179 Response 2: 116; Response 12: 218; Response 13: 231.

180 On excommunication as temporary, see e.g. Response 9: 177. On its connections to secular power, see Vodola 1986: 12–14. Response 13: 228–9 shows a series of moves in dealing with a sinner, starting with episcopal warnings, then royal coercion and finally excommunication.

181 Response 5: 135; Response 10: 182; Response 13: 227–31; Appendix Response 7: 305–6.

182 Response 10: 179; cf. Response 1: 102; Response 5: 135.

sentence themselves, meant it was dangerous to excommunicate the powerful.[183] If people ignored episcopal orders and continued to associate with those excluded by excommunication, the credibility of the sanction might be undermined; moreover, many people's eternal salvation might be put at risk. Thus, although Hincmar often used sentences of excommunication on his enemies, he never imposed it on a king.[184]

Justice and oaths

Hincmar, then, made distinctions, albeit not always consistently, between different sources of law, and different ways of reaching a legal resolution. However, all these distinctions were ultimately transcended by the underlying notion of divine justice.[185] For Hincmar and his contemporaries, the innocent had to be protected and wrongdoers punished in all contexts. All judgements had to be just and impartial, following the example of the only truly just judge, God.[186] There must be no 'taking account of persons', that is either deferring to the rich and powerful from fear or desire for favour, or being unduly lenient towards the poor, for this was 'bad' mercy, dangerous for all concerned.[187] Family ties must similarly be ignored.[188] These rules were not a matter of narrow legality, and applied equally to Christian rulers and to Church leaders.[189]

The overriding importance of justice ensured that the distinction between secular and ecclesiastical law could not be an absolute one.[190]

183 Vodola 1986: 5–9, 16–17. cf. Appendix Response 7: 314–5.

184 See Vodola 1986: 15–18; Screen 2015: 85–6. Perhaps as a result of Hincmar's frequent excommunications, some ninth-century texts, including Pseudo-Isidore, lessened the penalties for associating with an excommunicate (Vodola 1986: 17–18).

185 On Carolingian ideas of justice, see Fouracre 1995; McKitterick 1997; Stone 2012: 159–73. Appendix Response 4: 294: even if someone 'cannot legally be convicted' for a crime, they will not escape God the Judge.

186 Preface: 87–9; Response 12: 202. The same principles applied when giving penance (Response 13: 224, 230).

187 On respecting of persons, see Preface: 88; Response 12: 202; Response 13: 223–4; Appendix Response 6: 304. On 'bad' mercy, see Response 12: 218; Response 22: 274–6; Appendix Response 5: 296. Response 1: 102 shows God telling Samuel not to weep for Saul, since He had rejected him.

188 Appendix Response 5: 296.

189 On kings' relationship to law, see below, 70. Hincmar frequently quotes Proverbs 8:15 on kings ruling through divine wisdom (Response 5: 134; Response 13: 222; Appendix Response 6: 300).

190 Cf. Firey 2009: 47: 'For Hincmar, penitential confession and the judicial ordeal had the same purpose: the affirmation of the truth known to God.' Response 13: 228–9 combines Gospel instructions for how the Church should deal with sinners with appeals to 'the royal power'.

Hincmar several times highlighted the parallels between Roman law and Old Testament rules, using a text (the *Mosaicarum et Romanarum legum collatio*) probably written by a fourth-century Christian author.[191] There was plenty of this kind of crossover in the Frankish world. Church canons could be incorporated into royal capitularies, while ecclesiastical courts cited secular law in their decisions, and Frankish emperors worked together with ecclesiastical councils.[192] A secular judgement on a person could be sufficient proof for excommunication, and conversely, ecclesiastical laws about trial *in absentia* could be applied to the demand for Hubert's appearance before a secular court.[193] Rules about the good character required of accusers and witnesses easily crossed from one tradition to another;[194] so did expectations about the need for 'proof' of a charge.[195]

In fact many key Frankish legal procedures are difficult to categorise as either secular or ecclesiastical. Oaths, for example, were an important element in ninth-century Frankish society in both secular and ecclesiastical procedure.[196] They might be used to assert innocence, whether of oneself (purgation), or on behalf of somebody else (compurgation) as a kind of character witness. Hincmar was keen to justify such oaths in the face of New Testament prohibitions on swearing, which he interpreted as merely banning *unnecessary* oaths: oaths were useful in 'doubtful and obscure matters' or where there were no reliable witnesses.[197] In *De divortio*, he was especially concerned with the relationship of oaths to

191 Response 12: 193, 204–5. On this text, see Frakes 2011; Corcoran 2015: 140–1. The ninth-century manuscript Berlin, Staatsbibliothek, Lat. Fol. 269, perhaps from St-Denis, contains a text similar to that which Hincmar used.

192 The *Admonitio generalis* 789, MGH *Capit.* I, no. 22: 53–61, is the first of a long line of capitularies citing from canons. Response 5: 133–4 discusses such interactions. The *Tomus prolixus* (Response 1: 107) describes how 'a council of bishops was held at a general meeting (*generalis conventus*) of the magnates'.

193 Response 10: 179–80; Response 11: 188; Response 12: 204. There were, however, some ecclesiastical sources which justified judgements *in absentia* (Response 10: 180; Appendix Response 6: 304–5).

194 Response 10: 179; Response 12: 217. On Roman and medieval concepts of *infamia* and those unsuitable to accuse others, see Peters 1990.

195 See e.g. references to the fact that Judas was not 'condemned' as a thief (Response 10: 180; Response 13: 231; Appendix Response 7: 316).

196 Oaths have been widely discussed as part of the debates about feudalism: see e.g. Reynolds 1984; Becher 1993; Esders and Mierau 2000. On their use in Frankish courts, see Wood 1986: 14–18; Nelson 1986: 59–60. Response 7: 169 refers to oaths taken by bishops to kings.

197 Response 6: 145, 161.

systems of justice, noting that oaths might be requested to ensure fair treatment for defendants, or for wives returning to violent husbands.[198]

Oaths raised, however, the obvious problem of false oaths, or perjury, a subject on which Hincmar was invited to comment, although neither Lothar nor Theutberga was explicitly accused of perjury.[199] For Hincmar, perjury encompassed several different sins. One was breaking a sworn vow by later actions.[200] Another was making an untruthful statement under oath.[201] Related to both of these was swearing 'deceitfully': using a form of words to make someone believe wrongfully that you had promised or claimed something.[202] Whatever form it took, perjury was as serious as murder, because it offended God, by showing contempt towards the name by which someone had sworn.[203] God would exact punishment for this sin, but perjurers also faced very severe secular penalties.[204]

However, even perjury needed to be considered in the round. Hincmar was ambivalent about whether a cleric who learned about perjury through a secret confession should report it to the authorities.[205] And he was clear that a sworn oath ought to be broken if keeping it would have worse consequences – if, for example, the oath bound someone to carry out a sinful act.[206] Borrowing from Gregory the Great and Bede, Hincmar compared such a situation to jumping off a high wall: falling into sin cannot be avoided, but one should choose the wall's lowest point to minimise the damage.[207] The point seems to have been that Lothar II could not claim to be compelled by any promises he might have made to Waldrada. Of course, as Hincmar smoothly pointed out, such situations were best avoided by not making such oaths in the first place.[208]

198 Response 12: 206 referring to Hubert's case; Response 22: 272–3 on those seeking sanctuary in church. On protection against wives being killed, see below, 55–6.

199 Question 6: 144.

200 Response 6: 146–7.

201 Response 6: 147–8.

202 Response 6: 147; Response 9: 177. Cf. Response 10: 183 on 'false witnesses'. Such deceptions, did not, however, deceive God (Response 6: 150; Response 7: 167).

203 Response 6: 146–7.

204 Hincmar cites Pseudo-Cyprian calling for the execution of perjurers (Response 6: 149), and Carolingian laws penalised perjury with the loss of a hand (Stone 2012: 169).

205 Response 1: 102–3; Response 7: 168–9.

206 Response 6: 149; Response 14: 232.

207 Response 14: 150, 232–3.

208 Response 6: 149.

The ordeal

Another judicial procedure impossible to classify as either secular or ecclesiastical is the ordeal, which Hincmar and other simply called a 'judgement' (*iudicium*). Although they were a feature of secular trials, ordeals required the involvement of priests for what was in effect an invocation of God's power.[209] God would reveal the party with right on their side through direct intervention, whether by stopping them from being scalded by boiling water, by ensuring they sank in (cold) water, by not making them cough when eating Eucharistic bread or by giving them victory in a duel or other physical challenge. These ordeals were a novelty in the post-Roman Latin West; even in their heyday, they were reserved for cases where other methods of proof were lacking.[210] As Robert Bartlett puts it, the ordeal 'was a device for dealing with situations in which certain knowledge was impossible but uncertainty was intolerable'.[211]

Given that the issue was revisited just a couple of years later, Theutberga's ordeal in 858 evidently did not provide certainty. The success of her champion, who was judged to be unharmed (literally 'uncooked') by the boiling water, might simply have been due to chance, but since the outcome of any ordeal was subjective and so required interpretation, it might instead have reflected a lack of support for Lothar II.[212] Either way, the result was a major set-back for Lothar II's cause, so we should not be surprised that some of his supporters cast doubt on the validity of the ordeal as a mechanism for establishing guilt and innocence, following earlier sceptics like Agobard of Lyons.[213]

209 On types of ordeals and the rituals associated with them, see Bartlett 1986: 4–11; Firey 2009: 47–50; Heidecker 2010: 65–7. Response 6: 152 states that the cold water for the ordeal was consecrated as for a baptism. Response 3: 122: 'many bishops' had been consulted about the ordeal in 858.

210 Bartlett 1986: 25–33. Response 6: 145, : like purgation by oath, the ordeal is used for 'doubtful and obscure matters', which cannot be settled by normal means and therefore was appropriate for Theutberga's case, where there were no witnesses (Question 1: 95). Bührer-Thierry 1992: 305–7 points out the additional symbolism of the ordeal's use in cases of sexual sin: the accused body demonstrates its own innocence.

211 Bartlett 1986: 33. See the differing views of Brown 1975 and Bartlett 1986: 34–69 on the relationship of the ordeal to norms of 'community justice'.

212 Response 1: 95; on interpretation of ordeals, see Bartlett 1986: 39–40. Other uses of a champion by a queen instead of undergoing the ordeal herself are not known from early medieval sources: see Bartlett 1986: 16–18; Bührer-Thierry 1992: 307–11.

213 Scepticism about the outcome of Theutberga's ordeal is expressed in both the Booklet of Seven Chapters and the *Tomus prolixus* (Response 1, c. 2: 105; c. 16: 108–9). Bartlett 1986: 72–5 discusses Agobard and other ninth-century critics of the ordeal.

In response, Hincmar in *De divortio* provided one of the few extended justifications of the principle of the ordeal.[214] One part of his argument was simply to emphasise the importance of faith in God. Those who did not believe in ordeals showed their own lack of faith.[215] Another element of his argument was that it was customary. Hincmar claimed that the ordeal had been used 'since antiquity', had been 'handed down by authority', and had been approved by Charlemagne himself.[216] Although he was also aware that Louis the Pious had banned the use of the cold water ordeal, Hincmar rather surprisingly declared that this ruling was not found in 'established synods'.[217]

But Hincmar also did his best to draw on possible biblical precedents. Alongside references to the biblical trial of bitter waters, he argued that the Flood and the punishment of Sodom showed God's judgement through the elements of fire and water; as a result, the ordeal of boiling water was particularly appropriate as it combined these two elements.[218] He then devoted several pages to explaining away difficulties with this analogy. For reasons now unclear, Hincmar was particularly concerned with the ordeal of cold water, in which the accused was tied up and submerged in water. He explained at length why if the Flood is a precedent for ordeals, the innocent Noah floated on the water, whereas in the cold water ordeal the innocent sank (although they had a rope around them so that they could be hauled up quickly).[219] His ultimate answer was that in the cold water ordeal, the innocent person is received by the water as in baptism, and has their sins washed away; they metaphorically die and are reborn as innocent.[220] One may wonder how convinced Hincmar's questioners would have been by this.

Hincmar also dealt with the specific question of whether Theutberga's ordeal could have been invalidated in some way. He was emphatic that God would not behave deceptively in order to show mercy to Theutberga.[221]

214 Responses 6–9: 144–77. Schrörs 1884. 191 claims that Hincmar almost turns the ordeal into a sacrament, with its misuse as sacrilege.

215 Hebrews 11:1; Response 6: 164.

216 Response 6: 150–1. On Charlemagne's approval of the ordeal, see Response 6: 165.

217 Response 6: 163.

218 Response 6: 151, 153. Nevertheless, the ordeal is not a punishment, since it is intended to make the guilty 'confess and repent' (Response 6: 161). On the biblical ordeal of bitter waters (Numbers 5:11–31), see Response 6: 145, 152–3; Response 21: 268–9; Response 22: 277 and Bartlett 1986 : 83–5.

219 Response 6: 152, 153–8.

220 Response 6: 151–2, 156–7, 159.

221 Response 7: 166–7, rejecting the implicit suggestions in the Booklet of Seven Chapters and the *Tomus prolixus* (Response 1, c. 2: 105, c. 16: 108–9).

And Hincmar also forcefully rejected the idea that God could be tricked in the ordeal, for example by Theutberga thinking, at the crucial moment, of a different Hubert from the one she had sinned with.[222]

Yet despite initially stating that the ordeal's outcome in 858 should be accepted, Hincmar did concede the possibility that its result had not been correct. Perhaps this was from concern to maintain the general validity of ordeals if Theutberga should be proved guilty by another method, or perhaps it stemmed from his reluctance to come down too firmly on one side.[223] Whatever the case, such a possibility raised serious questions that needed further investigation in Hincmar's eyes. Theutberga might have already confessed her sin to Archbishop Gunther and been absolved of her sin – but how could she think to trick God in this way, and how had Gunther then dared to allow the ordeal to take place?[224]

Hincmar offered another possibility for the ordeal's failure: that it was not due to any deceitful action or magic by Theutberga, but that the devil may have worked an illusion, so that Lothar II and his supporters wrongly believed that her champion had passed the ordeal.[225] That they were deceived, however, was in itself a proof of their lack of faith. Here, as elsewhere in the text, Hincmar made concessions to Lothar II accompanied by sideswipes at his sinfulness.[226]

5 Penance and confession

Formal judgement was not the only way in which sinful acts were addressed within the Church. Hincmar's account of a young man unable to consummate his marriage, who eventually sought his bishop's help to end his bewitchment, is a good example of an alternative route. Although the bishop in question held *placita* to help resolve

222 Response 8: 170–2. Such ways of deceiving the ordeal by verbal trickery are found in later medieval stories, such as that of Tristan and Isolde: see Bartlett 1986: 18–19.

223 Compare Response 6: 166 and Response 9: 176. In Response 10: 178 he states that even if the ordeal was decided correctly, a further judgement on the case was possible.

224 Response 7: 168.

225 Response 9: 172–6. Response 6: 157 mentions that one reason to tie up those undergoing the ordeal of cold water is to prevent 'trickery'. Filotas 2005: 255, 267 discusses how using certain amulets or chrism (consecrated oil) was believed by some to allow fraudulent passing of the ordeal. On Hincmar's view of the devil, see below, 64–7.

226 See below, 76.

the difficulty, there was no judgement as such.[227] The key concepts here were instead confession and penance; these were pastoral procedures, rather than judicial ones, designed to help offenders rather than punish them. The distinction, though, was situational rather than absolute, and it is striking how Hincmar intertwined metaphors of healing with ones of punishment when he talked about penance. Bishops might offer 'medicinal judgements' to offenders or use 'medicinal severity' or the 'medicinal blade' to cut out illness or to stop the spread of contagion.[228]

Penance

Penance had developed in the early Church to provide a formalised method to express repentance, allowing the sinner to be reconciled to God and the Christian community after offering due 'satisfaction'.[229] It normally involved a set period (sometimes a penitent's whole life) during which penitents were excluded both from full participation in Church services and also some aspects of daily life, such as eating meat, bearing arms or sexual intercourse.[230] The period was fixed by the priest or bishop who imposed the penance, and depended both on the seriousness (and health) of the sin and the attitude of the sinner.[231]

By the ninth century, penance had become more elaborated. Some Carolingian churchmen made a distinction between a formal 'public penance' and a 'secret' penance, even if penitential practices did not always reflect this binary.[232] Imposition of public penance was increasingly reserved to bishops (and we know Hincmar was keen to ensure

227 Response 15: 236–7, see below, 68; Böhringer 2007: 284 thinks that Count Stephen of the Auvergne may similarly have been seeking for advice about his marriage dispute in 860 from the Synod of Tusey rather than a formal judgement. On this case, see below, 50.

228 Response 1: 101; Response 4: 126; Response 5: 135; Response 11: 180. On the idea of contagion see Response 5: 136; cf. Response 13: 231 and Appendix Response 7: 309 justifying excommunication by this metaphor. On the tradition of such language, see Firey 2009: 97–100, 109–10.

229 On the history of penance and its early medieval practice, see Hamilton 2001; Meens 2014.

230 Meens 2014: 15–19. Some councils imposed continuing restrictions on former penitents even after they had completed their penance: see Response 20: 258; Hamilton 2001: 6.

231 Response 17: 253–4; Many of the canons cited discuss whether the *viaticum* (last communion) could be given to a penitent near death, as an act of mercy (see 26 n. 142 above): see e.g. Response 4: 131; Response 12: 218; Response 13: 223; Response 17: 252–3.

232 Hamilton 2001: 4–9; Meens 2014: 118–23.

that he kept control of procedures in his diocese).[233] It theoretically brought with it such harsh restrictions in lifestyle that it might be most suitably performed in a monastery, making it difficult or perhaps impossible to hold public office or to remain in a marital union.

From the sixth century, this kind of penance could be imposed coercively on laity and clerics alike, and Hincmar often referred to the possibility that a judgement by a secular court might be followed by the imposition of penance, in addition to other penalties.[234] Secret penance by contrast was less solemn, and its implications, though highly varied, were generally less severe in scope and duration. It was 'secret' not because others did not know it was being performed, but because the penitent was not made the focus of public attention, and details of the sins concerned were not publicised.[235]

The choice between the two forms did not rest on the gravity of the sin alone, since very serious crimes could be absolved through secret confession and penance; Hincmar cited Pope Leo to argue that secret penance could often be the best procedure to follow, because people could avoid public humiliation and the danger of lawsuits brought against them.[236] The difference was rather about whether the sin had had implications for the whole community. Those who had committed secret sins could use secret confession and secret penance to put themselves right with God. By contrast, 'public' sins, often referred to as *scandala*, were those that had aroused God's anger against the kingdom, undermined social order or 'scandalised' the Christian community.[237] Since one important determinant of 'scandal' was the dangerous example set to others by the sinner, exemplary punishment via public penance was particularly justified in the case of high-status sinners.[238]

233 Hincmar, Third Capitulary, c. 1 (MGH *Capit. Episc.* 2: 73–4) gives a detailed description of procedures for dealing with 'public' sinners.

234 On coercive penance, see de Jong 1997: 876; Meens 2014: 75; Response 17: 251. As de Jong 1997: 892 states, the 'tension between non-compulsory sacrifice and coercive punishment was intrinsic to Carolingian public penance'. Response 5: 133–4 quotes a decree of Louis the Pious that someone who refused to perform public penance for wife-killing should be seized and chained. Cf. Appendix Response 4: 291: 'some are driven and forced to repentance'. Hincmar also mentions other examples of coercive penance: Response 1: 111 (Theutberga); Response 11: 189; Response 12: 201.

235 de Jong 2009: 233.

236 Response 11: 190–1; cf. Response 5:135.

237 de Jong 2009: 232. If serious sins were not already widely known, it was therefore better that secret penance was used to avoid 'scandal' (Response 5: 135).

238 de Jong 1997: 897; Response 5: 135; Response 12: 201–2.

And since another determinant was whether the sins might have damaged the community's standing in the eyes of God, the category could include even sins that were hidden from all but a few, such as incest.[239]

Yet despite a widespread emphasis on the distinction between public and secret penance in the Carolingian world, in practice there was a great deal of ambiguity. The precise implications of public penance were not clear-cut: as Rob Meens points out, before Louis the Pious's deposition in 833, rulers had done public penance while remaining in office.[240] Moreover, what counted as a public sin was necessarily a matter of case-by-case interpretation.[241] This was important for Theutberga's case, because Lothar II's supporters argued that what she had done was widely known, so that her offence was notorious and could not be hidden, and she therefore needed to perform public penance.[242] Because Theutberga should ideally carry out this penance within a monastery, they implied that this would put an end to her marriage to Lothar.[243] They also reported that she had confessed her sins 'openly, in the presence of all'.[244]

Hincmar took issue with this argument on a number of levels. He denied that Lothar II could remarry if Theutberga undertook public penance. Such penance might entail continence and marital separation, but it did not break the marital bond, so it could not be imposed on a spouse without the other spouse's commitment to continence too. If Theutberga retired to a monastery, Lothar would have to as well.[245] Moreover, Hincmar argued that it was really Lothar, not Theutberga, who should be carrying out public penance, for his adultery.[246] However, Hincmar's main argument

239 de Jong 1997: 898–901. The *Tomus prolixus* (Response 1, c. 19: 110) speaks of the 'pollution of incest, breathed out into the public'. On Carolingian ideas of 'pollution', a concept that overlapped with 'scandal', see Firey 2009: 61–100.

240 Meens 2014: 128–30.

241 Response 5: 135: 'whatever many know has been perpetrated should be healed by the knowledge of many'. Cf. Appendix Response 7: 305, where King David is punished publicly after a secret confession; Hincmar distinguishes between God's forgiveness and God's punishment to try to fit the case into his model.

242 Response 1: 110.

243 Response 1: 105, 107 and 110, c. 16. de Jong 1997: 877–86: 'voluntary' entry into a monastery to perform public penance became a key element of early medieval practice. Firey 2009: 25 points out that such ambiguity could have served all parties in Theutberga's case.

244 Response 1: 107.

245 Response 20: 258. Some Roman laws allowed the remarriage of one spouse if the other entered the religious life, but Gregory the Great forbade this. See Reynolds 1994: 227–38 and below, 52–3.

246 Hincmar several times states or implies that Lothar should do penance (Response 1: 112; Response 13: 223; Response 20: 258; Response 21: 269). On Lothar's adultery as 'public', see below, 56.

about Theutberga's penance revolved around the nature of the confession that she had supposedly made at Aachen.

Confession

Like oath-taking, confession was a method of proof in both ecclesiastical and secular courts. But confession was also at the heart of penance, when the sinner voluntarily admitted their own wrongdoing, and accepted a medicinal penance.[247] In *De divortio*, Hincmar moves between legal and penitential meanings of Theutberga's confession(s) in a way that is often difficult to follow. This blurring of terms partly reflects Hincmar's aim of discrediting the proceedings of the councils of Aachen in 860. But it also reflects the realities of the different structures and procedures for dealing with wrongdoing.

One of Hincmar's tactics was to cast doubt on whether Theutberga had confessed voluntarily. Early medieval churchmen were well aware that confessions might be forced, or be written for and not by the accused: such confessions were invalid.[248] The texts from the two councils of Aachen had been specifically designed to exclude later claims of a coerced confession by Theutberga.[249] Hincmar hinted that such emphasis was in itself suspicious, though without making direct accusations of improper pressure, possibly to hedge his bets.[250]

However, the core of Hincmar's argument was that Theutberga's confession should be considered to have been secret.[251] Hincmar admitted that details of the confession were now well known, and that he himself knew a lot about the accusations, but he emphasised that this knowledge was based on rumour, hearsay and gossip: this was the wrong kind of knowledge, and Hincmar was reluctant to hear more about it in this way.[252]

247 Response 1: 108–10, cc. 15–17. On this overlap, see Firey 2009: 11–37.

248 Response 10: 181–2 quotes both a papal decretal and a capitulary on the topics (ironically both forged). Cf. the reference in Response 11: 188 to 'a guided text' being used in a case.

249 Question 1: 98; Response 1: 109. This was indeed Theutberga's claim to Pope Nicholas: see Heidecker 2010: 100.

250 See e.g. Response 5: 135 with a reference to Theutberga being judged if she has 'publicly and willingly confessed'; Response 12: 204, where he refers to what people may say about any judgement.

251 Response 5: 136. As de Jong 1997: 894 explains, 'occult' (hidden) sins were those that were *not* notorious.

252 Response 1: 101–2; Response 3: 121, 123; Appendix Response 1: 284.

Classifying Theutberga's confession as secret in this way had major implications for the next steps in the procedure against her. Because a bishop could not reveal the contents of a secret confession, Hincmar argued that Theutberga's statement could not be used as evidence against her in any kind of trial, nor could it serve as the basis of public penance.[253] Moreover, Hincmar cited authorities to show that spouses could not be separated on the basis of a secret confession or a booklet (*libellus*) of confession or accusation.[254] A public judgement by bishops was required for a couple to separate, and Hincmar insisted this had not taken place.[255]

Hincmar's argument was complicated by the fact that at least three different accounts of the circumstances of Theutberga's confession were in circulation. According to the Booklet of Eight Chapters, Theutberga had confessed in private to Archbishop Gunther, who on her instructions repeated her confession to the other bishops.[256] This was said (in 860) to have happened 'recently', although in Question 6 it was claimed that she had confessed to Gunther before the ordeal in 858.[257] In the Booklet of Seven Chapters, however, Theutberga confesses to all the bishops in person on 9 January 860, and there is no mention of a previous confession to Gunther.[258] Finally, according to the *Tomus prolixus*'s account of the Second Council of Aachen, Theutberga first told Lothar II and then 'some bishops and laymen' the details of her sin, then publicly confessed she was unworthy of marriage and finally handed to Lothar II a written confession of her sin, which was (implicitly) read out.[259]

Hincmar clearly based his argument that the confession had not been public on the Booklet in Eight Chapters, and edged around the account

253 Response 1: 102–3; Response 11: 190–1. On the seal of the confession in cases of perjury, see above, 35.

254 Response 1: 111; Response 2: 120; Response 11: 187; Response 22: 271. Hincmar's argument exploits the fact that the same word (*libellus*) was used for the confession by Theutberga as for biblical discussions of the documentation by which a Jewish man could divorce his wife, a procedure that Jesus rejected (Matthew 19:7–9): see e.g. Response 2: 118.

255 Response 2: 119; Response 5: 134–5. See Firey 2009: 37–42 and on separation, see below, 52–3.

256 Question 1: 97–8. Firey 2009: 21 claims this text may accurately reflect Theutberga's responses.

257 Question 1: 96 Question 6: 114.

258 Response 1: 105–6. Firey 2009: 29 sees an open breach of confession by Gunther in this account, but this ignores the possibility of a 'public' confession.

259 Response 1: 107–9.

in the Booklet in Seven Chapters by claiming that confession to a number of bishops was the same as confession to one.[260] He was less clear about his objections to the procedure at the Second Council of Aachen, but stressed the involvement there of laymen (implying that it cannot have been a penitential confession) and the absence of a judgement (implying that it was not a juridical confession).[261] The modern reader might interpret this as casuistry, reflecting Hincmar's determination to classify Theutberga's confession as non-public come what may, not least because he never defines exactly how a public confession should be carried out.[262] Yet Hincmar did express a strong sense of the qualitative distinction between meetings that were secret and those that were public in other works, too, not least his account of government under Charlemagne, the *De ordine palatii*, written a couple of decades after *De divortio*.[263]

What made the matter particularly knotty for Hincmar, and perhaps explains some of his contortions over Theutberga's reported confession, is the similarity of events at the Second Council of Aachen to the Council of Thionville in 835 that had removed Ebbo from his office as Archbishop of Rheims.[264] Ebbo had publicly affirmed his unworthiness and offered a written confession of sins, without specifying in public exactly what these were. This seems so close to Theutberga's actions that the procedure at Aachen had perhaps been modelled upon it, and that presented Hincmar with a problem.[265] If after such a procedure Theutberga could remain married, why could Ebbo not have continued as archbishop of Rheims, instead of being replaced by Hincmar?[266] Hincmar responded, a little unconvincingly, by asserting that the cases of laity and clerics were simply different: a voluntary resignation of office by a cleric could not be reversed, even if based on a false confession, while the voluntary separation of a marriage could not be allowed without further investigation.[267]

260 Response 1: 102. These bishops, however, claimed that they had been given 'licence' to discuss the matter more widely (Question 1: 98).

261 Response 1: 111, 113. See Firey 2009: 41.

262 See in particular Response 11: 187–8.

263 *De ordine palatii*, cc. 29–30: 82–6 (Dutton 2003: 527–8). On the text, see McKitterick 2008: 142–8.

264 See above, 11–12.

265 The parallels were probably because the earlier council offered the useful precedent of a face-saving method to ensure someone's removal from a position of honour.

266 Question 2: 114. See above, 11.

267 Response 2: 115–20. In Response 10: 181 Hincmar returns to the question of secret and forced confessions, but does not mention Ebbo, while in Response 11: 187 he seems not to distinguish between the cases of a bishop resigning and a married couple separating, confirming the slightly haphazard nature of the text's construction.

6 Christian marriage and Frankish society

Marriage is a central issue for *De divortio*; it was also an important part of ninth-century Frankish society, both for Frankish elites and, so far as can be seen, for its peasantry, too.[268] However, then as now, marriage was a complex matter. That complexity derives from its position as both an important social practice and a debated theological concept: it was in the intersections of these aspects that much of Lothar II's attempt to rid himself of Theutberga was conducted.

Late Antique legacies

Christianity has been concerned with marriage ever since Jesus performed his first miracle at a wedding in Cana (to which Hincmar made frequent reference).[269] Some of the first judgements by the early Church were on marriage-related topics, and Late Antique popes deliberately positioned themselves as 'experts' on such household matters.[270] Among many Late Antique commentators on marriage, Augustine of Hippo's efforts to find a middle path between ascetics hostile to marriage and 'heretics' who considered it morally equal to virginity, proved particularly influential, especially on Hincmar. Augustine developed arguments that marriage was intrinsically good, possessing the three 'goods' of offspring, fidelity to one's spouse and *sacramentum* – a symbolic bond mirroring that between Christ and the Church.[271] Continence within marriage was certainly a good thing, but for those who were not capable of it, sexual activity within that marriage, for the sake of procreation, was acceptable.

Marriage in Late Antiquity, however, did not just have Christian connotations, for it was also a legal institution, recognised in imperial courts and legislation, as well as a key social institution.[272] For the elites, marriage was primarily a matter of making political alliances with other families. That is abundantly clear from Gregory of Tours's *Histories*,

268 Toubert 1996: 381–90. As Hincmar stresses (Preface: 86; Appendix Response 1: 283) a case about marriage is therefore automatically of general concern. For overviews of early medieval marriage, see Reynolds 1994; Stone 2012: 247–78.

269 See e.g. Response 4: 126; Response 5: 134; Response 21: 266. On the use of the story in early medieval preaching, see d'Avray 2005: 21–33.

270 See e.g. above, 29 n. 164 on St Paul's letter to the Corinthians discussing the case of a man who had taken his stepmother as his wife; Sessa 2012: 127–47.

271 Response 5: 138; Response 14: 234; Response 21: 263–7. On Augustine's ideas of marriage, see Brown 1988: 387–427; Reynolds 1994: 241–311.

272 On Late Antique marriage legislation see Reynolds 1994: 3–65; Evans Grubbs 1995; Cooper 2007: 143–60.

but it remained the case in the Carolingian period too.[273] As we have seen, Lothar II had probably married Theutberga in the first place because of the influence of her brother Hubert; moreover, the marriage should also be connected with that between Boso and Engeltrude, Theutberga's brother and Lothar's cousin respectively, and seen as part of a wider set of alliances.[274]

Nor should the function of marriage as a legal and religious institution make us forget that it also potentially involved personal bonds of affection and desire between a husband and wife. As already mentioned, the sources speak unequivocally and often of Lothar II's passion for Waldrada and hatred of Theutberga. Commentators like Hincmar were far from naïve – Hincmar discusses at length in *De divortio* the possibility of feigning emotions – but no one attempted to reduce Lothar's feelings to political calculation.[275] Indeed, the intimate nature of the marital bond was precisely what made it so important to those with a responsibility for Christian society.

Christianising marriage

From the early eighth century onwards, increasing demands were made by Church reformers such as Pope Gregory II and Boniface, in conjunction with certain of the Frankish lay elite, that marriages, particularly those of kings and the nobility, should conform more closely to Christian standards. Merovingian rulers had been able to repudiate wives or occasionally even kill them; if they were not technically polygamous, they certainly had both wives and mistresses simultaneously.[276] The Carolingian dynasty supported reformers' positions during and after its rise to power.[277] Clerics in the ninth century began to claim that Christian religious rituals were necessary for a proper marriage, as is particularly clear in the Pseudo-Isidore forgeries.[278]

This is often seen as part of a wider narrative, that of the Church's takeover of marriage. There is much truth in this, yet the narrative should nevertheless be treated with care.[279] Firstly, the process was far

273 For overviews, see Le Jan 1995: 263–332; Shanzer 2002.

274 Heidecker 2010: 59–62. On Engeltrude, see below, 50.

275 See e.g. Response 1: 111 on Lothar's 'bad' sadness, and Airlie 1998: 29–31.

276 Stafford 1983: 73–4, 187.

277 Heidecker 2010: 11–20; Ubl 2014: 144. Response 5: 133 cites Louis the Pious's decrees from the Council of Worms 829.

278 Reynolds 1994: 401–12; Response 4: 127 cites Pseudo-Evaristus on this topic.

279 For a recent helpful survey, see Karras 2015; cf. also Bof and Leyser 2016.

from instantaneous. Charlemagne's repudiation of the daughter of the Lombard king Desiderius around 772 seems to have encountered few objections, and, with his five wives and as many known concubines, he was hardly a model of conjugal self-control.[280] Some Carolingian moralists were indulgent on the question of concubines, and some royal concubines later became queens (as Waldrada intended to do).[281] For instance, Lothar II's brother, Louis II of Italy, would seem to have formalised his relationship with Angilberga only in 860, perhaps in response to the developing situation north of the Alps.[282]

That marriage practices did not change at once should not, however, necessarily be seen as reflecting lay resistance to the clerical view of marriage, as was once widely supposed.[283] Given that 'the Church' did not really have a unified position, such a generalisation is impossible to sustain. Faced with the authoritative yet confused legacy of Late Antiquity, Carolingian intellectuals broadly emphasised (Augustinian) strands in the Christian tradition that promoted monogamous marriage and to a certain extent sexual activity as positive forces in society, playing down equally venerable strands of thought much more hostile to both.[284] When it came to specifics, though, the diversity in their texts left a great deal of room for manoeuvre; or, put differently, the potential for conflicting interpretations.[285]

For example, classical and early medieval texts including *De divortio* refer only to concubines and wives: the concept of 'Friedelehe', a supposedly lesser form of marriage into which Waldrada entered, is a pure invention of early twentieth-century historians.[286] Yet there was no universally recognised definition of a concubine.[287] The text Hincmar

280 Desiderius's daughter: Nelson 1998: 178–84; concubines and wives: Esmyol 2002: 148–152.

281 On acceptance of unmarried men having concubines, see Stone 2012: 283. Hincmar, however, disapproved (Response 2: 119). There are disagreements on which Carolingian royal partners were actually concubines: compare Esmyol 2002: 154, 170–1 and Hartman 2007.

282 Hartmann 2007: 563–4.

283 See in particular Duby 1978.

284 Toubert 1977: 281–2; Stone 2012: 274–8, 298–310.

285 Smith 1998: 53: 'the classical and patristic heritage of late antiquity [on marriage, sexuality and gender] was vast, and neither coherent nor consistent'.

286 Karras 2006. Response 2: 119 distinguishes between 'legitimate marriage' and concubines.

287 Esmyol 2002: 165 in contrast argues that there were clear boundaries between concubines and wives, but that rulers sometimes simply ignored these. On concubinage in the Middle Ages, see Esmyol 2002 and Karras 2012; on royal concubines, see Stafford 1983 and Hartmann 2007.

cites most often is a letter of Pope Leo I to Rusticius, dealing specifically with converting a concubine to a wife.[288] As noted above, however, this letter was written at a time when concubines were assumed to be unfree, and was thus awkward to apply to a noblewoman like Waldrada.[289] That Hincmar referred to Waldrada only as a concubine (rather strikingly, he never gives her name in the text) was more a statement of his opinion than an acknowledgement of a simple fact.[290]

More broadly, there was no single authoritative statement on what made a marriage valid in general.[291] Similarly, although most patristic authors were clear that remarriage was not possible while both spouses were alive, an author whom Carolingian writers identified as Ambrose of Milan nevertheless permitted it for men, though not for women.[292] Even the Gospels themselves seemed inconsistent. Mark, Luke and John forbade separation from a spouse on any grounds, but Matthew made a – much-cited – exception on grounds of fornication (sexual activity outside of marriage).[293] While Christians were increasingly clear that divorce was rarely possible, the Old Testament showed its previous acceptability to God and gave examples of men having more than one wife simultaneously.[294] What is more, no Carolingian cleric claimed that marriage was simply a matter of clerical expertise. Even Hincmar was perfectly happy to acknowledge that clerics were no experts on matters like the mechanics of human reproduction (though that did not stop him from researching the matter, adding material to *De divortio* that came to light after he had finished the first draft).[295]

In any case, laymen were not necessarily opposed to the principle that their marriages should measure up to Christian standards. As de Jong points out, the Carolingian extension of prohibitions against incestuous marriage drew on widespread social beliefs in the polluting force

288 See e.g. Response 4: 128–9; Response 21: 262–3. Sometimes he reduces this to the phrase 'legally betrothed, endowed and honoured with a public wedding' (Response 13: 222; Response 22: 277).

289 Böhringer 2011: 152; Karras 2012: 31–2.

290 Airlie 1998: 15–18 prefers to talk of Lothar and Waldrada's relationship as a 'weak union', in contrast to the 'strong union' of Lothar and Theutberga.

291 Heidecker 2010: 16–25; Karras 2012: 31–7. Response 4: 126–9 quotes a mixture of sources relating to this topic, without attempting to integrate them into a coherent whole. Response 14: 234 refers to men making women a 'pledge of faith' (perhaps a promise of marriage) and later abandoning them.

292 See below, 53: the author is today known as Ambrosiaster.

293 Matthew 19:9. On interpretations of this text, see Reynolds 1994: 173–226.

294 See e.g. Response 21: 267 on Ahasuerus repudiating Vashti.

295 Response 12: 200–1.

of incest.[296] Similarly, while some of Lothar's leading churchmen supported his attempts to repudiate his queen, there were laymen within his kingdom who thought that his marriage to Theutberga should not be dissolved simply at his will. Carolingian laymen certainly did try to bring their marriages to an end, but they often did so by manipulating the Church's rules, not by ignoring them.[297]

Some members of the laity seem to have adopted certain clerical ideas about marriage with enthusiasm. That might have been less the result of a mass change in morality, and more the growing sense that these ideals had instrumental value. Kings and queens loomed particularly large here.[298] Correct marital behaviour by kings was increasingly seen as a marker for their virtue, a public measure of their own self-control and their ability to govern their own household.[299] The accusations made about the alleged infidelity of Empress Judith in the early 830s represented a turning point in this regard: they were transparently intended to damage her husband, Louis the Pious, presented as an ageing weakling able neither to restrain nor to satisfy his wife's sexual appetite.[300]

Debates about marriage had implications for succession, too. Legitimacy was not yet such a crucial factor in regulating royal succession as it would later be; several illegitimate sons of Carolingian rulers did succeed to rule.[301] Still, illegitimacy could increasingly be exploited as a weakness by rivals;[302] unsuccessful Carolingian princes might have had their legitimacy brought into question *post factum*.[303] The belated appearance of the argument that Lothar had in fact been formally married to Waldrada before he met Theutberga could have been an attempt retrospectively to confer legitimacy on their son, Hugh, as much as

296 See below, 61 n. 388. Ubl 2008: 377–83 argues that Carolingian couples did largely adhere to incest prohibitions.

297 See below, 53.

298 Joye 2015 shows how Carolingian condemnations of *raptus* in both secular and ecclesiastical legislation linked together and reinforced the authority of kings and fathers.

299 Staubach 1993: 172–81 sees Sedulius Scottus's mirror *Liber de rectoribus christianis* as propaganda linked to Charles the Bald's takeover of Lotharingia in 869 which implicitly contrasted Charles's exemplary marital control with that of Lothar II. Such views built on an Antique tradition that wives' behaviour reflected on their husbands (Cooper 1992). See also Airlie 1998: 20–4, 32–3; MacLean 2003b: 3–12.

300 Ward 1990; de Jong 2009: 191–212.

301 Arnulf is the most striking example.

302 See e.g. *AF (B)* 889: 118 on Arnulf's illegitimate sons.

303 Karras 2012: 37: the status of Himiltrude, Pippin the Hunchback's mother, may have been affected in this way.

another tactic to end the marriage with Theutberga. By 863 when the claim was made, Lothar had celebrated Waldrada as his queen; he (or they) might well have started to think seriously about planning their children's future.[304]

Hincmar's view of marriage

Many historians have compared Hincmar's statements on marriage across his writings, and concluded that he was inconsistent, in particular on the question of whether marriage was a matter for bishops or for secular courts.[305] On some occasions, he clearly argued for the ability of a secular court to judge marital matters. In Theutberga's case, he suggested that the matter should first of all be examined by the laity, drawing on a case (that of Northild) apparently discussed at the Council of Attigny in 822.[306] He came to a similar conclusion in the case of Engeltrude, touched on in *De divortio.*[307] Engeltrude, the wife of Count Boso (probably the brother of Theutberga and Hubert), had run off with a vassal of Boso to Lotharingia in around 857, and despite condemnation by several synods refused to return to her husband.[308] Hincmar rejected the idea that because Engeltrude had appealed to Archbishop Gunther of Cologne, she should not therefore be judged by a secular court.[309]

Yet in the almost contemporary case of Count Stephen of the Auvergne, Hincmar encouraged investigation by a Church council. Stephen claimed that he had tried to break off his betrothal, because he had previously slept with a relative of his fiancée and realised the marriage would therefore be incestuous. Although forced into the marriage by fear of his would-be father-in-law, he had not consummated it. Hincmar wanted the council to investigate these claims, including questioning Stephen's wife.[310]

304 Konecny 1976: 117.

305 See e.g. Heidecker 2010: 99.

306 Response 5: 136–7, 'through men of this order, that is married men'; cf. Response 1: 111. On the case of Northild, see Böhringer 2007: 268–72; Nelson 2012; Joye 2015: 195–6.

307 Responses 22–3: 270–81; Appendix Response 5: 295–8. Hincmar also wrote a letter to Gunther of Cologne on the case in late 860, *De uxore Bosonis, Epistola* 135 (MGH *Epp.* 8: 81–7), which is essentially an expanded version of his argument in *De divortio.*

308 On the case, see Stone 2007a; Heidecker 2010: 97. Engeltrude was Lothar II's first cousin once removed: see Heidecker 2010: 70–2 and his Genealogy 4.

309 Response 22: 270–8. This contradicts the claim by Daudet 1933: 112 that laypeople were able to choose their jurisdiction in such matters.

310 Hincmar, *Epistola* 136 (MGH *Epp.* 8: 88–107). On this case, see Böhringer 2007: 277–84 and Stone 2007a. In Appendix Response 6: 299 Hincmar quotes Deuteronomy's statements that the hardest cases should be brought to priests.

Hincmar's apparently inconsistent statements on these cases, combined with his silence about the second marriage of Louis the Stammerer (Charles the Bald's eldest son), has led to accusations of hypocrisy.[311] However, Letha Böhringer has argued that bishops were concerned to intervene when disputes between powerful families might lead to violence, and to adopt whatever strategy was most likely to lead to peace.[312] Hincmar's repeated calls for a 'general council' to be involved in settling Lothar's case should perhaps be seen as part of this strategy.[313] One might note too that in none of these cases does Hincmar make any programmatic claims concerning ecclesiastical jurisdiction in marital disputes.[314] This is significant, since he did make substantial claims about the Church's jurisdiction over some other categories of case.[315] Consistency was perhaps less important to Hincmar than finding a workable solution which would help create peace.[316]

Flexible though he was about how marital problems should be resolved, Hincmar nevertheless had a clear view of certain key principles. He considered marriage to be an institution as old as humanity itself, given by God to Adam and Eve.[317] He followed Augustine in considering the Christian marriage bond as lifelong and loving.[318] Although it was not an equal relationship (wives might refer to their husbands as their lord (*senior*)), husbands were supposed to show greater virtue in reflection of their superior position.[319] A specifically female weakness was acknowledged, but balanced against general human fragility.[320] Hincmar had

311 Brühl 1964: 76–7 sees Hincmar as supporting Louis the Stammerer's repudiation of his first wife and remarriage, although Böhringer 2007: 286–7 points out that we do not know sufficient details to be certain of Hincmar's role. On Hincmar's relationship to Louis the Stammerer, see McCarthy (2015).

312 Böhringer 2007. Cf. *AB* 862: 97, where Baldwin's abduction of Judith was subject to both a judgement by 'secular law' and a 'canonical sentence'.

313 Preface: 86; Response 1: 101; Response 3: 122–4, Appendix Response 1: 284; In Response 3: 123 Hincmar demands a 'large-scale meeting, consultation and consensus' to solve the matter and claims that Adventius agreed to the need for a general council. In Response 12: 217 he speaks of Hubert being brought before an ecclesiastical court.

314 Contrary to the claims of Daudet 1933: 101–22; Heidecker 2010: 91.

315 See above, 28.

316 Böhringer 2007: 267; cf. Bof and Leyser 2016.

317 Response 3: 124; Response 21: 269; Response 22: 274; Appendix Response 1: 283. Marriage was also given by God to non-Christians (Response 5: 134 and Response 21, 268).

318 Response 15: 237.

319 Husband as 'lord': Response 1: 98; virtue: Response 5: 140.

320 Response 1: 108; Response 15: 245; Response 20: 258. Airlie 1998 is fundamental on the gender politics of Lothar's case.

a relatively elevated view of wives' status, attributing more power to them within the household than can be deduced from Augustinian theology alone.[321]

Hincmar was also quite clear on the circumstances in which a legitimately married Christian couple might be separated.[322] One possibility was for them to become continent, that is, to abstain from sexual activity altogether, as opposed to chastity (*castimonia, castitas*), which encompassed legitimate sexual activity within a marriage.[323] Both spouses had to agree to this and if the separation was intended to be permanent, both had to obtain their bishop's permission to enter the religious life.[324] The second situation in which separation became possible was if one partner had committed fornication.[325] This position had a biblical foundation (Matthew 5:32 and 19:9), provided one ignored corresponding verses in Mark and Luke, which omitted the exception.[326] In such cases, Hincmar agreed that the spouses could be separated, with the consent of the local bishop.[327] But the bishop should then endeavour to reconcile the couple – and Hincmar saw no problem with a concept of 'reconciliation' that compelled the adulterous Engeltrude to return to her husband, or gave Lothar a choice between Theutberga and celibacy.[328]

Hincmar, however, stated consistently (perhaps more consistently than his sources and some of his contemporaries) that such separation

321 Contrast Response 5: 140–2 and with Augustine's view in Response 18: 255–6. Hincmar also hints that women could have considerable power within the family: according to Response 15: 236, it was unusual for a husband to be able to arrange a marriage for his son against his wife's opposition. Nevertheless, Hincmar did not see wives as having complete freedom: see his comments on Engeltrude in Appendix Response 5: 296.

322 'Mixed marriages' between a Christian and a non-believer were not necessarily indissoluble: see Response 21: 260.

323 Response 2: 115–6; Response 5: 130.

324 Response 5: 131, 134; Response 23: 279–80; Appendix Response 4: 293. On the tradition of such separation and changing views of whether it could be done unilaterally, see Reynolds 1994: 227–38. Response 10: 186 and Response 23: 280 cite a letter by Gregory the Great dealing with a woman called Agathosa, whose husband had entered a monastery without her consent.

325 Response 2: 115; Response 5: 131, 134.

326 On interpretations of these texts from Matthew, see Reynolds 1994: 173–226. Hincmar does not cite Mark 10:11 at all. Luke 16:18 is cited only when quoted in a letter by Innocent I (Response 5: 132).

327 Response 5: 132–3 cites Council of Agde 506, c. 25 on the episcopal role in separation; cf. Response 5: 131, 134, 137; Response 22: 277.

328 On Lothar's choice between reconciliation and celibacy, 'with free choice completely removed', see Appendix Response 4: 291–4; Heidecker 2010: 168; On Engeltrude see Appendix Response 5: 295–8.

did not mean divorce.[329] Drawing on Jerome and Augustine, Hincmar argued that a separated couple may be living apart, but they were still married to each other, and so could not marry anyone else.[330] The fourth-century writer Ambrosiaster had claimed in his commentary on St Paul's First Epistle to the Corinthians that although a woman could not remarry if her husband committed fornication, a man could remarry if his wife had.[331] Although Hincmar makes considerable use of Ambrosiaster's text in *De divortio,* he never cites this statement. Instead he stressed that there was a single law in marriage for both men and women.[332] For Hincmar, marriage only ended (and the marriage bond was finally broken) when one of the spouses died; divorce, in the sense of terminating an existing marriage, was impossible.

Historians have often assumed that Hincmar was therefore categorically opposed to Lothar II's attempts to be rid of Theutberga. Yet this is not quite right, because Hincmar accepted the argument of Theutberga's accusers that if she were guilty of the offences that were charged to her, in particular of incest, then she had not been capable of entering into the marriage, which was therefore made invalid, or as we might say, annulled.[333] Other commentators at the time disagreed, and perhaps Hincmar was simply keen to leave Lothar II the possibility of exit (see below, 62–4). Still, the strategy of using canon law to break a marriage by arguing that it had never been valid in the first place for reasons of incest is attested elsewhere, too.[334] Hincmar himself was open to the idea that non-consummated marriages were incomplete, and so could

329 Gaudemet 1988: 16–20.

330 Response 2: 115; Response 5: 138–9; Response 21: 263–5, Appendix Response 4: 291–3

331 Ambrosiaster, *Commentarius in Epistolam I ad Corinthios*, 7, 11, 2: 75 (Bray 2009: 150–1); Heidecker 2010: 14, 105–7. This argument was cited by Lothar's supporters at the Council of Aachen 862 (Ubl 2008: 349–50). On Ambrosiaster, see Hunter 2009. In the Carolingian period his works were believed to be written by Ambrose of Milan, and hence had considerable authority.

332 Response 5: 131, 140; Response 10: 187; Response 13: 222; Response 20: 258; Response 21: 259, 267–8.

333 In Response 5: 138 Hincmar specifically states the conditions for the separation of a 'marriage legally entered into'; cf. Response 11: 189 on marriage being 'usurped'; Response 12: 219; Response 13: 222. He discusses other examples of where marriages 'insulting' to God may be dissolved in Response 19: 256–7 and Response 21: 259–60. On incest, see below, 60–4.

334 Other tactics used by husbands included orchestrating an affair with their mother-in-law, and 'accidentally' sleeping with a sister-in-law (both of which broke norms about incest), and even the drastic step of self-enslavement. See Ubl 2008: 381–2; Stone 2012: 271–4; Ubl 2014: 153–7. On the related case of Stephen, see above, 50.

be broken, allowing the spouses to marry other people, though he worried about wives making false allegations of impotence.[335]

7 Theutberga's offences

It has often been said that Lothar II's attempts to divorce Theutberga failed for political reasons, since other Frankish kings managed to rid themselves of their wives without comparable struggle.[336] It is certainly true that Lothar's opponents were not solely motivated by respect for legal or theological niceties. The king clearly anticipated some political difficulties in ending the union, since Theutberga was well connected, which is doubtless why, instead of simply casting her aside, he arranged the 858 ordeal. Yet we should not rush to over-simplify and reduce everything to mere power politics. For after the ordeal went against him, Lothar calculated that the best way forward was on technical grounds, which brought theological and legal issues to the fore.

The arguments chosen by Lothar II's advisers centred on allegations made about Theutberga's conduct prior to marriage: specifically, accusations of abortion, unnatural sex and incest.[337] This cocktail of charges was designed to inflict maximum damage on her, while leaving Lothar himself unscathed. Unfortunately for Lothar, his advisers seem to have chosen their ground poorly. It did not necessarily matter that not all Carolingian clerics agreed that conduct before a marriage was relevant to its ending, provided the offending spouse had behaved correctly within the marriage.[338] All that was needed was a charge plausible enough for consensus to be built around it. But none of the arguments and charges that Lothar's supporters advanced before 862 proved strong enough to create that consensus, let alone offer protection from the political consequences of the king's decision to leave Theutberga.[339]

335 Response 2: 119. On Hincmar's views and those of other Carolingian authors on male impotence and marriage, see Gaudemet 1980; Reynolds 1994: 346–61; Rider 2006: 39–41.

336 See e.g. Hartmann 2007: 564; Heidecker 2010: 186–7. MacLean 2003a: 170–8 argues that Charles the Fat's separation from Richgarde on the grounds of non-consummation potentially allowed Charles a remarriage.

337 Question 1: 95.

338 Different conclusions are reached by Hincmar in Response 12: 220 and by Ratramnus in 862 (MGH *Conc.* 4, no. 9D: 84–6). (On Ratramnus's authorship of this text, see below, 63.) Hincmar does raise queries about the issue, however: see Response 12: 202.

339 Ubl 2008: 251–2.

Adultery

We should begin, however, with an allegation that was never formally lodged against Theutberga, but that hovered in the background.[340] If a 'legally entered' marriage ended only with a spouse's death, there was one obvious way in which Lothar II could rid himself of Theutberga: by killing her. The second set of questions sent to Hincmar suggests that Lothar II was considering executing her for adultery, as permitted by Roman law and by the Old Testament.[341] Punishing female adultery by death was also sometimes acceptable in Frankish society, as a means of restoring a husband's lost honour.[342] Claims by Carolingian moralists that such killing of wives was widespread may be exaggerated, but there are known examples.[343]

Hincmar was very cautious on this subject. He noted that Jesus had chosen to prevent the death penalty in the case of an adulterous woman and instead forgave her (John 8:1–11).[344] He also repeated earlier Carolingian demands that men could not kill their wives before a formal judgement against them had taken place, to prevent the murder of innocent women.[345] In the case of Engeltrude, an adulteress who refused to return to her husband, Boso, claiming to be in fear for her life, Hincmar suggested that sureties should be sought from Boso before she was sent back, to the effect that he would not murder her.[346]

The question, however, that Hincmar never directly addresses is whether an adulterous wife could be executed *after* some form of legal judgement.[347] Hincmar may have felt that the issue raised thorny questions about the contradictions between Old and New Testament precedents.[348] He hints that an adulterous woman should not be killed, but

340 On allegations concerning adulterous queens in the early Middle Ages, see Bührer-Thierry 1992; Bührer-Thierry 2007.

341 Appendix Question 4: 290–1.

342 Response 5: 142.

343 See Böhringer 2007: 259; Stone 2012: 202–5. Response 5: 141–3 has a lurid denunciation of men who carry out such murders, copied from Hincmar's earlier work *De raptu*. Response 15: 236 recounts an incident when a bewitched young man threatens to kill his wife.

344 Hincmar frequently discusses this story and the procedures used: see Response 5: 143; Response 11: 188; Response 21: 269; Response 22: 276.

345 Response 5: 133.

346 Response 22: 277–8; Appendix Response: 296.

347 Response 22: 277–8 implies that Engeltrude's adultery should not be judged in an ecclesiastical court.

348 Response 5: 143 and Response 22: 278 state that Jesus in John's gospel did not deny the validity of the judgement condemning an adulteress.

without explicitly ruling it out; and he cuts short an Augustine quotation which leaned heavily in that direction.[349]

Hincmar was not prepared to guarantee the life of adulterous wives absolutely. However, what he did do was turn the argument round, by suggesting that if anyone was guilty of adultery, it was Lothar II.[350] In Roman law, *adulterium* was an offence committed only by married women and their male lovers, but the New Testament had expanded adultery to include all extramarital activity by both married men and women, and this was very much the line taken by Hincmar.[351] Adultery by men was often hard to prove, but not in this case.[352] Since Lothar and Theutberga's marriage had not been ended by the councils of Aachen in 860 (according to Hincmar, anyway), Lothar's relationship with Waldrada was adulterous, even if Theutberga were subsequently to be found guilty.[353] Hincmar's view was clear: because the relationship with Waldrada had come 'to the notice of many', it was a public sin and therefore required public penance; he added that a priest should not spare even a king who had sinned.[354]

Abortion

According to the list of questions sent to Hincmar, Theutberga had been accused of aborting by means of a drink a child she had conceived with her brother.[355] This was a very serious matter. Christian abhorrence of abortion had been a major distinguishing feature from Roman norms, where abortion was predominantly understood to concern fathers' rights over children and husbands' rights over wives.[356] Although early medieval views differed on whether abortion at an early stage was akin

349 Appendix Response 5: 298. Response 5: 142 talks ambiguously of a judgement as 'releasing' husbands from adulterous wives; 143 refers to the 'healing' of adulterous wives, implying that they should undergo penance. In contrast, Ubl 2014: 52–3 cites late ninth-century texts which explicitly ruled out the execution of an adulterous wife and forbade her to be returned to her husband if that was a risk.

350 This is already suggested in the list of questions sent to him: see Question 13: 221; Question 18: 254.

351 Reynolds 1994: 122–6. Late Antique law often allowed husbands but not wives to divorce for adultery: see Böhringer 1992: 139 n. 36; Reynolds 1994: 49–53. On Carolingian attitudes, see Stone 2012: 289–92.

352 Response 1: 104.

353 Response 13: 221–2.

354 Question 13: 221; Response 13: 221–3, 228–31. On public penance: see above, 39–41.

355 Question 1: 95. On the use of abortifacients in the early Middle Ages, see Riddle 1992; on early medieval discourses around abortion, see Mistry 2015.

356 Mistry 2015: 25–39. Patristic writers associated abortion writers with other female sexual sins, imagining guilty women attempting to destroy the evidence of their

to murder, churchmen also saw abortion as sinful because procreation was the only justifiable reason for sexual activity (see below, 58).[357]

Yet abortion was by some margin the weakest charge against Theutberga. Hincmar does not go into details of punishments in *De divortio*.[358] Instead he observed that it was not a matter well suited to episcopal enquiry, urging that laymen should be consulted, who could ask their wives about matters of conception.[359] Hincmar, however, knew enough about human reproduction to make the point that the accusation was inconsistent with another charge against Theutberga, that of sodomy, in whose broad definition the impossibility of conceiving children was central; and he saw fit to expand the point considerably as he continued to work on the manuscript.[360] As Hincmar observed, only the Virgin Mary had conceived of a child in a non-standard fashion, so to some extent the accusation was even blasphemous.[361]

Though the accusation of abortion appears in the list of questions, it is striking that it is not actually mentioned in any of the records from the Aachen councils of 860 or indeed 862. Read closely, moreover, the list of questions specifies that the issue of abortion had been raised in 858, when Theutberga's champion was put to the ordeal.[362] This might have reflected an attempt to throw the book at Theutberga or to bring the case within the remit of a 'secular' court, on the grounds that abortion was linked to murder. Either way, it looks rather as if Theutberga's accusers had quietly dropped the charge by 860. It is even possible that the group who wrote to Hincmar had added or in some way embroidered this rather implausible charge to the list of accusations precisely in order to undermine the case against Theutberga.[363]

unchastity. See also Response 12: 220, citing Augustine on lustful spouses aborting their own children.

357 On varying views concerning foetal development, see Elsakkers 2001. Hincmar cites potentially contradictory texts in Response 12: 199 the Vetus Latina version of a key Biblical text [Exodus 21:22] on abortion which had different penalties depending on the development of the foetus, as well as Gregory the Great's view that conception and birth had the same meaning.

358 Response 12: 218 briefly cites penances from the Council of Ancyra.

359 Response 12: 201.

360 Response 12: 200–1. On definitions of sodomy, see below, 59.

361 Response 12: 200–1; this section of the response includes two later additions to the text.

362 Question 1: 95.

363 Mistry 2015: 250–3 comes to a similar conclusion, suggesting that the representation of Theutberga in 860 as an involuntarily polluted victim was difficult to square with an accusation of abortion. Cf. Heidecker 2010: 68.

Unnatural sex

An element of the 858 trial retained in 860 was that Theutberga had engaged in an unnatural sexual practice. One aim may have been to exculpate Lothar II from not having recognised that Theutberga was not a virgin when they married.[364] But Lothar II may again have been seeking to justify the execution of his wife.[365] As Hincmar points out, the Old Testament punished both incest and unnatural sex with death: how much more should the combination of the two be penalised?[366] Hincmar obliquely hints that such a death penalty should not be carried out even were Theutberga found guilty of her offences, but as mentioned already (55–6), he is perhaps deliberately vague on the subject.

The Second Council of Aachen was noticeably unclear on the question of precisely what Theutberga was supposed to have done, describing the alleged intercourse merely as 'against natural usage'.[367] The list of questions sent to Hincmar suggests that in 858 the accusation had been a little more specific, of 'masculine intercourse between the thighs'; the most plausible suggestion is that this was femoral intercourse.[368] But the exact act might well not have been obvious to contemporaries: there was no consistent way of talking about particular kinds of sexual activity.[369]

Hincmar was a little more concerned by the specific details of Theutberga's offence than were the Lotharingians, judging by the attention he gave to the matter. But for Hincmar, as for other Carolingian writers, the key point was that all sex was unnatural if it was not potentially procreative.[370] Hincmar cites several texts which give hierarchies of sexual sins, in which unnatural sexual activities are even worse than (potentially procreative) incest.[371] Hincmar devoted considerable time

364 Response 12: 201 hints at the existence of such an argument. At the Council of Aachen 862, it was indeed explicitly claimed that Theutberga had not been a virgin when Lothar married her: see *Gutachten einiger Bischöfe*, Council of Aachen 862 (MGH *Conc.* 4, no. 9D: 84).

365 See above, 55.

366 Response 12: 193–4, 195. Hincmar claims vaguely that Roman law decreed similar penalties.

367 Response 1: 108.

368 Response 1: 95: 'masculinus concubitus inter femora'. See Olsen: 2011: 35–40.

369 Olsen 2011: 6–8, 13–26, 38, 41; Stone 2012: 292–3. In Response 12: 198 Hincmar describes a wide range of sexual sins, including incest and bestiality, as included under the term 'fornication'.

370 Response 12: 194. On the Carolingian category of 'unnatural' sex, see Olsen 2011: 197–200; Stone 2012: 292–8.

371 Response 12: 194–5. Hincmar at 194 also cites Augustine saying that it is worse for a man to commit unnatural sex with his wife than with another woman.

in *De divortio* to showing that unnatural sexual activity of whatever kind ought to be condemned, whether between men and men, men and women or women and women.[372] (Hincmar rather unusually discusses female same-sex intercourse at length, even mentioning the use of sex toys.)[373] He also includes masturbation in this condemnation; as Hincmar summarises it: 'it is uncleanliness when males work shamefulness in males, or women in women, or males in women, or whoever by themselves in whatever way works shamefulness'.[374]

As a result, it is not surprising that he explicitly took issue with unnamed opponents who argued, rather adventurously, that the specific category of sodomy applied only to anal sex. That was not how Hincmar saw it.[375] In fact, *De divortio* has the first known reference to sodomy as an abstract concept. Hincmar quotes a letter of Gregory the Great, but where Gregory had written of the sin of the sodomite (*scelus sodomitae*), Hincmar removed the letter 't', and so wrote of the sin of sodomy (*scelus sodomiae*) – and indeed introduces Gregory's text by using this term too.[376] Whether this tiny but significant alteration was already present in his source manuscript, it suited his argument by collecting all kinds of deviant sexual behaviour under a single label, with its connotations of the destruction by fire of the city of Sodom for its depravity.[377]

Although the accusation of sodomy was useful before a secular court in 858, it was less so in the more strictly ecclesiastical context of 860. Claims about unnatural behaviour were certainly humiliating for Theutberga, and provided further grounds for her to do public penance, which her accusers may have hoped would have effectively ended her marriage with Lothar.[378] However, such acts did not necessarily require lifelong penance

372 Response 12: 196–9. In the Preface: 94 and Response 12: 193 Hincmar excuses himself for writing about such shameful matters by saying he is following the example of St Paul.

373 Response 12: 197–8. On lesbians in the Middle Ages, see Murray 1996; Benkov 2001.

374 Response 12: 197.

375 Response 12: 196–9. This passage is an addition to the original text (Olsen 2011: 41), which suggests a continued concern about definitions of such a serious sin.

376 Response 12: 206. On the possible significance of this, compare Jordan 1997: 35–6 and Olsen 2011: 33–6. There are some manuscripts of Gregory's letters with this variant reading, but they are later in date than Hincmar's text; that does not of course rule out a lost intermediate manuscript.

377 Genesis 19:1–28; Leviticus 20:10–17. Hincmar refers to the story of Sodom several times (Response 6: 150, 152; Response 12: 195). The sins of Sodom were also intertwined with ideas of idolatry: see Response 12: 198–9, 206.

378 Response 12: 218 cites a council decreeing a ten-year term of penance for the sins of abortion and unnatural sex.

in a convent, and as we have seen, Hincmar emphasised that public penance was not a bar to subsequent marriage or to the continuation of a marriage.[379] He also quoted statements by Church Fathers that sodomitical acts did not in themselves end a marriage, nor even necessarily justify separation.[380] The accusations of sodomy therefore had more impact at a rhetorical than a practical level, and Theutberga's accusers devoted most of their efforts to a third, more serious accusation: incest.

Incest

Incest was a major concern for Carolingian moralists, with both secular and religious gatherings repeatedly legislating against it and demanding action against perpetrators. It was used to label sexual relations with someone with whom one already had specific social ties (endogamy): relatives by blood, but also certain relatives by marriage or those to whom one was tied via godparenthood. By extension, it was also used to label marriages to such people.[381]

In the twelfth century, attention concentrated on the second of these meanings. Marriage became technically forbidden between people who shared the same great-great-great-great-great-grandparent, some of whom might well have lived two or three centuries ago. All it took to annul a marriage under these rules was a little research into family history.[382] Hincmar's *De divortio* makes the earliest known reference to a key text in the development of this tradition, a forged letter supposedly sent by Gregory the Great to Bishop Felix of Messina.[383] In this letter, Gregory retracted the leniency demonstrated in an earlier (probably) genuine text, the *Libellus responsionum*.[384] Whereas the *Libellus* had allowed the newly converted Anglo-Saxons to marry within four degrees (*generationes*), the forged letter to Felix emphasised that for the 'properly taught', the prohibitions extended to the seventh degree.[385]

379 See above, 41 n. 245.

380 Response 5: 139; Response 12: 220. However, in Response 12: 195 he also cites Ambrosiaster saying that a wife should neither be returned to a husband seeking unnatural intercourse with her, nor allowed to remarry.

381 For overviews of the topic, see Ubl 2008; Stone 2012: 255–67.

382 Ubl 2008: 477–8.

383 Pseudo-Gregory, Letter to Felix of Messina (J †1334).

384 Ubl 2008: 220–7, 336–42. In the late ninth century, the letter to Felix was included in John the Deacon's life of Gregory the Great, through which it was widely disseminated. This letter does not appear in the two main early recensions of Pseudo-Isidore (see Fuhrmann 2001: 169), but Ubl 2008: 336–40 believes it was also probably by the Pseudo-Isidore workshop.

385 Response 12: 219.

However, such distant ties of relation were not so important in the early Middle Ages. That was partly because of uncertainty about the way of calculating 'degrees' of relation (*generatio, geniculum, gradus*). Alongside the (later dominant) canonical method, which counted back to the common ancestor of a couple, making first cousins into a relationship of the second degree, some commentators seem to have used the much more generous Roman method, which counted every step between the couple and their common ancestor as a degree, making first cousins a relationship of the fourth degree.[386] In any case, in the absence of written genealogies for the nobility, it is not clear whether anyone could have credibly established distant degrees of relation.[387] Given the nature of the Carolingian aristocracy, Theutberga and Lothar II may well have been related within prohibited degrees according to the canonical method, but no one suggested it, perhaps because no one could prove it.

The relevance of incest in the case of Theutberga was not, then, about prohibited degrees within a marriage, but about the polluting effects of sexual relations with a close relative. The charge was that Theutberga had been 'stained' by sexual intercourse (willing or not) with her brother Hubert while she was growing up.[388] Such intercourse with close blood relatives is discussed by early medieval penitentials, but very rarely by other Carolingian texts.[389] The accusation was clearly intended to shock hearers and stigmatise Theutberga, and the Lotharingian bishops treated it as a previously unknown sin, calling for severe punishment so that brother–sister intercourse should remain taboo.[390]

In order to redeem such a polluting sin, a long period of penance would have been required.[391] But Lothar II's circle went further, arguing that Theutberga's polluted state had in fact rendered her incapable of marriage altogether. To make this point, Lothar II's supporters drew on the records of the Council of Epaon, a synod held in Burgundy in 517 (though Carolingian writers, misled by their sources, wrongly identified it as from

386 Ubl 2008: 14–27.

387 Stone 2012: 265. As Bauer 1994b: 71–2 points out, brother–sister intercourse was obviously unacceptable under either method of counting.

388 On incest as pollution, see de Jong 1989: 48–9, 52–3; Stone 2012: 263–4. On the question of coercion, see Response 1: 106, c. 4, 7, 107, c. 15.

389 Payer 1984: 30–2; Stone 2012: 257.

390 Response 1: 110, c. 18. Incest was sinful and also dishonourable (see Stone 2012: 132). Ubl 2008: 351 sees the accusation as intended not only to end the marriage but to blacken Theutberga's name.

391 On penances, see Ubl 2008: 299–301, 316–19. The Old Testament had punished incest between brother and sister with death (Response 12: 192–3, 195).

the Council of Agde 506).[392] This council originally declared that incestuous marriages, that is ones between relatives, were invalid, but in one version of the canons, a tiny textual alteration (deliberate or accidental) changed the meaning to state that people who had committed incest were not capable of marriage.[393] This altered phrase appeared in the forged letter from Gregory the Great to Felix on prohibited degrees, suggesting that the concept circulated widely.[394]

As already noted, Hincmar's general position in *De divortio* seems to be that 'divorce' and remarriage was not an option (he is quite clear about this in Responses 2 and 23). Crucially, however, Hincmar accepted in principle the Lotharingian argument that incest cast doubt on whether a subsequent marriage was legitimate.[395] He cited both versions of the Epaon canon, but more often the version banning 'incestuous people' from marriage.[396] Hincmar also reinterpreted two other phrases from Pseudo-Gregory's letter to Felix in a similar vein, implicitly applying the statements that a man should not marry a woman previously 'polluted' by one of *his* relatives, and that a man forbidden an incestuous marriage might be allowed an alternative one, to Lothar's non-incestuous marriage to a woman who had slept with one of *her* own relatives.[397] He also hinted that canon law about the dissolution of marriages between Christians and non-Christians (*infideles*) might be relevant.[398] Hincmar concluded that, should Theutberga be properly proved guilty of incest as alleged, then after a suitable penance Lothar could marry someone else, including even Waldrada.[399]

392 Response 12: 220; Response 19: 257. On the transmission of this canon, see Ubl 2008: 202, 313.

393 The editor reconstructs the original phrase in the council as: 'Incestus vero nec ullo coniugii nomine praevelandus' (*Concilia Galliae a. 511–695*: 31–2) (incest is not to be established by any name of marriage), although the manuscripts he cites include many variants. One version, found in some manuscripts of the *Collectio Hispana*, was 'Incestos vero nullo coniugii nomine deputandos' (incestuous marriages are not to be reckoned by the name of marriage). The altered version has 'Incestuosos vero nullo coniugii nomine deputandos' (incestuous people are not to be reckoned by the name of marriage). See Ubl 2008: 348; d'Avray 2015: 51–2.

394 On the letter, see above, 60.

395 Response 1: 113 'whether this coupling … had been a marriage'; Response 13: 222: 'was not a legitimate marriage'.

396 'Incestuosos' version: Response 12: 194, 219 (in Pseudo-Gregory); Response 12: 220 and; Response 19: 256 (in Pseudo-Gregory). 'Incestos' version: Response 19: 257.

397 Response 12: 219; see Ubl 2008: 348–9.

398 Response 21: 260. He was perhaps suggesting that Theutberga could be considered as *infidelis* in the light of her actions.

399 See especially Response 21: 265.

Incest remained the central charge at the Third Council of Aachen in 862. However, by this point Lothar's supporters had slightly changed tack. The emphasis was now on the moral and social impossibility of a king remaining married to a woman who had committed such terrible acts, not on her incapacity to enter into marriage in the first place. Lothar II appeared before the council and pleaded for help. The bishops had forbidden him from his wife, as wholly unsuitable for a king, and had prohibited him from having a concubine: so as a young, virile man, what was he meant to do?[400] The bishops took pity, and granted him permission to marry again.

The reason for the change in emphasis may have been that Theutberga had by this point left Lotharingia and could no longer be put under pressure, but it may also have been the realisation that the incest argument was fragile.[401] Its weakness was laid bare by another contemporary commentator, identified by recent research as the monk Ratramnus of Corbie, who around 862 wrote a short text that systematically took the incest allegation apart.[402] Ratramnus firstly pointed out that the Council of Epaon did not remove the capacity for marriage from those guilty of incest, but only forbade them to marry their relatives. Since Lothar II and Theutberga were not related, her previous incest was no impediment to their marriage. Secondly, provided Theutberga had repented of any sinful acts committed before the marriage, these had no bearing on her marriage to Lothar afterwards. Like penance and baptism, marriage was a fresh start. Separation remained possible, but only if both partners wanted to become continent. Sure of his ground, Ratramnus stated the position bluntly: Lothar II's choice was between continence and reconciliation with Theutberga.[403]

There is no reason to think that Ratramnus's text circulated widely, but the supporters of Lothar may have realised that they were on thin ice. In 863 they abandoned the incest argument entirely, claiming instead that Lothar II had in fact already been married to Waldrada.[404] This

400 *Libellus proclamationis Lothars II*, Council of Aachen 862 (MGH *Conc.* 4, no. 9B: 74–5).

401 Contrary to the view of Kottje 1983 and Bauer 1994b.

402 Edited as *Gutachten einiger Bischöfe*, Council of Aachen 862 (MGH *Conc.* 4 no. 9D: 78–86). The identification of Ratramnus as the author was suggested by Ubl 2008: 350–1 and further strengthened by Hoffman and Pokorny 2011: 11.

403 On Ratramnus's text see Heidecker 2010: 107–9.

404 Adventius, *Epistolae ad divortium Lotharii regis pertinentes*, 5 (MGH *Epp.* 6: 215–17; Dutton 2003: 386–9). Airlie 1998: 17–18 points out that the non-royal name of Lothar and Waldrada's son Hugh suggests that he was not originally intended to succeed his father. In contrast, the couple's daughters were given 'royal names': see Böhringer 2011: 152–3.

not only conferred legitimacy on their children (as discussed above), but if proved, would have made the marriage with Theutberga definitively illegitimate, since it was theologically impossible to marry while one's spouse was still alive.

Yet even before this dramatic tactical swerve, it seems unlikely that Hincmar, known for his acuity in interpreting Church councils, would have been unaware of the incest argument's flaws. Indeed, he seems to allude to them himself in a conspicuously awkward passage.[405] The fact that in *De divortio* he nevertheless accepts this argument is therefore in itself good evidence that, however thorough his critique of the procedures may have been, he was not as hostile to Lothar II's divorce as has sometimes been thought.[406]

8 Magic, witchcraft and the workings of the devil

In *De divortio,* Hincmar responds to a question put indirectly to him: might Lothar have been bewitched by Waldrada?[407] The questioners may have seen this as the mostly likely explanation for the strength of Lothar II's emotional attachment to Waldrada. They might, though, have also been attempting to represent Lothar II as under a woman's control, to frame his actions as a sign of her power and his weakness – and of course to blacken her name, thus making it harder for Waldrada ever to become queen.[408] If so, they seem to have succeeded in the long run, for a (probably) tenth-century source depicted Waldrada as a witch.[409]

Magic and the demonic

Whatever the motivation behind the question, Hincmar addressed it squarely, making his treatise an important source on early medieval magic.[410] Central to Hincmar's concept of magic were two assumptions, both founded on a learned tradition from Late Antiquity and before. The first was that that people could indeed exercise magical power. That was emphasised by many sources at Hincmar's disposal, not least the Bible, which includes examples of magic and witchcraft, such as the

405 Response 21: 261: 'almost illicitly'!

406 For example, in Response 1: 99 where he accepts that the bishops could have been divinely inspired. For claims of his hostility, see above, 14.

407 See Question 13: 221.

408 On the long history of such rhetorical practices, see Cooper 1992.

409 *Vita s. Deicoli,* ed. G. Waitz, MGH *SS* 15, 2 (Hanover, 1888), c. 13: 678.

410 See e.g. Flint 1991; Filotas 2005; Rider 2006.

Egyptian magicians who turned sticks into snakes (Exodus 7:11–13) or the 'witch of Endor' (1 Samuel 28 7–25), who raised the spirit of Samuel for Saul.[411]

The second assumption concerned the source of magical power, and was a matter of definition: that what made magic magical was not the intention or the nature of the activity that was carried out, but the nature of the unseen powers that were harnessed.[412] Facing the Egyptian magicians, Aaron's rod had also become a snake and swallowed up their snakes, but this was done through the power of God, and so was a miracle, not magic.[413] There was no such thing as 'white magic', since all magic was linked to evil forces, powers permitted by God for reasons known only to Him.[414]

It is for this reason that Hincmar refers interchangeably to 'demonical arts', 'magical arts' and 'wicked (*maleficia*) arts', as well as using a variety of more specific terms.[415] For churchmen like Hincmar, magic was different from superstitious practices. Superstition was a more fluid category, blending into pious or devotional practices in the cases of amulets; for some Carolingian writers (though not Hincmar) it included the cult of the saints or pilgrimage.[416] None of these practices, however, was ever considered magical, and Hincmar cites approvingly texts from the 'Council of Braga' which permitted a number of unorthodox practices, provided only they were accompanied by the invocation of God, and

411 Hincmar mentions these examples several times: see e.g. Response 8: 172; Response 9: 173, 175; Response 15: 238.

412 Kieckhefer 1989: 14: 'That which makes an action magical is the type of power it invokes: if it relies on divine action or the manifest powers of nature it is not magical, while if it uses demonic aid or occult powers in nature it is magical.' The definition by Flint 1991: 3 which sees all use of preternatural control over nature as magical is therefore excessively broad. Jolly, Raudvere and Peters 2002: 8: distinctions between the manipulation and supplication of supernatural powers are also unhelpful.

413 On the varying attitudes of Carolingian reformers towards miracles, see Smith 2003; Noble 2009: 287–313. In Response 13: 228, Hincmar claims that miracles are no longer necessary in the Church, an argument already made by Gregory the Great (see Markus 1997: 56–7), but his section of the *Annales Bertiniani* include accounts of miracles (see e.g. *AB* 862: 101).

414 Rider 2006: 29.

415 See e.g. Response 9: 174; Response 17: 250. Hincmar does not use the term 'magia'.

416 See on superstition Response 15: 239–40 and on piety Response 6: 163; Filotas 2005: 252–6. Hincmar condemns amulets in Response 15: 239. For criticism of the cult of the saints by the Carolingian writer Claudius of Turin, see Noble 2009: 288–95.

not of demons.[417] Like paganism, magic was a category largely invented and defined by clerics, and applied on a case-by-case basis.[418]

More open to debate than whether magical or demonic arts worked was the question of exactly how they worked. For some Late Antique authors, magic, and demonic power in general, were primarily illusionary in their effect. Augustine of Hippo, much cited in *De divortio*, did not believe that the devil and demons were able actually to affect the material world, but could only deceive people by the illusion that magic had been worked.[419] In this way, it was people's belief in demons itself that gave demons power.[420] However, other writers quoted by Hincmar, such as Bede, disagreed, claiming that the devil might be able to foresee the future, or that demons might cause very real ulcers to appear on someone's body.[421]

Hincmar tended to follow Augustine, citing several stories showing how magic and the devil worked more by apparitions and deception than by altering reality.[422] Hincmar was also certain that the devil often took advantages of people's weaknesses: for instance, persuading them to perjure themselves or, more subtly (because it seemed honourable), tempting them to commit some terrible crime simply to avoid perjury.[423] Hincmar draws on biblical and Late Antique stories of magic and witchcraft, such as King David's son Amnon, who was inspired by the devil (and a male companion) to commit incest.[424] The devil was allowed by God to test the faithful in this way, for reasons which were hidden to humans, but were undoubtedly just.[425] The key point

417 Response 17: 252; these were in fact translations by Martin of Braga (d. 580) of Eastern canons.

418 On early medieval paganism and problems in defining it see Filotas 2005: 12–25; Palmer 2007. In *De divortio*, Hincmar uses the term 'paganus' in connection to magical practices only in a quotation from the 'Council of Braga' (Response 17: 252).

419 Response 8: 172; Response 9: 173. On Augustine's ideas on magic, see Graf 2002.

420 Response 9: 175.

421 Response 9: 175; Response 15: 247–8.

422 See above, 38. Cf. Response 9: 173–4. Cut "citing Gregory the Great and Pseudo-Clement" to allow space for extra line in n. 423 citing Gregory the Great and Pseudo-Clement, alongside other texts.

423 On perjury, see above, 35. Response 10: 182–5 suggests that the devil uses the possibility of redemption through future penance; Hincmar adds a passage about the temptation to avoid perjury to a quotation from Gregory the Great.

424 Response 15: 235–6.

425 Response 8: 172; Response 9: 173; Response 16: 248–9. The exemplar for this practice was the biblical account of God allowing the devil to attack Job (Response 9: 173). Cf. Response 8: 170–1.

for Hincmar was that people, whatever their sex or status, should resist such temptation.[426]

Frankish magic

Authoritative texts taught Hincmar that the devil and magic were to be taken seriously; but he appears to have had first-hand knowledge, too. Discussing the different types of demons, some specialising in particular types of sins, he mentioned that he himself had experience of magical practices, but (frustratingly) opted not to give more details 'for the sake of brevity'.[427] Other sources also confirm that magic was perceived as a reality in the Frankish world. Hincmar's contemporaries in Francia followed a range of practices relying on unseen powers to protect against harm and to influence the world, and many of these would have been classified by Hincmar as magical. Such practices are abundantly attested by penitentials' lists of sins and appropriate penances for them.[428] Their use was not confined to peasants in the countryside; accusations of magic can be found amongst the Frankish elite, too. Indeed, Lothar II's own father Lothar I had arranged for Gerberga, the sister of the highly placed nobleman Bernard of Septimania, to be drowned in 834 'as if a witch'.[429] It is hardly surprising then that Hincmar was quite open to the idea that magic and the devil were involved in Lothar II's attempt to rid himself of Theutberga.[430]

Still, separating out what in *De divortio* comes from Late Antique sources and what comes from Hincmar's contemporary experience can be difficult. For example, in Response 15, Hincmar gives a long list of types of magicians and the material they use.[431] Most of this is taken from Isidore of Seville's *Etymologia*, but there are a number of additions to Isidore's text. These might reflect Hincmar's own contributions, and thus possibly practices in his own diocese; but they might simply reflect

426 In Appendix Response 6: 299, 304 he implies that Lothar is being ruled by the devil.

427 Response 15: 242. Details of demons and their attacks might be needed in order to effect a cure (Response 15: 247).

428 Filotas 2005 shows the wide range of such practices.

429 Astronomer, c. 52: 496: 'tamquam venefica' (Noble 2009: 286). Scholars have therefore often seen a 'common tradition' of understanding magic, rather than distinct 'popular' and elite views: see Kieckhefer 1994: 833; Filotas 2005: 26–7.

430 See e.g. Preface: 94. By the time he wrote Appendix Response 1: 283 he was more specific: the devil's operation in the matter 'cannot be doubted'.

431 Response 15: 238–9.

interpolations to Isidore's original text at any point in the 200 years before Hincmar read one particular manuscript of it.[432]

There is, however, one passage that has not been traced to any other text and thus has been thought to reflect Hincmar's own pastoral experience.[433] He recounts the story of how a newly married husband, though not previously impotent, was unable to consummate his marriage, and sought separation from his wife. The bishop responsible refused to agree (as mentioned above, 38–9), and after a great deal of effort 'the works of the devil were dissolved by the grace of God'; Hincmar noted with satisfaction that the married couple now 'rejoice in numerous children'.[434] Hincmar does not specifically mention in this story any human as magically responsible for the husband's impotence. By implication, though, it may have been the man's previous concubine, or his mother, who had opposed the marriage.

This is particularly interesting because in the penitential and conciliar literature from the early Middle Ages, magic is often associated with women;[435] and the list of questions that Hincmar received specifically referred to women as allegedly able to carry out love magic.[436] Though Hincmar's Lotharingian questioners asked him about the punishment of both (male) sorcerers (*malefici*) and female enchanters (*incantrices feminae*), Hincmar's discussions concentrated on men being magically attacked by 'witches' (*strigae, lamiae*) and weaving women (*feminae genichiales*).[437] Yet before concluding that the exercise of magic was strongly gendered in Hincmar's Francia, we should consider whether this simply reflects the context of the questions, implicitly about Waldrada. Hincmar also cites Late Antique stories and canons that show men and women as practising and believing in magic.[438] For instance, he quotes at length a story, originally from the Byzantine world, in which a servant goes to a (male) sorcerer and later makes a pact with the devil in order to gain the love of his master's daughter.[439]

432 Our thanks to Karl Heidecker for this point. On the arguments over whether early medieval pastoral literature reflects its own culture or earlier ones, see Filotas 2005: 8–9.

433 Rider 2006: 32–4.

434 Response 15: 236–7.

435 Compare the index entries for 'men' and 'women' in Filotas 2005.

436 Question 15: 235.

437 Response 15 237–8; Question 17: 249. There was a long association of magic with the female activity of weaving: see Filotas 2005: 73–4, and Response 17: 252, citing canon 73 of the 'Council of Braga'.

438 Response 17: 250–2.

439 Pseudo-Amphilocus's story is in Response 15: 243–7.

If it is difficult to separate out popular practices from Hincmar's wider reading, or to read past the particular circumstances of *De divortio* to broader Frankish practice, the treatise at least reveals something about the attitude of one influential Frankish cleric to magical practice. One striking feature is Hincmar's fundamental optimism about the capacity of the Church to deal with magic. His main concern with magic in *De divortio* is to demonstrate both its existence and the role of the Church in healing people from magical attacks; his discussion of punishments for those who inflict such attacks is surprisingly cursory.[440] In particular, he does not cite Exodus 22:18, which in the Vulgate version, states that *malefici* should not be allowed to live.

Hincmar, in other words, treats magic in a fairly matter-of-fact way, which seems to reflect his confidence in the Church's ability to deal with it. Sometimes elaborate programmes were required to cast off demons or break magical spells, involving communal prayer and hymns.[441] Hincmar also cites Bede's account of how a priest used holy oil and salt to heal a nun from demonic illness.[442] But sometimes a holy man's prayers alone might be enough to cast demons off.[443] And Hincmar notes that demons were routinely driven out from the sick at saints' shrines (though they might also enter perjurers there).[444] In short, apparitions or real, manifestations of demonic power were dangerous, but they could be countered, and were being countered, every day. For Hincmar, unlike some other Carolingian authors, the use of magic was not a threat to the whole of society, but a specific form of sinfulness which the Church could deal with effectively.[445]

9 Kingship and bishops

Hincmar's works have often played a key role in discussions of Carolingian 'political thought'.[446] Recent studies of such thought have tended to move away from purely abstract theories to look at

440 Response 15, which discusses whether love magic is possible, takes up nine pages of the MGH edition; Response 17, on punishment, is three pages long, of which one page is taken up with general questions about the severity of penance.

441 Response 15: 245–7.

442 Response 15: 247–8.

443 Response 9: 173 cites stories of St Benedict and St Peter.

444 Response 6: 149.

445 Compare the denunciations of sorcery and soothsaying in the royal palace by Paschasius Radbertus, *Epitaphium Arsenii*, II, 8 (Cabaniss 1967: 160–2) from the 850s.

446 See e.g. Nelson 1977; Fried 1982; Nelson 1994.

intellectuals' responses to particular political events;[447] we should remember that in *De divortio* Hincmar was primarily concerned with the behaviour of a specific king, Lothar II, and that his focus on kings and bishops (and his relatively few mentions of lay noblemen) reflects the specific issues in Lothar's case. Nevertheless, embedded within the text are pointers to wider theories of how kings and bishops should behave and how they should relate to one another.

When it came to kings, Hincmar drew not only on the Old Testament, but also on a long tradition of Christian moral thought on kingship from Augustine onwards.[448] Within this tradition, the king did not simply inherit his throne, but was granted it by the grace of God.[449] Hincmar was especially keen to stress the ruler's role as a law-maker and guarantor of justice, acting on behalf of God.[450] Such a role required that the king honoured God and kept his own laws.[451] Only the good and just king was a true king, and not a tyrant permitted to rule by God as punishment for his people's sins.[452] The good king must punish the unjust, not protect them, or his own good deeds would not avail him.[453]

All this meant that kingship carried a heavy moral responsibility. The essence of kinship was reflected in the 'name of the king': a king (*rex*) was so called from 'ruling' (*regendo*), so only a man who ruled himself could truly be called a king.[454] That meant that the king needed to control both his mind and body; Lothar II's argument that he needed to remarry to contain his sexual desire lawfully could be turned against

447 Compare e.g. Anton 1968 and de Jong 2009.

448 Anton 1968 is fundamental.

449 Appendix Response 6: 301–3. Appendix Response 7: 320: the sons of an unjust king would not inherit his throne. Response 12: 208 stressed that God had granted the single kingdom of the Franks to the Carolingians.

450 Nelson 1977: 242–3; see above, 29.

451 Response 11: 189–90; Response 12: 209–10; Appendix Response 5: 295–6; Appendix Response 6: 302. In Appendix Response 6: 300, however, Hincmar accepts theoretically that a good king need not be subject to the law, drawing on St Paul's statements on the law as intended only for those who act badly.

452 Response 12: 86, 215; Appendix Response 6: 300–1; Preface: 86: unlike a tyrant, a king is marked by gentleness, patience and love; Appendix Response 7: 309: a good king loves free speech from his subjects.

453 Response 12: 207 (criticising Charles the Bald's protection of Hubert); Appendix Response 5: 295–7 (criticising Lothar's protection of Engeltrude). Queens had similar responsibilities: Response 13: 230 cites a letter from Gregory the Great to the Merovingian queen Brunhild.

454 Appendix Response 6: 300; this royal name came from God and could be damaged by sinful behaviour (Response 12: 210, 214). On classical and Carolingian ideas concerning the 'name of the king', see Anton 1968: 384–404.

him, as proof of a lack of self-control that in turn showed unfitness for rule.[455] But a king must also rule his own household, including his children and his wife, so Lothar II's 'shame' at public rumours of his wife's bad behaviour was entirely understandable.[456]

As well as this more or less traditional view of kingship, some of Hincmar's thought in *De divortio* reflected his own priorities and anxieties. He emphasised that the king must especially respect laws and documents signed by his own hand (copies of some of which Hincmar had helpfully kept).[457] Since Hincmar was extremely concerned with the protection of Church property, he included a long digression on the need for kings not to remove land from churches, including land they had themselves granted.[458]

Hincmar's thinking also reflected distinctively Carolingian concepts and vocabularies of rule. Charlemagne's reign had seen the development of the idea of *correctio* (reform and rectification of the whole of society) as a key task for the ruler.[459] The idea was refined by Louis the Pious in the early 820s. Louis saw his imperial *ministerium* (God-ordained role within society) as caring for the Church and the kingdom. Within this scheme, bishops had a special role, sharing in this *ministerium* as Louis's 'helpers' (*adiutores*); they had a particular authority (*auctoritas*), and a key part of their role was *admonitio*, warning about the sins of those under their pastoral care.[460]

This theory was further developed by the bishops themselves at the Council of Paris in 829, focusing on the need for kings and bishops to collaborate in ensuring the salvation of the Christian people entrusted to them.[461] The conciliar canons issued in Paris explicitly drew on a formula first used in Pope Gelasius's letter to Emperor Anastasius at the end of the fifth century, that there were two powers by which the world was chiefly ruled: the sacred authority (*auctoritas*) of priests (*pontifices*) and royal power (*potestas*).[462] Pope Gelasius had thought bishops

455 Airlie 1998: 25–6; Appendix Response 7: 317–8.

456 Response 1: 108–9, c. 16. See above, 49.

457 Response 12: 209; Morelle 2004: 297–301 argues that references to the king's 'hand' on such documents should not be taken too literally.

458 Response 12: 212–7.

459 Nelson 1994: 60; de Jong 2005: 115–16.

460 Patzold 2008: 140–6; de Jong 2009: 37. The ruler's role also involved *admonitio* (de Jong 2009: 131–5).

461 Patzold 2008: 149–68.

462 Preface: 91; Response 11: 190; Appendix Response 6: 299–300; Appendix Response 7: 319. On Gelasius's letter (J 632) and its Carolingian reception, see Sassier 2005 and Patzold 2008: 140 n. 240, 155–7.

should obey the ruler's laws on public discipline, and that the ruler in turn should obey bishops.[463] However, of these two, the priesthood had a greater responsibility, because they were answerable to God himself for the conduct of kings.[464] The Frankish bishops in 829 interpreted this as placing the king *within* the Church, making him ultimately subject to their authority.[465]

Hincmar similarly argued that bishops had jurisdiction over kings, but he never explicitly claimed that this allowed bishops to depose their king.[466] Instead, the emphasis in *De divortio* is on the shared responsibility of the king and bishops for the well-being of the kingdom.[467] They would be held answerable to God after death not only for their own sins, but the evil deeds of all those subject to their control, and their exalted position would make their subsequent punishment in the afterlife harsher.[468] Indeed, that punishment might come sooner than expected: biblical precedents showed that God might take immediate vengeance on notorious sinners, but also on those who 'consented' to their sins, which meant failing to repress sin in subordinates or to warn those who could not be coerced.[469] At the worst extreme, unchecked sinfulness might bring destruction or disaster on an entire people, as had happened several times in the Old Testament.[470]

463 Response 11: 190.

464 Appendix Response 6: 300.

465 Patzold 2008: 156–7. Cf. Appendix Response 6: 301.

466 Nelson 1977: 272–7; as she points out (243–4) the bishops in 833 had similarly not claimed the right to depose Louis the Pious. Cf. Response 12: 210, 215. In Appendix Response 7: 306 Hincmar states that a king who sets a bad example would be better off in 'private life' (*vita privata*).

467 In Response 13: 230 Hincmar says that a letter of Gregory the Great to Queen Brunhild contains advice for 'bishops and kings and all those endowed with human power': power could to some extent transcend gender boundaries.

468 Preface: 90, 91; Response 12: 210, 211, Appendix Response 7: 305–7.

469 See e.g. Response 6: 153–4 on the earth swallowing up Dathan and Abiran and their families; Response 10: 186 on Ananias and Sapphira; Response 13: 229 on Eli's sons; Response 21: 269–70 on David's punishment for adultery. On the idea of 'consent' to sins, see Preface: 91; Response 6: 161; Response 12: 205; Response 13: 229, 230; Response 17: 250; Appendix Response 5: 297; Appendix Response 7: 307–8, 314–15. Such failure to repress evildoers was regarded as *negligentia* (negligence), a key term in Carolingian reform texts: see de Jong 2009: 121–2.

470 See e.g. Response 6: 150–2 on the Flood and the destruction of Sodom. Appendix Response 7: 320–1 quotes Pseudo-Cyprian warning of the many dangers to the kingdom ruled by an 'unjust king'.

Lotharingian kingship

Though Hincmar's theories of kingship are already visible in outline in the first part of the treatise, they come much more sharply into focus in the second part. But now his tone changed. This is partly because the political situation had altered between spring and summer, but it also reflects his response to a new series of questions. In Karl Heidecker's words, Hincmar reacted to some of these as if he had been 'stung by a hornet'.[471] Most controversial of all was the suggestion that no king could be judged or excommunicated by anyone, since 'he is subjected to the sovereignty of God alone'.[472]

Some historians, most notably Hans Hubert Anton, have argued that we can detect in this statement a distinctive Lotharingian concept of kingship.[473] Karl Heidecker suspects instead that the questioners had deliberately exaggerated Lothar II's position to bring him into disrepute, since it seems at odds with Lothar's earlier submission to episcopal authority.[474] Yet we should not assume that Lothar's court necessarily shared a single strategy for bringing about the end of the marriage; different advisors could have recommended different solutions. And, notwithstanding Hincmar's harsh response to these questions, he continued to have a great deal of respect for kingship as a divinely ordained institution. When he revised the manuscript of *De divortio*, he even added extracts from royal capitularies and, in the conclusion, provided a lengthy discussion of what made a good king and the benefits his rule could bring.[475]

Nevertheless, Hincmar also had an exalted view of the role of bishops, as the successors to the apostles and to the prophets.[476] In both parts of *De divortio* he stressed that their duties encompassed advising and, if necessary, admonishing and even judging kings.[477] His models included

471 Heidecker 2010: 96.

472 Appendix Question 6: 298.

473 Anton 1993: 114–18; Böhringer 2011: 150 similarly sees such claims by Lothar's supporters as a 'radical' statement about an 'absolute' ruler. On the problems with Anton's arguments of a distinctively Lotharingian view, see Airlie 2011: 341–4.

474 Heidecker 2010: 95–6. However, he accepts (128–9) the similarity of some of the views and citations to later statements by Lotharingian bishops.

475 Appendix Response 7: 319–21.

476 Preface: 93; Response 1: 99; Response 12: 209; Response 21: 269; Appendix Response 6: 301. In Appendix Response 6: 299 Hincmar even cites Deuteronomy 17:12, saying that men who do not obey priests should be killed!

477 Preface: 111–112; Appendix Response 4: 294; Appendix Response 6: 299–300, 301. On the Carolingian tradition of admonishing rulers, see de Jong 2009: 112–22.

the Old Testament prophet Nathan, who reproached King David for his sins, but also Ambrose of Milan's insistence in the fifth century that Emperor Theodosius must do penance for a massacre that he had ordered.[478] If kings did not accept the Church's capacity to censure, they were implicitly denying its ability to absolve sins.[479] Hincmar stressed though that episcopal authority relied not only on holding an office, but also on performing it correctly.[480] A bishop who behaved wrongly might himself need to be 'rebuked, reproached and corrected'.[481] The term 'bishop' itself indicated that they should be watchmen.[482] They must speak out and warn all sinners, or they would face judgement for their neglect.[483]

The Frankish Church

In principle, Hincmar cherished the autonomy of bishops within their dioceses, and, following Gregory the Great, warned against bishops who judged or gave penance to parishioners from other dioceses.[484] In the case of Theutberga (as in similar cases), Hincmar claimed he was only responding to requests for advice and not attempting to judge. Although elsewhere Hincmar was keen to emphasise his metropolitan control over his suffragan bishops, in *De divortio* he called himself

478 On David, see Response 11 189; Appendix Response 6: 299. On Ambrose, see Response 13: 230; Appendix Response 6: 300; Appendix Response 7: 309–14 and Meens 2014: 21–3. The precedent was an important one for Carolingian reformers: see de Jong 2009: 122–31 on texts connecting it to the penance by Louis the Pious at Attigny in 822. While a priest could impose penance, only a bishop could reconcile a penitent sinner to the Church: see above, 39.

479 Response 12: 217.

480 Response 13: 224 and Appendix Response 7: 307, 314–5 condemn clerics who flatter the powerful; Appendix Response 2: 286 states that a bishop's authority depends on him judging 'rightly'.

481 Appendix Response 3: 287; Appendix Response 3: 289 deals with the bishop who has acted 'violently or negligently against those subject to him'. Hincmar also quotes extensively from Pseudo-Cyprian on the dangers of the 'negligent bishop' in Appendix Response 7: 321–2.

482 On the bishop as watchman, see Appendix Response 7: 310, 321.

483 Preface: 90–1; Response 13: 231 states that if bishops do speak out, they will be 'acquitted' by God of others' sins; cf. Response 13: 229. Response 12: 210 warns bishops who might be tempted to conceal the sins of a king.

484 Hincmar, *De uxore Bosonis* (MGH *Epp.* 8: 83), discusses Gunther of Cologne's handling of the case of Engeltrude; Hincmar argues that since she is the wife of Boso, the matter must be dealt with in the province where he lives. Response 3: 123–4: any wider involvement required the agreement of fellow bishops.

simply a bishop, drawing on the biblical and canonical resonances of that position.[485]

Yet his discussions of kings and bishops took place within a wider framework of a distinctively Frankish Christendom.[486] Although the Frankish people were divided amongst several different kingdoms, many observers still regarded them as a single unit, as Lothar II's brother, Louis II, would later make clear in a sharply worded letter to Emperor Basil I of Byzantium.[487] In 860, Hincmar shared this view: the Franks were one people, united under one Church, and that Church was led by its bishops.[488] When challenged on why he should be involved in a case from a different province and kingdom, he was quick to insist that since this was a general matter, he had a right to be involved in the decision making.[489]

Hincmar had a sense of the universal Church too, 'spread far and wide across the world'.[490] He took care to acknowledge the pope's pre-eminent position in the Church, even setting out a theoretical hierarchy in Appendix Response 2: appeals from an individual bishop's judgement should go to a provincial synod; appeals from a provincial synod should go to a general synod; the pope could overrule or confirm the judgements of both provincial and general synods.[491] Yet it is revealing that Hincmar did not discuss the possibility of an appeal to Rome in his text: *De divortio* throws into relief that papal intervention was still not a matter of routine in the ninth century.[492] Nicholas I's very forceful involvement in the case from 862 onwards reflected his

485 Response 3: 121 refers briefly to Hincmar's metropolitan authority, contrasting 'his son' Hincmar of Laon, with other bishops not subject to his authority. On the use of the title 'archepiscopus' in the Carolingian period, see Pangerl 2011: 29–31: it was used both for metropolitans (the highest-ranking bishop within a province) and as a personal title of honour for some non-metropolitans.

486 See de Jong 2006.

487 Costambeys, Innes and MacLean 2011: 14, citing MGH Epp. 7: 385–94.

488 Response 12: 208; Appendix Response 1: 283.

489 Appendix Response 1: 282–4. Even though his archiepiscopal province extended into Lotharingia (see above,), Hincmar did not attempt to use this to justify his involvement. Possibly he feared this might raise further difficulties with one of his suffragan bishops over episcopal and archiepiscopal jurisdiction. Hincmar already had difficult relations with these: see Stone 2015: 13–14.

490 Response 5: 135.

491 Preface: 85; Appendix Response 2: 286. In Response 3: 125 he says that it is proper that the pope should be told about the case, but implies he should not be told too much! Response 12: 203 cites a letter from Gregory the Great referring to the pope's right to retract the sentences of others.

492 See de Jong 2015: 273, 279–81.

unusual desire for political influence, and may have been unexpected.[493] Hincmar's focus was firmly on the need for a gathering of Frankish bishops.[494]

10 Aftermath

As already suggested, *De divortio* was partly intended to hedge Hincmar's bets. Its overall verdict cannot be simply seen as either pro- or anti-Lothar II.[495] On the one hand, Hincmar did not claim that the ordeal's result in 858 had been definitive, and he accepted the principle that if Theutberga's prior incest were proved, Lothar II could remarry.[496] On the other hand, he went to considerable lengths to deny that the procedure at the councils of Aachen had been valid and that Theutberga had made a proper public confession. In his view, only after a judgement by laymen and a general council had taken place could the marriage be declared invalid;[497] moreover, Lothar II needed to do (public) penance for his own sexual sins.[498]

Hincmar might have been setting up a possible future compromise which would allow Lothar to marry Waldrada, but only if he made concessions. The need for Hubert and Theutberga to be present at a future judgement, for example, gave considerable opportunity for Charles the Bald to be obstructive, since both had fled to his kingdom. Similarly, the holding of a general council (and the possible need for Lothar II to make some formal act of penance during it) would confirm the collective standing of the Frankish bishops, with Hincmar leading the way. Even as Hincmar offered possible support for Lothar II in the first part of *De divortio*, that support was accompanied by a stream of barbed comments about the king and his episcopal supporters.[499]

As mentioned above, Hincmar probably presented his thoughts on Lothar's marriage at a meeting of the kings in Koblenz in June 860, and

493 On Nicholas I, see Scholz 2006: 185–211; Heidecker 2010: 149–72. On connections between the Frankish Church and the papacy and especially on judicial appeals, see de Jong 2015.

494 See above, 51.

495 Böhringer 2011: 147–8.

496 Above, 38, 62.

497 Above, 28, 43, 52.

498 Above, 41.

499 See e.g. Response 1: 111 on Lothar's wicked grief; Response 1: 112 on possible sacrilege by Lothar; Response 7: 168 on Gunther; Response 12: 201 on Lothar's failing to claim that Theutberga was not a virgin.

again at a meeting in Tusey in October/November of that year. Whether anyone paid much attention is difficult to say, however, for events were moving rapidly. Lothar II and his advisers pressed on with their plans, acting as if the decisions of the councils of Aachen had not been challenged. They sent envoys to Rome in 861, but did not wait for the pope's reply before holding the Third Council of Aachen in April 862. Whereas the first two councils in 860 had merely permitted Lothar and Theutberga to separate, this council gave formal permission for Lothar to marry again. This he duly did, and 'Queen Waldrada' is attested in some charters.[500] Charles the Bald made his disapproval clear at a meeting at Savonnières in 862, where he refused to speak with his nephew, but Louis the German negotiated on Lothar's behalf, and things were smoothed over.[501]

In November 862, however, Pope Nicholas finally took action. He sent legates into Lothar's kingdom, and ordered a synod to be held to consider the question once again in their presence. This took place at the Council of Metz in June 863. To Lothar II's satisfaction, the papal legates confirmed that his marriage to Theutberga was over, and that Waldrada was his wife and queen. When the king dispatched archbishops Theutgaud of Trier and Gunther of Cologne with a record of the council (now sadly lost) for the pope's approval, he might have considered this a formality.

If so, he was wrong, for in a dramatic turn of events, Pope Nicholas held a synod in Rome in October 863 at which he annulled the Council of Metz, peremptorily deposed the two Lotharingian archbishops and threatened the king himself with excommunication. Considerable political lobbying, and a degree of political calculation, must have lain behind Nicholas's action, but it nevertheless represented a turning point in the affair, as well as a quite unprecedented assertion of papal authority over the Alps, which inspired later commentators.[502] Lothar II persuaded his brother, Louis II of Italy, to intervene on his behalf, but Nicholas remained steadfast. By 865, Lothar II and his bishops had bowed to the pressure, and Theutberga was formally reinstated as his queen, though to Hincmar's irritation Lothar avoided doing penance.[503]

500 The first mention of Waldrada and Hugh is from May 863 in DD. Lot II, 19, *Die Urkunden Lothars I. und Lothars II.*, ed. T. Schieffer, MGH *Diplomatum Karolinorum* III (Berlin, 1966): 415.

501 Heidecker 2010: 100–20.

502 Bonizo of Sutri, *Liber ad amicum*, Book III: 579 (Robinson 2004: 173), writing during the papal reform movement of the late eleventh century, claimed that Nicholas had excommunicated and then deposed the 'emperor' Lothar.

503 Heidecker 2010: 168.

Theutberga, however, had had enough. Doubtless under pressure from her husband, but plausibly reflecting genuine unhappiness too, she wrote to the pope requesting that she be allowed to divorce and retire to a convent. Only now was reference made to her sterility. Nicholas, however, remained intransigent.[504] He pointed out that sterility was the result of sin and could be overcome by prayer. Only if Lothar II also committed himself to a life of continence would separation be possible. And for good measure (and without much legal or theological justification), he added that under no circumstances would Lothar ever be able to marry Waldrada. The belated argument that Lothar had actually been married to Waldrada all along, prior to the 'marriage' to Theutberga, did not sway his mind. For Nicholas, the issue was now less the issue of marriage, and more the assertion of papal authority.[505]

Lothar II did not change his mind, either, and contemplated accusing Theutberga of adultery and testing the accusation with a duel.[506] Only on Nicholas's death on 13 November 867 did the opportunity for some resolution present itself, as the new pope, Hadrian II, seemed more accommodating. But time had run out for Lothar II, who died from a fever in August 869 as he returned from a meeting with Hadrian, struck down along with many of his supporters. As the survivors amongst his followers hastily made their way back to Lotharingia to prepare for the inevitable crisis, they did not bother to bring his body with them, instead abandoning it in Piacenza. Deprived of a marriage with Waldrada, Lothar was also deprived of a ceremonial funeral. Contemporaries, not least Hincmar, predictably saw all this as divine vengeance.[507]

Charles the Bald with remarkable – pre-arranged? – speed invaded Lotharingia, and on 9 September 869, it was none other than Hincmar of Rheims who presided over his coronation as king of Lotharingia in Metz.[508] Charles was not able to hold on to the whole kingdom for long, though, and Lotharingia remained contested between kings of Western and Eastern Francia for decades, indeed generations.

504 Heidecker 2010: 153–4.

505 For varying opinions on Nicholas's attitude to the case, see Kottje 1983; Heidecker 2010: 152–68; d'Avray 2015: 50–62.

506 Nicholas I, *Epistola* 48 (MGH *Epp.* 6: 330).

507 *AB* 869: 156; cf. also Regino, *Chronicon* 869: 159–60. As Airlie 2006: 199 points out, Regino was writing with hindsight. On other contemporary views, see Heidecker 2010: 183–4.

508 For the argument that Charles had been planning to invade in any case, see Staubach 1982: 242–50.

As for Theutberga and Waldrada, the former retired to a convent in Metz and the latter to the convent of Remiremont.[509] Theutberga may have found consolation in the marriage of her niece, Richildis, to the newly widowed Charles the Bald in 870, as Charles sought to consolidate his grip on the kingdom. Waldrada may still have been alive to see her son with Lothar II, Hugh, mount a credible defence of his rights to inherit his father's kingdom; but perhaps also to hear in 885 that he had been captured, blinded and confined to the monastery of Prüm, where his grandfather Lothar I was buried.[510] Later, however, another of Waldrada and Lothar's children, Berta, married one of Theutberga's nephews, Theobald 'of Arles'. The names they gave two of their children show that in the early Middle Ages, the bitter struggles of previous generations were not always carried over into enduring feud: Theutberga and Hugh, later king of Italy.[511]

11 Conclusion

Few who have read Hincmar's *De divortio* would consider it a masterpiece, or even his masterpiece. Wordy, often confused, it leaves too many loose ends untied, and readily betrays its origins as a composite, slightly hurried piece of work written for a specific political purpose. Yet whatever its shortcomings as a treatise and as a political intervention, as evidence for the politics and society of ninth-century Francia we consider it to be absolutely first-rate. This is because developing an argument about Lothar II's attempt to divorce Theutberga required Hincmar to articulate principles on a whole variety of topics, seldom treated so extensively anywhere else in this period.

More than just a window onto these topics, however, *De divortio* stands as a kind of monument to Carolingian intellectual and political culture. It may be, as has been suggested by Karl Heidecker, that the eventual outcome of Lothar II's case was decided more by politics than by learned appeals to ancient authorities in a battle over the meaning of marriage.[512] It is nevertheless true that the political struggle was at least in part articulated through reasoned argument over principles, and nominally based on evidence collected from a remarkable range of sources. In this it stood

509 Heidecker 2010: 184.

510 On Hugh's career, see MacLean 2003a: 149–52; Airlie 2011: 353–5.

511 Lazzari 2007: 137–8.

512 Heidecker 2010: 186.

in a tradition of ninth-century Frankish political contests involving competition for the 'moral high ground'.[513] This should not be understood in a triumphalist sense, for much of the debate, on all sides, had a vicious edge, particularly for the women concerned.[514] In Hincmar's learned and accomplished *De divortio*, we see in plain view the impact of the so-called Carolingian Renaissance on politics and society; we also see its darker side.

Principles of translation

This translation is based on Letha Böhringer's excellent MGH edition from 1992, which also includes an extensive apparatus and introduction in German. Readers interested in learning more about how the text was put together, or in identifying the precise stages of redaction, are strongly encouraged to consult this edition; we have indicated the page numbers in Böhringer's edition in angle brackets (< >) to make that consultation easier. The only other English translation of *De divortio*, by Priscilla Throop, appeared while we were putting together the final draft. We benefited from consulting it, though the translations remain very different.[515]

Our translation includes the additions made after the main text was completed (as discussed above, 20), which we have indicated with arrows (→ ←). The only part of the text that we have omitted is the *capitulatio* – effectively 'contents pages' summarising each Response – at the front. This part of the text is fragmentary, and anyway adds little (the exception is the summary of Response 12, which is clearer than the text it condenses, as noted in our translation). All ellipses (marks of omission) in the translation are ours: we use them to indicate to the reader where Hincmar has silently abbreviated a citation.

We have generally preferred to translate literally rather than idiomatically, although we have broken up some of Hincmar's long sentences, and some of Hincmar's paragraphs, too, in the interests of comprehensibility. Hincmar's Latin is often deliberately ambiguous, and we hope some readers may want to use our translation to make sense of the original Latin text. Our translations of biblical passages are based on the King James Bible, with the aim of capturing something of the resonances that the Vulgate would have had for Hincmar's contemporaries.

513 de Jong 2009: 5. On the same moral competition during the civil war of 840–43, see Nelson 1985.

514 This is emphasised by Airlie 1998: 22–4.

515 P. Throop, *Hincmar of Rheims on Kingship, Divorce, Virtues and Vices* (Charlotte, VT, 2014). Throop's translation is without commentary or introduction.

A number of words are ambivalent, and we have sometimes left them in the Latin (or else given the Latin in brackets):

- *fidelis*: faithful, either in a religious sense (Christian) or a political one (loyal)
- *iudicium*: judgement, but also ordeal
- *res publica*: we have translated this as 'state', but the term is contested[516]
- *sacerdos*: either priest or bishop
- *sacramentum*: sacrament or oath
- *servus*: servant or slave.

Notes have been kept to a minimum, and we have not marked up short or insignificant quotations, instead concentrating on explaining Hincmar's often convoluted argument and on selective references to the extensive secondary literature. For more extensive citations, we have relied on Letha Böhringer's work; her apparatus should be consulted for the full details of Hincmar's sources and how he reworked them. Where possible, we give both page numbers of the source edition and of an English translation of the source, with a preference for the most easily accessible, for instance those freely available online. This is so that readers without strong Latin can quickly see for themselves the context of the quotations and the extent to which Hincmar faithfully reflected his sources' arguments. We have consulted these translations, but not copied them. We have, however, cited directly translations of the *Annals of St-Bertin*, *Annals of Fulda* and Regino of Prüm's *Chronicle*, which are already available in the Manchester Medieval Sources series (and have not given page numbers for the Latin text of these sources).

516 Sassier 1988: 23–8. The term is used four times in *De divortio* (Preface: 88; Response 2: 116; Response 12: 218; Question 22: 270). For recent scholarship discussing early medieval polities and the use of the concept of 'state' see Airlie, Pohl and Reimitz 2006; Pohl and Wieser 2009.

HINCMAR OF RHEIMS, *DE DIVORTIO*

Preface

<107> To the glorious lord kings, to our venerable fellow bishops and to all those placed in the bosom of the catholic Church, Hincmar, by name but not merit bishop of Rheims[1] and servant of the people of God, together with my lord colleagues and brothers, venerable bishops of the diocese of Rheims.[2]

The holy Roman Church, as the mother and teacher, nurse and instructress of all churches, is to be consulted about all doubtful and obscure things which concern the continuity of the right faith or the dogmas of piety, and her healthful admonitions are to be kept.[3] This should be done particularly by those who live in those regions in which divine grace, through her preaching, gave birth to all in faith, and nourished with catholic milk those whom it preordained to eternal life.[4] For just as the blessed Innocent wrote to Decentius, Bishop of Gubbio:[5]

> 'it is clear that in all Italy, Gaul, Spain, Africa, Sicily, and the islands lying between them, there were no churches instituted except those founded by bishops that the venerable Peter or his successors appointed. Therefore it is necessary that they follow what the Roman Church keeps, from which church without doubt they received their origin, lest when they favour foreign assertions, they seem to have lost the head of the institutions.'

1 This is how Hincmar usually referred to himself, though he insisted on the distinction between bishop and archbishop in theory: see Introduction, 74–5.

2 Hincmar claimed to be writing on behalf of his suffragan bishops, so perhaps he had consulted with them. The address also shows that Hincmar intended his treatise to be of general interest, neither restricted to those who had asked his opinion nor confined only to Lothar II's kingdom, on grounds that he justifies below. On the dating and dissemination of the text, see Introduction, 16–17.

3 On the relations of the Frankish church to Rome, see Introduction, 75–6.

4 Predestination, the question of whether God had already decided who was going to heaven and who to hell, was a controversial question at the time Hincmar wrote *De divortio*. For the context, see Gillis 2015.

5 Innocent I, Letter to Decentius of Gubbio (J 311): 18–20 (Connell 2010: 20). The notion that all the churches in Gaul had been founded by missionaries sent personally by St Peter or other disciples of Christ was gaining ground in the ninth century. See Herrick 2012: 129–30.

But also because blessed Celestine, bishop of the same first see, said to Venerius and the other Gallican bishops that 'the universal Church is disturbed by any novelty whatever', and writing to Nestorius of Constantinople decreed that 'all ought to know what is happening, whenever the case of all is being dealt with',[6] the voice of our humility speaks to all.[7]

For, although this is a matter of a king and queen [Lothar and Theutberga], namely man and wife, who according to holy authority are 'no more twain but one flesh' [Matthew 19:6], the case of all is generally affected, since marriage is called by the holy apostle 'a great sacrament in Christ and the Church' [Ephesians 5:32], in which the health of all is believed to consist.[8] For the apostle Peter testifies about Christ <108> that 'there is none other name under heaven given among men, whereby we must be saved' [Acts 4:12]. And just as all whom the Ark did not preserve perished in the Flood, thus no one can be saved who does not remain in the unity of holy Church with right faith and good works.[9]

But as is also shown by this spiritual reason, the case brought forward for discussion, far from being trivial, is about the dignity of such a most eminent name and about such people, that the 'kings of the earth and all the people, princes and all the judges of the land, young men and maidens, old men and young' [Psalms 148:11] ought to apply their mind to this case. And they ought to apply truth of judgement, priestly agreement and zeal for royal gentleness, patience and love towards its honour. Whence it is written: 'the honour of the king also loveth judgement' [Psalms 98:4] and 'justice strengthens his throne' [Proverbs 25:5] and again 'Justice and judgement are the habitation of thy throne' [Psalms 89:14]. And although there may be other virtues without which one cannot reach the eternal kingdom, yet without these three which we have mentioned, though a tyrant can be created, no one can healthfully obtain an earthly kingdom.[10] That is, without gentleness,

6 Celestine I, *Epistola* 21 to the bishops of Gaul (J 381): col. 530; *Epistola* 2 to Nestorius of Constantinople (J 374): 12; both also cited in Appendix Response 1: 284; the same phrase from *Epistola* 21 is cited in Response 3: 124.

7 On Hincmar's right to intervene in the case, see Introduction, 13–15.

8 On marriage as sacramental and a matter of general concern, see Introduction, 45–54.

9 In the introduction, Hincmar goes to considerable lengths to justify his intervention in the dispute, all the while carefully showing respect for the papacy's authority.

10 For Hincmar's views on kingship, see Introduction, 69–70.

'since the gentle will inherit the earth' [Psalms 96:10]; without patience, since 'He that is slow to anger is better than the mighty; and he that ruleth his spirit than he that taketh a city' [Proverbs 16:32], and 'in your patience possess ye your souls' [Luke 21:19]; and without true love, about which is said, 'Ye that love the Lord, hate evil' [Psalms 96:10], since 'he that loveth iniquity hateth his own soul' [Psalms 10:6]. And again in the Psalms it is written: 'Aim, proceed fortunately and rule because of truth and gentleness and righteousness' [Psalms 44:5], since 'he will keep truth following gentleness with justice, so that neither will he abandon zeal of righteousness in the weight of gentleness nor on the other hand will weight of gentleness disturb zeal of righteousness'.[11] Since as Wisdom says, 'the king that sitteth in the throne of judgement scattereth away all evil with his eyes' [Proverbs 20:8], and again, 'The king that faithfully judgeth the poor, his throne shall be established for ever' [Proverbs 29:14].

Concerning indeed priestly agreement and discrimination, it is said to the Lord:

> 'For thy loving-kindness is before mine eyes: and I have walked in thy truth. I have not sat with vain persons, neither will I go in with dissemblers. I have hated the Church of evil doers; and I will not sit with the wicked. I will wash mine hands in innocency: so will I compass thine altar, O Lord, that I may publish with the voice of thanksgiving, and tell of all thy wondrous works' [Psalms 25:3–7].

But, as St Gregory says:[12]

> 'I see others, to whom through the position of authority are committed the duties of exhorting and correction, who see that something illicit has been committed, and yet since they fear to offend the favour of certain powerful people, they do not presume to reprove. Whoever that person is, what else is he doing except seeing a wolf coming and fleeing? He flees, because he was silent; he was silent because, despising eternal grace, he loved temporal glory more, and before the face of the powerful man he hid himself away in the hiding places of his silence, and gave way to a secret fear as to a public persecution. It is well said about such: They love the glory of men more than God. If these things are strictly judged, whoever is like this has denied Christ by his silence, even though public persecution was lacking.'

<109> For judges are ordered: 'if you truly speak justice, judge rightly, sons of man' [Psalms 57:2], 'so that when any mortal gives public

11 Gregory I, *Moralia in Iob* I, 12, 16: I, 32 (Bliss 1844: I, 39).

12 Gregory I, *Moralia in Iob* XXIX, 7, 16: III, 1444–5 (Bliss 1844: III, 313).

judgement, if he speaks the truth let him also judge the truth, and let him not set with flattering speech the mousetrap of deception, through which he secretly destroys innocents',[13] taking care, since man sees the face but God the heart. 'And if the eye (that is the intention) of the heart should be straightforward, the whole body (that is every action) will shine.'[14] But if, however, the intention itself should be shadowy, then shadows will be in the action in such a fashion that they can hardly go beyond the name of shadows. And St Gregory says:[15]

> 'For I see several who thus take into account the person of the powerful man, so as not to hesitate, when requested by him as a favour, to deny the truth in the case of their neighbour.[16] And what is Truth except He who said: I am the way and the truth and the life? For John the Baptist died when asked about the truth of justice, not the confession of Christ; but since Christ is Truth, he therefore went all the way to death for Christ, that is namely for truth.'

And blessed Bede:[17]

> 'Many today abhor the crime of Judas, who sold his lord and teacher and God for money, as immense and criminal, yet do not take caution.[18] For when they utter false testimony against anyone for gifts, certainly, since they deny truth for money, they sell the Lord for money, for He Himself says: I am the Truth. When they stain the society of brotherhood with whatever plague of discord, they betray the Lord, since God is love. Even if no one gives money, they sell the Lord for thirty pieces of silver, since they assume the image of the prince of this world ⌜Satan⌝, that is the exemplar of the old enemy, neglecting the image of the creator, in whose image they were made. That person too sells the Lord who, neglecting love and fear of him, is shown to love and care more about earthly and perishable things, nay rather criminal things.'

Since matters are like this, it is necessary for both ecclesiastical judges and judges of the state (*res publica*)[19] that, under the eyes of the celestial Judge, they decide judgement in no matter what case and about

13 Pseudo-Jerome, *Breviarium in Psalmos* 57, 2: cols 989–90.

14 Gregory I, *Moralia in Iob* XXVIII, 11, 30: III, 1418 (Bliss 1844: III, 285).

15 Gregory I, *Moralia in Iob* XXIX, 7, 16: III, 1444–5 (Bliss 1844: III, 312–13).

16 On Carolingian concepts of justice, see Introduction, 33–5.

17 Bede, *In Lucae evangelium expositio* VI, 22, 5–6, 21: 374, 379; parts also cited below, Response 13: 225–6.

18 John 12:6 states that Judas was a thief, and he was often seen as motivated by greed in betraying Jesus.

19 Note that Hincmar holds secular and ecclesiastical courts to the same standards of divine justice: see Introduction, 33.

whatever person in such a way that there may not be anything in that judgement of 'the passion of evil, of fraud', mildness, simulation, or desire or hope of whatever kind of gain, but that the whole should be the 'unleavened bread of sincerity and truth' [1 Corinthians 5:8], that is the judgement of justice, the equity of truth, the purity of truth. Otherwise (may it not happen), we judges may incur the curse which is invoked by us and by the whole Church in the words of the prophet: 'Let the lying lips be put to silence' [Psalms 30:19] and 'With flattering lips and with a double heart do they speak. The Lord shall cut off all flattering lips' [Psalms 12:3], which say one thing and conceal in the heart another. Sometimes what these lips say is valid, but they interpret what they say in a sense different from what, with their conscience as a witness, they perceive. And St Jerome in the commentary on Matthew says:[20] 'He is a false witness who does not understand words in the same sense in which they are said.' And about such is written again: 'Let the mischief of their own lips cover them' [Psalms 140:9], 'let them cover themselves with their own confusion, as with a mantle' [Psalms 109:29], <110> that is 'made as a fiery oven in the time of the anger of God' [Psalms 21:9], namely so that they may burn inside and outside in the eternity to come. We cannot be free judges before His gaze, to whom the thought of man is confessed, unless we say true things truly 'from heart and mouth', since then we may judge justly; and that also with fear and trembling, lest perhaps we sin through ignorance, for as it is said: 'With what judgement ye judge, it will be judged about you' [Matthew 7:2], and: 'If our heart does not censure us, God is greater than our heart, and knoweth all things' [1 John 3:20]. And therefore also in those things which are certain before men, we cannot be secure, knowing, as Paul says, that 'he that judgeth me is the Lord' [1 Corinthians 4:4], we who are often justified by human judgement.

Therefore we write to kings, whom God has thus placed in such an excellent position so that they are able to be observed by all subjects and be had in place of a mirror;[21] that since they ought to be feared by the wicked and loved by the good, let them ensure to do those things about which none of those subject to them may be able justly to reproach them; and let them take the greatest care to avoid those things which, for the sake of the ministry imposed on them by God, it will be

20 Jerome, *Commentariorum in Matheum* IV, 26, 61: 259 (Scheck 2008: 306). Also cited below, Response 10: 183.

21 On the role of kings, see Introduction, 71–2. On the mirror as a Late Antique and Carolingian metaphor for self-reflection, see Darling 2013: 227–9.

necessary to correct in those subjected to them.[22] Otherwise they may hear themselves refuted by the apostle: 'And thinkest thou this, O man, that judgest them which do such things, and doest the same, that thou shalt escape the judgment of God?' [Romans 2:3]. And again it is written: 'a sharp judgment shall be to them that be in high places' [Wisdom 6:5]. And the Holy Spirit confirms, through the holy men Benedict and Cyprian, that every individual king will render account about all his judgements to the most equitable judge God in the Day of Judgement, and that he will render account for as many people 'as he has under his care, without doubt added to his soul'.[23] And 'just as he who is constituted first on the throne of men', he will have above him in 'that future retribution, as a punishment, as many as he had sinners underneath him in the present world', unless he should rule himself and those committed to him well (as much as he is able with God as his helper).[24]

<111> But our speech is directed to our fellow bishops and through this to us ourselves, so that we may teach what the Lord taught, we may preach what we ourselves steadfastly keep. For, just as it is written 'Ask now the priests concerning the law' [Haggai 2:12], thus likewise the Lord says: 'Hearing from me, you will announce to them', hearing indeed either by heavenly inspiration or divine reading, about which is written: 'I will hear what God the Lord will speak' [Psalms 84:9], and 'Scrutinise the Scriptures' [John 5:9], and 'The law of the Lord is perfect, converting the soul, the testimony of the Lord is sure, making wise the simple' [Psalms 18:8]. Indeed, this follows: 'Give them warning from me' [Ezekiel 3:17]. 'From me', he says, not 'from you', since the preacher ought to propose things that he learned from God whether by holy Scripture or by the doctrine of the holy masters to his hearers, not fawningly or changeably according to human will, but sincerely and constantly. And it is said to the listeners, just as to us (may it not be for our judgement): 'Ask thy father, and he will shew thee; thy elders, and they will tell thee' [Deuteronomy 32:7], and through us is added

22 *Correctio* – literally 'correction' – had been presented as the key duty of Carolingian kingship since the reigns of Charlemagne and Louis the Pious; on this and the concept of 'ministry', see Introduction, 71.

23 Benedict of Nursia, *Regula Benedicti* 2:38: I, 450 (Clarke 1931: 13). For the importance of monastic conceptions of rulership, see de Jong 2005: 130–1.

24 Hincmar draws here on the apocryphal work of Pseudo-Cyprian, *De XII abusivis saeculi*, c. 9: 53, whom he also cites in Response 6: 149 and at length in Appendix Response 7: 318–22. On this text, which probably comes from seventh-century Ireland, see Anton 1982; Meens 1998. Hincmar, who was greatly influenced by it, may have been the first writer to attribute it explicitly to the third-century African bishop Cyprian.

to the same as an order: 'Come, ye children, hearken unto me: I will teach you the fear of the Lord' [Psalms 34:11]. So too elsewhere we are complained about, where it is said: 'they are shepherds that cannot understand' [Isaiah 56:11], since 'a good understanding have all they that do his commandments' [Psalms 111:10]. Also he says: 'they that handle the law knew me not' [Jeremiah 2:8], since those who do not faithfully preach to those committed to them about works, life and morals, by word and example, although they may worship by name, they do not know the Lord according to truth, as is written: 'But if any man be ignorant, he will be ignored' [1 Corinthians 14:38], that is will be condemned.

Therefore there is nothing about which we may be certain except the mercy of God. On the day of great judgement, from our hands the blood of so many will be demanded as perish in their iniquities without our admonitions. For the Lord says to each bishop, that, 'When I say unto the wicked, Thou shalt surely die; and thou givest him not warning, nor speakest to warn the wicked from his wicked way, to save his life; the same wicked man shall die in his iniquity; but his blood will I require at thine hand' [Ezekiel 3:18]. For it also to be feared that the Inspector of consciences and even more of deeds may say to us: 'ye have taken away the key of knowledge: ye entered not in yourselves' [Luke 11:52] and although you admonished others by word, who might have been able to enter, you destroyed them by deed. And it should be known, and always contemplated with the 'greatest fear and trembling', that since the episcopal ministry is more spiritual and consequently greater than the royal ministry, it is as much more perilous, 'to the extent that we are going to render account for kings themselves to the King of kings' and Pastor of pastors in the day of trembling examination.[25]

We have decreed these things to be said here to all those gathered in the bosom of the catholic Church, so that they themselves should also beware doing such things, and as much as they are able, they should not consent to those doing them and not favour them with flattery. About such people the apostle marvellously says: 'That they who do such things shall not inherit the kingdom of God' [Galatians 5:21], and again: 'that they which commit such things are worthy of death, <112> not only those who do those things, but also those who consent to those doing' [Romans 1:32]. We have omitted to list these things in this schedule, lest we might seem

25 Gelasius I, Letter to Anastasius (J 632): 20 (Tierney 1964: 13). On this famous letter, the first articulation of the theory of the 'two powers' and the relationship of priestly to royal authority, see Introduction, 71–2. It is also cited below, Response 11: 190; Appendix Response 6: 300; Appendix Response 7: 319, 322.

to have done injury to other lords and our fellow bishops, who know those things sufficiently well and know better and more suitably than us how to expound them to their hearers, especially since they are impressed on all those visiting church in frequent apostolic readings.[26]

This introductory speech of ours begins in this way, because recently some people from the clerical order, and some indeed from the lay order – persons who, because of the place of their office and the merit of religion and also because of the refinement of their devotion and nobility, ought not to be despised – sent a certain booklet (*libellus*) to us setting out questions, whose text we include below.[27] Through our Lord Jesus Christ (who said, 'Take heed that ye despise not one of these little ones' [Matthew 18:10]; and 'Give to him that asketh thee' [Luke 6:30]; and 'from him that would borrow of thee turn not thou away' [Matthew 5:42]; and 'Say not unto thy neighbour, Go, and come again, and to morrow I will give; when thou hast it by thee' [Proverbs 3:28]; and who ordered the rulers of his Church through blessed Peter, 'that they should be ready to give an answer to every man that asketh you a reason' [1 Peter 3:15], since 'he who withholdeth corn', that is the documents of holy eloquence, 'the people shall curse him, but blessing shall be upon the head of him that selleth it' [Proverbs 11:26], since he teaches the things which he learned from the Lord as teacher, receiving the greater grace of teaching, and he himself will merit to receive from the hearers the prize of faith and confession), they asked that we might in no way neglect their requests, nor dissimulate, nor delay by some excuse. Instead they asked that, as quickly as possible and keeping secret the names of those by whom these matters were raised and to whom we should reply about these things, we should briefly respond, through each of the points they raised, with whatever the Lord will bestow upon us about these matters, according to scriptural authority and the doctrine of the catholic Fathers.[28] We would have preferred to write nothing about these things, but rather to hear the doctrine of the wise, or to announce what we perceive by spoken word alone.[29] And although it had to be written, perhaps we would have been able

26 Most of the sins listed in these two biblical passages are not obviously relevant to the case; note, however, Hincmar's assumption that his audience would know these texts well.

27 On these questions, see Introduction, 16–8.

28 The fact that those who commissioned Hincmar's work requested him to keep their identity secret is significant. See Introduction, 6.

29 Is this Hincmar trying to evade responsibility, or just a literary trope of reluctance?

to construct an order better suited for reading out, if we had wanted or had been able to neglect the request of such and so many people.[30]

So, when they read these things from holy Scripture and the traditions of the Fathers by which we reply to their propositions, let them not grow angry with us about the disordered order of responses. And if we should drift from the thrust of their questions to things which perhaps do not pertain to this matter, let them not shun us for superfluity, nor let anyone fling back our sincere response to his own injury. For we remember the Lord's words: 'Thou shalt not respect persons in judgement' [Deuteronomy 16:19] and again the holy apostles (on whose behalf although unworthy we act, imitating according to our measure) saying: 'For we cannot but speak the things which we have seen and heard' [Acts 4:20]. We have taken care therefore to respond to those propositions about which we were asked, or rather questions which were proposed, not with our own words[31] but with those of divine Scripture or of those through whom the Lord has spoken and from whom we have learned those things, as far as the brevity of time has allowed and as occurs to the memory, putting first what they requested, and giving solutions without flattery.[32]

<113> We have written generally to all, since we know this case pertains to persons of every order, and we are prevented by the aforesaid adjuration from betraying those who transmitted the proposals to us.[33] So, may the Lord give a direct and well-sounding word to our mouth, so that, concerning those things we were asked about, we may be able to proffer the suitably collected words of those to whom the Lord said: 'For it is not ye that speak, but the Spirit of your Father which speaketh in you' [Matthew 10:20]. May the grace of our Lord Jesus Christ, who wants all men to be saved and wants no one to perish, grant that the words of the saints excerpted through the service of our humility may be pleasing in the sight of those hearing them, to whom God says generally: 'He that is of God heareth God's words' [John 8:47], and who said to his disciples 'He that heareth you heareth

30 It is interesting that even for this unwieldy text, Hincmar had in mind an oral recitation ('dicendi ordo'). This tells us nothing about the literacy or otherwise of Frankish society, but it shows his aspiration to reach a broad public audience. On the circulation of *De divortio*, see Introduction, 18.

31 For Hincmar's emphasis on authorities, see Introduction, 20–4.

32 Hincmar's stress that he wrote the *De divortio* under pressure of time is important in explaining its chaotic and rambling structure.

33 In other words, Hincmar's generalised response is designed in part to maintain the anonymity of those who commissioned his report.

me'. May He who ordered the stone to be removed from the tomb of Lazarus remove the hardness of disobedience from the inner hearing of the hearts of all those hearing. May He who formerly promised through the prophets that 'I will take away the stony heart out of your flesh, and I will give you an heart of flesh. And I will put my spirit within you, and cause you to walk in my statutes, and ye shall keep my judgments, and do them' [Ezekiel 36:26], bear away the senselessness of the disobedient, lest (may it not happen) to those despising the counsels of his saints (to whom He said: 'He that despiseth you, despiseth me' [Luke 10:16]), He may say what is very terrible, 'ye therefore hear them not' (that is do not obey), 'because ye are not of God' [John 8:37].

And let no one curse us as shameless for conversing about shameless matters of this kind, which modest ears shun by blushing, since Paul disputed about such matters, among other things, from the fear of Christ, which he truthfully said had spoken in him. We shall in no way dare to be silent about those things which we shall be able to perceive from the questions, since He [Jesus] frightens us and says: 'For whosoever shall be ashamed of me and of my words, of him shall the Son of man be ashamed, when He shall come in His own glory, and in His Father's, and of the holy angels' [Luke 9:26]. For no one ought to be exasperated by hearing the wickedness of the infirm, which the poisoned cunning of diabolical malignity inflicts on human fragility, knowing himself according to the apostle to be surrounded by infirmity and considering his own self, lest perhaps he might be tempted.

Nor ought he to fear, as blessed Gregory in the *Pastoral Rule* says:[34]

> 'that, when he stoops to know another's temptations, he also may be struck by the same temptations, since the water through which the multitude of the people is cleansed', as the Lord ordered to be done through Moses, 'is without doubt contaminated. For when it receives the dirt of those who wash, it loses as it were the serenity of cleanliness. But the pastor is in no way to fear these things, since under God who subtly considers all things, the more compassionately he is wearied by others' temptations, the more easily he is rescued from his own.'

And as much as he ought both to hear the impurities of others' sicknesses and to come to the assistance of the sick with medicinal counsel in all ways, just as it seems useful to each one, so much he is not able to be unaware that God, as He Himself said through the prophet, works

34 Gregory I, *Regula pastoralis* II, 5: I, 202 (Barmby 1895: 14). Hincmar in Response 1: 101–2, however, claims that he is too burdened by his own sins to want to hear about Theutberga's.

by putting up with our iniquities, and sees our hidden disgraces and the uncleanliness of thoughts themselves and mercifully bears them with enduring expectation. Whence St Augustine says in the fourth book of *Against Julian*:[35]

> 'Certainly, if we allow those over whom we have power to perpetrate crimes before our eyes, we shall be guilty with them. But how innumerable are those things He permits to happen before our eyes, which He would in no way permit, if He did not want? And yet He is just and good, and, not wanting anyone to perish, after showing patience He gives the opportunity for repentance.'

<114> St Gregory demonstrates why this should be, explaining the witness of Scripture:[36] 'For the Most High is a patient repayer, since He both suffers our evils and repays. For those whom He tolerates for a long time so they may convert, He condemns more harshly if they do not do so.'

Question 1

They [the Lotharingian bishops and laymen] say in their first chapter:[37]

> 'The wife [Theutberga] of the lord king Lothar was indeed first accused of debauchery (*stuprum*), that her brother[38] had committed a dreadful deed with her in masculine intercourse between her thighs (*masculinus concubitus inter femora*), as "men are accustomed to commit shameful deeds with men" [Romans 1:27], and that she had conceived from that.[39] Therefore, in order that the disgrace might be hidden, she had drunk a potion and had aborted the foetus.[40] This she denied. For the sake of proof, and in the absence of witnesses, it was decided by the judgement of the lay nobles, by the counsel of the bishops, and by the agreement of the king, that a champion of this woman should go to the ordeal of boiling water.[41] After he was found to be unharmed (*incoctus*), that woman was restored to the marital bed and to the ordained royal union, from which she had been suspended.[42]

35 Augustine, *Contra Iulianum* V, 4, 14: cols 791–2 (Schumacher 1957: 256–7).

36 Gregory I, *Homiliae in euangelia* I, 13, 5: 93 (Hurst 1990: 154).

37 This is the first section of the document sent by a group of Lotharingian bishops and laymen to several bishops in February 860: on the date, see Introduction, 16–18.

38 On Hubert, see Biographical notes xiv–xv and Introduction, 3.

39 The exact nature of the act is debated: see Introduction, 58. Hincmar discusses the medical possibility of such a conception below, Response 12: 200–1.

40 On abortion, see Introduction, 56–7.

41 On this ordeal, which usually required putting the hand into a cauldron of boiling water and taking out an object, see Bartlett 1986: 4–9 and Introduction, 36–8.

42 The ordeal and the restoration of Theutberga took place in 858: see Introduction, 4.

Then, after a length of time, the booklet which we have sent to you [the Booklet of Eight Chapters][43] was written by some bishops, though we do not know whether it was about the same act or concerned something done after the beginning of the marital union.[44] And it was widely suggested by some people that because of the secret confession which the booklet mentioned, all you remaining bishops should take up speech, and should definitively remove her from marital union, and, if you should demand more, that she should be compelled to give you a booklet confirmed by her own signature.[45] This way, just as Ebbo, the former bishop of Rheims, was removed from his seat and his [episcopal] order thanks to a booklet of secret confession, so she should be removed from marital union through a booklet of secret confession.[46]

Concerning the venerable archbishop of Rheims [Hincmar], we were told that he consents to this procedure, and that through bishops, that is Archbishop Wenilo of Rouen and Bishop Hildegar [of Meaux], he has passed on his verbal agreement.[47] And that through Adventius [of Metz],[48] who had spoken to him at Rheims about this case, he [Hincmar] has sent letters of consent to the royal meeting (*placitum*) and to the bishops' meeting (*conventus*), and that he has sent letters to the apostolic seat [Rome] through this same Adventius. Now, we demand that you send back word to us, by Truth, which is God, how much of all this should be authoritatively accepted as truth.'

<115> Now, the text of the Booklet of Eight Chapters runs like this:

'Chapter 1. We bishops, who were recently convened at the palace of Aachen,[49] have taken care to bring to the attention of our brothers and co-bishops what we learned and what we discovered there, so that they, preparing their bodily ears and spiritual hearing, might discern and

43 This booklet (the text of which Hincmar gives a little later, 96–8), contains a report of the First Council of Aachen in January 860 (see Introduction, 5) and includes the 'confession' of Theutberga (cc. 6–8).

44 There was no consensus on whether sins committed before a marriage could invalidate it: see Introduction, 63.

45 Some scholars have seen this as demonstrating that the authors of the questions sent to Hincmar wrote before the Second Council of Aachen, when just such a written document was provided: see Introduction, 17. On secret confessions, see Introduction, 42–4.

46 On Ebbo of Rheims and the significance of his case to Hincmar, see Biographical notes xiii and Introduction, 11–12 and 44.

47 These two bishops took part in the Second Council of Aachen in 860: see 107. Hincmar describes his earlier part in the proceedings in Response 3: 121–5.

48 On Adventius, see Biographical notes, xiii and Introduction, 5.

49 Probably a reference to the First Council of Aachen in January 860: see introduction, 5.

work out in unanimous counsel what conclusion and end they might put to this matter.[50]

Chapter 2. The glorious king Lothar had an intimate and secret conversation (*colloquium*) with us. Humbly and in devoted purity, he set forth his own particular and personal needs, and sought advice and a remedy. Admiring his good will, we were led and bent to compassion, by God's inspiration, through his tears and sighs. To the king as he asked, sought and knocked [Matthew 7:7] we gave counsel and medicinal remedy.[51]

Chapter 3. Then the king, in a melancholy tone of voice, began to tell us about his wife, to which we listened not without grief and sadness. He wanted to keep her, but she was demanding with constant and insistent requests that, freed from marital bonds, as by her own account unworthy of the marital bed, she should merit to take the veil and to serve Christ the Lord.

Chapter 4. Meanwhile a messenger of this queen summoned us, begging that we would not delay to go to her. As we went, she hurried to meet us. She almost threw herself at our feet, and began to implore us in these words: "For the sake of God and of your ministry, I implore you, give me true counsel."

Chapter 5. We replied to her immediately: "May God give us counsel, which we can truthfully and beneficially pass on to you. So tell us, in a clear and true confession of your conscience: What is it that you seek advice about with such a visibly earnest entreaty? For unless we know the truth of the matter, we cannot give you what you seek. But we warn you first, and carefully command by God's authority and our own: you must not confess any crime falsely ascribed to you, whether because you have been allured with other rewards (*honores*), by the persuasion, or rather deception, of anyone or from fear of any punishment or death.[52] For you would lead us into error, which God forbid. Rather, as we advised previously, reveal the truth of the matter to us, just as it is, neither more nor less. And with God's help, we will strive to give you advice and assistance (*consilium et auxilium*),[53] so that you will not be cheated of your rights in any respect."

Chapter 6. "With God and my conscience as my witnesses", she said, "and my confessor also as a witness, I shall stray neither to the right

50 This document was evidently intended for dissemination, perhaps in preparation for the Second Council of Aachen.

51 The priest or bishop as doctor is a recurring metaphor in Carolingian (and earlier) texts: see Introduction, 32 and 39

52 Lothar II's bishops repeatedly tried to pre-empt any claim that Theutberga's confession had been coerced: see Introduction, 42.

53 A famous phrase: see Devisse 1968.

nor to the left in any respect in what I say and confess about myself, saying nothing except what is truthful. I recognise and know this about myself", she said, "I am not worthy to remain in the marital bond (*coniugalis copula*). And I present to you here as a witness this bishop Gunther,[54] to whom I have confessed. He knows that I am not worthy." And she turned to this bishop, and pleading, said, "I ask, bishop, that you make your co-brothers understand, as you know best, that the matter is just as I bore witness about myself."[55]

The bishop replied to her, "It would be good", he said, "that you yourself should reveal to my co-brothers what still remains hidden, so that they might hear what they should judge upon from your own lips." But she said, "What need is there that I should say anything other than what you know? For the sake of God, you do it, you tell them my necessity, so that all of you, together with my lord (*senior*) [Lothar], might give me permission to do what I want to.[56] Since even for the whole world, I am unwilling to lose my soul [Mark 8:36]. And so I ask you, for the sake of God and the ministry which you took on, do not deny what I demand for the salvation of my soul."

<116> Chapter 7. Then we bishops asked as a test, whether if her request were to be granted, she would later make some complaint or prepare a trap. To this she replied without constraint: "Through the faith which I nourish, I promise to you in the presence of God that I shall never in eternity make an accusation, either directly or through any cunning."

Chapter 8. What we finally learned from our co-brother [Gunther] about this matter, while he grieved, anguished, lamented and sorrowed greatly that he had ever been aware of this confession, these things we shall tell our brothers and co-bishops face to face, according to the licence given us.[57] So that, as we said in the beginning, they might understand the evidence (*argumenta*)[58] of this hitherto hidden matter, and then everyone, with one counsel and agreement, might dispel error and raise up truth.'

54 On Gunther, archbishop of Cologne, see Biographical notes, xiv, and Introduction, 9.

55 Firey 2009: 21–6 sees Theutberga here attempting to manipulate proceedings, by stressing the penitential rather than legal aspects of the procedure, but her argument relies on the assumption that the Booklet is a verbatim transcription of events.

56 It was common for wives in this period to call their husbands 'senior' as a term of respect.

57 Perhaps a reference to the Second Council of Aachen.

58 *Argumentum* is a difficult word to translate. Lewis and Short 1879: 159 define it as 'The means by which an assertion or assumption may be made clear, proved, an argument, evidence, proof', but for Isidore of Seville, it meant something more like 'plausible account': *Etymologiae* I, 44, 5 (Barney 2006: 67).

Response 1

We think it unnecessary to go over in detail each of the points of this booklet, as if in response. It itself reveals sufficiently clearly what it contains, and neither needs the vindication of our praise, nor avoids censure. Yet it is remarkable what we reread in the fifth chapter about the woman concerned:[59] 'But we warn you first, and by God's authority and our own we carefully command: you must not confess any crime falsely ascribed to you, either because you have been allured through other rewards, by the persuasion, or rather deception, of anyone or from fear of any punishment or death. For you would lead us into error, which God forbid.' Why were such things said to this woman before her confession, if it was not known before what she was about to say? And if the things that were going to be said were known to many beforehand, then why did they listen to them as if to a secret confession?[60]

But we think this could have happened in this way. As we read in the divinely inspired letters: 'The Spirit of prophecy is not always with the prophets: as Elisha said to his boy Gehazi about the Shunamimite: "Let her alone; for her soul is vexed within her: and the Lord hath hid it from me, and hath not told me" [2 Kings 4:27].'[61] And the Spirit is again with the prophets when it wishes. Therefore Ahijah, inspired by the Holy Spirit, said to the wife of Jeroboam, as soon 'as he heard her footstep entering the door, "Come in, thou wife of Jeroboam; why feignest thou thyself to be another?"' [1 Kings 14:6]. Therefore, since as the apostle testifies the pastors of the Church are prophets,[62] if the Spirit of God disclosed to the ears of those addressing the woman who perhaps approached them in deceit, so it is within the power of that Spirit, who 'bloweth where it listeth' [John 3:8], to suggest to these [bishops] in secret revelation that they should command this woman by God's and their authority not to dare tell them anything in deceit.[63]

59 See above, <115>.

60 Hincmar raises one of the most contentious points in the case here: the status of Theutberga's various 'confessions'. See Introduction, 42–4.

61 Gregory I, *Homiliae in Hiezechihelem prophetam* I, 1, 15: 12 (Tomkinson 2008: 36). The example of Ahijah is also taken from this book (I, 1, 7: 8; Tomkinson 2008: 31).

62 On the Old Testament prophets as models for bishops, see Introduction, 73.

63 Though some modern readers suspect Hincmar of sarcasm in this paragraph (e.g. Firey 2009: 21), he may be trying to show open-mindedness. Later on in this response, however, he points out a series of flaws in the account by the bishops.

We do not wish to dispute uncertain things at length, since we can instead bring forth certain things from the authority of the Scriptures.[64] For concerning exhortation to confession, we read that it is written: 'Reveal thy way unto the Lord, and trust in Him' [Psalms 36:5]. And on exhortation to a subsequent confession, we again read: 'I said, I will confess my transgressions unto the Lord, and thou forgavest the iniquity of my sin' [Psalms 31:5]. The Lord proffers forgiveness, not punishment, to a confession that is not extorted by fear, but rather brought forth in hope of indulgence through medicinal encouragement, as again he [the Psalmist] says: 'And of my own will shall I confess to Him' [Psalms 27:7]; a confession which is not induced by present glory, but by future bliss, since it is written: 'It is vain for you to rise before light, rise after you have sat, you that eat the bread of sorrows' [Psalms 126:2]. For 'he rises before light who, separating himself from God's care by neglecting his commands, falls, and who puts seeking to be exalted with honours and to profit in this life, which is similar to night, before the day of the world to come'.[65] <117> 'So first we should sit in penitence, so that afterwards we may rightly arise through mercy, since whoever does not willingly humble himself through penitence will not be exalted by the coming glory.'[66]

But how we should not be exalted but rather humbled by confession and penance, the Lord shows in the Gospel of Luke, saying of the condition of the penitent: 'they had a great while ago repented, sitting in sackcloth and ashes' [Luke 10:13]; and in the psalm: 'I humbled my soul with fasting, and I put on sackcloth' [Psalms 34:13] and 'I became troubled' [Psalms 29:8]; and 'For I have eaten ashes like bread, and mingled my drink with weeping' [Psalms 101:10]; and 'I watch, and am as a sparrow alone upon the housetop' [Psalms 101:8]. Therefore the sacred canons order that,[67] 'at the time when they seek penance, penitents should receive the laying on of hands and sackcloth upon their heads from the priest, as is everywhere established'. And let him whose crime is well known (*vulgatus*) receive that laying on of hands, which every public penitent should receive from the bishop from whose

64 The following row of scriptural citations concern only the general importance of confession, and do not deal with the specific issues raised by the questioners. They are presumably intended only to impress his audience before Hincmar gets down to serious argument.

65 Gregory I, *Homiliae in Hiezechihelem prophetam*, Fragment 19: 432 (Tomkinson 2008: 494).

66 Gregory I, *Moralia in Iob* VIII, 47, 80: I, 444 (Bliss 1844: I, 481).

67 Council of Agde 506, c. 15: 201.

diocese he comes, in front of the apse.[68] That, however, which harms the Church in general, should be medicinally healed by a synod, that is by a meeting of bishops. And in an extraordinary way, that booklet speaks of an episcopal meeting, which should take place for a general matter, yet describes a secret confession, which demands a special medicine.[69]

The seventh chapter, in which the aforementioned woman is tested with questions, seems suspect to our slow and paltry understanding, since it is written there:[70] 'whether if her request were to be granted, she would later make some protestation or prepare a trap', as is shown by the oath she gave. So we shall not respond to that, lest we seem to deviate from the course of the law or the path of the chapter.[71]

About what is written in the eighth chapter of this booklet:[72] 'What we finally learned from our co-brother ⌜Gunther⌝ about this matter, while he grieved, anguished, lamented and sorrowed greatly that he had ever been aware of this confession, these things we shall tell our brothers and co-bishops face to face, according to the licence given us. So that, as we said in the beginning, they might understand the evidence (*argumenta*) of this hitherto hidden matter, and then everyone, with one counsel and agreement, might dispel error and raise up truth', let them (and also whatever venerable bishops and glorious kings, and all those placed together in the bosom of mother Church) know that, under these circumstances, we would rather not know about this hidden matter than know about it, for reasons which we shall explain.[73]

That is, because we have too many of our own sins, as well as sins confessed to us by those confessing in secret devotion, and sins publicly and with great responsibility committed by those subjected to us, all of which our eyes cannot manage to weep away, let alone all those sins which lie hidden and can be better healed and washed away by

68 The apse as the place for the imposition of hands is first mentioned by the fourth-century *Breviarium Hipponense*, c. 30c: 41, and was often repeated by other canons.

69 On the distinction between secret and public confession, central to Hincmar's argument, see Introduction, 42–4; on the need for a general council, see Introduction, 51.

70 See above, 98.

71 Hincmar's aim in making this statement is not clear: is he trying to hint at mistaken procedures without being specific, or was he planning when he wrote this to tackle the issue of forced confession at a later stage?

72 See above, 98.

73 Hincmar's point is that the content of a secret confession, which he insists Theutberga's was, should not be divulged (though he also thinks that the accusations need to be brought up properly at a general council). See Introduction, 42–4.

others than by us.[74] By what curiosity, <118> which as Gregory says 'is a great defect',[75] should we seek to learn and to hear those? Under such a greatly aggravated burden, we would lament just as that pious and holy man [Gunther] lamented to whom the woman confessed, as was written:[76] 'grieving greatly, anguished and sorrowing that he had ever become aware of her confession'. For we read that Samuel lamented for Saul, after the Lord had cast him out, so that the Lord said to him: 'How long wilt thou mourn for Saul, seeing that I have cast him out?' [1 Samuel 16:1]. But we do not read that he [Samuel] disclosed to anyone, except Saul himself, what sin he mourned about him, and how much his own tears recounted it to the ears of the Lord.[77]

The second reason is that it is known by the oracle of the Holy Spirit to be prudent that sinners should lay bare 'the hidden matters of their sins to spiritual seniors, who know to cure their own sins and those of others, and not to expose them and make them public'.[78] And so it is written in the holy canons of the African Council:[79]

> 'Whenever a bishop says that someone had confessed to him alone his crime, and that man denies it, the bishop should not think it an insult that his word alone should not be believed, even if by the scruple of his own conscience he says that he is unwilling to associate with the man denying the charge. For as long as that bishop does not associate with this excommunicated man, so long that bishop will not have communion with other bishops, in order that the bishop should rather take care not to say anything about anyone which cannot be proven with documents.'

For what is the crime to be unwilling to associate with the confessed, except that of making public the confession of the crime? And no matter to how many bishops that women detailed her offence in secret confession, it should be kept secret as if she had told it to only one.[80]

74 On the responsibilities of bishops for the sins of their flock, see Introduction, 72.

75 Gregory I, *Homiliae in euangelia* II, 36, 4: 335 (Hurst 1990: 316).

76 See above, 98, c. 8.

77 In revealing Theutberga's confession, Gunther is therefore not following the example of the prophet Samuel, as a bishop should.

78 Benedict of Nursia, *Regula Benedicti*, c. 46: II, 596 (Clarke 1931: 69).

79 *Registri ecclesiae Carthaginensis excerpta*, c. 132: 232. We have translated *communicare* as 'to associate' here and elsewhere, though *communicare* has the additional ecclesiological sense of being 'in communion' which 'to associate' lacks. On excommunication, see Introduction, 32–3.

80 In other words, even if she confessed to a number of bishops, it was not a proper public confession: see Introduction, 44.

For as the holy Augustine says, explaining the judgement of Leviticus, 'If anyone sins, in that he hears someone swearing, and is a witness, whether he hath seen or known of it; but does not utter what he knows, then he shall bear his iniquity' ⌜Leviticus 5:1⌝:[81]

> 'This appears to say that a man sins when another in his hearing swears falsely, and he knows this to be sworn falsely but stays silent. He knows if he was a witness or saw or was aware of the matter about which the oath was sworn. That is, he was able to be aware, if in any way he knew or saw with his own eyes, or he who swore disclosed it to him. But between the fear of this sin, and the fear of betraying people, there is a frequent and not insignificant temptation. We are able to call back someone prepared to perjure themselves from such a grave sin by warning or forbidding. But if he should not hear us and should swear falsely in front of us on the matter which he had disclosed to us, it is a very difficult question whether he should be betrayed, if being betrayed he risks danger of death. But since it does not expressly say to whom this should be disclosed, whether to him to whom the oath is sworn, or to the priest, or to someone who is able not only to impose punishment on someone who cannot be pursued, but is able to pray for him,[82] it seems to me that the man frees himself from the fetter of sin if he discloses it to those who are more able to help than to harm the perjurer, whether by correcting him, or by praying to placate God for him, <119> if he should apply medicine to the confession …'

And the rest which follows on from there. What we say about one sin should be understood also to apply to others. And Solomon says: 'He who walks deceitfully reveals his secrets, but he that is of a faithful spirit concealeth the matter' ⌜Proverbs 11:13⌝.

And St Gregory says in his *Pastoral Rule*:[83]

> 'Those who are in charge of others should show themselves to be such that their subjects may not blush even to disclose their secrets to them; that the little ones, suffering the waves of temptation, may run back to their pastor's heart as to a mother's bosom, and wash away in the solace of exhortation and in the tears of prayer, what they foresee will pollute them with the filth of buffeting sin.'

And it is agreed that everyone knows there is no one who would not blush to reveal his sins to his prelate, if he thought he would be exposed and publicly known. And it is commanded in the Council of Carthage:[84]

81 Augustine, *Quaestionum in heptateuchum libri septem* III, 1: 175.

82 Augustine presumably means a bishop, who can excommunicate an absent sinner. On whether there was a duty to denounce perjurers, see Introduction, 35.

83 Gregory I, *Regula pastoralis* II, 5: I, 200 (Barmby 1895: 13).

84 Actually *Statuta ecclesiae antiqua*, c. 14: 168.

'that a bishop shall hear the case of no one, which it will be necessary for him to judge publicly, without the presence of his clerics, for the judgement of the bishop will be invalid unless confirmed by the presence of his clerics'. And the Lord orders in the Gospel that a delinquent is to be warned in the presence of one or two people, lest when the matter is taken to the Church, he who warned is judged to be not a corrector, but a slanderer, in the absence of witnesses.[85]

The third reason [not to hear details of the matter] is that we are not able to judge, and nor should we judge, about hidden things which lurk out of our sight, like this matter, which is described as hidden in the above-mentioned booklet,[86] and which we desire never to be known by us, if it cannot be cured by secret counsel. And that one cannot judge about hidden things, the blessed Innocent wrote to Bishop Exsuperius of Toledo, who was asking 'why, since the Christian religion condemns adultery in both sexes equally, it is not suitable for husbands taking communion (*communicantes*)[87] to remain with adulterous wives, when on the contrary wives are seen to remain in the company of adulterous husbands'. Because, Innocent says:[88]

> 'Women cannot easily accuse their husbands of adultery, and hidden sins cannot be punished. Husbands, however, are accustomed more easily to bring their adulterous wives to the priests, and so communion is denied to these women when their crime has been revealed. But as [the crime] of husbands is committed secretly, it is not easy for anyone to be kept away due to suspicions, who will certainly be removed [from communion] if his shameful act should be laid bare. So although the case is the same, yet the reckoning of vengeance falls silent in the absence of proof.'

→ The text of the Booklet of Seven Chapters[89] is as follows:

> 'Chapter 1. After our lord the most serene and glorious king Lothar joined Theutberga to himself in marriage, in royal fashion, with the

85 Hincmar here again blurs distinctions between different forms of episcopal action, in this case informal warnings by bishops and their formal judgements.

86 See above, 98, c. 8.

87 On excommunication, see Introduction, 32–33.

88 Innocent I, *Epistola* 6 to Bishop Exsuperius of Toulouse (J 293), c. 4: cols 499–500. On Roman and early medieval understandings of adultery, see Introduction, 56.

89 This is a second document about the First Council of Aachen in January 860. It is probable that Hincmar received this from a different source from that of the Booklet of Eight Chapters, since it was inserted into the manuscript on additional pages. See Introduction, 16–20.

agreement and by the will of his faithful men,[90] and after complaints of discord between them began to arise, some people told the prince that this Theutberga had some dreadful crime and a wickedly inflicted secret wound in her soul or body, by which she had seriously offended God, and because of which it was not appropriate nor was it lawful, nor did it behove him, to have her in union any longer.

<120> Chapter 2. The king often consulted both secretly and openly in the sight of his faithful men about this rumour about her, which was circulating in the conversations of various people.[91] He discussed it with them, and as a result an ordeal (*iudicium*) took place through their advice, but Divine Piety leniently did not wish to show forth the truth of the matter. But afterwards when he had gone to his brother the emperor Louis [II] in Italy, there the wicked deed became more apparent to him.[92]

Chapter 3. So, lest this suspicion and this most vile rumour about the royal wife should remain unexamined or untested any longer, and so that our lord should be made more certain and safer about this matter, so that what should be done might be carried out more freely in royal fashion, Gunther the archchaplain, Archbishop Theutgaud, bishops Adventius[93] and Franco,[94] abbots Eigil[95] and Odelinus[96] and other of his faithful men met at the palace of Aachen at the order of the prince, in the year of our Lord's Incarnation 860, in Lothar's fifth year, the eighth indiction, the fifth Ides of January [9 January]. The king told them all the above things, and, sending these bishops and abbots to Theutberga, instructed them with a command that they should enquire of her the whole truth about this rumour: which they did. And she confessed to them, before God and his angels, everything that she had done, and revealed to them completely the whole secret according to the rumour

90 Lothar's marriage to Theutberga was publicly celebrated in 855. See Introduction, 3–4.

91 On the significance of such rumours, see Introduction, 41.

92 The implication is that God allowed Theutberga to pass the ordeal in 858, despite her guilt, and that subsequent evidence justified a retrial; see Introduction, 37–8. Lothar's visit to Louis II took place in the summer or autumn of 859.

93 On Gunther, Theutgaud and Adventius, see Biographical notes xiii–xvi.

94 Franco, bishop of Liège (before 859–901), celebrated in several poems by Sedulius Scottus: see Heidecker 2010: 74.

95 Eigil, abbot of Prüm (853–60). Eigil's departure from Prüm later this year, and arrival in West Francia (where he became archbishop of Sens), was probably related to the politics of the divorce: see Regino, *Chronicle* 860: 136 n. 59.

96 Odelinus, abbot of Inden (Kornelimünster) (before 860–after 866).

that had arisen.[97] And they, returning, announced to the king that he would not be allowed to have her as a wife.[98]

Chapter 4. Gunther spoke first. "She confessed to God and to us that she had an interior wound, not inflicted on her willingly but violently, on account of which she judged herself wholly unworthy to come any longer to the royal marital bed.[99] And on account of this wound, of which is shameful to speak, [she said that] she was in no way able to be in intimate union any longer with him, or with anyone else. And so she asked for permission to be given her to change her secular dress and to leave manly intercourse (*virilis commixtio*).[100] This was not because of any deceitful anger or will against the king, but so that, once she had left, he might be relieved in soul and body, and she, through God's mercy and the prayers of the bishops, might be able to repent for what she had wrongly done."

Chapter 5. Adventius said "This crime and deed was hidden from me till now: it is sinful that you should live together any longer as male and female.[101] And even if she were beloved and cherished by you as she was before, I would counsel you, according to the ministry committed to me, and I attest that she should in no way any longer be at your side as a wife, but that you should permit her to take the veil and change her dress, according to her request."

Chapter 6. Archbishop Theutgaud spoke similarly, and agreed.

Chapter 7. Abbot Eigil, on behalf of Theutberga, urged that this should be done, and asked that since she had committed this abominable deed not voluntarily but overcome by violence, she should be given the possibility of taking the veil, and a place to go where she might heal this wound, which indeed she asked for the love of God, and for the salvation of her soul, straightforwardly, and without any oppression, any kind of pretext or intention.'

97 The circumstances of this confession are reported differently from how they appear in the Booklet of Eight Chapters (see above, Question 1: 96–8). For Hincmar's response to these confessions, see Introduction, 43–4.

98 Unlike the Booklet of Eight Chapters, which does not include an episcopal judgement, Lothar is here given no discretion in the matter. Firey 2009: 28–9 points out the legal rather than religious emphasis of this text. On incest, see Introduction, 60–2.

99 Incest is here treated as a matter of pollution, rather than of intention, though the fact that Theutberga had not consented seems nevertheless relevant, according to Eigil's comment a few lines below.

100 That is, to enter a convent.

101 Adventius is similarly evasive in a later letter to Pope Nicholas I, explaining that he did not know that Lothar had married Waldrada before he married Theutberga: *Epistolae ad divortium Lotharii regis pertinentes* 5 (MGH *Epp.* 6: 216 (Dutton 2003: 388)).

We think it more reasonable to be silent concerning this booklet than to respond. For as it is similar in the most part to the previous one in unreason, so it is so dissimilar to truth and reason that it should not be believed to have been produced by these bishops.[102]←

→ <121> But also in a certain volume, which we have avoided writing out in full here because of its great length, and which starts:[103]

> 'In the year of our Lord 860, the eighth indiction, in the middle of February, on the command of the glorious kings Louis [the German], Charles [the Bald] and Lothar the younger, a council of bishops was held at a general meeting (*generalis conventus*) of the magnates from the kingdom of the propitious Lothar, at the palace of Aachen, present being Gunther of Cologne, Theutgaud of Trier, Wenilo of Rouen, Franco of Tongeren [Liège],[104] Hatto of Verdun, Hildegar of Meaux and Halduin of Avignon',[105]

we find what follows in its chapter 15, concerning the woman this is about:

> '15. For she [Theutberga], assured by no guarantee that this would be concealed or passed over, narrated first to the king an account of the perpetrated deed, just as the rumour had been, and then explained the same in detail to some bishops together with some laymen. Afterwards, she passed into the hands of the glorious king Lothar a small charter (*cartula*) of her confession, written out on her own request, in the presence of all of us [bishops] and many laymen, and then she spoke these words openly, in the presence of all: "My lord king", she said, "for the sake of God, and for your mercy, I ask that I may be permitted to do penance, since I confess in words and in writing that I am not worthy of the marital bond (*coniugalis copula*). Prostrate, I therefore humbly demand that you will not deny me now and henceforth what is able to succour my salvation."[106]

102 Hincmar decides just to ignore this booklet, though it is not clear whether he is claiming that it is a forgery or simply inaccurate. His hostility is perhaps because it suggests that Theutberga's confession in January was public rather than private, since it was given to a number of clerics (though above, 102, he dismisses this as an issue). See Introduction, 31.

103 The *Tomus prolixus* (literally 'verbose volume') contains the acts of the Second Council of Aachen, and is known only from the extracts in *De divortio* here and in Response 22: 276–7. Like the Booklet of Seven Chapters, the text of the *Tomus* and Hincmar's comments on it were inserted on additional folios in the manuscript, suggesting that Hincmar obtained copies of them only partway through his writing of the first section. See Introduction, 17.

104 The bishopric of Tongeren-Maastricht moved to Liège around 720, so Hincmar's terminology here is archaising: see Webb 2013: 514.

105 The presence of bishops from outside Lothar's kingdom (Halduin/Hilduin, Wenilo and Hildegar) is noteworthy. See Introduction, 5.

106 On the disputed significance of this confession as 'public' or 'secret', see Introduction, 44–5.

The text of this writing contained these words and this meaning: "I Theutberga, deceived by the imprudence of the feminine sex and by human fragility,[107] and stung by the consciousness of transgression, declare, for the hope of my soul's salvation and for the sake of loyalty to my lord (*senior*), this my true confession in the presence of God, and his holy angels, and of venerable bishops and noble laymen. My brother the cleric Hubert corrupted me when I was growing up, and performed and carried out on my body a fornication against natural usage (*fornicatio contra naturalem usum*).[108] This I confess, with my conscience as my witness, neither persuaded by any ill-willed suggestion, nor compelled by any violent necessity, but declaring the truth of the matter, just as it really was, with a straightforward will. May God who comes to save sinners and promises forgiveness to those straightforwardly and truthfully confessing their sins help me, since I invent nothing, I pronounce in my own voice, and I confirm what was done in a chirograph.[109] For it seems more tolerable to me, an imprudent and deceived woman, to confess my fault straightforwardly amongst people, than to blush before the tribunal of the Lord, and to have everlasting misery."

16. When this was read out, horror and grief equally struck the hearts of those present, and groans filled the breasts of the priests for such unrestrained devilish trickery. But although this confession of hers seemed believable, yet in case this woman was lying for any deception or from fear of anyone, we spoke with the king once more, requesting him with many entreaties that he should confess to us if he had compelled her by persuasion or threat deceitfully to incriminate herself. But he declared to us with the greatest attestations that he had persuaded her to confess only the truth of the matter, nor had he overzealously done anything further in the case.[110] And he recounted to us at the same time how after he had first heard of this unspeakable matter and believed it to be true, how much he grieved, and how much this unexpected evil, this unwished-for accident displeased him, <122> but how he wished to bear the filthy matter patiently, and, if so much rumour had not spread, to keep it hidden, and he had done this as far as he could. And that he had accepted the false ordeal (*iudicium*) as a truthful examination,[111] and tolerated it,

107 On the gender politics of the case, see Airlie 1998 and Introduction, 51–2.

108 As in the Booklet of Seven Chapters (above, 106, c. 4), Theutberga's lack of intent is stressed and coercion is implied. On Hubert, see above, 95. On the category of 'unnatural' sexual practices, see Introduction, 58.

109 A document written or signed in her own hand: on the significance of these, see below, Response 12: 208–9.

110 As with the Booklet of Eight Chapters, Question 1: 97–8, cc. 5, 7, there is an attempt to forestall claims that Theutberga had been coerced.

111 A repeat of the claim that the outcome of the ordeal in 858 was invalid: see Introduction, 36–8.

while himself knowing the truth, so that, if it were possible that such an incredible disgrace should appear and then fade away from the world, he would not have to remain in such shameful disgrace and ruinous offence in the world's sight. But after the pestilence once revealed was not able to be hidden, and he was not able to bear the weight of such shame, he trembled at the too widely divulged and spread filthiness, especially when travelling through Burgundy and Italy, and could not bear this matter to spring up any longer without the examination of bishops. In truth, he repeated not without groans and with tearful sighs, that many times this had been impressed upon him concerning this woman, and also affirmed by very many people even within this kingdom.[112]

17. Returning back, we approached the woman first in secret, then in the presence of laymen, and exhorted her with holy oaths and with many admonishments that she should not in any way make a false accusation against herself, and we took care to deter her with threats of eternal punishments should she do so. And again we guaranteed her our counsel and advice, and safety and defence against all plots and violence, if only she should now confess faithfully to us whether she had been persuaded or compelled to incriminate herself. To this she replied with a bitter look: "Do you think that for anything in the world, I should wish to destroy myself in this way? For just as I have confessed, thus I confess now, and thus I shall confess. I simply beg of you, for the love of God, now give to my prayers the mercy I desire."[113]

Our Solicitude asked whether she should wish to pursue further any other complaint or to prepare any plots, if her petition were granted. Our Unanimity continued in this way about her pledge, "O daughter, know that if you await our sentence on you and your confession, the censure of divine and canonical authority will grasp you firmly, and the indestructible priestly bond will begin to bind you, so that what you are still able to regain now, if indeed you are, henceforth we doubt that you will be able to regain later."[114] In this way, very many laymen also advised her, especially those close to her and her friends, repeatedly insisting that she should not trap herself.[115] She, however, remained totally obstinate in

112 Since a good king was expected to rule his own family (see Introduction, 71, rumours about Theutberga's behaviour brought shame on her husband.

113 Theutberga's 'bitter look' was presumably interpreted by Lothar's supporters as showing her fixed determination to confess, but those who favoured Theutberga might instead see it as her registering the only protest she was able to make (see Airlie 1998: 37).

114 The language of confession and legal judgement are intertwined: see Introduction, 42.

115 This may be a reference to Theutberga's support within Lotharingia, but it is more likely simply emphasising that she was not under any pressure.

her confession, as if the secret of her conscience were visible to the eyes of those peering in.[116]

18. Why should we delay any further? With all doubt now removed, and the truth of the matter established, it was clear that this wickedness, new to human ears and dreadful in its abominable pollution, should be treated with no trivial attention or easy indulgence, lest if it were not strictly and diligently uprooted it should cause pestilential infection to those in the present and the future, especially since rumour had dispersed its stench for a long time, and far and wide among innumerable people.[117] There is no doubt that natural intercourse between brother and sister should not deserve the mercy of earthly honour, so nothing remains other than punishment and penance, so that the damnable crime does not have the opportunity to develop any further, the crime which immediately inwardly cuts off from transgressors many things which would have been licit.[118] For the more rarely such a thing occurred in the world, the more it is obvious that no one dared take it as a precedent, which could never have been pardonable in the presence of the glory of the world. But rather, when anyone at different times has fallen into this misery, it has happened not from the example of someone else, but by the ancient trick of the Devil, and by a similar impulse and slip of fragility, the fall was always fresh, as if new. We must beware this sort of contagion, which now begins afresh and was unheard of to us before, lest it should transmit a sickly plague and an incurable pestilence to humankind. It should clearly be wholly eradicated at its pernicious source, to leave no precedent nor opportunity to the weak, lest perhaps – may it never happen – it should become a custom, so that he who ought to avoid natural intercourse with his blood relatives should think the evil of fornication against nature in his own kin to be a trivial offence, and should more boldly be accustomed to it.[119]

19. All these things considered and carefully ascertained, we decreed that this lamentable pollution of incest, breathed out into the public, "should be purged by the performance of public penance".'[120]

116 A vivid metaphor that underlines the public nature of Theutberga's confession.

117 Both Lothar II's supporters and Hincmar stress the novelty of Theutberga's crimes: the former to argue for particularly harsh treatment of her, the latter to argue that careful study of older authorities is called for. See below, Response 3: 124–5.

118 The bishops' argument is that Theutberga's incest made her incapable of a later marriage. On incest, see Introduction, 60–2.

119 The bishops argue implausibly that if Theutberga were let off, incest between brother and sister (and even 'unnatural' sexual acts between them) might become widely accepted.

120 Leo I, *Epistola* 167 to Rusticus of Narbonne (J 544), c. 14: col. 1207 (Feltoe 1895: 111). Hincmar drew on this letter repeatedly: see below, Response 2: 117;

<123> Here we briefly set out, and shall show more fully in due course, that a booklet of confession of this sort was expressly forbidden by Pope Leo,[121] and that sacred authority does not allow for a wife to be able to separate from her husband in this way. Since, as was written there, the woman gave her booklet of confession not to the bishops, but to the king and uncovered her crimes to laymen, let the king arrange a legal judgement, let the married laity judge according to law and justice the wife of the king, a layman (*laicus*),[122] and if the matter passes from their judgement to episcopal judgement, let the bishops assign a medicinal judgement according to the laws of the Church.

Concerning where it is written that the king grieved over the deed and that this sad action greatly displeased him, he must take care that (may it not happen) his grief 'might not be the washing away of a wicked deed, but its confession.[123] For this is', as the doctors of the Church write, and the venerable priest Bede says, following their judgement:[124]

> 'the justice of heavenly judgement, that often the wicked both recognise and confess that they have gone astray, and bear a certain penitence for their error, but yet they do not rest from going astray. So by that same confession and repentance they give witness against themselves, that they do not commit the offence unknowingly, when they refuse to restrain themselves from the sin that they censure. They perish the more justly, since they neglected to turn away from the pit of perdition that they were able to foresee.'

Therefore it is written about Herod, that 'the king was saddened' by the request of Herodias [Matthew 14:9].[125]

> 'But indeed Herod's sadness was such as was the repentance of the Pharaoh and Judas, each of whom in madness added to their misdeeds

Response 3: 124; Response 4: 128; Response 13: 222; Response 20: 258; Response 21: 261, 262; Appendix Response 7: 318–9. On Theutberga's sins and therefore her penance as 'public', see Introduction, 41–4.

121 Leo I, *Epistola* 168 to the bishops of Campania, Samnium and Picenum (J 545): c. 2: col. 1211, cited below, Response 11: 190.

122 Note that Hincmar here is clear that the king is a layman. On lay judgement of the case, see also below, Response 5: 137–8 and Introduction 50.

123 See above, 108, c. 16. Hincmar thus turns the tables on the staged emotionalism of the council and raised the question of Lothar's sincerity: see Airlie 1998: 28–31; Firey 2009: 41–2.

124 Bede, *Homiliarum euangelii libri ii* II, 23: 353 (Martin and Hurst 1991: II, 234). Cited below, Response 6: 149–50 and Response 14: 232–3.

125 Bede, *Homiliarum euangelii libri ii* II, 23: 353 (Martin and Hurst 1991: II, 234). See Matthew 14: 3–12 and Mark 6: 17–29 on Herodias requesting the head of John the Baptist from Herod.

> after they had unwillingly betrayed themselves by the accusation of their conscience.[126] Thus Herod, asking for John's head, simulated sadness on his face, and so condemned himself, by showing openly to all that he knew him to be innocent and holy whom he was about to hand over to be killed. In truth, if we peer carefully into that wicked heart, it was secretly rejoicing, for what was sought he would have done earlier had there been an excuse. For if the head of Herodias had been requested, there can be no doubt that he would not have wished to give it and, genuinely sad, would have refused it.'

So let this our lord king direct his thoughts to the eyes of the heavenly Onlooker, who sees into the hearts of all and to whom human thought reveals itself, and let him very carefully consider if he would receive with equal sorrow and with equal serenity on his face someone who might then perhaps say: 'Since you have released this woman from you, you shall permit neither this woman nor that one ever to approach you in any way in future.'[127]

Concerning the fact that the king declared that he had accepted a false judgement as a truthful examination while himself knowing the truth,[128] we know that we shall have to give very precise account for all our judgements to the most equitable judge, the King of kings, and that which we perceive we must declare, without respect of persons, compelled by truth. That is, since he [Lothar] dared to act contrary to legal decree and the Gospel truth which says: 'Thou shalt not tempt the Lord thy God' [Deuteronomy 6:16], who, as is again written, 'scorneth the scorners' [Proverbs 3:34], so he should accept and accomplish worthy penance as a sacrilegious man, who acted in contempt and by deceit against the holy sacraments. And those who consented to his action, if there were any, should be subjected to legal and ecclesiastical judgements.[129]

<124> As for the rest that follows on from there, that this woman in accordance with her many requests was commanded to purge herself through the satisfaction of public penance:[130] if, placed in legal

126 See Exodus chapters 7–11 on the 'hardening of Pharaoh's heart' and Matthew 27: 3–10 on Judas's suicide.

127 Hincmar implies that Lothar's reaction might be different if told that he cannot marry Waldrada after his separation from Theutberga, as Pope Nicholas later stated (see Heidecker 2010: 154).

128 See above, 108.

129 Hincmar several times refers to Lothar's need to do penance for various sins: see Introduction, 41.

130 See above, 110.

judgement, she rationally and justly escaped it, by kind equity or the piety of forgiveness, this [penance] would have been good in every respect, so long as the permission to separate was not made a stumbling block (*scandalum*) for the weak, against the apostle, and she did not make her husband commit adultery.[131] For otherwise, she and her supporters ought to have heard the words of the apostle, 'Ye ask and receive not, because ye ask amiss' [James 4:3]. But since she had accused herself in writing in front of the king and noble laymen, as according to Roman law anyone can accuse another under the conditions set by these laws,[132] it does not appear to follow that, neither legally judged by these, nor acquitted by the indulgence of princely judgement, she should be punished by the bishops with public penance. For in a legally ordered judgement, even executioners cannot drag off the guilty to torture without a judgement being offered, nor can they release those bound from their chains without the indulgence of the prince.[133]

After powerful testimonies of authorities, which however confirm very little or not at all the things done concerning this woman, indeed are often opposed to them, the text continues:[134]

> 'About our king and the fragility of his youth and his wavering incontinence, there is great need for advice, lest he transfer his danger to the people and the kingdom. Therefore we demand with the greatest urgency that with the advice and sincere assistance of your brotherhood, we might be swiftly consoled and strengthened in the Lord.'[135]

But this sentence seems in a remarkable way uncertain to us, for it does not explain what is demanded by way of consolation, nor is the matter described about which advice must be given. We were more explicitly questioned by others, about whether this coupling (*copulatio*) between the lord king and the aforementioned woman had been a marriage (*coniugium*): we shall show in the course of this work what we think, as sacred authority teaches. We shall show whether there

131 Hincmar here allows spouses to separate, where the woman is guilty of a sexual sin, in order for her to do penance, but does not allow remarriage for the 'innocent' spouse: see Introduction, 52–3.

132 *Codex Theodosius* VIII, 1, 5, 12, 15 and 19.

133 On Hincmar's views on public penance, see Introduction, 39–40. Here his point is that the right procedure has not been followed.

134 The *Tomus prolixus*. Hincmar is always keen to point out the inadequate use of sources by his opponents: see Introduction, 27.

135 On the 'fragility' of Lothar, which his supporters claimed required him to remarry, see Introduction, 71–2. The wording here does not prove that the *Tomus prolixus* was a letter, as is sometimes thought: see Böhringer 1992: 124 n. 93.

was lascivious intercourse or incestuous pollution, and what we have found collected in the sacred pages about these things. Meanwhile, however, we advise with forbearance the writer of this volume that it would have been safer to await and to seek advice of the general brotherhood (*collegium*) about those things which were done concerning the woman,[136] and in that advice which is now being sought, <125> advice about the lord king might also have been taken, rather than now, as the old proverbs are accustomed to say, sounding the trumpet after the storm has blown over,[137] for it is written 'Let your gaze precede your steps' [Proverbs 4:25] and 'Do everything with counsel, and thou shalt not repent when thou hast done' [Ecclesiasticus 32:24].[138] ←

Question 2

Concerning that which is written to us, that some are saying the issues of this hidden matter ought to be judged from the secret confession of the aforesaid woman, in the fashion of the secret confession of the former bishop Ebbo [of Rheims].[139]

Response 2

Perhaps laymen and people of this sort are saying [these things], who do not know ecclesiastical laws and who did not take part then in the episcopal judgement of the time, but infer what happened from corrupted hearsay. Therefore we, who were in that council [Thionville, 835], can show from firm acquaintance, both from the episcopal records, and from that writing itself which Ebbo offered to the council, confirmed by his hand, that the aforesaid bishop [Ebbo] was accused in synod, chose judges for himself, and offered to the sacred synod the booklet signed by his own hand about his withdrawal from the episcopal ministry because of the burden of his sins. He himself confessed according to the tenor of his booklet, and brought in witnesses. Thus at last, according to his confession, supported by witnesses and writings, he accepted the synodal sentence that by the

136 On Hincmar's call for a general council, see Introduction, 51.

137 This may be a Frankish proverb.

138 This is the Vetus Latina version of Ecclesiasticus 32:24; the Authorized Version omits this verse from its translation.

139 The attempt to draw parallels between Ebbo of Rheims and the case of Theutberga was potentially embarrassing for Hincmar. See Introduction, 11–12; 44.

judgement of the chosen judges he should leave the episcopal ministry, and he left and departed.[140]

Therefore let those who say such things also know from our notification, what they cannot not know from the usage of Christine doctrine, that just as the social order (*ordo*) is different, so is the case different. And the law of the case of a husband and wife is different not only from that of a bishop, but indeed a priest and a deacon, for as the Gospel and apostolic truth teaches, 'the man hath not power over his body, but the woman; and the woman hath not power over her body, but the man' ⌈1 Corinthians 7:4⌉. By which 'power of the body' is designated the use of the genitals, just as authors explain, which the married ought not to abuse with others, <126> but use nuptially with each other. Otherwise, just as the apostle says about himself, whoever fears God has the power of restraining his own body and subjecting it to service and bearing it as far as death for Christ, and, according to common and licit usage, of moving his other limbs and giving care to his body. In which sense the same apostle continued: 'And a woman is bound by the law of her husband', as long 'as her husband liveth. But if her husband be dead, she is loosed from the bond of her husband, let her marry whom she will, yet in the Lord' ⌈1 Corinthians 7:39; Romans 7:2⌉. And a husband cannot send his wife away for any cause whatsoever, but for no other except for fornication alone.

And if he should send her away, he cannot take another while she is alive, nor can she marry another while her husband is alive, since it is written:[141]

> 'What God has joined, let man not separate. For God joined by making one flesh of man and woman; man cannot separate this, but only perhaps God alone. Man separates when because of desire for a second wife, he sends the first one away. God separates, who also joined them, when by consent, for the sake of service of God since time may be short, he thus has a wife as though not having one.'

But God does not separate from a husbandly and wifely conjunction (*coniunctio*), initiated according to God, but from carnal commerce and the practice of wifely intercourse (*commixtio*). If they cannot endure

140 The acts of the Council of Thionville of 835 to which Hincmar here makes reference, and at which he was apparently present as a young cleric, unfortunately do not survive; the confession of Ebbo does, but in two different versions (*Apologetici Ebonis forma prior* and *Apologetici Ebonis forma posterior*). The matter was less clear-cut than Hincmar here suggests, for Ebbo denied that he had actually been judged. See Introduction, 11.

141 Jerome, *Commentariorum in Matheum* III, 19, 6: 166 (Scheck 2008: 215). Hincmar stresses that separation does not end a marriage: see Introduction, 52–3.

this, 'let them not keep themselves fraudulently from each other, except it be with consent for a time, so that they may be free for prayer, and let them again return to it, so that they might not be tempted by Satan because of incontinence' [1 Corinthians 7:5]. Whichever of them should fall into Satan's temptation through incontinence, by committing adultery, will be able to achieve the remedy of repenting through the antidote of healthy penance, and to seek perfection through ecclesiastical authority.

But we read that, according to the Synod of Valence [of 374], bishops, priests or deacons who say they are polluted by mortal crimes 'should be removed from their above-mentioned ordinations, since they are guilty either by a true confession or by a lie of falsehood'.[142] For nor can he be absolved, who pronounces against himself a capital case, which when said would be punished in another person, since everyone who is his own cause of death is a greater murderer. About which death St Augustine says,[143] explaining the sentence of Deuteronomy 'If a man be found stealing his brethren from the sons of Israel and accepting a price for him being sold, then he will be killed; and thou shalt put evil away from among you' [Deuteronomy 24:7], that:

> 'Scripture says this repeatedly, when it orders evil men to be killed. The apostle uses the same way of speaking when he says: "For what is it for me to judge about those who are outside? Do not you judge them that are within? Bear away the evil from you yourselves!" From which it appears that he wanted it to be understood, that he who did such things deserved excommunication. For now in the Church excommunication does what killing used to do.'

Thus also what the civil laws in the ministry of the state (*ministerium rei publicae*) condemn with death, the ecclesiastical laws punish by the judgement of degradation or excommunication.[144]

→ Also we read in the African canons that a bishop who has lied about himself, that he had been in communion with those not to be associated with, should lose the episcopate.[145] But a wife cannot be separated from

142 Council of Valence 374, c. 4: 40 (also cited below, Response 10: 180–1). The passage may originally have applied to those on the point of ordination, rather than to those already ordained: see *Conciles gaulois du IVe siècle*: 107.

143 Augustine, *Quaestionum in heptateuchum libri septem* V, 39: 296 (shortened), also cited below, Response 12: 218.

144 Hincmar here asserts that clerical courts cannot impose the death penalty. On excommunication, see Introduction, 32–3.

145 *Registri ecclesiae Carthaginensis excerpta*, c. 124: 227, though misleadingly quoted, since the original canon criticises those lying about others, not themselves.

a husband by such deception. In addition to this, there comes what we placed a little above:[146] a bishop, f. priest or deacon cannot be absolved who pronounces a capital case against himself, which pronounced would be punished in another. Since this case, it is said, is not pronounced by this woman against herself alone, but rather more concerns her brother, so she is not able to be separated for such a statement, before she has clearly confessed or been convicted by means of him to whom the case refers.[147]←

But also bishop, priest and deacon are not thus like husband and wife, who 'if they should fall into the snare and temptation of the devil' [1 Timothy 6:9] can receive the remedy of penance through the imposition of hands, but, just as Leo writes:[148] 'a private retirement is to be sought by those who have lapsed in this way, in which a satisfaction if worthy may also be fruitful'. Nor will they be able to obtain by penance the perfection of returning to their ecclesiastical grades, whereas a man and woman, if they should commit adultery, will be able to obtain the perfection of communion. As Gelasius writes:[149] 'If perhaps people of this kind have slipped in [to the clergy], it is as necessary for those found to have sinned previously to be expelled, as that those forgetful of the vow of profession, violators of holy conduct, should without doubt be removed.' And Siricius:[150]

> 'We should make provision in equal measure, that just as it is not conceded to any clerics to do penance, thus also after penance and reconciliation it is not ever allowed to any layman to obtain the honour of clerical office, since, although cleansed of contagion of all sins, yet they who were formerly vessels of vices ought to receive no instruments for bearing the sacrament.'

And just as someone who is mutilated in some part of the body or is publicly doing penance cannot canonically reach or remain in an ecclesiastical grade, so neither can the twice-married man, whether detected before or after baptism, enjoy to the full the gift of an ecclesiastical grade, as sacred authority teaches, although the same authority does not drive back from the lay order those mutilated or publicly doing

146 See above, 116.

147 Hincmar repeats this demand for Hubert to be examined before Theutberga's guilt can be decided in Response 12: 204–5.

148 Leo I, *Epistola* 167 to Rusticus of Narbonne (J 544), c. 2: cols 1203–4 (Feltoe 1895: 110).

149 Gelasius I, *Epistola* 14 to the bishops of Lucania, Bruttia and Sicily (J 636), c. 18: 372.

150 Siricius, Letter to Himerius of Tarragona (J 255), c. 14: 110.

penance in adolescence or twice married.[151] For just as the body has one duty of the head and another of the limbs for the sake of diversity, thus the case of a priest is one matter and the case of a common man (*plebs*) another; a pastor's case is one thing, that of a member of the flock another.

And according to canonical authority, a man and woman, even separated for the sake of fornication, can be rejoined in marriage by mutual reconciliation after penance; but a bishop or priest or deacon degraded justly and according to ecclesiastical laws is not able to aspire to the grade again. Let him who wishes read the letters of Leo the Great and the decrees of Gregory, in which he will find that a bishop or priest or deacon aspiring to ecclesiastical grades after canonical deposition ought to be banished into exile or sent into a monastery under penance.[152] <128> There is also the fact that a woman is not able to give a man a notification (*libellus*) of repudiation, and that the Lord himself prohibited a man from giving a woman a notification of repudiation, which Moses but not God permitted, as the Gospel attests.[153] And Paul taught that 'the law is written not with ink but with the Spirit of the living God in the hearts of the just';[154] and the holy canons, as Damasus and Leo teach, are written by the same Holy Spirit.[155] About which it is written, 'The spirit of your Father which speaketh in you' [Matthew 10:20], and 'If any man have not the Spirit of Christ, he is none of his' [Romans 8:9] and 'The spirit is God' [John 4:24], and 'bloweth where it listeth' [John 3:8] and 'He divides severally as he wills' [1 Corinthians 12:11]. By the authority of these canons, a bishop can also remove himself, because of infirmity of soul or illness of body, from the

151 On prohibitions on ordaining as priests men who had married more than once, see d'Avray 2005: 131–4.

152 Leo I, *Epistola* 134 to Marcian (J 508), c. 2: col. 1095 asks for the heretic Eutyches to be banished to a more remote place. Hincmar conflates two letters of Gregory the Great: Gregory I, *Registrum* XI, 53 to Anthem, sub-deacon of Campania (J 1845): II, 956–7 (Martyn 2004: III, 799) ordering a sub-deacon who had made a false accusation to be deprived of his office, publicly beaten and sent into exile; and XII, 10 to John, bishop of Justiniana Prima (J 1860): II, 982–4 (Martyn 2004: III, 816–17), ordering that a deposed bishop who had subsequently tried to regain his see should be deprived of communion and kept in a monastery for life to do penance.

153 Matthew 19:7–9 has Jesus rejecting the Jewish tradition allowing a husband to divorce his wife by means of what the Vulgate calls a 'libellus', the same word used for Theutberga's booklet.

154 Hincmar here combines together phrases from Romans 2:15 and 2 Corinthians 3:3.

155 Hincmar here refers to Pseudo-Damasus, Letter to Bishop Aurelius of Carthage (J †241): 21 (part of the Pseudo-Isidore forgeries) and Leo I, *Epistola* 14 to Anastasius of Thessalonika (J 411), c. 2: col. 672 (Feltoe 1895: 16–20).

church over which he presides and from his office, if he should wish, by giving a notification subscribed by his hand, just as:[156]

> 'blessed Gregory indicates in his letters many times, as is clearly known from those to Bishop Marianus of Ravenna, to the clergy and people of Rimini, and also to the deacon Anatholius, and to Bishop Aetherius and Queen Brunhild, and also in the Gallican canons about Potamius, bishop of Braga'.

→ But we do not read that a woman ought to be separated from her husband by a notification (*libellus*) brought to a synodal meeting, or that she is able to be unyoked from the yoke of marriage (*coniugale iugum*) without a public judgement of examination. For often we endure women protesting with the greatest incivility, who try to affirm with an oath, and still more by providing a booklet (*libellus*), that the husbands who legally received them cannot render the debt to them when lying together (*concubitus*), and they present many other deceits.[157] But the husbands on the other hand reply that they lie, just as the result of the matter proves in many cases. But husbands too are accustomed to reproach their wives about very many things, which we reckon would be very shameful and superfluous to insert here. If we were to offer assent easily to these things, an innumerable crowd of separated people would violate the legal bond of marriage instituted by the Lord. For if men or women being wanton could be separated from the yoke of marriage in whatever way they should wish, <129> in order either that they might be joined in other marriages or pollute themselves in furtive adulteries, they would separate themselves very willingly. This is what we discern in adolescent widows, who receive the sacred veil after the passing on (*absolutio*) of their husbands, in order that they may licentiously abuse themselves with more men.[158] But meanwhile men also check themselves from legitimate marriage so that they may usurp the embraces of very many concubines.[159] Foreseeing this by the

156 Hincmar here cites a text concerning the deposition of Ebbo, the *Libellus* of Bishop Theoderic of Cambrai (Council of Soissons 853, no. 27 Anhang, MGH *Conc.* 3: 292).

157 This statement, presumably based on Hincmar's personal experience as bishop, perhaps attests to the knowledge on the part of these women of canon law, which in certain circumstances accepted impotence as grounds for separation. Alternatively it may simply testify to the importance of consummation in Frankish concepts of marriage: see Gaudemet 1980.

158 On Carolingian churchmen's suspicion of widows and demands for episcopal control over their veiling, see Nelson 1995: 90–4.

159 Hincmar's comment on contemporary Frankish mores is interesting. See Introduction, 47 on concubines.

Holy Spirit and teaching to beware other things of this kind, the apostle says: 'I want the younger widows to marry, bear children, be *matres familiae*' [1 Timothy 5:14].

Hence the disciplinary discretion of ecclesiastical authority provides very cautiously and prudently that ecclesiastical men may be able to remove themselves from the office of sacred ministry, with their conscience providing evidence, and may apply themselves to the worthy fruits of penance, since in this business, no occasions of pleasure or craftiness can intervene, only the devotion of humility and salvation. But a husband and wife, since holy authority says now they are not two but one flesh, cannot separate by secret confession or by presenting a notification (*libellus*), just as it is written: 'Whom God has joined together, let not man separate' [Matthew 19:6] for whatever other reason 'except manifest fornication' [Matthew 5:32]. And separated, they must either thus remain or be mutually reconciled, nor can they thus be separated so that part of one body in the man or woman preserves continence and part remains in pollution. However, those joined together more completely by common consent are able to be at leisure from marital work (*opus uxorium*) so that they may be free for God in perpetual love of continence.[160] ←

Question 3

An account ought to be given about what is written [in the booklet of questions from the Lotharingian bishops]:[161]

> 'Concerning the venerable archbishop of Rheims [Hincmar], we were told that he consents to this procedure,[162] and that through bishops, that is Archbishop Wenilo of Rouen and Bishop Hildegar [of Meaux], he has passed on his verbal agreement. And that through Adventius, who had spoken to him at Rheims about this case, he [Hincmar] has sent letters of consent to the royal meeting (*placitum*) and to the bishops' meeting (*conventus*), and that he has sent letters to the apostolic seat [Rome] through this same Adventius.'[163]

For if the 'shepherd of the Church and the first of the apostles [Paul], performing exceptional signs and miracles did not disdain humbly when reprimanded to give an account for why he had gone to the Gentiles,

160 On separation (but not divorce) so that both spouses could enter the religious life, see Introduction, 52–3.

161 See above, Question 1: 96.

162 That is, to the proceedings at the Second Council of Aachen.

163 On Adventius's planned trip to Rome, see Introduction, 14.

why he had eaten with them, and why he had received them in baptism', as we read in the Acts of the Apostles [Acts 11:1–18], 'how much more ought we, sinners that we are, when we are accused of something, to appease our accusers with a humble account?'.[164]

Response 3

So I, servant of the Church of Rheims, assure all those who wish to believe in the truth, that I confirmed neither my consent nor dissent in this matter through the above-named deputies, nor through any other venerable bishops, verbally or in writing. Nor did I speak with the above-mentioned bishops <130> between the Calends of last November [1 November 859] and when these events took place, nor does it lie in my power that I should authoritatively enjoin them to do anything, except only just as they can command me to do what they want in the spirit of charity.[165]

However, the venerable Bishop Adventius and my son Hincmar, bishop of Laon,[166] came to Rheims to visit me on the eighth Calends of February [25 January 860], and on the order of their lords[167] and in the name of our colleagues, they forcefully enjoined me to go to the then impending meeting at the palace of Aachen, if my bodily infirmity allowed;[168] and if I myself were not able to go, that I should send one of our co-bishops, who might be present in their discussions. We talked about other things too, including those things of which, according to the rumour spreading through the mouths of the laity – and not just the nobles, but the commoner people (*plebiores*) too – I had heard the lord King Lothar's wife had been accused.[169] I said that if perhaps royal command and a priestly summons should order me to go to the meeting, it would be safer and more reasonable that the discussion and

164 Gregory I, *Registrum* XI, 27 to Theoctista (J 1817): 907, 908, rearranged (Martyn 2004: III, 767).

165 Wenilo's and Hildegar's sees did not come under the archbishopric of Rheims, and thus they were not subject to Hincmar's authority.

166 On Hincmar of Laon, Hincmar's nephew and protégé, see McKeon 1978; West 2015b.

167 Lothar II for Adventius, Charles the Bald for Hincmar of Laon.

168 The Second Council of Aachen in mid-February 860. Devisse 1975–76: II, 1104–5 notes Hincmar's tendency to suffer from illness at times of crisis, which he sees as possibly having psychological causes, but see also Schröder 2014.

169 Again, Hincmar wishes to stress that the laity already know about the case, not just bishops, and that it was not therefore a matter just for clerics to decide. Hincmar accepts that the matter was widely known, but that it was known in the wrong way – through rumour and the spreading of a secret confession.

settlement of that matter, which by its novelty quite made hearers' ears ring, or made them deaf, should be entirely put off to a general synod.[170] For weighed down by ill health, I was not able to go, nor was I able to send a co-bishop of my province without the agreement of a provincial synod, and nor should matters which so generally affected everyone be settled by a few bishops.[171]

Lord Adventius pressed me, that I should go, or that I should send our co-bishop in my place, and the reason would then be explained to us for which the smallness of my person, or the presence of a legate of my province, had been requested. But the evening hour put an end to our conversation. Adventius was neither questioned by me about the secret matter which the aforementioned booklet indicates,[172] nor did he reveal it to me spontaneously, although as it happened I realised that it was that matter, which, as I said, I had heard about, and about which I had learned that many bishops had been consulted when the trial of purgation was performed,[173] and which, it is said, even the women in their weaving sheds discussed.[174] As dusk approached, the venerable Adventius went to his lodgings, and Hincmar, bishop of Laon took himself off to his usual quarters. After lying in bed ill, however, I began to feel better, and various things came into my mind, since pious Adventius had not told me why I was called to the synod. I had spoken much with him about the question of the woman, which had been pressed upon me, and I grew suspicious, as I said before, that this question could be the cause of the summons. So I thought it would be best that I should send a letter to him about our conversation of the day before.[175] If anyone wants to read a copy of this letter, here it is:[176]

170 On Hincmar's calls for a general council, see Introduction, 51, and on 'novelty' see Response 1: 110, c. 18.

171 On excuses made by Carolingian bishops not to attend ecclesiastical councils (which ranged from lack of money to Viking attacks), see Schröder 2014.

172 The Booklet of Eight Chapters: see above, Question 1: 96–8.

173 The ordeal of 858: see Introduction, 36–8.

174 On women's textile workshops, see Herlihy 1990: 77–91. Again, Hincmar represents public knowledge about the affair as only rumour, so he could argue that Theutberga's confession had been secret.

175 Hincmar is here carefully covering his back. He claims that Adventius had not provided him with any details, so he cannot have agreed to the bishops' decision to bring Theutberga's confession before a council, without explicitly saying that he disagreed with it. His supposed ignorance also reinforces his argument that Theutberga's confession had been made secretly (see Introduction, 42).

176 Also edited as Hincmar, *Epistola* 132 (MGH *Epp.* 8: 74–5). On Hincmar's archival practice, see Devisse 1975–76: II, 940–50.

<131> 'Hincmar, in name, not by merit bishop of Rheims, servant of the people of God, to my beloved and faithful brother and venerable bishop Adventius, very many greetings in the Saviour.

Yesterday, as far as my ill health permitted it, we spoke much in conversation concerning that question which I had not expected at the time, about which I had heard so often and so much that I had not thought I would hear anything more about it. We decided at last that it was best and most reasonable to save the matter for a general synod.[177] But what I touched on with you very little for lack of time in the evening, so I now more clearly with friendly advice beseech your most faithful Charity to do. Detained by illness, I am unable to go to your meeting, as requested by the lords' command,[178] and the fellow priests' summons. Nor am I able to send any co-bishops in canonical fashion, instructed by a regular meeting and commended with accompanying letters, on my behalf.[179] The urgency of the mission, and the shortness of time, do not allow me to consult my lords and fellow bishops on these issues. And as you know best yourself, unless they are consulted, the venerable rules permit me "to do nothing except what pertains to one's own diocese",[180] and no one acts against these rules without danger of retribution.

I am worried that the lord king may think that I wish to suspend the service (*servitudo*) I owe in deference to him,[181] and that the venerable bishops will suspect that if anything is decided according to the sacred rules, I wish to retract whatever does not suit me. Hence, just as I trust in your goodness, may your Love, which learned of my devotion speaking face to face, allow me to be excused without any scruple, since I set out to your Wisdom whatever I felt to be most healthy. And as such a tiny little man, I do not dare to produce a definitive judgement or to join a consensus in a matter which is so great, involving such eminent persons, in which so many things have been done by such important men, and about which so many and so important people have been consulted, in the absence of large-scale meeting, consultation and consensus, and

177 Hincmar here claims that Adventius agreed that a general synod was required. The Second Council of Aachen indeed had bishops from beyond Lothar's own kingdom in attendance.

178 The three kings nominally convening the synod, Charles, Louis and Lothar.

179 Cf. *Statuta ecclesiae antiqua*, c. 9: 167.

180 The phrase is used frequently by Pseudo-Isidore, but also has parallels in genuine councils: see Böhringer 1992: 131 n. 23.The independence of dioceses was one of Hincmar's favourite themes: see Introduction, 74–5.

181 Presumably this means Charles the Bald, although it might be Lothar II, since Hincmar's archdiocese extended into Lothar's kingdom. On the relationship between bishops and kings, see Introduction, 71–4.

> before I have read over the authorities of the Scriptures about this kind of thing, and the decrees of the Fathers.[182]
>
> I should neither praise nor criticise before I hear whatever you decide upon according to the rules, and whatever conclusion your meeting, pleasing to God, comes to, or whatever should seem best and most reasonable to me. And so at the bottom of this letter of our Tinyness, I think it appropriate to place, not my words, but those of the great Leo to Rusticus, Bishop of Narbonne:[183] "In matters which were doubtful or obscure, <132> we thought it best to pursue whatever was found to be neither contrary to the Gospel precepts, nor to the decrees of the Holy Fathers." And finally, I beg your loving Charity to read out this letter in your holy council as my excuse in addition to the speech of your Prudence.'[184]

In the course of time, this same lord Adventius sent a messenger to me, and through this messenger I again sent letters to Adventius as follows:[185]

> 'Hincmar, bishop of Rheims to his beloved brother and venerable bishop, Adventius, very many greetings in the Saviour.'

And, after certain initial comments about the matter for which Adventius had sent the messenger:[186]

> 'As for the rest, although you did not mention the issue to me at all, I bring up the matter of your mission. It is necessary, as – thanks be to God – your prudence teaches you, to act very cautiously and carefully. The matter is such, involving such eminent persons and of such a nature, that it will be necessary that it is known to all, and pondered by all. For as Celestine writes, "the universal Church is struck by any novelty whatever".[187] It is a matter between the King of kings and an earthly king, about the first law given to the first man in Paradise and strengthened by God and man in the Gospel; it is also a matter about an issue previously unheard of by us. So it will be necessary to read over the holy authorities and to interrogate the Christian laws very

182 On Hincmar's reliance on authoritative texts, see Introduction, 20–3; and on his insistence on a general council, see Introduction, 51.

183 Leo I, *Epistola* 167 to Rusticus of Narbonne (J 544): col. 1202 (Feltoe 1895: 110). See Response 1: 110, with note 120.

184 Note that the letter was designed for oral recitation.

185 Also edited as Hincmar, *Epistola* 133 (MGH *Epp.* 8: 75–6).

186 This probably concerned Adventius's planned embassy to Rome in 860: see Introduction, 14.

187 Celestine I, *Epistola* 21 to the bishops of Gaul (J 381), already cited above, Preface: 86.

subtly, to advance pontifical authority in its examination with sincere and cautious tread, and not to send any Christian astray from the right path.[188]

It is indeed proper that you let the Apostolic See know about these matters, for "whatever is offered truthfully from the heart and from the lips"[189] – as I know you will do – should be apparent to heavenly eyes. And it is proper, so that no one can later be able to contrive otherwise, to suggest nothing to the Apostolic See about the consent of the bishops or whatsoever laymen, for the sake of anyone's concealed intent, on anyone's behalf, except to set out the case whose handling you know.[190] Moreover, thus pursue the things enjoined so that as far as possible, you will not be able to offend your lord [Lothar II]. And above all, whatever you do should not deviate from the holy rules, or – may it not happen – go against divine equity and justice. I write this to your Wisdom, although it is superfluous, because you are dear to me, and you deigned to promise me that I may commit myself to your faith in safety, and you wished to demand of me that I should zealously repay you with my own devotion.'

Up till now, I have sent no other letters about this matter, either to the Apostolic See or to any bishop.

Question 4

'We ask to be sent back to us in the second chapter, if actions committed after marriage has been entered into are to be considered, how a marriage should be entered into, and what the law of marriage is; and how, and for what issues, it can be separated (*separari*). And whether, after a separation, the husband or wife can aim for another bond, and whether either of them sinning within marriage should be judged according to an equal judgement.'[191]

188 On the case as unheard-of and novel, see Response 1: 110, c. 18, Response 3: 122. Note that Hincmar here suggests that marriage as a state goes back to the Garden of Eden; and that the matter needs public discussion rather than just rumour: see Introduction, 51.

189 Benedict of Nursia, *Regula Benedicti* 4, 28: I, 458 (Clarke 1931: 16).

190 This sentence is difficult to understand, but its main point is to advise Adventius to be conscientious about how he presented the question to the papacy. Hincmar had already experienced misleading accounts of cases in which he was involved coming before the papacy: see Stone 2007a: 471–2 on the case of Falcric.

191 The Lotharingian bishops in 862 used Ambrosiaster to claim that the rules for remarriage were different for husbands and wives. See Introduction, 53.

Response 4

<133> It is written in the eighth chapter of the above-mentioned booklet,[192] as we have shown, that 'understanding the evidence (*argumenta*) of this hitherto hidden matter, we should dispel error and raise up the truth' (and we read that the *argumentum* is something which, although it may not yet exist, is able to happen).[193] Further, the matter is all about marriage, before which sins are frequently committed due to human fragility; and frequently in the act itself of entering into marriage, and frequently too after entering marriage, still more serious sins are committed. Accordingly, starting from the root, we shall set out how marriage ought to be entered into, then we shall show what the law of marriage is, then we shall explain judgement and the procedure for judgement, if a sin is committed within marriage. For a sin is an evil thing, and evil is not natural, and because of this is not substantial, but rather it becomes established in a good substance.[194] And as a developing illness is driven out by medicine, when a rule, that is natural soundness, and medicine is applied to the illness,[195] just so the wickedness may be more clearly understood, and, as this happens, we shall be able to drive out the error in the evidence (*argumentum*) we have understood in this hitherto secret matter, and we shall more easily establish the truth.[196]

How marriage (*coniugium*) should be entered into, both the Old and the New Law teach, as the Lord commands through Moses and shows in the Gospel: 'when Mary the mother of Jesus had become engaged to Joseph', He said, 'before they had come together in nuptial celebration' [Matthew 1:18]; just as He showed the same thing in the nuptial celebrations, which He deigned to sanctify by His presence and to make renowned by the miracle accomplished there.[197]

192 The Booklet of Eight Chapters. See above, Question 1: 98.

193 Isidore of Seville, *Etymologiae* I, 44, 5 (Barney 2006: 67): a passage on the writing of history. On the concept of *argumentum*, see 98 n. 58 above.

194 On the argument, made by Augustine among others, that evil has no independent existence, see Evans 1999.

195 Like goodness, health is seen as natural, and illness as an unnatural state.

196 Böhringer 1990; Böhringer 1992: 66–68; and Heidecker forthcoming show that the texts cited in Responses 4 and 5 are largely compiled from an earlier dossier of texts that Hincmar had created. As his citations show, there was no single authoritative statement on what made a valid marriage: see Introduction, 48.

197 The wedding feast at Cana [John 2:1–11]. Hincmar frequently mentions this passage: see Introduction, 45.

And the blessed Evaristus, the fourth pope from St Peter, wrote in the decretals on this point as follows:[198]

> 'Likewise we have it preserved and handed down to us, that a wife may legitimately be joined to her husband. But as we accept from the Fathers, and find handed down from the holy apostles and their successors, a marriage may not be entered into legitimately unless a wife is sought from those who are seen to have domination (*dominatio*) over the woman, and by whom she is guarded, and she is engaged by her nearer relatives and endowed according to the laws. And, when the time comes, she should be blessed in priestly fashion, as is the custom, with prayers and offerings by a priest; and guarded and accompanied by bridesmaids as custom teaches, and requested from her relatives according to the laws at the appropriate time, she may be endowed and solemnly received. Then let them spend two or three days in prayer, keeping chaste, so that good children might be brought forth, and that they might be pleasing to God in their actions.[199] In this way, they will be pleasing to God, and they will bring forth legitimate sons able to inherit, and not bastards.[200]
>
> Therefore, dearest and justly renowned sons, know that marriages enacted in this way with the aid of the catholic faith are legitimate. Otherwise, do not doubt that these are not marriages, but just adulteries or living together (*contubernia*), or debaucheries (*stupra*) or fornication, rather than legitimate marriage, unless their own will should support it and legitimate vows should hasten to aid.[201] For to keep the divine commands is divine reward; and there is no doubt that to desert them is presumption. Why therefore should it be unworthy to preserve the unity of the Church? Therefore let us all realise and decide the same. If matters are assumed differently, then the transgressors at once lose themselves, for they deceive themselves.'

<134> And the angel spoke to Joseph about this type of marriage, 'Joseph, thou son of David, fear not to take unto thee Mary thy wife (*coniunx*)' [Matthew 1:20], that is fiancée (*desponsata*).[202] And the

198 Pseudo-Evaristus, Letter to the bishops of Africa (J †20), c. 2: 87 (part of the Pseudo-Isidore forgeries). On the role of Pseudo-Isidore in developing Carolingian ideas of marriage, see Introduction, 46.

199 On this abstinence, the 'nights of Tobias', an idea developed by Jerome in his Vulgate version of the Book of Tobit, see Reynolds 1994: 334–7.

200 On legitimacy, see Introduction, 49.

201 On the contradictory ending of this text, which suggests that the formalities previously mentioned were not strictly required, see Reynolds 1994: 406–7.

202 In Matthew 1:18, Mary is called 'desponsata' (fiancée), in Matthew 1:20, 'coniunx' (spouse); hence Hincmar argues that marriage exists from the time of the betrothal.

blessed Pope Siricius said in the fourth chapter of the decretals to Bishop Himerius of Tarragona:[203]

> 'That it is not permitted in the laws of marriage to choose the fiancée of another. You asked about a violation of marriage, whether one man is able to receive in marriage a girl engaged to another. We prohibit this from happening in every way, for violation by any transgression of the blessing which the priest gives the girl to be married is a form of sacrilege for the faithful.'

And in the tenth chapter of the Council of Ancyra:[204] 'Concerning fiancées subsequently corrupted by other men. Fiancées abducted by other men are to be taken away and returned to those to whom they were previously engaged, even if violence had been inflicted upon them by their abductors.' We also read multiple and repeated decisions by holy men on this topic, but these should suffice, and more than suffice, to demonstrate this type of marriage.[205]

Although we do not condemn second marriages, but rather accept them,[206] we understand that there is another type of marriage, as the apostle teaches, and we know how it ought to be entered, as Pope Leo showed in the decretal to Rusticus, bishop of Narbonne. For he said in chapter eighteen:[207]

> 'Not every woman joined to a man is that man's wife, just as not every son is his father's heir. Legitimate bonds of marriage are those between free and equal persons, as the Lord established long before the beginnings of Roman law existed. A wife is one thing, a concubine another, just as a slave-girl is one thing, and a free woman another.[208] Because of this, the apostle brought evidence for showing the distinction between these persons from Genesis, where it is said to Abraham "Cast out your slave-girl and her son [Hagar and Ishmael], for the son of a slave-girl shall not be an heir with my son Isaac" [Galatians 4:30, citing Genesis 21:10]. Since from the beginning, the fellowship of marriage (*societas nuptiarum*) was so arranged that it should

203 Siricius, Letter to Himerius of Tarragona (J 255), c. 4: 90.

204 Council of Ancyra 314, c. 10: 83 (Percival 1900: 68).

205 Hincmar has an extensive discussion of *raptus* (marriage by abduction) in his treatise *De coercendo et exstirpando raptu viduarum, puellarum ac sanctimonialium*. See Stone 2009 and Joye 2015.

206 Apparently 'second marriages' here means the remarriage of the widowed: in Response 2: 117–18 Hincmar states that such marriages are acceptable for the laity.

207 Leo I, *Epistola* 167 to Rusticus of Narbonne (J 544), cc. 4–6: cols 1204–5 (Feltoe 1895: 110). Hincmar frequently cites this passage in *De divortio*: see above Response 1: 110, n. 120.

208 The Roman legal distinction that Leo is following here is between slave concubines and free wives. On the changing position of concubines, see Introduction, 47–8.

> have in it, besides (*praeter*) the union of the sexes, the sacrament of Christ and the Church, so it should not be doubted that the woman in whom there is shown to have been no nuptial mystery does not belong to marriage.[209] So, if anyone[210] gives his daughter in marriage to a man who has a concubine, it is not to be interpreted as if he gave his daughter to a married man, unless perhaps that other woman should be seen to be made free, legitimately endowed and honoured with a public ceremony. Those joined by paternal will to men lack fault if the women these men already have are not married to them, for a married woman is one thing, a concubine another.[211] And to cast out the slave-girl from the bed, and to take a wife, if she is of proven free status, is not a second marriage, but a progress towards honesty.'

And St Ambrose says in his book *Concerning the Fallen Virgin*:[212] 'Any woman joined to a man, whose betrothal was completed in the presence of ten witnesses, once the marriage is consummated, commits adultery only with great mortal danger.'

<135> But since Church order does not neglect those outside the common order, but rather welcomes those who recant and spurns those who despise it, it is written in the third chapter of the Council of Neocaesarea about multiple marriages:[213] 'About those who have entered multiple marriages. A prescribed time ⌜of penance⌝ is made clear to them, but their confession and faith can shorten that time.' 'It also happens, through the disaster of war and most serious enemy raids, that the wife of a captive is joined to another man, and that contrary to right order and the laws, widows, virgins and nuns are abducted. Medicine for this is set out by the holy canons',[214] which I do not think it necessary to include here.[215]

209 On the construal of this sentence, and in particular 'praeter', see Franssen 1983: 141–3.

210 Leo's original (and the text of Hincmar's earlier dossier) discusses the specific case of a cleric who has given his daughter in marriage, but Hincmar here generalises the rule. Whether this is a legitimate extension or a distortion of Leo's meaning is a nice point.

211 Hincmar takes the three steps by which Leo says a slave concubine can be converted into a free wife (freeing the woman, endowing her and publicly wedding her) as the key distinction between a valid marriage and other kinds of relationship. On Hincmar's use of this text in discussions of the case of Count Stephen, see Franssen 1983; Böhringer 1992: 134 n. 11.

212 Pseudo-Ambrose, *De lapsu Susannae*, c. 20: 10–11, also cited below, Response 12: 215; Response 22: 270.

213 Council of Neocaesarea, c. 3: 123 (Percival 1900: 80). On attitudes to the remarriage of the widowed, see Stone 2012: 268.

214 Leo I, *Epistola* 159 to Nicaetas of Aquileia (J 536), cc. 1–4: col. 1137 (Feltoe 1895: 102–3).

215 On the remarriage of those whose spouses had been captured, see Reynolds 1994: 131–8; Sessa 2011.

So these are the ways in which marriages are established, or living together (*contubernia*) is taken up.

Question 5

> '[And tell us] how or for what causes, according to authority, marriages can be separated once they have been entered into, and without which causes they must not be separated. → And whether after a separation, the man or woman should hope for another union, when both are alive;[216] and whether, sinning within marriage, they should each be judged by the same judgement.' ←

Response 5[217]

Firstly, [separation is possible if] it happens from love of eternal salvation, according to the Gospel admonition, as St Augustine says in his book *On the Good of Marriage*, where marriage is said to be better, rather than dissolved (*dissociatus*), as it is more spiritually maintained.[218] And St Augustine says in book five of *Against Julian*:[219]

> 'Luke the evangelist said about the Lord that He was "thought to be the son of Joseph" [Luke 3:23], because this was thought in order that He might be believed to have been born from Joseph's sexual relations.[220] He [Luke] removed this false opinion from the people, but did not deny, against angelic witness, that Mary was the wife of this man. You yourself admit that she took the name of wife from the pledge of betrothal. And this pledge remained perfectly inviolate. Nor indeed, when he [Joseph] had seen the holy virgin bestowed with divine fertility, did he seek another wife, for nor indeed would he have sought this one, had she not needed a husband. But he did not therefore judge that the bond of

216 Separation of a couple was always permitted under some circumstances, e.g. if they both decided to enter the religious life. The argument was over whether separation could be followed by remarriage: see Introduction, 52–3.

217 Like Response 4, this response is derived from an earlier dossier of Hincmar: see above, n. 196. On Hincmar's construction of this response, see also Bof and Leyser 2016.

218 In other words, separation is permitted for the sake of continence, though this does not end the marriage.

219 Augustine, *Contra Iulianum* V, 12, 47–8: col. 811 (Schumacher 1957: 289). Augustine is arguing, against Julian, that sexual relations are not necessary to make a marriage valid. Hincmar, however, accepted that an unconsummated marriage could be dissolved in some circumstances: see Introduction, 53–4.

220 Joseph's marriage to Mary was seen by many Church Fathers as intended to protect Mary from the shame of unmarried motherhood, and as remaining unconsummated. See Reynolds 1994: 338–45.

faithful union should be dissolved because the hope of sharing the flesh was taken away.'

<136> Second, equally according to the Gospel truth, ⌜a marriage may be separated⌝ in the case of fornication.[221] Medicine of this kind is applied in the canons of the Council of Ancyra:[222] 'If anyone's wife is an adulteress, or if he himself has committed adultery, it is fitting for him to pursue perfection with a penance of seven years, according to the prescribed stages.' And about their separation, it is written in the Council of Africa, chapter 69:[223]

> 'It pleased us that, according to gospel and apostolic discipline, neither a husband dismissed by his wife nor a wife by her husband may be joined to another, but let them remain thus or be reconciled to one another. And if they ignore this, let them be brought back to repentance.'

Authority then continues, that in whatever way marriages legitimately entered into should be separated, they should not be separated without sacerdotal awareness and without legal judgement.[224] And again in the Council of Elvira:[225]

> 'A believing (*fidelis*) woman who leaves her believing adulterous husband and takes another, is forbidden to marry. If she does marry him, let her not receive communion, unless the man she left departs this world, except perhaps if the necessity of illness compels it to be given.'

And a similar judgement is to be held regarding the husband, for, as Innocent wrote to Exsuperius, bishop of Toulouse, and Augustine wrote in his book *On the Ten Strings*, → and Jerome in his letter to Oceanus about the death of Fabiola, ← they are held by one law of divine judgement, if they are disunited (*dissocientur*) for whatever cause.[226]

221 On the 'Matthean exception' ⌜Matthew 5:32 and 19:9⌝ allowing a wife to be 'sent away' for fornication, see Introduction, 52.

222 Council of Ancyra 314, c. 19: 107 (Percival 1900: 73), also cited below, Response 13: 223.

223 *Registri ecclesiae Carthaginensis excerpta*, c. 102: 218. (In the *Collectio Dionysio-Hadriana*, it is numbered c. 69.) On this canon and its varied forms, see Bof and Leyser 2016. Also cited below, Appendix Response 4: 291.

224 No specific source for this statement is known, but several councils demanded that bishops should be told about marital separations: see Böhringer 1992: 136 n. 8. Hincmar cites the Council of Agde 506, c. 25, which makes a similar statement below, 132–3. See Heidecker forthcoming on this passage.

225 Council of Elvira, c. 9: 3 (Laeuchli 1972: 127). On the *viaticum* (communion before death), see Introduction, 26 n. 142 and 39 n. 231.

226 That is, they could remain married (Böhringer 1992: 136 nn. 11–12 identifies the sources mentioned). On contradictory patristic views on whether women and men should be treated in the same way, see Introduction, 53–4.

Innocent wrote about this to Exsuperius, bishop of Toulouse, chapter 7:[227]

> 'Your Goodwill also asked about those who join themselves to another in marriage after a repudiation (*repudium*). They are clearly adulterers on both sides. For whoever rushes to another union (*copula*) while his wife is alive, although the marriage may seem to be dissolved, cannot be seen not to be an adulterer. So much that even those female persons who are joined to them are also seen to have committed adultery,[228] according to what we read in the Gospel: "Whoever putteth away his wife and marrieth another, committeth adultery: and similarly whosoever marrieth her that is put away committeth adultery" [Luke 16:18]. And therefore they must all abstain from the communion of the faithful. But nothing of the sort can be decreed for their parents or relatives, unless they are revealed to have incited the illicit union.'

→ <137> And St Ambrose writes in his book on Abraham:

> 'I warn you men, especially those who are reaching for the grace of the Lord, not to become mingled with an adulterous body: for he who joins himself to a prostitute is made one body – nor to give to women this opportunity for divorce. Let no one delude himself with the laws of men. All sex outside marriage (*stuprum*) is adultery, and what is not allowed for a woman is not allowed for a man. The same chastity (*castimonia*) is required from a man as from a woman. Whatever should be done with a woman who is not one's legitimate wife is condemned as the crime of adultery.[229] Therefore watch out for that which you must beware, so that no one offer himself to the sacraments unworthily.'[230] ←

Chapter 4.[231] In the Council of Agde, it is written about those who leave their wives without cause as follows:[232]

> 'About those laymen who send away or who have sent away their conjugal partner for no serious fault, and, without offering plausible reasons for the separation, therefore set aside their marriages, so that they may undertake either other ones or illicit ones. If they do this before they

227 Actually Innocent I, *Epistola* 6 to Bishop Exsuperius of Toulouse (J 293), c. 6: cols 500–1.

228 In Roman law, adultery was an offence of married women and their lovers; a married man sleeping with an unmarried woman was not therefore committing adultery. See Introduction, 55–6.

229 Ambrose thus rejected the Roman definition of adultery (see above, n. 228).

230 Ambrose, *De Abraham* I, 4, 25: 519.

231 Hincmar here accidentally includes the numbering from his source dossier: see Böhringer 1990: 42.

232 Council of Agde 506, c. 25: 204, also cited below, Response 22: 277. On the role of bishops in separations, see Introduction, 50–1.

> have explained the cause of the separation to the provincial bishop, and if they cast off their wives before they are condemned by judgement, they are to be excluded from the communion of the Church and from the gathering of the holy people, because they stain the faith of marriage.'

And again in the Council of Elvira:[233] 'Women who leave their husbands without any preceding cause, and join themselves to others, may not receive communion even at the end [of life].' And there are other incestuous unions and separations and judgements about them, which we pass over from discussing here, hastening to other matters.

Let all those who are reading this recognise that the holy and apostolic men, the successors that is of the apostles, did not establish laws from their tradition – which we have included here, so that none of the faithful should dissolve a marriage established by divine authority without his bishop's knowledge – so that we should despise and wish to trample upon the Christian laws of the world. For the Church is often accustomed to demand that these should be promulgated even for matters of the Church by emperors and kings, and episcopal authority frequently uses and accepts their decisions in their judgements, together with the sentences of the canons. So much so that Damasus and Leo and St Gregory made these sentences of law canonical, as we find in their letters, and St Gregory drew up a letter of instruction for John the *defensor* going to Spain about sacred orders wholly from the instituted laws.[234]

→ <138> And amongst other kings and emperors throughout the various courses of time who have decreed legal rights (*iura legalia*) is the emperor of our own time, Louis of pious memory. In a synod and general meeting (*placitum*) at Worms [829], in the presence of the legate of the Apostolic See and Pope Gregory [IV] and many others, he [Louis] decreed concerning those things which the bishops had recently found to be necessary and useful for the matter in synods held at four places of his empire, commanding thus, with everyone's agreement, bishops as well as faithful laymen:[235]

> 'Whoever takes another wife, having left his own wife or having killed her although innocent, let him put down his weapons and perform public

233 Council of Elvira, c. 8: 3 (Laeuchli 1972: 127).

234 Böhringer 1992: 137 n. 23 lists the parallels. On Hincmar's views of the relationship between secular and ecclesiastical law, see Introduction, 28.

235 *Capitulare pro lege habendum Wormatiense* 829, c. 3 (MGH *Capit.* II, no. 193: 18–19). On Hincmar's attitude to this meeting, at which he may well have been present, see Depreux 2015: 160–1. On the killing of adulterous wives, see Introduction, 55; and on coercive penance, see 40.

penance. And if he should be contumacious, let him be seized by the count and bound in chains, and held in custody, until the issue is brought to our attention.' ←

Let Christ, the power (*virtus*) of God and the wisdom of God, speak of Himself: 'I, wisdom, dwell with prudence, and am present in learned thoughts. By me kings reign, and lawgivers decree just things. By me princes reign and the powerful decree justice' [Proverbs 8:12, 15–16].

And therefore both the deputies (*vicarii*) of Christ and the successors of the apostles [bishops] established these laws, and we howsoever presiding over the Church of God in their place, insert them here, so that the blessing which the Lord first gave to Adam and his wife in paradise, saying 'Increase and multiply' [Genesis 1:28], which given once is to this day and to the end not denied <139> not only to the faithful but also to infidels, may be given individually by the mouths of the priests to the faithful and the devout, as a holy mystery – which Christ brought through His presence to the wedding where He made water into wine.[236] And so, those who are joined through God, that is through their [priests'] ministry, by the laws of the world, which are sanctified by the justice of God through which everyone is made just, may not be separated without their [priests'] knowledge. And if, for the sake of God, they are separated spiritually from commingling of the flesh, so that cleaving to the Lord they may be made one spirit, as Paul says about many in the Church, including certain ones who were publicans and prostitutes, murderers and adulterers, 'For I have espoused you to one husband, that I may present you as a chaste virgin to Christ' [2 Corinthians 11:2], they may be joined to the Lord more fully with the blessing of sacerdotal awareness.[237]

If, however, the spouses have separated by a just civil law, and in concordance with the holy precept of the Lord because of the sin of fornication, which is accustomed to snatch away [people] through human fragility, they should seek the medicinal advice of episcopal care.[238] So that the bishop might know in what way, with respect to the quality and quantity of the form of injury, and to their virtue, he must apply the medicine of healing. Thus the Lord, the day before He suffered for

236 Marriage at Cana [John 2:1–11]. Hincmar sees marriage as originating in the Garden of Eden and so as enjoyed by non-Christians. On these biblical references, see Introduction, 45 and 51.

237 Hincmar demands several times that separation for the sake of a couple entering the religious life must be overseen by a bishop: see Introduction, 52.

238 On the Roman laws allowing men to divorce their wives for adultery, see Introduction, 55. Hincmar however sees this separation as temporary.

the reparation and salvation of all who perished in Adam, once for all blessed at dinner with His own hands a Eucharist composed of bread made of flour and water, and a cup from the holy altar mixed with water, and commended it to the mouth; which every day, in the whole catholic Church spread far and wide across the world, He consecrates though the hands and mouths of priests (*sacerdotes*) with those same unfailing words of His, for the redemption, the reparation and the salvation of believers.[239] Priests cut off from that life-giving communion with a medicinal blade those who publicly sin in serious crimes which the laws publicly condemn.[240] And after a satisfaction [of penance] that they see as appropriate, they attend to their reintegration into the wholesome refreshment, since the spiritual doctors of the Church, that is the priests of the Lord, are able to give medicinal and healing counsel for the infirmities of sinners secretly confessed to them.[241]

And they [the priests] are not able reasonably to separate anyone by an ecclesiastical judgement, that is the separation from the communion of the Church, or from a [ecclesiastical] grade or from a conjugal union, unless either he has publicly and willingly confessed to crimes or has openly been convicted of them. And confession or conviction in ecclesiastical grades has a form and an order, <140> which do not need to be included here.[242] And public confession or the conviction of laypeople has its form and order, in which they ought publicly to be judged.[243] Serious crimes too can be absolved by secret confession and penance, 'so that the weak in the Church should not be caused to stumble (*scandalizentur*) by seeing punishments whose causes they know nothing about';[244] but whatever many know has been perpetrated should be healed by the knowledge of many.

And he who sins against the purity of the Church, let him apply himself to showing due satisfaction to it. And he who has destroyed many, as much as himself, by his own example, let him cure many with the antidote of his humility.[245] As Paul says about himself, 'I before was a

239 For Hincmar's conception of the universal Church, see Introduction, 75.

240 On excommunication as 'medicinal', see Introduction, 32–3.

241 On the distinction between public and secret confession and penance, see Introduction, 40–1.

242 Hincmar has already discussed a supposed distinction between how someone might be removed from an ecclesiastical grade and a marriage in Response 2: 114–20.

243 On rituals for public penance, see Hamilton 2001: 34–8.

244 Hrabanus Maurus, *De institutione clericorum* II, 30: 376.

245 The 'scandal' resulting from public sins by prominent sinners therefore needed exemplary punishment: see Introduction, 40.

blasphemer and a persecutor and contumelious' [1 Timothy 1:13], and 'They saw how he who first fought against this faith now preacheth it, and they glorified God in me' [Galatians 1:23–24]. It is the case that whoever offends God in many things will attain a cure more quickly with many people praying for him to the Lord, as St Gregory wrote to Felix, the bishop of Sicily:[246]

> 'The wicked should be segregated from the good, the evil from the just, so that at least in their shame they may recognize their consciences, and be converted from their wicked deeds. And if they should appear incorrigible, let them be segregated from the faithful until satisfaction, according to the sentence of the Lord Saviour, who amongst other things instructed about a sinning brother: "But if thy brother shall trespass against thee" and what follows, up to where it is said "let him be unto thee as an heathen man and a publican" [Matthew 18:15–17]. The bad should be segregated from the good by these and many other authorities of the holy Fathers, lest the just perish for the unjust, as is written: "the just perishes for the unjust" [1 Peter 3:18]. There must always be discrimination between the good and the bad, as there is between sheep and goats. Open sins should not be purged with hidden correction, but rather those who are openly harmful should be openly complained of, so that when they are healed by open rebuking, those who offend by imitating them are corrected. For when one is corrected, many are emended. And it is better that one man should be condemned for the salvation of many, than that many should perish through the licence of one person. It is no wonder if this notion is observed amongst people, since we have very often known this to happen amongst cattle. Those which are seen to have scabies or some skin disease are separated from the healthy, lest all should be condemned or perish from their disease.[247] → It is indeed preferable that the wicked should be openly corrected than that the good should perish for them.' ←

These things have been said to explain why we set down the laws that spouses might be separated, whether from the love of God or the admission of sin, with sacerdotal awareness, from whom they took the blessing of entering into marriage. But since we are currently concerned with the separation of a man and wife, which took place not because of love for perpetual continence, nor, until now, as is said, for an open crime, but on account of a certain suspicion,[248] <141> it is necessary that

246 Pseudo-Gregory, Letter to Felix of Messina (J †1334): 752. On this forged letter, which Hincmar frequently cites, see Introduction, 60. This passage is also cited below, Appendix Response 7: 308.

247 The metaphor of sin as a contagious disease is a frequent one in Carolingian thought: see Introduction, 39, with n. 228.

248 Hincmar again claims, despite Theutberga's 'confessions' at the Councils of Aachen, that her offence is still a secret: see Introduction, 42.

this dispute be aired through men of this order, that is married men, and that it be judged and settled according to Christian laws set down by God with a most fair investigation.[249] And wherever sacerdotal piety or the medicinal severity of Church authority finds its place in this business, let it not only offer itself without difficulty to the sons of the Church and the judges of justice, but let it truly force itself upon them.

And since it is written: 'Pass not beyond the ancient bounds which thy fathers have set' [Proverbs 22:28], whose true doctrine should be imitated by us as examples, we thought it necessary to recall to the memory that some of us were present in the palace of Attigny in the time of the Lord Louis, the pious emperor of holy memory, when there was a universal synod of the whole empire, including even legates of the Roman see.[250] In the general meeting (*placitum*), a certain woman of not ignoble ancestry (*non ignobilem natione*) called Northild publicly complained to the emperor about certain shameful matters (*inhonestae*) between her and her husband named Agembert. The emperor sent her to the synod, so that episcopal authority should decide what should be done. But the entirety of the bishops sent her back to the judgement of the laymen and of the married, so that those who knew about these matters, and who were very sufficiently familiar with the laws of the world, might judge between her and her husband.[251] This was so this woman should subject herself to their legal judgements, and should hold without appeal to what they decided about the matter. <142> If there were to be some crime, for which after their judgement she would demand a measure of penance from episcopal authority, they would not refuse to impose it upon her according to what the holy canons constituted.[252] This sacerdotal discretion pleased the lay nobles, because judgement about their wives was not taken away from them, nor was any prejudice inflicted upon civil laws by the sacerdotal order. And they gave the law to the woman's complaint, and conveyed a settlement by legal judgement to the question.

249 Hincmar argues here that the judgement about the case must be made by a secular court, and that ecclesiastics' role is limited to imposing suitable penance afterwards. On Hincmar's views of procedure in other marriage cases, see Introduction, 50–1.

250 On the Council of Attigny in August 822, at which Louis did penance for the blinding of his nephew Bernard, see de Jong 2009: 35–6, 122–31, It is likely that Hincmar was present at the events, but not a participant: see Böhringer 1992: 1; Nelson 2015: 44.

251 On the case of Northild, known only from this passage, see Introduction, 50.

252 On this combination of secular judgement followed by penance, see Introduction, 40.

In the same way, let them call this matter [between Lothar and Theutberga], whose discussion concerns most important people, to the middle of a judgement, and let them judge very carefully following what they see to be appropriate to a judgement of equity; recognising that a marriage legally entered into is able to be dissolved for no reason, except, as we have said above, a joint spiritual separation, or a clear confession or open conviction of bodily fornication. For as St Augustine says in the book *On the Good of Marriage*, it is not licit for a woman to leave her husband or a husband his wife even because of sterility (*sterilitas*):[253]

> 'nor is it allowed to join oneself to others for the sake of children, for whose sake the wife was taken. And if they were to do this, they and those to whom they joined themselves would commit adultery. The bond of marriage (*vinculum nuptiarum*) remains, even if children, for whom it was entered into, do not follow, because of obvious sterility.'

And again in the same book:[254] 'Just as it is preferable to die of hunger than it is to eat sacrifices made to idols, so it is better to die childless than to seek descendants from an illicit sexual union (*concubitus*).'

→ And in his books to Pollentius, *On Adulterous Marriages*, the reader will find it is stressed over and over again that a husband cannot be separated from a wife, nor a wife from a husband, except only for the cause of fornication. For that reason they are able to be separated, on condition, however, that they remain unmarried or are reconciled to each other.[255] ←

And St Jerome says in his commentary on Matthew:[256]

> '"The disciples said to the Lord, 'If the case of the man be so with his wife, it is not good to marry'" [Matthew 19:10]. The burden of wives is a heavy one, if it is not permitted to leave them except for the cause of fornication. What then? Should such a wife be kept if she is drunken, if she is angry, if she has wicked habits, if she is wanton, greedy, roving,

253 Augustine, *De bono coniugali* 15: 209, rearranged (Wilcox *et al.* 1955: 31), also cited below, Response 21: 265–6. Despite Augustine's belief that sexual intercourse was acceptable only for the sake of procreation, he thought a marriage could not be ended if procreation proved impossible.

254 Augustine, *De bono coniugali* 16: 211 (Wilcox *et al.* 1955: 32). Augustine goes on to state that children born from illicit unions can be good, a point which Hincmar chose not to stress.

255 Augustine, *De adulterinis coniugiis*. Augustine thus makes remarriage after a first legitimate marriage impossible during the lifetime of one's repudiated spouse, and Hincmar follows him.

256 Jerome, *Commentariorum in Matheum* III, 19, 10: 167 (Scheck 2008: 217).

abusive and slanderous? Like it or not, she is to be kept. For when we were free, we voluntarily subjected ourselves to servitude.'

→ And again in his letter to Amandus the priest:[257]

> 'The apostle cut through all the excuses, and very clearly defined that woman to be an adulteress, who marries another while her husband is alive. <143> I do not want you to object to me about the abductor's violence, the mother's persuasion, the father's authority, the swarms of relatives, the traps of slaves and relatives, the damage to the family property: as long as her husband is alive, even if he is an adulterer, even if he is a sodomite, even if he is buried deep in every wickedness and the wife leaves him because of these evil deeds, he is still considered her husband, and she is not allowed to take another.[258] And the apostle did not decide this on his own authority, but Christ spoke through him, who said in the Gospel, "whosoever shall send away his wife, except for the case of fornication, causeth her to commit adultery: and whosoever shall take the woman sent away is an adulterer"' [Matthew 5:32].

And the apostolic [popes] Innocent, Leo and Gregory, and the African Council, Ambrose, John of Constantinople, Origen in his books amended by St Jerome, the venerable priest Bede and all other catholic doctors all agree with this gospel truth and apostolic doctrine.[259] If there were not such a clear precept of the Lord – so that even Paul when asked about virgins and giving counsel did not dare to change anything at all of it, saying 'Concerning the wife, yet not I but the Lord, let not the wife depart from her husband, and that if she departs, let her remain unmarried or be reconciled to her husband' [1 Corinthians 7:11] – or if there were a passage in Scripture such that authors would understand it differently, though not contrary to faith, then we would follow the decision of the great majority and of greater authority which we have in the canons.[260] But now we are not able to, nor should we think or understand differently, except according to what we read again in the divinely inspired writings. St Paul joined fornicators and adulterers with worshippers of idols, saying that they will not possess the kingdom of God [1 Corinthians 6:9], and ordered that bread not be broken with them [1 Corinthians 5:11]. And again he wrote that God will judge fornicators and adulterers [1 Corinthians 11:3]. And these

257 Jerome, *Epistula* 55, c. 4: I: 493 (Fremantle 1893: 110), also cited below, Response 12: 220.

258 On adultery and sodomy, see Introduction, 55–6 and 58–60.

259 Böhringer 1992: 143 nn. 62–9 notes the relevant passages.

260 For how Hincmar negotiated through the body of sometimes conflicting Church tradition, see Introduction, 26–7.

men, who as we have shown are held by the same judgement before God as are women if they have committed adultery, will be condemned with a greater punishment, to the degree that they are the heads and governors of women, the more fragile sex and weaker vessels.[261]

And they must not presume an undue licence, so that they condemn their adulterous wives without judgement.[262] <144> For the Lord said in the Law about the slave (*servus*), who is the property of his master: 'Who smites his slave or slave-girl (*ancilla*) with a rod, so they die at his hands, will be guilty of a crime' [Exodus 21:20]. And 'if anyone should kill his own slave without the awareness of a judge', the holy canons command them to expiate the spilling of blood with excommunication for two years.[263] And 'if a mistress should beat her slave-girl with blows, whence she dies, and if this happens on purpose, let her be admitted to communion after seven years, or if there was an excuse, after five, saving the authority of the gift of *viaticum* [final communion]', which is to be denied to none in their last breath.[264]

If therefore such equity and goodwill should be preserved even towards the servile condition in the house of every Christian, between master and slave (*servus*), how much more and more generously and fully should it be kept between a husband and wife, a man and his spouse, the head and the body? For, as the apostle teaches:

> 'the husband is the head of the wife, even as Christ is the head of the Church, and he is the saviour of the body. … So ought men to love their wives as their own bodies. He that loveth his wife loveth himself. For no man ever yet hated his own flesh; but nourisheth and cherisheth it, even as the Lord the Church' [Ephesians 5:23–29].

And let the Christian man pay attention: if his foot or hand or genitals or whatever other limb should begin to rot away or to be eaten up by cancer, with how much diligence, inspection and medical judgement he will either bear it, so that it might heal, or cut it from himself, if it

261 Hincmar here reaffirms both male superiority and the equal moral standards demanded of men and women: see Introduction, 53.

262 Most of the rest of the text of this Response, discussing killing wives, had been previously used in another text by Hincmar, his treatise on *raptus*. On this text, see Böhringer 1992: 68–71; Stone 2009; and Joye 2015. On Hincmar's ambiguous response to such killing, see Introduction, 55–6.

263 Council of Epaon 517, c. 34: 33.

264 Council of Elvira, c. 5: 2 (Laeuchli 1972: 127): i.e. the penalty is excommunication for this period of time. Response 17: <216–17> repeats that the *viaticum* should not be denied, citing a number of decretals and canons. On the *viaticum*, see Introduction, 39 n. 231.

should be unable to heal. And so let him do with his limb, that is his body, that is his wife.[265] And again the apostle says: 'Husbands, love your wives, even as Christ also loved the Church, and gave himself for it; That he might sanctify and cleanse it with the washing of water by the word' [Ephesians 5:25–26]. For indeed so much and so great and excellent a love between man and wife is commended by apostolic men, that nothing is able to be nor should be greater in that union, instituted once by God and legitimately connected, saving however the superiority in that marriage of the husband and the subjection of the woman. For what should be more venerable than the conjugal mystery (*coniugium mysterium*) of Christ and the Church? What should be more holy, than that men should love their wives as Christ loved the Church, giving Himself for it, so that He might sanctify and cleanse it? What should be dearer and more conjoined than that a man should be head of a woman as Christ is the head of the Church, the saviour of the body? He even testifies in the Gospel about the unity of this marriage, saying: 'And now they are not two, but one flesh' [Matthew 19:6]. They will be, he said, two in one flesh]. And the apostle adds to this, saying 'Men, love your wives and be not bitter against them' [Colossians 3:19].

If therefore men ought not to be bitter to their wives, how much less should they be savage, cruel, bloodthirsty, keeping no law for them, no reason, no judgement, which in the Christian religion is even to be kept for slaves? But as soon as they want, provoked with indignation and an impious fury, <145> they have them led as if to the butcher's to be torn to pieces, and they order them to be slaughtered by the knives of their cooks like sheep or pigs; or they themselves butcher them with their own hand and their own sword, not at all handing themselves over for their sake in imitation of the Lord Jesus Christ that they might sanctify and cleanse them.[266] Instead, destroying them for ever through the zeal of their lust, they impiously pollute themselves with their blood: when in such a case, the more easily murder can be committed by a husband's zeal, the more justly should legitimate judgement be awaited.

Some of these men are found to be so unmerciful, having not human affection but bestial cruelty, that they kill their first wives from suspicion of adultery, without any law, without reason, by no judgement, but simply from hatred and cruelty, or lust towards another wife or concubine. And drenched in fresh blood from the slaughter, not only

265 That is, he must either endure his wife's sins or at most separate from her.

266 On the murder of wives in Carolingian Francia, see Introduction, 55–6.

are they pricked by no repentance, nor making satisfaction to God in humility but exulting in their pride, they arrive at Christ's altar without delay, and carelessly dare to touch the sacred mysteries. Christ always says about such people taking His mysteries what He said about Judas: 'Behold, the hand of my betrayer is with me at the table' [Luke 22:21]. When they are able to be released from their sinning wives without any mortal peril by a judgement, they do not wait for it, but forestalling the judgement of divine law, they incur the judgement of damnation.[267]

Let men defend themselves as much as they like, those of this sort, through worldly laws, if there are any, or through human custom. But if they are Christian, let them know that on the Day of Judgement, they will be judged not by Roman or Salian or Burgundian laws, but by divine and apostolic laws.[268] Although in a Christian kingdom even those public laws should be Christian, that is fitting and harmonising with and consonant to Christianity. For the law of the Almighty God divides all things into three kinds, which men are seen to have subject to them in earthly matters or to possess, since in the Ten Commandments He determines and declares, 'You shall not desire the wife of your neighbour, nor his slave (*servus*) nor his slave-girl (*ancilla*), nor his ox nor his ass, nor all the things that are his' [Exodus 20:17]. In these words the dignity of the wife should be considered in one way, the condition of slaves and slave-girls in another, and in another the cheapness of brute animals or unfeeling things. And so all these are to be dealt with according to their own merits, and distinguished and judged in their own degrees.

We say this so that the sort of men who in a disordered order preserve amongst themselves a meaner condition for their wives than for their young slaves (*servioli*), should think about it. And if a master is guilty of murder for a slave killed without the awareness of a judge, and is not able to expiate the shedding of blood except through penance, what should be understood for the case of a wife? We do not say this, however, to trample upon or prohibit proper judgments, but rather we exhort that these should be sought and followed.[269] For we know that the law of God – by which every Christian will be judged on the Day

267 Hincmar's leaves the matter of whether 'release' means separation or the execution of adulterous wives ambiguous, since he is primarily concerned with the procedure, not the decision. See Introduction, 56.

268 On Hincmar's views on secular law, see Introduction, 28.

269 Again, Hincmar conspicuously does not rule out execution following a judgement in a secular court.

of Judgement, so that he will receive according to his works – allows no guilty person, not even adulterers or adulteresses themselves, to be punished except through legitimate judges and witnesses. He commanded these [adulterers and adulteresses] to be stoned in a public judgement by the people.[270] And we read that Susanna, <146> when she was falsely accused of the crime of adultery, was both condemned in public judgement and was absolved in public [Daniel 13].[271] And the woman truly caught in adultery was first led, according to the law, to the Pharisees, who exercised the power of judgement over the people, and then, for the sake of tempting Him, to the judgement of the Lord. And He did not deny the judgement but ordered it to be carried out justly and by the just [John 8:3–11].[272] Therefore, if any woman caught in adultery according to the law of Moses, which the Lord promulgated in the Old Testament, or to the public laws of Christians, which the Church embraces, should come to episcopal judgement, there is a very obvious and very sufficient medicine prepared by the wholesome tradition of the apostles, by which without any error of ambiguity she will be able to be cured, through divine grace and ecclesiastical piety.[273]

Question 6

'In the third chapter,[274] we request that we be advised what to do about the above-mentioned woman, accused of debauchery and abortion, for which she has now undergone an ordeal (*iudicium*): what do you think about this?[275] For some say that ordeals accustomed to be done by boiling or cold water, or by red-hot iron, are of no authority or credence, but that they are inventions of human opinion, in which, through deceptions (*maleficia*), very often falsehood takes the place of truth, and so they ought not to be trusted.[276] And we ask you to write back to us what you

270 A reference to the Old Testament punishments for adultery: see e.g. Leviticus 20:10.

271 On the figure of Susanna, see Introduction, 31.

272 Hincmar frequently refers to this biblical example: see Introduction, 55.

273 Though Hincmar is not explicit here, the reference to medicine and curing implies that bishops should give penance to an adulterous wife, in preference to her execution.

274 From the list of questions sent to Hincmar in February/March 860.

275 On ordeals, see Introduction, 36–8. Given that Theutberga had been cleared in 858, Lothar's argument for the divorce relied heavily on proving either that ordeals were an unsafe method of proof in general, or that this particular ordeal process had somehow been flawed.

276 There was a Carolingian tradition of scepticism about the ordeal: see Bartlett 1986: 72–5.

> think about purgation by oath, what authority this has;[277] and whether it might be true, as some people say, that because of the secret confession that the woman [Theutberga] made, as he [Archbishop Gunther] is a witness who heard it, her champion who went to the ordeal escaped unharmed.[278] And they also say that the woman was thinking of someone else with the same name as her brother when she sent her champion to the ordeal, and therefore he was not harmed in that ordeal.[279] And also [tell us]: if any cheating should be found in an ordeal or an oath after purgation has been given, whether that matter, cleared by ordeal or oath, might be brought back legally into judgement.'

Response 6

Well, if this is a question of debauchery and abortion before the marriage was entered into, which is what we understand has been ascribed to this woman, then we must first consider the ordeal of examination, according to which, we have heard, she was as it were cleared (*quasi purgatam*).[280] Then we shall set out some of the other things we perceive. This way, if perhaps the purgation by oath should be considered valid, then the question can be put to rest without further effort, while if it is justly and reasonably proven to be invalid, <147> then we shall turn to the main part of the question. For as St Paul says, 'Faith is the substance of things hoped for, the evidence for things not seen' [Hebrews 11:1]. John the Constantinopolitan expounds on this:[281]

> 'For those things which cannot be seen, but exist in hope, might be thought to be without substance. But faith gives substance to them, just as the resurrection has not yet happened,[282] and as yet has no substance, but the faith of certain hope makes it remain in our soul. Faith is the evidence (*argumentum*), that is the interpretation (*coniectio*), of those things which are not seen. For an interpretation is for things already shown clearly; while faith is the vision of things which are not apparent,

277 Clearing one's name by oath-taking was a common practice in many post-Roman legal systems: see Introduction, 34–5.

278 This question seems odd, because the ordeal took place in 858, while Theutberga's confession to Gunther was in 860. The implication may be that Theutberga had also made an earlier secret confession, and so been cleared of her sin by God before the ordeal took place: see Introduction, 43.

279 On the possibility of cheating the ordeal, see Introduction, 37–8.

280 Hincmar's caution about the outcome of the 858 ordeal may be to allow room for manoeuvre on the question of its validity.

281 John Chrysostom, *Homiliae in Epistolam ad Hebraeos* 21: cols 369–70, loosely quoted (Gardiner 1890: 463).

282 That is, the resurrection of believers at the Last Judgement.

> a vision which leads to the same satisfaction as those things do which are seen. It cannot be called faith unless someone has more satisfaction about those things which are not seen than about those things which are seen.'

Authority approves two means of investigating, testing and as it were bringing into sight any kind of doubtful and obscure matters → which cannot be proven or settled by the law in judicial procedure. ← These are the ordeal (*iudicium*) and swearing (*iuramentum*), which is usually called the oath (*sacramentum*), for in these a matter is seen by the eyes of faith, which is not perceived by earthly eyes.[283]

Concerning the ordeal (*iudicium*), it is written in the Book of Numbers:

> 'Speak unto the sons of Israel, and say unto them, If any man's wife goes aside, and commit a trespass against him, and lie carnally with another man, and the husband be unable to prove it, and the adultery stays hidden and there is no witness to it because she was not caught in the act: if the spirit of jealousy provokes the man against his wife, who is either defiled or is accused on a false suspicion ...' ⌈Numbers 5:11–14⌉.[284]

And after the judgement (*iudicium*) to which she should be put has then been explained, it continues: 'And if she should not be defiled, she will be innocent, but if she is found to be defiled, then shall the man be guiltless from iniquity, and this woman shall bear her iniquity' ⌈Numbers 5:27–28⌉.

The apostle Paul writes about swearing or the oath in the letter to the Hebrews: 'For when God made promise to Abraham, because he could swear by no greater, he sware by himself. For men verily swear by the greater: and an oath for confirmation is to them an end of all strife' ⌈Hebrews 6:13, 16⌉. The younger Pope Gregory ⌈II⌉ writing to Bishop Boniface through the priest Denwald said:[285]

> 'If a priest or any ordained cleric (*sacerdos*) is accused by the people and there are no true witnesses who can vouch for the truth of the alleged crime, then let him swear an oath in the presence of all, and let him offer as a witness about the purity of his innocence Him to whom all things are uncovered and open, and so let him remain in his clerical grade.'

283 If God should be believed to exist and act, even though he is not visible, then he should also be believed to act in the ordeal or oath-taking. See Introduction, 36–8.

284 The passage from Numbers describes the 'ordeal of bitter water'; see Bartlett 1986: 83–5.

285 Gregory II, Letter to Boniface (J 2174), ed. as Boniface, *Epistola* 26: 45 (Emerton 2000: 32).

Clearing oneself by an oath is extremely common, both in Church law and in laws outside the Church, and is known to have arisen even from the earliest of times, according to the truth of the faith.[286] And let us respect in silence what is said in the Old and the New Testament, or by the Deity Himself, such as 'By myself have I sworn, saith the Lord' [Genesis 22:16]; and 'The Lord hath sworn and will not repent' [Psalms 110:4], and many other instances. Also:

> '"Amen, amen, I say to you." The Lord saying this promises much indeed, for in a way, if it is right to say it, this is His oath, "Amen I say to you." <148> For Amen is translated "truly", but it cannot here be understood as if He might have said "Truly I say to you"; no Greek or Latin speaker would dare to translate it thus. Let it stay thus untranslated, not so that it should be denied, but so that it should be honoured under a secret veil, so that it should not be cheapened by being bared.[287] For the Truth which surely could not lie at all, even if it had not said "Truly I say to you", says this to commend, to drive home in a certain way, to awaken the sleeping, to make them alert, and [He] does not wish to be scorned.'[288]

For Abraham said to his slave, 'Put thy hand under my thigh and swear to me by the God of heaven' [Genesis 24:2–3]. And the king [Abimelech] said to Abraham, 'Swear unto me by God', and Abraham said 'I will swear' [Genesis 21:23–24]. And Isaac and King Abimelech swore to each other in turn [Genesis 26:30]. And in Jeremiah: 'I have sworn by my great name, saith the Lord' [Jeremiah 44:26], and David, 'I have sworn and will perform it' [Psalms 119:106]. And in the New Testament we read the apostle to have said, 'God is my witness' [Philippians 1:8], and 'Behold, before God, I am not lying' [Galatians 1:20], and 'I die daily in your glory, brothers' [1 Corinthians 15:31]. And anyone who should wish to seek more will find plenty in the letters of Leo and Gregory.[289]

→ But the Lord shows in Exodus how much one should beware perjury in an oath, saying 'Thou shalt not take the name of the Lord thy God in vain; for the Lord will not hold him guiltless that taketh his name in vain' [Exodus 20:7].[290] In vain indeed, and for nothing, yet this is not of no consequence, but so that it may be harmful to him who takes the

286 On Hincmar's positive attitude towards the oath, see Introduction, 34.

287 That is, 'Amen' is left in the original Hebrew.

288 Bede, *In Lucae evangelium expositio* VI, 21, 32: 370.

289 Böhringer 1992: 148 n. 12 cites letters on oaths by Gregory I; letters by Leo on the topic have not been traced.

290 Hincmar inserts a passage on perjury from here to 150: see Introduction, 20 (on the insertions) and 34 (on perjury).

name of the Lord his God in vain, as it is to a man guilty of a crime. And again, the Lord says in Leviticus: 'Ye shall not swear by my name falsely, neither shalt thou profane the name of thy God: I am the Lord' [Leviticus 19:12]. And holy David said in the Psalms, 'He that sweareth to his neighbour, and deceiveth him not' [Psalms 15:4]. Cassiodorus says:[291] 'To swear in human terms means promising something with God as a witness. For "to swear" (*iurare*) sounds like "to plead by law" (*iure orare*), that is to speak justly. Now, someone speaks justly when those things which he promises are fulfilled.' And St Ambrose in his letter to Emperor Valentinian:[292] 'What is it to swear other than to confess the divine power of Him whom you attest as the protector of your good faith?' And again it is said in the Psalms: 'Nor did he swear by trickery to his neighbour' [Psalms 24:4]. 'For he swears by trickery who intends to do other than what he promises, believing it not to be perjury to wickedly deceive someone who makes the mistake of believing him.'[293] And St Jerome adds:[294] 'There are many who swear treacherously to deceive their neighbour, which the Father of heaven abominates, for as Peter says, "Thou hast not lied unto men but unto God"' [Acts 5:4].

And in the Book of Kings, it is written that:

> 'Then there was a famine in the days of David three years, year after year; and David enquired of the Lord. And the Lord answered, It is for Saul, and for his bloody house, because he slew the Gibeonites. The children of Israel had sworn unto them: and Saul sought to slay them in his zeal to the children of Israel and Judah' [2 Samuel 21:1–2],

saying that for the sake of Joshua, He had permitted those same Gibeonites to live.[295] Here it is made clear how impious perjury is, for which the Lord imposed such a vengeance. And the prophet Jeremiah says: 'Behold, ye trust in lying words, that cannot profit ye to steal, murder, and to commit adultery, and to swear falsely' [Jeremiah 7:8–9]. Here is to be weighed up how much a crime swearing falsely is, since the prophet links it with adultery, murder and theft, the perpetrators of

291 Cassiodorus, *Expositio psalmorum* 14, 4: I, 135 (Walsh 1990: I, 158–9).

292 Ambrose, *Epistula* 72, 9: III, 15 (Beyenka 1954: 34).

293 Cassiodorus, *Expositio psalmorum* 23, 4: I, 217 (Walsh 1990: I, 243).

294 Pseudo-Jerome, *Breviarium in psalmos* 23, 4: col. 886.

295 In Joshua 9, the inhabitants of Gibeon trick Joshua into swearing an oath not to kill them by claiming that they are not inhabitants of Canaan. Even when Joshua subsequently discovers their deception, he cannot reverse his sworn decision. Saul, by killing them, is therefore breaking this oath.

which the apostle said do not possess the kingdom of God [1 Corinthians 6:9]. And Jerome says in his commentary on this prophet:[296]

> 'It had come to pass that some could be found amongst the people who pretended to worship God and swear by the Lord. <149> This he [Jeremiah] foresaw, that God delights not at all in vain speech, but in the truth of faith. And He says "I do not cherish those who swear by Me and swear in falsehood, but those whose hearts and tongues are in accord".'

And in the prophet Zechariah:

> 'For every one that stealeth shall be judged; and every one that sweareth shall be judged likewise. I will bring it [a curse] forth, saith the Lord of hosts, and it shall enter into the house of the thief, and into the house of him that sweareth falsely by my name: and it shall remain in the midst of his house, and shall consume it with the timber thereof and the stones thereof' [Zechariah 5:3–4].

And in the prophet Ezekiel: 'As I live, saith the Lord God, surely in the place where the [Babylonian] king dwelleth that made him king, whose oath he despised, and whose covenant he brake, even with him in the midst of Babylon he shall die' [Ezekiel 17:16].[297] 'For', says Jerome:[298] 'Zedekiah had spurned the oath, breaking the covenant, and since he did all these things, he will not escape.' And again Jerome, 'Behold, he gave his hand to the king of Egypt and handed himself over and committed the sacrilege of perjury against God.' And Jerome once again:

> 'It [the passage of Ezekiel] continues "in the prevarication in which he had despised me", so that we should not think the oath, the covenant and the agreement to be of the king of Babylon or of Zedekiah who made it. For he who despises an oath despises him by whom he swore it, and does an injury to him in whose name his adversary believed. Whatever Nebuchadnezzar did against Zedekiah, he did not by his own strength, but by the anger of God, in whose name Zedekiah had perjured himself. For we read that Zedekiah was captured and taken to Riblah, and there his sons were killed, he was blinded, and like a wild beast he was shut up in a cage and taken to Babylon.'

296 Jerome, *In Hieremiam* I, 92, 2: 52 (Graves 2011: 33). Most of the following biblical citations can also be found in Jerome's discussion.

297 On the reign of Zedekiah, who rebelled against Nebuchadnezzar once he had been made king of Judah, see 2 Kings 24:17–25:7.

298 Jerome, *Commentariorum in Hiezechielem libri XIV* 5, 17, 11–18: 219–20.

And St Cyprian says in the ninth grade of abuse[299] that the ministry (*ministerium*) of the king is 'to make away with the impious from the land, and not to permit parricides and perjurers to live'. And St Gregory in his homily on the Gospel says about the martyrs:[300] 'The living who are sick come to their dead bodies and are healed; perjurers come and are afflicted by demons; those possessed by demons come and are freed.' Hence it should be considered how great a sin it is to commit perjury in the name of the Lord and His saints, which Jerome, as we have mentioned, says is a sacrilege.

And one should be aware how greatly rashness in swearing should be avoided, unless great necessity demands it, or it is for the benefit of those who do not believe in the truth, in order that they might believe and the matter may be resolved through an oath (*sacramentum*), with peace and concord.

> 'The Lord shows this in the Gospel, saying "Do not swear" [Matthew 5:34], and James in his letter says: "But above all things, my brethren, swear not, neither by heaven, neither by the earth, neither by any other oath: but let your yea be yea; and your nay, nay; lest ye fall into condemnation" [James 5:12]. This is the judgement to which Herod fell victim, <150> so that he had either to commit perjury, or, fearing to perjure, to carry out another sin.[301] But if it should happen perhaps that we swear incautiously, that is, an oath which if kept would lead to a worse result, then we should openly recognise that the oath can be changed by more healthy counsel. By force of necessity, we shall have to perjure, rather than fall into a more serious crime in order to avoid perjury. For David swore by the Lord to kill Nabal, a foolish and impious man, and to destroy all that belonged to him. But at the first intercession of his [Nabal's] prudent wife Abigail, he revoked his threats, sheathed his sword, and did not grieve that he had committed something sinful by such perjury.[302] And Herod swore to give to the dancer whatever she demanded of him, and, lest he be called a perjurer by the banqueters, he defiled the banquet itself with blood, making the death of a prophet into a dancer's reward. Moderation is to be carefully observed not just in swearing, but in all things that we do. So if perhaps we fall into the traps of the wily enemy, from which we cannot escape without some stain of

299 Pseudo-Cyprian, *De XII abusivis saeculi*, c. 9: 51. On this text, see above, Preface: 90.

300 Gregory I, *Homiliae in euangelia* II, 32, 6: 285 (Hurst 1990: 264).

301 On Herod's execution of John the Baptist at Herodias's daughter's wish, see Matthew 14:1–12.

302 The story of David, Nabal and Abigail is in 1 Kings 25, though there is no specific mention of David swearing an oath to kill Nabal.

> sin, let us ask to escape it by seeking the approach in which we bear less risk. And so, following the example of those shut in by enemy walls, and who, desiring to escape, see all exits forbidden to them: it is necessary that they choose some place from which to jump down, a place where the wall is lower, so they run the least risk in falling.'[303]

And a certain orthodox and famous poet wrote about this, among other things from the Holy Scriptures and the sayings of the catholic Fathers:[304]

> 'But if the matter demands and forces you to swear,
> Do it with pure words, do it with pious mind.
> Do not think that you can deceive the Thunderer with artifice of words.
> To Him nothing is hidden, to Him your heart is open.
> Who hears your oaths not as you swear, but as he to whom you swear thought you swore
> And so you are guilty towards both,
> certainly to God, whose name you wish to take in vain,
> and to your comrade, whom you prepare to deceive with black fraud.
> If you swear to do a crime, may your vow not be fulfilled.
> Though both are wounds, that one is worse
> The smaller wound torments less, the greater more,
> Happy he who goes away unharmed by any wound.'[305] ←

But more about the ordeal. When the Lord spoke of his coming for the future Judgement, which will be by fire, he recalled into mind that judgement which was by water, saying: 'And as it was in the days of Noe, so shall it be also in the days of the Son of Man' [Luke 17:26–28], and he referred to the fact that Sodom was judged by fire, saying 'Likewise also as it was in the days of Lot'.[306] From antiquity, Christianity, which is between the judgements already performed and those to come,[307] has

303 Bede, *Homiliarum euangelii libri ii* II, 23: 352–3 (Martin and Hurst 1991: II, 233), also cited above, Response 1: 111 and below, Response 14: 232–3.

304 Theodulf of Orléans, 'Versus contra iudices', *Carmen* 28, vv. 833–44 (MGH *Poet.* 1: 514) (Andersson 2014: 104–5). Hincmar's reluctance to credit Theodulf by name suggests uncertainty about the authority of his writing.

305 The inserted folio (f. 35) in fact finishes a few lines down, in mid-sentence, but it probably includes original material that had been erased and recopied: this is the most likely end of the added text. See 146 n. 290 above.

306 For the stories of Noah and of Lot and Sodom, see Genesis, chapters 6–8, 18–19.

307 That is, between the Flood and the Last Judgement.

sanctified and approved the ordeal. It can be performed by water, as was done in the time of Noah in the Ark of faith, freeing the innocent and condemning the guilty. Or it can be by boiling water, as was done in the time of Lot in fire, and as it will be at the coming of the Son of Man:

> 'as Peter testifies, saying: "that by the word of God the heavens were of old, and the earth standing out of the water and in the water. Whereby the world that then was perished. But the heavens and the earth, which are now, by the same word are kept in store, reserved unto fire against the Day of Judgement and perdition of ungodly men" [2 Peter 3:5–7]. <151> By this he clearly teaches that the heavens which will perish by the flames are the same as those which were ravaged by the waters, that is, this empty and cloudy zone of the wind. For the waters of the Flood which cleared the mountain peaks by only fifteen cubits cannot be believed to have reached beyond the limits of the air and the ether. However far they reached, the flames of judgement will, without doubt, reach that far, according to the word of Peter. And since it is written "Heaven and earth shall pass away" [Matthew 24:35] and "The earth remains for eternity" [Ecclesiastes 1:4], it is to be understood that heaven and earth pass away from that shape which they now have, but will remain in essence for eternity. For "the shape of this world will pass away" [1 Corinthians 7:31], and there will be, he [St John] says, "a new heaven and a new earth" [Revelation 21:1] and these are not other ones to be established, but these ones, renewed. So they pass away and they will remain, since that appearance which they now have will be veiled, but they will always be preserved in their nature. Hence it is written "Thou shalt change these things, and they shall be changed"' [Psalms 102:26].[308]

Therefore authority is believed to have handed down to the Church, which the Ark of the Flood symbolises, the ordeal of boiling water, in which two investigative judgements are joined together in one: that which has been done by water and that which will be done by fire. Although these are dissimilar in terms of their varying times, yet they are one in the mystery of their operation, through which the holy are freed unharmed, and the wicked are handed over to be punished. This authority also established that the Holy Spirit is breathed into the water of baptism by the priest's exhalation. This is the Holy Spirit which 'moved above the waters at the beginning of the world, so that the nature of the waters might take on the virtue of sanctification', and by which the stain of all sin is removed. Candles, kindled from the holy

308 Bede, *In Lucae evangelium expositio* VI, 21, 33: 371 (shortened).

place by a light, are held submerged, until the consecration of the font is completed by Him:

> 'who, washing away the crimes of a guilty world with water, signified a form of regeneration in that cascading Flood, so that by the mystery of one and the same element, there should consist both an end to sins and the source of virtues. And He will come again, to judge the living and the dead and the world, through fire.'[309]

For in that same baptism, which the prophet Moses symbolised when he threw a piece of wood as if into the font of myrrh, and the water was sweetened,[310] it is proclaimed through the priest of the Lord that the blood of Christ on the cross is three in one, not by nature, but by the mystery of operation. That is the blood of redemption, the spirit of sanctification and the water of cleansing, when the unclean spirit, blown away and exorcised, leaves the person, and the world is judged, and the prince of the world is cast outside. And since he [the devil], a liar and the father of lies, does not stand in truth, he is cut off from the truth of nature, which, made in the image of God, and reborn through water and the Holy Spirit, is reshaped back to its pristine condition, and, inwardly and outwardly cleansed by faith, is proven innocent of all traces of lying and of any malice.[311]

And it makes no difference whether someone is tried by cold water or by a judgement of any heated element in the name of the Author and Director of the elements – whom all the elements recognise, when He is faithfully invoked. As when by Moses' staff, both waters were turned to blood, and blood into waters, and in the rock which gave forth water.[312] And as under Elisha, the salt or wood was placed into water for anyone of doubting faith – faith which is 'the evidence of things not seen' [Hebrews 11:1].[313] <152> For cold water [for the ordeal] is consecrated just as in baptism.[314] In the Flood, the innocent were lifted up to the heavens with the Ark, and the guilty were destroyed, and the Sodomites were punished with fire.[315] And in the Book of Numbers,

309 These two quotations are adapted from the liturgy of the Gregorian Sacramentary (no. 85: 186, 188) for blessing baptismal water on Easter Saturday. On Carolingian baptismal liturgy, see Keefe 2002: I, 41–51.

310 See Exodus 15:23–24 on Moses miraculously sweetening the waters of Marah.

311 Just as the baptised person is cleansed from evil by the baptismal water, so the innocent person who undergoes an ordeal is cleansed from the accusation.

312 See Exodus 7:17–22 (River Nile turned to blood); 17: 6 (rock at Horeb gives water).

313 See 2 Kings 2:20–21 (Elisha uses salt to make the waters of Jericho wholesome); 6:4–6 (he throws a stick into the Jordan to make a lost axehead float).

314 On prayers for blessing the water for an ordeal, see Heidecker 2010: 67.

315 See above, 150.

cold water, in which the Lord commanded curses to be washed, when drunk by an adulterous woman is read to have caused her thigh to rot [Numbers 5:11–31]. And John the apostle escaped unharmed from the cauldron of bubbling oil.[316] And whoever queries the burning water, let him know that storm and fire will accompany the terrible Judge coming to the future Judgement, as it is written: 'A fire shall devour before him, and it shall be very tempestuous round about him' [Psalms 49:3], so that 'the storm will test those whom the fire burns',[317] and that fire will be a pathway for the saints, 'who will be caught up in the clouds to meet the Lord in the air' [1 Thessalonians 4:17], 'and a fire burneth up his enemies round about' [Psalms 97:3].

Since indeed reason reveals itself in the ordeal of purgation, through boiling water or through cold, let us mention what some wise men contributed as they investigated the matter:[318]

> 'Certainly it is clear that the guilty are scalded by boiling water, and the innocent are freed without harm. For the just man Lot escaped the fire of Sodom unburned.[319] And the fire to come which will go on ahead of the terrible Judge will be harmless for the saints, and will burn up the wicked. Just like the former Babylonian furnace, which did not touch the boys in any way, and neither harmed them nor caused them any nuisance, but in its flames, burning off their chains, it burnt those Chaldeans, ministers of the king, who had kindled it [Daniel 3:46–50]. But it seems not to be clear why in the judgement of cold water the innocent should go under, and the guilty float on the water.[320] Because in the judgement of the Flood, the innocent were lifted up, and the guilty perished by submersion.[321] And the Egyptians, who pursued through the Red Sea the Hebrews, for whom the Lord cared by a morning watch through a column of smoke and fire, "sank like lead in the foaming water, so that not one of them should survive. And the sons of Israel saw the Egyptian dead upon the sea shore" [Exodus 14:28, 31]. And the earth could not hold up the unfaithful and the sinners when it opened up and swallowed Dathan, and engulfed the flock of Abiram

316 The tradition that the apostle John survived being thrown into a cauldron of boiling oil at Rome is first recorded in Tertullian, *De praescriptione haereticorum*, c. 36: 138 (Bindley 1914: 84–5).

317 Gregory I, *Homiliae in euangelia* I, 1, 6: 10 (Hurst 1990: 19).

318 It is unclear whether what follows is a direct quotation, and on what source Hincmar is relying. One possibility is a lost treatise by Hrabanus Maurus on the ordeal, but Hincmar seems only to have read this text years after *De divortio*: see Böhringer 1992: 152 n. 41.

319 On Sodom, see above, 150.

320 The verdict of the cold water ordeal seems reversed from what might be expected: see Introduction, 37.

321 See above, 152.

[Numbers 16:1–33]. And the unsteadiness of water bore up Peter as he trod upon it, trusting in his faith, but almost swallowed him up as he sank when he faltered in his faith, until Christ lifted him up by his right hand [Matthew 4:28–31]. And the catholic Fathers, explaining the passage of the Epistles about the Ark of the Flood as a symbol of baptism, say that "the heretics" and bad Christians "are submerged in the depths by the same waters which raise up the orthodox and just to the heavenly Kingdoms".'[322]

<153> But we should know, as the blessed Gregory said:[323]

'that divine work is not wonderful if comprehended by reason, and that the faith to which human reason offers proof has no merit. And since Paul the apostle says: "Now, faith is the substance of things hoped for, the evidence of things not seen" [Hebrews 11:1], it is clear that faith is the evidence for those things which are not able to appear. For those things which appear no longer involve faith, but recognition. But these works of our Redeemer which in themselves cannot be comprehended should be considered in the light of other works of his, so that His more marvellous deeds should provoke faith in the marvellous.'

...

'And so the Lord deigned to explain some things in the Scriptures through Himself, so that we should know to seek the signification of things also in those things which He wished to explain through himself.'[324]

So let those who demand the proof of human reason in divine judgements and miracles accept in response,[325] that the Ark which contained the just designates the Church of the faithful, the faith of the Holy Trinity built through the incarnation of Jesus Christ. And all those people about whom the Lord said: 'The end of all flesh is come before me, the earth is filled with violence through them, and, behold, I will destroy them with the earth' [Genesis 6:13] were covered by the flowing waters. And not all were drowned, covered by the overflowing waters, but the innocent were freed and the guilty were punished, as is written: 'And Noah went in and his sons, and his wife and his sons' wives with him into the ark, because of the waters of the flood' [Genesis 7:7]. And a little later: 'All the fountains of the great deep were broken up, and the windows of heaven were opened. And the rain was upon the earth forty days and forty nights' [Genesis 7:11–12]. And again: 'And the waters increased, and bare up the Ark, and it

322 Bede, *In Epistolam I Petri* III, 19–21: 249, 250 (shortened and rearranged, with Hincmar's addition of the words 'and bad Christians').

323 Gregory I, *Homiliae in euangelia* II, 26, 1: 218; II, 26, 8: 224 (Hurst 1990: 201, 207).

324 Gregory I, *Homiliae in euangelia* I: 15, 1, 104 (Hurst 1990: 88).

325 All these biblical examples are taken from Ambrose, *De sacramentis.*

was lift up above the earth' [Genesis 7:17], and after a little: 'And all flesh died that moved upon the earth. And Noah only remained alive, and they that were with him in the Ark' [Genesis 7:21–23]. And a little later, 'And the fountains also of the deep and the windows of heaven were stopped' [Genesis 8:2].

And the same cloud was made dark to the Egyptians and bright to the Hebrews, and again it is written:

> 'and the angel of God, which went before the camp of Israel, removed and went behind them; and the pillar of the cloud went from before their face, and stood behind them: And it came between the camp of the Egyptians and the camp of Israel; and it was a cloud and darkness to them, but it gave light by night to these: so that the one came not near the other all the night' [Exodus 14:19–20].

And one and the same rod was held up over the waters, which became as 'a wall unto them on their right hand, and on their left' [Exodus 14:29], and He led across the sons of Israel, as it is written, through the very great waters, and He 'overthrew the Egyptians in the midst of the sea' so that 'there remained not so much as one of them' [Exodus 14:27], and the Israelites saw the Egyptians dead upon the sea shore, whom the Lord had looked over in the morning watch, as we said, in a pillar of fire and cloud [Exodus 14:31]. And 'He spread a cloud for a covering; and fire to give light in the night' [Psalms 105:39] – that is:[326]

> 'Christ, who is the column of light dispersing the shadows of unfaithfulness, and pouring forth the light of truth and spiritual grace on the humans He loved – and through the column of cloud, which is the Holy Spirit. In which baptism there is now a type of baptism, just as was also shown in the Flood.'

And let us add also that Elijah invoked the name of the Lord his God, and 'there came down fire from heaven' [2 Kings 1:10]. <154> And 'Elisha invoked the name of the Lord, and the iron axe rose from the water to the wood handle, and floated on the waves' [2 Kings 6:6–7].[327] 'The element of iron is heavier than liquid water, so let us realise that grace is greater than nature.'[328]

Let the explanation of Ambrose suffice for all these things, so that the comparison can be deduced, why in the ordeal of cold water there

326 Adapted from Ambrose, *De sacramentis* I, 6, 22: 24 (Thompson 1950: 56).

327 Adapted from Ambrose, *De sacramentis* II, 4, 11: 29; IV, 4, 18: 54 (Thompson 1950: 62, 89).

328 Ambrose, *De mysteriis* IX, 51: 111 (Thompson 1950: 146).

should on the one hand be sinking, on the other hand floating. For he says in his book *On the Sacraments or Mysteries*:[329]

> 'Baptism was indeed invented so that the trickery and ambushes of the devil should not prevail in this world. About this baptism, hear what Scripture, or rather the Son of God, says: "But the Pharisees and lawyers rejected the counsel of God against themselves, being not baptized of him [John the Baptist]" [Luke 7:30]. Therefore baptism is the counsel of God.' And a little later: 'By your submerging this sentence is dissolved: "For dust thou art and unto dust shalt thou return" [Genesis 3:19]. When this sentence is fulfilled, there is room for the heavenly benefit and remedy. This is water from the earth, therefore, because the conditions of our life do not allow that we should be covered by earth and rise again from the earth. Further, it is not earth but water that washes. Therefore the font is, as it were, a tomb.'

→ For the rest, as the apostle says, 'All Scripture is given by inspiration of God, and is profitable for doctrine, for reproof, for correction, for instruction in righteousness, that the man of God may be perfect, thoroughly furnished unto all good works' [2 Timothy 3:16–17]. And as we read in the sayings of the catholic Fathers: 'divine speech is a pearl, which can be inspected from every angle'.[330] And the person who offers testimony from the Scriptures for the instruction of the faithful is not a fabricator of lies, even if he expounds upon them differently from how those through whom it was offered understood it. So without prejudice to the intellect of our betters, I shall say what I, according to the smallness of my little intellect (*ingeniolum*), believe can be dug out from their words.[331]

The holy apostle teaches that the Red Sea, which our fathers crossed over under Moses as leader (*dux*), was a baptism coloured red by the blood of Christ. And this Moses prefigured Christ the leader, who through baptism brought us from Egyptian servitude to the promised land, that is from the slavery of sin and the domination of death into the freedom of the glory of the sons of God, and into the kingdom of eternal life, just like the Rock [Christ] following the people through the desert, who follows us in the wasteland of this world with his mysteries.[332] Therefore the same apostle said about baptism: 'So many of us as

329 Ambrose, *De sacramentis* II, 6, 18–19: 33–4 (Thompson 1950: 66): because water comes from the earth, baptism is a symbol of passing through burial into new life.

330 Jerome, *Epistula* 22 to Eustochia, c. 8: I, 155 (Fremantle 1893: 25).

331 Hincmar here justifies his own interpretation of Scripture, rather than relying on patristic interpretations (a reminder that Carolingian exegetes were by no means trapped in tradition). See 26–7. The insertion here continues to 159.

332 See 1 Corinthians 10:1–5.

were baptized into Jesus Christ were baptized into his death. Therefore we are buried with him by baptism into death' [Romans 6:3–4]. John Chrysostom says:[333]

> 'What does it mean, "baptized into death"? That we ourselves also shall die, just like him. For the cross is baptism. What the cross and the tomb were to Christ, baptism has become for us, though not in the same way. Therefore he [St Paul] did not say those "planted together in death", but "in the likeness of his death" [Romans 6:5]. For He Himself both died and was buried in the flesh, but we both died and were buried in our sin.'

With all these sayings gathered together, it seems possible that someone who is buried with Christ through baptism into death [Romans 6:4], and freed through the same baptism from death, and through sin returned to the same slavery and death – 'the soul that sinneth, shall die', he says [Ezekiel 18:4] – is placed into the water in likeness to death, so that the wicked will be proven so, whether he wishes it or not, for often good things are offered to the unwilling. And so he may confess, and through the confession of emendation and correction may be freed again from the death of the sin committed. <155> Or if proven innocent by the judgement of God, he may not be considered by us amongst those guilty of a sin, when 'planted together in likeness to death' in the water. The sea indeed, designating baptism as was shown above, kept none of the dead in itself, since, as is written: 'it threw the dead Egyptians on the shore' [Exodus 14:31]. So the dead Egyptian, that is the man subject to sin, will not be received, not be held by water sanctified by the invocation of truth, which is Christ, so long as by denial he remains in the death of his sin.

Let him who is tied up by the bonds of his iniquities come forth from the shadows of bad conscience, by confessing. And through a confession of truth, let him be buried in the water as if in some way planted together in likeness to death, very truly of that truth, freed by that truth. Let him who is sent into the water to be tested be tied with a rope, because as it is written, every individual is tied up by the ropes of his sins.[334] He is tied up for two reasons: so he cannot do any trickery in the judgement, and so that if the water should receive him as if innocent, he can be pulled

333 John Chrysostom, *Homiliae in Epistolam ad Romanos* 10: col. 480 (Morris and Simcox 1889: 405), via Augustine, *Contra Iulianum* I, 6, 27: col. 660 (Schumacher 1957: 33).

334 An interesting detail concerning Carolingian practices of the ordeal.

out in time, lest he be endangered by the water.[335] For Lazarus, dead for four days, by whom is signified anyone buried under a heap of sins, was buried, bound up with bands and, tied up by the same bands, is read to have left the tomb when the Lord called, and at his order was untied by the disciples.[336] And so anyone to be examined in a judgement is sent to the water tied up, and is pulled out tied up. And either having cleared himself, he is immediately released by the judgement of the arbiters, or, tied up, he is examined in judgement until he is cleared.[337]

And in the sacred history we read that:[338]

> 'Elijah came with his disciple Elisha to the river Jordan. And rolling up his cloak, he struck the waters, which were parted, and both crossed over. Afterwards, Elisha picked up the cloak of Elijah which had fallen from him, and coming to the Jordan he struck the waters, and, invoking the God of Elijah, he parted them and crossed over. Rightly the flow of our mortality is expressed by the River Jordan, for in Latin "Jordan" means "their descent"',

that is, of the Christians. For, Gregory says:[339]

> 'since the Author of our redemption deigned to be baptised in the River Jordan, it is appropriate that the name Jordan represent the multitude of those who have received the sacrament of baptism. And it is written in Job about the old Enemy of the human race, "And he trusteth that he can draw up Jordan into his mouth" [Job 40:23], since after seizing so many of the unfaithful from the beginning of the world, he still trusts he is able to scoop up the faithful too; for every day he devours in his mouth of pestilent persuasion those in whom a blameworthy life is at odds with a profession of faith.'

And it is just like the waters, struck and divided by the rolled-up cloak of Elijah [2 Kings 2:14], through which a crossing was prepared, when those, as we have just set out in the words of Gregory, are tied up and sent down into the water. Since it is as if the waters are divided, when the water [of the ordeal] receives some and shows them to be innocent, or rejects others, and shows them to be guilty. And a crossing is

335 Hincmar here for the first time mentions that interference with an ordeal is possible: see Introduction, 38.

336 John 11:39–44.

337 Perhaps a reference to the use of multiple ordeals (discussed by Hincmar below, <156>) where someone already found guilty of one charge might face the ordeal again for additional accusations.

338 Bede, *Homiliarum euangelii libri ii* II, 15: 287–8 (shortened) (Martin and Hurst 1991: II 145), commenting on 2 Kings 2:8–14.

339 Gregory I, *Homiliae in euangelia* II, 26, 9: 225 (shortened) (Hurst 1990: 208).

prepared either when some accused of crimes are judged to be placed among the innocent, or on the contrary, when the judgement has been declared, and they are counted amongst those guilty of crimes. ←[340]

For when anyone who is thought to be guilty, and who is, is sent to be tested in the waters, the Lord is invoked by those who send him according to a certain measure of the form of baptism, <156> so that the truth which is sought may be shown forth, and He might deign to enlighten the shadows of our ignorance.[341] So that no one who is innocent might be unjustly condemned by us, or else, guilty, might escape unpunished, by denying it or by devilish trickery in any way. And he who is sent to the water to be tested confirms the invocation of those invoking, by his response and devotion, according to the formula before baptism. For as St Ambrose says in his book *On the Sacraments*:[342]

> 'You were asked, "Do you believe in God the Almighty Father?" You said "I believe", and you were immersed, that is buried. And again, you were asked, "Do you believe in our Lord Jesus Christ, and in his cross?" You said "I believe", and you were immersed, and so you were buried with Christ. For he who is buried with Christ rises again with Christ. And a third time you were asked, "Do you believe in the Holy Spirit?" And you said "I believe", and you were immersed a third time, so that a triple confession might absolve the multiple falls of an earlier time of life. Finally, so that we may offer you an example, the holy apostle Peter, after he seemed to have fallen by the human condition during the passion of our Lord, and who previously denied him, was later asked three times by Christ if he loved Christ: that he might abolish and dissolve that fall. Then he said "Yea, Lord; thou knowest, that I love thee" [John 21:15–17]. He said it three times so that he might three times be absolved.'

→ Just so the man found guilty in the judgement, if perhaps he was accused on many counts, should be examined by a repeated judgement, until he should be found to be proven by the confession of emendation.[343] And for this point we take the words of St Ambrose, saying:[344]

340 The interpolation ends a few lines down, but the additional text probably finished here: see n. 331 (and n. 305), above.

341 These parallels to baptism were potentially problematic: Hincmar later discusses opposition to the cold water ordeal on the grounds that baptism could not be repeated: see below, 163.

342 Ambrose, *De sacramentis* II, 7, 20: 34–5 (Thompson 1950: 67).

343 Hincmar here suggests the possibility of multiple ordeals, although other sources do not mention the practice.

344 This repetition of a previous quotation is part of the many additional notes made by Hincmar in the manuscript version of the text of *De divortio*.

> 'Finally, so that we may offer you an example, the holy apostle Peter, after he seemed to have fallen by the infirmity of the human condition during the passion of our Lord, and who previously denied him, was later asked three times by Christ if he loved Christ: that he might abolish and dissolve that fall. Then he said "Yea, Lord; thou knowest, that I love thee" [John 21:15–17]. He said it three times so that he might three times be absolved.' ←

And since, as we show above by divine authority, baptism is a judgement, and the baptism of Jordan is interpreted to indicate the stream of judgement, by which the Prince of the world, a liar and its father [the Devil] is cast out, and baptism is the counsel of God, so holy men devised the judgement of cold water to investigate the unknown. In this judgement of cold water for the invocation of truth, which is God, the person who wants to cover up the truth by his falsehood cannot be submerged in the waters, above which the voice of the Lord God's majesty intoned. For the pure nature of water does not recognise as pure a human nature which was cleansed of every stain of sin by the water of baptism, but is once again infected by falsehood. And therefore it does not receive it, but rejects it as foreign.

→ And as in baptism, the unclean spirit which is the prince of this world is cast out from a man, so anyone who through his sin is reoccupied by the devil, that is the prince of this world – as it is written, although he leaves the man, he returns to him lacking in good deeds, indeed empty, with another seven spirits still worse than himself [Matthew 12:43–45] – <157> is rejected by the water blessed by the invocation of the holy name. ←

For the water perceives the man [who is guilty] not to be natural, as if he is reborn from water and the spirit, cleansed 'not by the putting away of the filth of the flesh, but the answer and confession of a good conscience toward God' [1 Peter 3:21]. But rather he is perceived to be one of those about whom Leviticus writes: 'Whosoever he be of your lineage that goeth unto the holy things, which the children of Israel hallow unto the Lord, in whom there is uncleanliness, that soul shall perish before the Lord' [Leviticus 22:3]. He did not say: 'in whom there was uncleanliness'.[345] For uncleanliness is in him who covers the truth with falsehood. And so anyone from the sacerdotal lineage (*stirps*) – 'you', he said, 'a chosen generation, a royal priesthood' [1 Peter 2:9], and in the Book of Apocalypse, he says: 'You hath made us a kingdom

345 Humans have their uncleanliness removed by baptism, but someone who lies about their guilt before the ordeal has once again made himself unclean.

for God and priests' [Revelation 1:6] – who approaches those things which are consecrated to God, as long as he has uncleanliness in him, would not be able to be immersed in waters sanctified by the invocation of God, so that he may appear innocent, but will be shown to be the one who must perish.[346]

→ 'Purge out therefore', says the apostle, 'the old leaven, that ye may be a new lump, as ye are unleavened' [1 Corinthians 5:7]. As if he says openly: Someone accused of a crime and denying it, and whom you are unable to test by judicial order (*iudiciarius ordo*) with suitable witnesses, you should purge either by oath or by the judgement of God, lest with him remaining in your midst, a curse might be said to you: 'There is an accursed thing (*anathema*) in the midst of thee, O Israel: thou canst not stand before thine enemies' [Joshua 7:13].[347] And again the apostle said: 'And have no fellowship with the unfruitful works of darkness' [Ephesians 5:11]. And Augustine says: 'Have no fellowship, that is do not consent. And since not to consent was not enough, if it should be followed by the neglect of discipline, rather also argue against it. For wickedness will not harm you in two ways: if you do not consent to it, and if you argue against it.'[348] So the sinner is to be argued with. And if he denies it, and it cannot be proven by judicial order, let him be examined, so that the good person may be made obvious, and the reprobate may be unable to hide. ←

Once caught, however, let him confess and repent, and he will not be held by the rope of his sins by which he was bound, so that he might not sink; and drenched by tears, let him be washed in the water of salvation.[349] And let them, like the Egyptians and those who had been corrupted in fleshly corruption, be submerged in the presence of the Lord like lead in foaming waters, and according to the prophet, let his iniquities be cast into the depths of the sea [Micah 7:19]. For previously, with his falsehood, he was unable to be submerged to be washed, until by his confession that iniquity is cast into the depths, and he emerges washed.

346 Hincmar extends the remarks in Leviticus about unclean priests to all Christians, and hence any unclean person who comes to consecrated things will die, even if the water of the ordeal refusing to accept them may appear like their miraculous preservation from danger.

347 The ordeal is seen here as the second or third choice of legal procedure to be used, when other evidence is lacking: see Introduction, 36.

348 Augustine, *Sermo* 88: 93 (MacMullen 1888: 385), also cited below, Appendix Response 7: 307. On the need not to 'consent' to wickedness, see Introduction, 72.

349 In spiritual terms, the purpose of the ordeal is to provoke the guilty party to confession, following which he can then be absolved and spiritually cleansed.

Just like the iron of Elisha was pressed under by the water until at the invocation of the Lord's name it returned to the wooden handle,[350] so someone denying a sin before confession is pressed down by the weight of an anxious conscience, until he announces the impiety of his sin to the Lord, by the wood of whose cross, as St Ambrose says, the infirmity of all men was lifted up.[351] For this is the Flood, which is the baptism, by which the sins of all are washed away. The mind of the just, long since dead indeed from the denial of sin, is revived by grace alone.

Let the devout person read the *Dialogues* of St Gregory, and he will find there nuns who were not corrected, and who were excommunicated by St Benedict after their death because of their lack of correction.[352] <158> They left their tombs in the church at the moment of communion, because they were not in communion. But after reconciliation, they stayed in their tombs.[353] And he will find that the ground was not able to hold the body of a boy monk, since it did not have the grace of St Benedict;[354] and a glass vessel was broken at the sign of the cross made by St Benedict;[355] and another glass vessel was thrown by his orders because of disobedience into an enormous precipice, strewn with piles of rocks, and kept intact;[356] and his disciple, Maurus, walked on the waters of the lake,[357] and in the manner of Elisha, that a piece of iron was recalled by him onto a handle from the depths of the lake.[358]

→ And as it is written in the divine pages, the holy fire, hidden for a long run of years, changed into a thick liquid, was found again, and the same liquid poured over the offered sacrifice was changed by divine power, consumed by fire [2 Maccabees 1:20–22]. And the sacrifice of Gideon, though covered in broth which in abundance usually puts out fire, was consumed by tongues of fire, with the fire even licking the rock, through angelic ministry [Judges 6:19–21]. And in 'the mystery of one and the same element there is the end to sins and the origin of virtue',[359] with the Holy Spirit working in the water of holy baptism. ←

350 See above, 155 n. 327.

351 Ambrose, *De sacramentis* II, 4, 11: 30 (Thompson 1950: 62).

352 On the Carolingian concept of 'correctio', see Introduction, 71.

353 Gregory I, *Dialogi* II, 23: II, 206–8 (Zimmerman 1959: 91–3).

354 Gregory I, *Dialogi* II, 24: II, 210–11 (Zimmerman 1959: 94).

355 Gregory I, *Dialogi* II, 3: II, 142 (Zimmerman 1959: 62).

356 Gregory I, *Dialogi* II, 28:II, 218 (Zimmerman 1959: 96–7).

357 Gregory I, *Dialogi* II, 7:II, 158 (Zimmerman 1959: 69).

358 Gregory I, *Dialogi* II, 6: II, 156 (Zimmerman 1959: 68–9).

359 A quotation from the blessing of the baptismal water in the Gregorian Sacramentary, already cited above, 152.

Let the careful reader read this, and he will not be amazed that in the ordeal of cold water the innocent are received by the water and the guilty are not, just as in the ordeal of boiling water the guilty are scalded, the innocent preserved unharmed. For Christ, the medicine of the heavenly Father, the true doctor of human salvation, when called upon by his faithful followers, cures by opposites, treating cold with warmth, warmth with cold, just as doctors of the flesh are accustomed to do, inspired by Him.[360] And of those involved in one and the same insurrection in the old synagogue, some the earth swallowed up, some the hungry flames consumed [Numbers 16:31–35]. 'While the innocent flesh is washed by the cold waters of the Saviour, so the fiery sword of paradise formerly set against the sinners is extinguished.'[361] 'And by the disposition of the Creator and Director of the elements, by one and the same sun, mud is hardened out and wax is liquefied.'[362]

These things should be said, since the unstable element receives some as they sink for the sake of the faith of the believers, and does not receive others. And some are scalded by the heat of the same element, and others escape unscalded. It should not be omitted that we read in the capitularies of the emperors that the ordeal of cold water was forbidden. But this is not in those synodal decrees which we have from established (*certus*) synods.[363] Some absurd people say that it was forbidden because anyone submerged in water in the name of the Lord is as if rebaptised. But we do not find this written anywhere there, and nor are we unaware that St Ambrose talks of many baptisms, that is, he notes down many indications of baptism.[364] The holy canons forbid rebaptism to all, since it should be avoided. <159> However, there is hardly one amongst the faithful who immerses himself in water, even for washing, without making the sign of the cross, or invoking the holy name: for the apostle commands all things to be done in the name of the Lord [Colossians 3:17]. But no one thinks he is thereby baptised by that baptism through which he is reborn from water and spirit.[365]

360 Gregory I, *Moralia in Iob* XXIV, 2, 2: II, 1189 (Bliss 1844: III, 50–1).

361 Bede, *In Lucae evangelium expositio* I, 3, 21: 83–4.

362 Gregory I, *Homiliae in Hiezechihelem prophetam* II, 5, 10: 283 (Tomkinson 2008: 341), cited again below, 164.

363 This is a peculiar comment, because it was the Council of Worms in 829 which banned the cold water ordeal (see *Capitulare missorum Wormatiense* 829, c. 12 (MGH *Capit.* II, no. 192: 16), a council which Hincmar earlier praised (see Response 5, 133). It is possible, however, that Hincmar came across this quotation in Benedict Levita (see Introduction, 23).

364 Ambrose, *De sacramentis* I, 6, 20–II, 1, 2: 24–6 (Thompson 1950: 55–8).

365 On superstition, see Introduction, 65.

For speech and the work of God and all the sacraments are heavenly manna, which, as is written, 'had every deliciousness, every sweetness of flavour' [Wisdom 16:20]. Just as this, for the wishes of those taking it, was formerly made to the taste of those eating, so these things [the sacraments] were made to be shown for the devotion of believers. Just as the incarnation of the Lord is 'the ruin and the resurrection of many' [Luke 2:34], and His 'cross is to them that perish foolishness, but unto us which are saved it is the power of God' [1 Corinthians 1:18]. And His preaching is 'to the one the savour of death unto death; and to the other the savour of life unto life' [2 Corinthians 2:16]. It is a mockery for the unbelievers, but for the faithful it is redemption. The sacraments of the altar are life for those who approach devoutly, but a judgement for the undevout. Just as 'bread strengthens the life of the strong, but kills that of small children. And soft whistling calms horses, but excites puppies.'[366] The sun softens wax, but dries up mud,[367] it is light to the healthy eye, and darkness to the sore-eyed. As 'venom is death for men but life for the snake',[368] so this judgement is a display of truth to those who believe firmly and rightly, but to the hesitant and doubtful, error seems to be involved.[369] For as St Paul says: 'Now faith is the substance of things hoped for, the evidence of things not seen' [Hebrews 11:1]. And as St Gregory expounds:[370] 'It is clear that faith is the evidence for those things which are not able to appear. For those things which appear no longer involve faith, but recognition.'

So in this divine judgement, we must give credence to those things about which we doubted after they have been shown by divine display, contemplating with the eyes of faith those things which we cannot see with bodily eyes. Just as Thomas who used to doubt:[371]

> 'when he felt the Lord, saw one thing and believed another. For divinity could not be seen by mortal man – therefore he saw the man and confessed the God, saying "My Lord, and my God" [John 20:28]. By seeing, he therefore believed, and he proclaimed him [Jesus], in appearance a man, to be a God, which he was not able to see.'

366 Gregory I, *Moralia in Iob* XXX, 3, 12: III, 1499 (Bliss 1844: IV, 370).

367 See above, 163 n. 362.

368 Gregory I, *Moralia in Iob* III, 9, 15: I, 124 (Bliss 1844: I, 140).

369 Lothar's supporters had suggested that Theutberga's ordeal may not have revealed the truth about her guilt. Hincmar here is implicitly accusing them of lack of faith.

370 Gregory I, *Homiliae in euangelia* II, 26, 8: 224 (Hurst 1990: 207), cited above, 154.

371 Gregory I, *Homiliae in euangelia* II, 26, 8: 224–5 (Hurst 1990: 207).

So also we ought to praise and proclaim the truth of the matter about which we were in doubt, since we were unable to see it with earthly eyes, believing the truth, which is God, through heavenly display.[372]

We say this not to reprove anyone, for it is not written there why this ordeal ought not to take place,[373] but only to prevent such a statement; nor to try to defend our arguments as if they were wiser than those which other people will succeed or are succeeding in finding in the examples of the saints. 'Let every man be fully persuaded in his own mind' [Romans 14:5], so long as he cautiously makes sure that he does not differ from the catholic faith and the tradition of the Apostolic seat. But humbly offering what we think, we are prepared to yield without contention to a sound intellect, if anyone can explain things to us more appropriately; and not just very willingly to agree, but also even to learn.[374]

<160> These things being so, if by this form of judgement – which, as we have heard, the emperor Charles called Great[375] accepted in his lifetime in good faith – this woman was cleared about the things of which she was accused, 'by the counsel of the lay nobility, the agreement of the bishops and by royal decree'[376] – for any other way would not have been appropriate, and if this woman was restored to and received into the marital bed → not only by the agreement of the noble laymen, but also, as we have heard, with the reconciliation and blessing of the bishops ← we are not able to understand why we should bring the matter into question once more.

For the Lord says, 'Do not tempt the Lord thy God' [Deuteronomy 6:16]. And let us hear what the Lord heard from the man who said to him: '"Master, I beseech thee, look upon my son. And, lo, a spirit taketh him, And I besought thy disciples to cast him out; and they could not." And the Lord said, "O faithless and perverse generation, how long shall I be with you, and suffer you?"' [Luke 9:38–41]. For he heard how by that word 'he [the father] secretly accused the apostles about an impossibility, when the impossibility of the cure came not from the

372 The argument here is that an ordeal is used when a person's guilt or innocence is not known by others. The ordeal, by demonstrating God's judgement on the person, is therefore a visible indication of an invisible mental state.

373 That is, in the questions sent to Hincmar.

374 Personal theological and scriptural interpretations are thus permissible, within certain limits, though Hincmar also accepts that he might be wrong.

375 One of the first references to Charles as 'the Great', i.e. Charlemagne. Note Hincmar's reference to oral transmission.

376 Quoting from Question 1, 95, c. 1.

powerlessness of the healers, but from the faith of those who needed healing'.[377] We too shall hear this, although not with earthly ears, but because of infidelity, if we should revisit (*removere*)[378] such matters [the ordeal] without cause or due reason, as if the fraudulent matter in this judgement should be the doubtful revelation of God and not our unfaithfulness. If the woman appeared guilty in the ordeal, why was she received back? And if she was guiltless, why is the case revisited (*remota*)? Especially since it should be believed in every way that if her champion who went to the judgement for her had been burned, she would have been judged guilty, and her accuser would not have wished to have her admitted to a hearing again.[379] And it should also be held that just as in the judgement of baptism, the liar and the Father of Lies is cast out from those who are baptised, by the faith and mouths of those acting and professing for them, so the falsehood of this accusation should have been removed from this woman by the faith and profession of the champion she sent, through the action of that champion, and by divine judgement, and the truth of her innocence declared. For 'if we receive the witness of men, the witness of God is greater' [1 John 5:9]. He testifies to us, by the display of His virtues, what we ought to believe about those things of which we were doubtful before the display.

Question 7

> <161> 'And they say that it was on account of a secret confession made by this woman that her champion escaped unburned from the ordeal.'[380]

Response 7

In the same way, so we read, certain people attempted with false piety to defend St Peter, that he was saying he did not know that man whom he recognised to be God, when the Truth said: 'Thou shalt deny me' [Matthew 26:34].[381] So these, greater in iniquity because with impious falsehood they misrepresent the Truth as false while they proclaim Him as pious, say that He wished to free this woman [Theutberga], so

377 Jerome, *Commentariorum in Matheum* III, 17, 16: 152, probably mediated through Bede, *In Lucae euangelium expositio* III, 9, 40: 208.

378 Classically *removere* means to move back or to set aside, but here and elsewhere Hincmar seems to use it in the sense of 'moving again'.

379 In other words, Lothar II would not have accepted a retrial if the verdict had gone his way: why should he have one because he got an answer he did not want?

380 See above Question 6: 144.

381 That is, St Peter was not technically lying when he denied knowing the *man* Jesus.

that He might deceive those believing in her judgement, though it is said 'For the Holy Spirit of discipline will flee deceit' [Wisdom 1:5].[382]

And St Peter said to Simon Magus, who thought that he was able to buy the grace of the Holy Spirit through whom miracles and every sign were worked and which flees all falsehood: 'Thou hast neither part nor lot in this matter … For I perceive that thou art in the gall of bitterness and in the bond of iniquity' [Acts 8:21–23]. And, as the blessed Gregory says:[383] 'The simple Truth does nothing through duplicity', 'searching hearts and proving the loins' [Jeremiah 17:10] and 'piercing even to the dividing asunder of soul and body, and of the joints and marrow' [Hebrews 4:12] and the innards of the heart. And in order that Truth is near to those that call upon Him in truth, He orders judgement to be made in truth. For who called upon the Lord and was deceived? Faithfully invoked in a just judgement, He is not able to deceive anyone, 'for the Lord is righteous in all his ways, and holy in all his works' [Psalms 145:17].

And the catholic teachers say about the purgation of the oath (*sacramentum*), that just as it is received satisfactorily by that person to whom it is made, so it is judged by the Lord.[384] And Paul says, 'For, with the heart, man believeth unto righteousness, and with the mouth confession is made unto salvation' [Romans 10:10]. And in like manner, there is no confession (*confessio*) except confession (*fassio*) with the heart and by the mouth, so that our mind may be in concord with our voice.[385] And therefore in baptism, it is not the putting away of the filth of the flesh which cleanses, but the answer and confession of a good conscience towards God. For Peter, who had confessed 'the Christ, the son of the living God' [Matthew 16:16], knew Him to be the Lord and believed Him to be God, denied by his mouth that he was the disciple of Him who said 'Whosoever shall confess me before men, him I will confess also before my Father' [Matthew 10:32] and 'Whosoever shall deny me, I will deny him' [Matthew 10:33]. And just as we have read, to deny that he was his disciple, as Peter said 'I am not' to someone who claimed that he was one of that man's disciples, is nothing other than to deny that he is a Christian.[386] And so the sacred canons decreed those

382 On this argument, made implicitly in the proceedings of the Councils of Aachen, see Introduction, 37–8.

383 Gregory I, *Homiliae in euangelia* II, 23, 1: 194 (Hurst 1990: 177).

384 The specific source of this idea cannot be identified, but Hincmar repeats similar views elsewhere in the text: see Introduction, 35.

385 Böhringer 1992: 161 n. 5 suggests a glossary may have provided the rare word *fassio*.

386 Bede, *In Lucae evangelium expositio* VI, 22, 58: 391.

people to be among the apostates who believed in Christ in their hearts and denied him by mouth, when conquered by torture.[387] And again it is written, 'How then shall they call on Him in whom they have not believed?' [Romans 10:14].

<162> How, I say, did this woman [Theutberga] in this judgement call upon the Lord as her helper and liberator, in whom she did not believe? And if she faithfully believed in the Lord whom she called upon, she believed Him to be true and not false, and just and loving justice, and she knew Him not to be able to deceive or be deceived. Those who say to the contrary, what else do they say but assert that the Truth can deceive and be deceived? They are more obstinate than the demons, who, as the Gospel says, left those possessed confessing Him, because they knew Him to be the Christ.[388]

And we marvel if what is also said, that he [Gunther] who took the confession of this woman is also a witness of this [judgement], is in any way able to be true. And we would not dare to believe this, if we did not dare not to believe those men who sent word to us. For he [Gunther] would have known that what he reads again and again in the Book of Leviticus must not be understood perversely:[389] '"A soul who hears the voice of one swearing and is a witness, or who sees something and is conscious and does not make it known".' For as Origen says:

> 'By this, without doubt the soul receives the sin of him who unjustly either does or swears something. This too edifies us according to history, lest we should ever pollute our consciences with the sins of someone else, or lend consent to those who do bad things. I say "consent" not only about doing the same, but also keeping silent about actions done openly and illicitly.'

And if he [Gunther] knew and kept silent because of the secret confession, why – and, as is said, may it not be – did he agree that there should be a judgement about it, not respecting the sentence of both the law and the Gospel, 'Do not tempt the Lord thy God' [Deuteronomy 6:16; Matthew 4:7]? For if it is a loss of honour to act against canonical authority, which proceeds from the fountain of the law, the prophets and the Gospel, promulgated by the Holy Spirit by whom these things

387 See e.g. Council of Ancyra 314, cc. 1–5: 55–73 (Percival 1900: 63–5).

388 See e.g. Luke 4:41.

389 Origen, *In Leuiticum homiliae* 3: 301–2 (Barkley 1990: 53–4). Origen quotes in a free form the first part of Leviticus 5:1, which ends: 'then he shall bear his iniquity'. Origen goes on to warn against publicising the sins of someone else, which fits awkwardly with Hincmar's notion of public penance.

were spoken, he who tries to oppose the truth of the Gospel in such important matters cannot escape danger.[390] And again it is written, 'thou shalt perform unto the Lord thy oaths' [Matthew 5:33]. If he [Gunther] promised fidelity to his lord (*senior*),[391] how did he presume to consent to this trickery against him? And if then placed between two dangers, he chose the lesser, to neglect the oath, so that he might avoid the greater, lest he become a betrayer of confession, why does he now relate this confession?[392] For it is written: 'He that walketh deceitfully, revealeth secrets: but he that is faithful, concealeth the matter committed to his soul' [Proverbs 11:13], as if it should openly say: He that does not conceal the thing committed to his soul is not faithful. And Paul says to the faithful, 'What part hath he that believeth with an infidel?' [2 Corinthians 6:15].

More things could be said here, but that is not suitable for us. 'For every man shall bear his own burden' [Galatians 6:5]. We have said this briefly, not because we wish to believe in, or wish to be believed by anyone, any disparagement about whichever priest: but we have responded to the extent that we might, in the name of the Lord, point out to those witnesses this impious act of betrayal and duplicity, which we should very much avoid, and which is certainly detestable in all people.[393]

Question 8

<163> This also is said, 'that some people say that the woman was thinking of someone else with the same name as her brother when she sent her champion to the ordeal on her behalf. And therefore her champion was not burned in that ordeal.'[394]

390 If Gunther knew before the ordeal in 858 that Theutberga was guilty of incest, because she had secretly confessed to him, he should not have allowed her to perjure herself publicly, by taking an oath during the ordeal. Hincmar initially implies that breaking the seal of the confession (which is against canonical authority) is less serious than 'tempting God', by asking Him to demonstrate Theutberga's guilt in the ordeal, when this is already known to Gunther. On confession and perjury, see Introduction, 35.

391 That is, to Lothar II. On the fidelity promised by bishops to the king, see Odegaard 1945: 283–7 and Introduction, 34.

392 Hincmar here seems to equivocate over whether breaking the seal of the confession is worse than Gunther allowing Theutberga to lie on oath to both a king and to God. But whatever the correct decision in this dilemma is, Gunther is still in the wrong.

393 Hincmar frames his harsh criticism of Gunther with hints that Gunther's actions may have been misreported, thus allowing some leeway for further negotiation on the case.

394 See above, Question 6: 144.

Response 8

We can compare the idea that the Judge of all things which happen, and who knows all things even before they come to pass, could be led astray by that sort of mistake, with what Peter asked Gregory in the fourth book of the Dialogues: 'Is it the case, I beseech you, that some people are taken from their bodies as if by error?'[395] Gregory responded with reference to the two Stephens: for the Stephen who was brought to the infernal place to be judged was not the Stephen who had been ordered to be brought, who was Stephen the smith. So once the first Stephen was returned, Stephen the smith, who had been ordered to be brought, was brought.

Whenever this happens, says Gregory:

> 'if it is considered properly, it is not an error but a warning. For heavenly piety disposes from the great mercy of His generosity that some should suddenly return to the body after death and should at least greatly fear the torments of hell now they have seen them, which they did not believe when they heard of them.'

And after the story about Stephen, who was brought and returned, and afterwards was again taken to the torments, Gregory added:

> 'Therefore it is understood that those tortures of hell when revealed should be of help to some, but should be a witness against others. So that the first should see the bad things which they might guard against, and the others should be even more punished, because they did not want to avoid the tortures of hell, which they saw and recognised.'[396]

And thus from the Scripture of truth, God shows us something that either helps us as a warning of correction, or which grows by the retribution of justice into a heap of damnation for someone sinning more seriously. For it is written in the Book of Kings that Micaiah the prophet said:

> 'I saw the Lord sitting on his throne, and all the host of heaven standing by him on his right hand and on his left: And the Lord said: Who

395 Gregory I, *Dialogi* IV, 37: III, 124 (Zimmerman 1959: 237).

396 This is adapted by Hincmar from Gregory I *Dialogi*, IV, 37: III, 128–34 (Zimmerman 1959: 238–41). Gregory explains to Peter, his questioner in the *Dialogues*, how some dying people are given visions of hell, and then restored to life as warning. He cites the example of an acquaintance of Peter's called Stephen, who had such a vision while living in Constantinople. When Stephen died, he was brought before a judge in hell, but the judge said that instead 'Stephen the smith' should have been summoned, and the other Stephen was immediately restored to life. However, a soldier a few years later during a plague saw a vision of the afterlife in which Stephen was being pulled by competing good and evil spirits, since he had not reformed sufficiently.

> shall persuade Ahab, king of Israel, that he may go up, and fall at Ramoth-gilead? And one said on this manner, and another said on that manner. And there came forth a spirit, and stood before the Lord, and said: I will persuade him. And the Lord said unto him: Wherewith? And he said: I will go forth, and I will be a lying spirit, in the mouth of all his prophets. And He said: Thou shalt persuade him, and prevail: also go forth, and do so' [1 Kings 22:19–22].[397]

St Gregory explains in his books on Morals, very well known to devoted readers, what the evil spirit standing close to the Lord means, and what the questions the Lord is said to have put to the evil spirit mean, and how God speaks to the evil spirit and the evil spirit to God.[398] And it follows in the history of the Book of Kings, 'Now, therefore, behold the Lord hath put a lying spirit in the mouth of all these thy prophets, and the Lord hath spoken evil concerning thee' [1 Kings 22:23]. And a little later, 'And a certain man drew his bow at a venture, and smote the king of Israel (that is, Ahab) between the lungs and stomach' [1 Kings 22:34]. And a little later, 'and he died at even' [1 Kings 22:35]. And in that the word of the Lord was fulfilled through the hand of the prophet Micaiah, whom we mentioned earlier. Ahab said to Jehoshaphat the king of Judah who was searching for a prophet of the Lord, 'There is yet one man', said Ahab, 'by whom we may enquire of the Lord; Micaiah, the son of Imlah: but I hate him, for he doth not prophecy good concerning me, but evil' [1 Kings 22:8]. That is, he [Micaiah] told him the truth and so he hated him, and loved his lying servants (*ministri*) who were impious, <164> about whom it is written 'If a ruler hearkens to lies, all his servants are wicked' [Proverbs 29:12].

This should be feared by the king and all those wishing to believe in falsehood, as if God in an ordeal either could be deceived or deceive anyone rightly believing in Him. Or as if with undue mercy He ought to have mercy on those who have committed a crime and deny it and who tempt Him. For He prohibits having mercy on even the poor man in judgement under the guise of piety, lest they [those shown mercy] perish and fall into another trap, led astray by a lying spirit from the retribution of justice, because of the other sins they have perpetrated about which they have not given satisfaction to the Lord. Paul said about certain people, 'when they knew God, they glorified him not as God, neither were thankful: but became vain in their imaginations. And their foolish heart was darkened' [Romans 1:21]. Therefore 'God

397 God may therefore allow deception by spirits or devils, but only to lead astray the wicked (by implication, Lothar): see Introduction, 38 and 64–6.

398 Gregory I, *Moralia in Iob* II, 20, 38: I, 82–3 (Bliss 1844: I, 94).

gave them up to uncleanliness through the lusts of their own hearts; to dishonour their own bodies between themselves' [1 Romans 1:24], and because 'they did not like to retain God in their knowledge, God gave them over to a reprobate mind, to do those things which are not convenient' [Romans 1:28]. And to the Thessalonians, 'because they received not the love of truth, that they might be saved. And for this cause God shall send them the spirit of error, that they should believe a lie. That they all might be damned who believed not the truth, but had pleasure in unrighteousness' [2 Thessalonians 2:10–12].

→ Therefore St Augustine says in the third book of *On the Trinity*, speaking about the illusions worked by the magicians (*magi*) of Pharaoh as they resisted Moses:[399]

> 'It is given to be understood that not even those angels and powers of the air that transgressed, who have been thrust down from their habitation in that lofty ethereal purity into that lowest darkness as though into a unique prison, through whom magic arts have whatever power they have, can do anything except by power given from above. That power is given either to deceive the deceitful, as in the case of the Egyptians, and the magicians also themselves, in order that they might seem admirable in the seducing of those spirits, by whom they were becoming damnable in the truth of God. Or it is given for admonishing the faithful, lest they should desire to do anything of the kind as though it were a great thing, for which reason Scriptures have been also handed down to us by authority. Or lastly, it is given to exercise, prove and make manifest the patience of the righteous. For it was not by any small power of visible miracles that Job lost all that he had, and both his children and his bodily health itself. Whatever the transgressing evil angels do, the bodily creation does not serve for their will, but God's, from whom power is given.[400] So it is not on this account to be thought that the matter of visible things is subservient to the bidding of those transgressing angels; but rather to that of God, by whom this power is given, just so far as He, who is unchangeable, determines in His lofty and spiritual seat to give it. For water and fire and earth are subservient even to wicked men, who are condemned to the mines, in order that they may do therewith what they will, but only so far as is permitted.' ←

Question 9 and Response 9

But let us concede that there might have been deceit in this ordeal by the working of the devil, who although he lost the glory of angelic

399 Augustine, *De trinitate* III, 7, 12–13: 139 (Haddan 1887: 60). In Roman law, only the lower classes (*humiliores*) could be condemned to the mines as a punishment.

400 This sentence is an addition in one manuscript of Augustine.

spirit, 'did not lose its subtlety of nature'.[401] He is permitted to do many things, by divine judgement which is hidden but never unjust – permitted by the Lord either because of the unfaithfulness of those who do not rightly believe or for the cleansing of the faithful, as when the devil strangled Judas, sharing with Christ, full with wicked will, and buffeted Paul after he was taken up to the third heaven[402] – <165> just as many things were performed by the magicians of Pharaoh, which Moses the prophet of the Lord had done.[403] And the airs were disturbed to test Job, and 'fire from the airy heaven burned up his sheep and the servants' ⌜Job 1:16⌝. And the Antichrist will do many things himself and through his ministers, 'insomuch that, if it were possible, the elected shall be deceived' ⌜Matthew 24:24⌝. And through a sorceress (*pythonissa*) a vision of Samuel was shown.[404] And in the book of Dialogues which St Gregory wrote we read that 'an idol was found':

> 'which being for a little while by chance cast into the kitchen, fire was suddenly seen to come from it, and to the eyes of all the monks seemed to set the whole kitchen on fire. As if to extinguish the fire, the monks made such a noise by pouring water onto it, that the man of God Benedict, disturbed by the noise, came. He beheld that the same fire was in the eyes of the brothers, but not his own. He bowed down his head immediately in prayer, and then he recalled those brothers to their sight, whom he perceived to be deluded with a fantastical fire, so that they might behold the kitchen standing sound, and not see those flames, which the old enemy had fashioned.'[405]

And it is read in the *Itinerary of Peter* about the father of Clement, that he was anointed with an ointment by Simon Magus whom he had forsaken, so that he might be killed by the faithful, and he appeared to everyone's sight in the form of the same Simon. Only Peter observed who he was, and praying, he brought the disciples back to their sight, and returned his ⌜Clement's father's⌝ proper shape to the gaze of those observing, defeating the phantom.[406] And in the life of the monk John,

401 Gregory I, *Moralia in Iob* XXXII, 12, 17: III, 1642 (Bliss 1844: IV, 524). Having stressed the reliability of ordeals in general, Hincmar now concedes that God may have allowed the devil to mislead humans in this particular case. On Hincmar's attitude to the devil, see Introduction, 66–7.

402 On Paul, see 2 Corinthians 12:2–7. The sentence may be partially corrupt.

403 See e.g. Exodus 7:11–22.

404 1 Samuel 28:7–14.

405 Gregory I, *Dialogi* II, 10: II, 170–2 (Zimmerman 1959: 75–6).

406 Pseudo-Clement, *Recognitiones* 10, 52–67: 359–68 (Smith 1886: 206–9).

parents once saw their daughter as a mare by devilish working.[407] And in the Gospel we also read about the two disciples walking with Christ and doubting in him, 'that their eyes were holden, that they should not know him' [Luke 24:16]. We assume not unfittingly that the hindrance to their eyes was sent by Satan, so that Jesus might not be recognised, but that it was done with Christ's permission until the sacrament of bread, so that it should be understood that the hindrance of the enemy is removed by sharing in the unity of his body, so that Christ is able to be recognised. So it is no wonder if the Lord, who appeared externally to the sight of those doubting in the same way that He was considered by them within, should permit these things to happen in judgement, for the testing of the incredulity of those hesitating and doubting in faith.[408] This was done in their sight, not by the Truth's deceit, but because they were not capable of seeing the truth and thought the matter other than it was: as St Gregory says about Mary:[409]

> 'she was looking for the Lord, whom she did not at all believe had been resurrected, but because she loved and doubted, she saw and did not recognise, for love showed Him to her, and doubt hid Him'. And 'the Lord appeared to those aforesaid two disciples walking along the road who did not believe, but He did not show them an appearance which they would recognise. The Lord behaved externally before the eyes of their body, in accord with what was happening within them, in the eyes of their heart. The simple Truth did nothing through duplicity, but showed Himself to them in body as He was to them in mind.'[410]

→ <166> And St Augustine says in his book *On Christian Doctrine*:[411]

> 'Whatever men have arranged for [demonic] consultations is superstitious, and so are certain agreements about signs negotiated and arranged with demons, such as are employed in the magical arts, and the books of the soothsayers (*haruspices*) and augurs. In this class we must place also all amulets and cures which the medical art condemns, whether these consist in prayers, or in certain marks which they call characters, or in whatever things for hanging or tying.'

407 Hincmar's source cannot be identified, but a similar story is found in Palladius, *Historia Lausiaca*, c. 9: cols 354–5 (Meyer 1965: 56), in the life of Macarius the Egyptian.

408 That is, Hincmar claims that it is not that the result of Theutberga's ordeal itself was false, but that Lothar and his supporters might have been deceived about what they saw (her champion being unharmed). On demonic illusion, see Introduction, 66–7.

409 Gregory I, *Homiliae in euangelia* II, 25, 4: 209 (Hurst 1990: 192).

410 Gregory I, *Homiliae in euangelia* II, 23, 1: 193–4 (Hurst 1990: 176–7).

411 Augustine, *De doctrina Christiana* II, 20, 30: 54 (Shaw 1887: 545).

. . .

> 'And all these things are powerful just so far as they have been arranged with the demons by the previous understanding of the mind, as it were a kind of common language. But they are all full of harmful curiosity, torturing anxiety, and deadly servitude. For it was not because they had power that they were attended to, but it was by attending to and marking them that they came to have power. And so therefore they appear different to different people, according to their thoughts and conceptions. For those spirits who want to deceive take care to provide for each person the things in which they see his own suspicions and plots have already entangled him.'[412]

And the venerable priest Bede says in his *Commentary on the Book of Samuel*:[413]

> 'If anyone wonders how a woman is able to disturb and awaken a prophet after death by demonical art, let him know for certain that either the devil then showed a false shadow to those asking questions, or if it was really Samuel, only as much was permitted to the devil in doing these things as the Lord allowed. Nor is it astonishing that such things were for some hidden causes allowed to the wicked spirit who also set up the Saviour on the pinnacle of the temple, and who sought and took Job for testing.[414] For if we believe the phantom which appeared was rather an unclean spirit, nor should it disturb anyone how many true and prophetic things he was able to narrate. For we know that the devil is able to know in advance or predict many things of the future which he learned from the heavenly angels. But those things which he says should not be listened to at all, for all things which he says or does to men, he does with the intention of leading them astray.' ←

Lest that happen through the plots of demons, we should resist the devil, as the apostle says, strong in the faith which conquers the world, and through which the saints conquered the kingdoms. And about those who firmly believe in it, it is said, 'According to your faith, be it unto you' [Matthew 9:29], and the apostle says, 'Let him ask in faith, nothing wavering' [James 1:6]. And if something should happen in order to test our faith – for it is useful to test even the saints with the flames of temptation, so that either tempted, those who had been strong should be revealed, or so that once their weakness had been recognised through temptation, they might learn to be stronger, and

412 Augustine, *De doctrina Christiana* II, 24, 37: 59 (Shaw 1887: 547). On superstition, see Introduction, 65–6.

413 Bede, *In primam partem Samuhelis* IV, 28, 15–17: 256–7. The reference is to the story of the sorceress summoning Samuel's spirit: see above, 173 n. 404.

414 Matthew 4:5.

thus 'when they have been tested, they shall receive the crown of life' [James 1:12] – then we should not dispute the divine judgements, which are sometimes hidden but never unjust.

Nor must it seem astonishing if whatever deceit interferes by diabolical cunning in this type of judgement [the ordeal], with God's permission. For the water of baptism, in itself faithful, as Ambrose says 'is to some a deceptive water: the baptism of the faithless does not heal, it does not cleanse, but pollutes'.[415] And therefore according to the decrees of the canons, of St Innocent and of other Roman popes, <167> those baptised by heretics in the name of the Holy Trinity receive the grace of the Holy Spirit through the laying on of hands; but those not baptised in the name of the Holy Trinity are commanded to be baptised again.[416] But is it possible, although deceit is found in the baptism of heretics, that the baptism of catholics will not be found good? And if some deceit is found in the ordeal because of the faith of the unbelieving,[417] is the law of purgation to be rejected from the custom of those who believe? For just as private or public deceit is always to be punished, so, as we read is written, 'custom which does not impede the public good is to be retained as law'.[418] Therefore, if any deceitfulness is found in this judgement [of Theutberga], through whatever cleverness (*ingenium*), let the matter be brought back into question, as reason suggests, with a doubled vengeance of judgement, whether for the admission of sin or for the faithless deceit.[419]

But about the purgation of the oath (*sacramentum*),[420] we read in the letter of St Gregory to Secundinus, the bishop of Taormina, that the wife of Leo the *cartularius*[421] had left him for the crime of fornication and

415 Ambrose, *De mysteriis* 4, 23: 98 (Thompson 1950: 131). Hincmar has already compared the ordeal to baptism in Response 6: 155–63.

416 Böhringer 1992: 166 n.14 lists the relevant texts.

417 That is, because those who do not believe correctly, see things that are not actually real.

418 Theodosian Code V, 20, 1: I,2, 242 (Pharr 1952: 117). On Hincmar's concept of Roman law, see Introduction, 29.

419 Hincmar thus allows the possibility of a second trial of Theutberga, without conceding that ordeals in general are invalid.

420 Hincmar had already discussed oaths in Response 6: 145–50: see also Introduction, 34–5.

421 Gregory I, *Registrum* IX, 3 to Secundinus, bishop of Taormina (J 1527): II, 564–5 (Martyn 2004: II, 547–8). A *chartularius* was a late Roman administrative official, but by the Carolingian period could alternatively mean someone freed by a charter. Hincmar discusses this case several times: see below, Response 10: 187; Appendix Response: 291.

had put on religious clothing. But given an oath by him that since the start of their marriage he had not fallen into the sin of adultery, she returned to her husband without consulting the bishop, and therefore was excommunicated with her household.[422] And the holy pope decreed that her household should quickly be absolved. And if it were clear that the woman could find nothing to say against her husband, and moreover that her suspicion had been removed through that oath, and that after this she had returned to him of her own free will, then the censure upon her was to be moderated, and she was not to be deprived of communion for long. And he [Gregory] wrote again to Candidus the abbot:[423]

> 'Finally we dispose, so that it may be to the full satisfaction of everyone, that as well as his oath given bodily, he [Maurentius] should confirm that he twisted nothing in fraud, nor hid anything, but revealed all things truthfully. And if anyone, which we do not believe will happen, should in whatever way try to apply a contrary will about this matter, let him know that he who tries to rescind what has been settled usefully is guilty before God. For let him recognise that it is not his business to detract from this decision and this affair.'

And to Praeiecta:[424] 'It is very suitable to the moderation of the Church, that what has been ordered or decided should not be disturbed afterwards by any opposition.'

We have often heard, concerning this purgation of the oath, that many are accustomed to perform some deceit in it by swearing with a clever trick. But they are not so much swearing as perjuring, for just as we read, that oath will be judged by God in the same way as it was received in faith by him who was accustomed to be satisfied through it.[425] But in that purgation of the oath, deceit or rather perjury is revealed to have been committed, as we do not deny can happen in the ordeal (*iudicium*) through devilish cunning and by divine permission. And we find out about a deceitful oath in the Book of Kings and Maccabees, and in the prophet about an oath made to an unbelieving king, which did not rest unpunished.[426] And we think we have said enough about this above.

422 On bishops overseeing the separation of couples to enter the religious life, see Introduction, 52; on excommunication, see 32–3.

423 Gregory I, *Registrum* VIII, 12 (J 1499): II, 530–1 (Martyn 2004: II, 510), discussing an agreement made between Candidus, the abbot of the monastery of St Andrew on the Clivus Scauri in Rome, and the *magister militiae* Maurentius about the inheritance of Maurentius's deceased brother John.

424 Gregory I, *Registrum* IX, 23 (J 1547): II, 583 (Martyn 2004: II, 559).

425 See Introduction, 35.

426 1 Maccabees 6:62–7:4; Ezekiel 17:12–21.

Question 10

> <168> 'In the fourth chapter we ask you to send back word to us as follows.[427] If this case, about which we heard an ordeal was made (which indeed some of us saw),[428] is called back to judgement, how should the judgement be canonically arranged? And should the woman [Theutberga] be judged by the secret confession which, it is said, she committed to the bishops, or by the booklet proffered forth in the judgement?[429] And, if it were the case that she proffered this booklet under coercion or signed it unwillingly, could she legally be removed from the marital bed in this fashion?'[430]

Response 10

Even if in this judgement that we are discussing, as we said above, it had been made apparent with clear signs,[431] let a judgement be arranged just as St Fabian, pope and martyr, decreed:[432] 'That it is necessary for four persons always to be present in every judgement, that is chosen judges, accusers, defenders and witnesses.' For as Leo wrote to all the bishops appointed throughout Caesarea and Mauritania,[433] we are not able to judge anyone, unless present and 'standing there, and either proven guilty or confessed with certainty, he is able justly to be submitted to the sentence'.

→ And St Augustine says in his book on penance:[434]

> 'But very many good Christians bear the sins of others in silence although they know of them, because often they are lacking in proofs, and they are not able to prove to ecclesiastical judges the things which they themselves know. Although some [suspicions] may be true, the

427 This is the fourth section of the initial series of questions sent to Hincmar.

428 The 'judgement' (*iudicium*) being referred to here is presumably the ordeal of 858; some of Hincmar's questioners had apparently been eye-witnesses.

429 For these events at the First and Second Council of Aachen, see Question 1: 97–8, cc. 6–8; Response 1: 105–6, cc. 3–7, 107–8, c. 15 and Introduction, 42–3.

430 On coercion, see below, 182 and Introduction, 40.

431 That is, even if the ordeal in 858 gave the correct result, a further trial of Theutberga is theoretically acceptable.

432 Pseudo-Fabian, Letter to the Eastern bishops (J †93), c. 22: 165 (part of the Pseudo-Isidore forgeries). On judgement *in absentia*, see Introduction, 34.

433 Leo I, *Epistola* 12 to bishops of Mauretania (J 410), c. 12: col. 656 (Feltoe 1895: 16), also cited below, Response 11: 188.

434 Augustine, *Sermo* 351, 4, 10: col. 1546 (*De utilitate agendae poenitentiae*) (Hill 1995: 129–30).

judge should not readily believe them unless demonstrated with sure indications. We are not able to ban anyone from communion – although such a ban would be medicinal, not mortal – unless the person has either freely confessed, or has been named and convicted in some judgement, whether secular or ecclesiastical.[435] For who would dare take both roles, that he should be both accuser and judge to someone? Paul is understood to have briefly made known a rule of this sort when he gave an ecclesiastical court procedure similar to this in a certain way for some such crimes. He said "I wrote unto you in an epistle not to company with fornicators" [1 Corinthians 5:9], and the rest. And again, "If any man that is named as a brother be a fornicator, an idolater or covetous or a railer or a drunkard or an extortioner; with such an one no, [you are] not to eat" [1 Corinthians 5:11]. And it should be known that by "naming" the apostle wanted to be understood that which happens when a sentence has been carried out in full and judicial order. For if naming alone were enough, many innocent people would be damned, for many are often named falsely of a crime. Paul did not wish a man to be judged by a suspicious opinion, or even a usurped, extra-legal judgement, but either to have voluntarily confessed or been accused and convicted by the law of God according to Church procedure.'[436]

And in the Council of Toledo:[437]

'It is fitting that the life of the innocent should not be stained by the perniciousness of those who accuse. <169> Therefore if anyone is accused of something, let both accuser and accused be presented and let the sentences of the laws and the canons be consulted, so that if the accuser is found to be unworthy (*indignus*) to make an accusation, no one will be judged or condemned on his word.'

And in the Council of Chalcedon:[438] 'It is to be investigated in the judgement what sort of person it is who is accusing, and who is accused.' And again in the same council:[439] 'Those witnesses should not be admitted to give testimony who are not allowed to be accusers, or those whom the accuser brings from his own household.' ←

And St Cornelius, pope and martyr, and Felix Romanus the pope and all the other popes of that see decreed that 'Ecclesiastical judges should

435 On excommunication, see Introduction, 32–3.

436 Augustine (and Hincmar following him) here reinterprets a non-legal custom suitable for the small scale of the earliest Christian churches into a legal precept usable in a Christianised society.

437 Sixth Council of Toledo, c. 11: 241. On the Roman legal concept of *infamia* (those categories of people unsuitable to accuse others), see Introduction, 34.

438 In fact, *Statuta ecclesia antiqua*, c. 52: 174.

439 *Registri ecclesiae Carthaginensis excerpta*, c. 131a: 231.

be careful not to pass sentence in the absence of him whose case is being discussed. For [the sentence] will be invalid, and they will have to account for their action to their brothers.'[440] Except for certain cases, which the laws of the Church specify, just as the public laws set out to an assured extent.[441] In these cases, people may be judged in their absence: if the crime is extremely notorious (*famosissimus*), and those involved are extremely notorious too, so that neither are witnesses necessary for convicting, nor is the presence of that person required.[442] For this is what St Ambrose says about the letter to the Corinthians:[443]

> 'The judge should not condemn without an accuser, for the Lord did not cast off Judas, although he was a thief, since he had not been accused.[444] And anyone who does this deed[445] should be taken away from your midst: once the deed has been recognised, he should be driven out from the band of brotherhood. For all knew his crime and they did not accuse him: <170> publicly he had his stepmother in place of a wife [1 Corinthians 5:1]. In this matter, there was no need for witnesses, nor could the crime be hidden by turning one's back. "For I verily, as absent in body, but present in spirit" [1 Corinthians 5:3], that is absent in sight but present in the spirit of authority, which is never absent, "have judged already, as though I were present" [1 Corinthians 5:3] him who admits this.'

Although this is neither the time nor the place to demonstrate in which ways and to what extent it is possible and necessary to judge people in their absence according to ecclesiastical laws, let us bring to attention what is relevant to the matter now. The Council of Valence, following the Roman Church, showed that if anyone[446]

> 'pronounces himself to be guilty through either a truthful confession or a lying falsehood [he cannot be absolved], and nor can someone be absolved who accuses himself of a crime punishable by death (*causa*

440 Pseudo-Felix I, Letter to Bishop Paternus (J †142), c. 3: 198; cf. Pseudo-Cornelius, Letter to Bishop Rufus (J †115), c. 6: 174 (both part of the Pseudo-Isidore forgeries).

441 Böhringer 1992: 169 n. 8 lists canons and Roman law rulings on the matter.

442 There is no known source for this statement, but Hincmar may have derived it from Ambrosiaster's passage which he then cites. On the 'public' nature of some offences, see Introduction, 40.

443 Ambrosiaster, *Commentarius in Epistolam I ad Corinthios* 5, 2, 1–5, 3: II, 52–3 (Bray 2009: 141).

444 On Judas as a thief, see Preface: 88 n. 18.

445 The Corinthian Christian 'having his father's wife'.

446 Council of Valence 374, c. 4: 40, also cited above, Response 2: 116. The original text referred only to clerics who accused themselves of a 'mortal fault' (*mortale crimen*), i.e. a serious one that prevented them remaining in clerical orders.

mortis), which accusation would be punished in another. For anyone who is the cause of death to himself (*causa mortis*) is a greater murderer.'[447]

Since this can happen in the Church neither by secret confession nor through a third party, still less can it take place through priests, to whom it is not permitted to make public the sins confessed to them, unless he who committed the sin should himself spread the story of what he wrongly did.[448]

So far as he can, the bishop, to whom this duty is known to belong, ought to make sure that no one at all, seduced by error or coerced by fear, falsely incriminates himself, whereby he harms both himself and the Church. For it is decreed that an extorted confession or a coerced signature (*subscriptio*) has no force at all, as the glorious martyr St Alexander, the fourth pope after St Peter, judged:[449]

'If, which is inimical to every Christian by name, certain documents should have been extorted by whatever means, by fear, fraud or force by persons of this sort, or documents have been written or validated by them through whatever ingenuity so that they can free themselves [from accusations], we adjudge these to bear no prejudice or harm against them, nor any infamy[450] or bad faith, and nor do we allow them to undergo the confiscation of their property, by the authority of the Lord, the holy apostles and their successors. The confession of such people must not be forced but made spontaneously, as He attests who says: "For out of the heart proceed murders, adulteries, fornications, blasphemies" [Matthew 15:19] and the rest.'

And again:

'God pays more attention to your thoughts and your spontaneous will than to deeds performed through simple-mindedness (*simplicitas*) or necessity. A confession must not be extorted from such people, but should rather be freely uttered. It is dreadful to judge anyone from

447 The meaning of this passage is that lying about one's guilt in itself makes one guilty, and that a lie that results in one's own death is a particularly grievous form of murder (as the self-killing of an innocent person). Unlike in Response 2, Hincmar does not argue that this canon is applicable only to clerics, but takes a different approach: see next note.

448 Hincmar's argument is that although 'Ambrose' claims that a notorious sinner can be judged *in absentia*, and the Council of Valence equates a false confession with a true one, these conditions do not apply to Theutberga's case. Since according to Hincmar she has not made a (true or false) public confession, but only a secret one (see Introduction, 42–3), she is not a 'public' sinner.

449 Pseudo-Alexander I, Letter to all Christians (J †24), c. 7: 97–8 (part of the Pseudo-Isidore forgeries).

450 On infamy, see above, 179 with n. 437.

> suspicion or an extorted confession, for the Lord is an inspector of hearts more than of deeds, and requires pure thoughts and good wills rather than lying lips.'

This is the confession which ought to be made in church by him who sinned, just as it is written:[451] 'First confess your sins so that you may justify yourself.' 'First', indeed, so that in confession you may pre-empt the voice of the accusing devil and the gaze of the Lord, so you may justify yourself and not be condemned. For even this ecclesiastical excommunication is not an eternal punishment, but temporal and medicinal, so that the sinner may be converted to Him (who does not want the death of a sinner but their life) and live.[452] And again it is written 'For by thy words thou shalt be justified, and by thy words thou shalt be condemned' [Matthew 12:37]. <171> And so Jerome says:[453]

> 'There is no doubt about wicked words, that the man who offers them is condemned by God. But he can in no way be justified by good words unless he offers them with righteous intention, from the bottom of his heart. Even though they may be good words, they cannot justify the speaker if they are not offered from righteous zeal. For Caiphas is not found to be righteous after interpretation, who said "It is expedient for us that one man should die for the people, and that the whole nation perish not" [John 11:50]. Those words justify the speaker who keeps deep in his heart the good things he utters from his mouth, and utters them with holy intention. The working of human life consists in the weight of words, for as Solomon says, "Death and life are in the power of the tongue"' [Proverbs 18:21].

→ And in the capitularies of the emperors it is found that:[454] 'whoever, compelled by fear, says outside a judgement that he is unfree incurs no prejudice to his liberty, until he is presented to a judgement. So he may either obtain his liberty, if he can prove it in the presence of the judge, or if proven unfree, at once be returned to his master.' ←

Bishops, that is the judges of souls, must certainly take great care and also warn laymen that a devilish idea, as if under the pretext of a future confession and penance, should not secretly take hold of them as they go about the business of accusing, witnessing or judging, an

451 The exact source is not known, although there are parallels to the Vetus Latina version of Isaiah 43:26.

452 On Hincmar's view of excommunication, see Introduction, 32–3.

453 Source not identified.

454 Benedict Levita II, 153: II, 81. In Response 6: 163, Hincmar may have expressed reservations about this collection of capitularies.

idea speaking not in words, but by encouragement to everyone to follow the desires of his own heart.[455] 'Make sure', says the devil, 'that you carry out what you want to, and that you are not defeated in what you have begun. It is better for you to do penance afterwards than to be shamed in defeat.' To witnesses, he suggests, 'You are able to think up a way by which it will appear that what you say is true.' And the devil often persuades judges, so that they say 'How can I judge differently? As I hear, so I judge!'[456] Let them hear, let them listen to what is written: 'Woe unto you, who justify yourselves before men. But the Lord knoweth your hearts' [Matthew 24:27; Luke 16:15]. And: 'If thine eye', that is your intention, 'be single, thy whole body shall be full of light' [Matthew 6:22]. And: 'With what judgement ye judge, ye shall be judged' [Matthew 7:2], and 'a false witness shall not be unpunished' [Proverbs 19:5]. And let them read what St Jerome says in his commentary on Matthew:[457] 'A witness is false', he says, 'who does not understand statements in the same sense that they are said.'[458] How much worse is he who says things that were never spoken?

And let them set what Jerome says in this book against that thought which the devil proffers to ill-wishers, witnesses or judges, about obtaining penance.[459] Jerome says about Judas:[460]

> 'Then, when Judas, who had betrayed Him, saw that he was condemned, he was led by repentance to return the thirty silver coins to the princes of the priests and the elders, saying "I have sinned in handing over innocent blood" [Matthew 27:4]. The weight of impiety removed the greatness of avarice.[461] Seeing the Lord sentenced to death, Judas returned the price to the priests, as if it was in his power to change the sentence of the persecutors. And so although he changed his will, yet he did not change the results of his initial will. So if he who handed over the blood of the righteous sinned, how much more do they sin who bought righteous blood and provoked a disciple to betrayal by offering a price? "And they said, 'What is that to us? See thou to that.' And he cast down the pieces

455 On Hincmar's view of the devil, see Introduction, 66.

456 On the problems of corruption within the Carolingian judicial system, see Fouracre 1995; Stone 2012: 161–71. This long section (to 186) includes no specific references to Theutberga's case.

457 Jerome, *Commentariorum in Matheum* IV, 26, 61: 259 (Scheck 2008: 306). Already cited above, Preface: 89.

458 That is, who makes misleading statements. Hincmar refers repeatedly to this problem: see Introduction, 35.

459 See above, 182–3.

460 Jerome, *Commentariorum in Matheum* IV, 27, 3–5: 263–4 (Scheck 2008: 309).

461 That is, Judas's guilty conscience outweighed his avarice.

> of silver in the temple and departed, <172> and went and hanged himself" [Matthew 27:4–5]. It was of no benefit to do repentance if he could not correct the crime.[462] Whenever a brother sins against a brother, so that he is able to amend his sin, it can be forgiven him. But if the deeds remain, repentance is taken up with but vain speech. This is what is said in the Psalms about this most wretched Judas: "Let his prayer become a sin" [Psalms 108:7],[463] so that he was not only unable to amend the wickedness of his betrayal, but also added the crime of his own murder to his earlier wrongdoing.'

We should all fear this truthful sentence, we should all beware this most pernicious cunning of devilish wickedness aiming at our deception, by which the devil fraudulently deludes us by hope of repentance, and by counsel ties us up in fault, so that:[464]

> 'when we fall by sin from the state of justice, for the most part we fall also into the snare of desperation', and are ripped away entirely from the root of hope. 'Hence it is that the Lord through the prophet reproves not so much the evils of headlong hurry as the zeal for sin, saying, "Lest my fury go out like fire, and burn that none can quench it because of the evil of your doings" [Jeremiah 21:12]. Hence, again, in wrath He says, "I will punish you according to the fruit of your doings"' [Jeremiah 21:14].

Since then, as St Gregory says:[465]

> 'sins perpetrated through deliberation differ from other sins, the Lord does not censure wicked actions as much as the zeal for wickedness. For the sin in actions is often of weakness or of negligence, but in zeal it is always of malicious intent. He sits, as it were, in "the throne of pestilence",[466] who is lifted up with such elation of iniquity as to attempt even through deliberation to accomplish evil. Let those, then, who bind themselves in guilt even through deliberation understand what vengeance they must at some time suffer, they who are now become not the associates but the princes of the wicked.'

Also to be guarded against is the cunning

> 'of the crafty enemy, who when he sees that the mind he trips up by sin is afflicted by its fall, seduces it by the allurements of wicked security. And

462 The Latin here is 'egisse poenitentiam', which Carolingian readers would have read as 'to do penance', though they might have found the sentiment that penance is of little use without emendation difficult to agree with.

463 The Old Testament was thought to foreshadow events in the New Testament, and hence a statement about King David's enemies could be applied to Judas.

464 Gregory I, *Regula pastoralis* III, 32: II, 494–6 (Barmby 1895: 65).

465 Gregory I, *Regula pastoralis* III, 32: II, 496 (Barmby 1895: 65).

466 Literally the 'cathedra', the bishop's ceremonial chair.

> he calls before its eyes empty hopes and grounds of security so that he may withdraw from it the usefulness of sorrow. For he presents now the heavier offences of others', now he puts to it the shame [of breaking] the promise which he wickedly promised to fulfil, 'now that what was perpetrated was nothing, now he speaks of God's mercy', now he reminds the corrupted mind of the usefulness [of the sin] or whatever reward of grace or honour, now he shows another evil that can be excluded by the lesser evil, 'now he promises time afterwards for repentance; so that the mind, when led by this deception' may not turn back from what it has wickedly begun, and 'may be checked from the effort of repentance, so that it may receive no good afterwards, being saddened by no evils now, and so that who now rejoices in his transgressions may be more fully overwhelmed hereafter with punishments'.[467]
>
> 'Often indeed, through a special evil he perverts the hearts of the duplicitous through a trick of an old kind, so that while they deceive others by their crooked and double conduct, they glory as though they were surpassingly prudent beyond others. And, since they do not consider the strictness of retribution, they, miserable men, exult in their own losses. The prophet says about these, "Behold the day of the Lord comes, great and very terrible" [Joel 2:11], "against all fenced cities and against the high towers" [Zephaniah 1:16]. For in the highest judgement of wrath he will destroy human hearts closed off with defences against the truth, dissolving them, wrapped up in duplicities.'[468]

<173> Let accusers of the innocent, treacherous witnesses and judges hear what is said to them: 'Woe to them who set down unfair laws, writing down injustice' [Isaiah 10:1], and what the violent suffering inflicted by injustice says through Susanna.[469] For it has a voice, just like mercy, about which it is written, 'Hide away alms in the heart of the poor, and it will pray for you' [Ecclesiasticus 29:15]. For the violent suffering imposed as we said by injustice says:

> 'O everlasting God, that knowest the secrets, and knowest all things before they be. Thou knowest that they have borne false witness against me, and, behold, I must die; whereas I never did such things as these men have maliciously invented against me. And the Lord heard her voice' [Daniel 13:42–44].

And He gave back to the priests, who were the appointed judges of the people in that year and who had borne false witness, according to the

467 Gregory I, *Regula pastoralis* III, 29: II, 470–2 (Barmby 1895: 60–1), with frequent additions.

468 Gregory I, *Regula pastoralis* III, 11: II, 320 (Barmby 1895: 34).

469 On Susanna's story, found in Daniel 13, see above, Response 5: <145–6>.

evil that they had done, and they were killed [Daniel 13:62]. And let them hear that many also presently die in the flesh, like Ananias and Sapphira who while taking communion did not perceive the body of the Lord, as Paul said.[470] Many are alive in the flesh, but for their wicked deeds are dead in spirit, like her of whom it is written 'dead while she liveth' [1 Timothy 5:6]. The soul which sins always dies, and sinners who persevere are destroyed with 'double destruction' [Jeremiah 17:18], when they are made 'as a fiery oven' [Psalms 21:9], and covered 'with their own confusion as with a mantle' [Psalms 109:29], when they are destroyed 'both soul and body in hell' [Matthew 10:28]. We say this not to take away just judgements, but fearing lest we be judged to know injustice: not prohibiting bearing witness to truth, but fleeing from lies.

But although we adequately showed above from the decrees of St Gregory and from the decrees of other learned men the procedure for settling the matter in question, yet it is not displeasing to show what form the investigation and the settling of this sort of question should take.[471] If the question is about an issue [arising] after a marriage has been begun, he [Gregory] said to Hadrian:[472]

> 'Agathosa, the bearer of these presents, complained that her husband has, against her will, been converted in the monastery of the abbot Urbicus. And, since this undoubtedly extends blame and envy towards the said abbot, we order your Experience to investigate the matter by diligent enquiry, so as to see whether it may not be the case that the man's conversion was with her consent, or that she herself had promised to change her own status.[473] And should it be found to be so, see both to his remaining in the monastery, and compel her to change her status, as she had promised. If, however, neither of these things is the case, and you do not find that the aforesaid woman has committed any crime of fornication on account of which it is lawful for a man to leave his wife, then, lest his conversion should possibly be an occasion of perdition to the wife left behind in the world, we want you, without any excuse allowed, to

470 On their story, see Acts 5:1–10.

471 As this response and Response 11 show, Hincmar had very few authoritative ecclesiastical sources discussing procedural methods for cases.

472 Gregory I, *Registrum* XI, 30 to Hadrian, notary of Palermo (J 1820): 918–19 (Martyn 2004: III, 775), also cited in Response 23: 280. Hincmar omits the following from Gregory's letter to Hadrian: 'For, although secular law declares that marriage may be dissolved for the sake of conversion against the will of either party, yet divine law does not permit this to be done.' On changing views concerning separation for the sake of entering a monastery, see Reynolds 1994: 227–38 and Introduction, 52–3.

473 That is, that Agathosa had also promised to enter the religious life.

> restore her husband to her, even though he should be already tonsured. ... For, save for the cause of fornication, divine law on no account allows a man to leave his wife, seeing that after the husband and wife have been made one body by the bond (*copulatio*) of wedlock, it cannot be in part converted, and in part remain in the world.'

And that one single law about this is known to exist for husband and wife,[474] he [Gregory] shows in the letter which we inserted above, to Secundinus, the bishop of Taormina:[475]

> 'Leo the *cartularius*, bearer of this letter, came to us and spoke about his wife. She had left him for his crime of fornication, which he said greatly enraged her, <174> and because of this she had put on religious clothing. But he had not been at all blameworthy, nor had he fallen into the fault of fornication after the marriage had begun, and he added that – as he had sworn to his wife by the strictest oaths – he was innocent of the matter about which suspicion pained his wife. Therefore by her own will she had returned to him. But he said that she and her household had been deprived of communion by you because she had returned secretly to him, disregarding you. We wish that the household of this woman should receive sacred communion, and that penance will not long hold them in this affliction for the fault of their mistress. About the woman, that is the wife of this letter's bearer, it is necessary for you to observe that, if it is wholly clear that she was unable to say anything against her husband, and moreover that the suspicion shown by her was removed by an oath, as we were informed, and that afterwards she returned to him by her own will: then the censure of the judgement upon her should be tempered, so that by no means should she be deprived of communion for long.'

Question 11 and Response 11

We tried to show above by ecclesiastical authority that a husband cannot separate himself from his wife, or wife from her husband, by means of a written secret confession: just as a bishop cannot remove himself from the church entrusted to him or from his rank, nor can anyone in Church orders remove himself from his office (*officium*).[476] And nor

474 See Introduction, 53.

475 Gregory I, *Registrum* IX, 3 to Secundinus, bishop of Taormina (J 1527): 564–5 (Martyn 2004: II, 547–8), also cited in Response 9: 176; Appendix Response 4: 291.

476 That is, in Response 2: 114–120. In contrast to Response 2, Hincmar here does not distinguish between the case of a cleric resigning from office and a husband and wife separating: see Introduction, 44. Note however that a 'non' has been inserted into the text over an erasure. It is interesting that Hincmar talks of what he tried to show 'above' (*supra*): a reminder that he conceived of *De divortio* as a written text primarily, even if it was intended to be read out.

should anyone have to undergo public penance on account of an offered booklet of secret confession, and nor may someone be condemned on account of a guided text (*scriptura directa*),[477] or one presented by somebody else. Rather, the one who should be judged publicly should either be convicted or confess publicly, and in his own presence. The great Pope Leo wrote to Nicetas, bishop of Aquileia, saying:[478] 'A sentence can justly be imposed on someone who in their presence has been convicted or has undoubtedly confessed', because it is against reason for them to decide the punishments of those whose motives they are not able to know.[479]

Divine Scripture also demonstrates the procedure for judging, when accusers said about an accused woman in an arranged judgement: '"Send for Susanna the daughter of Chelchias, Joachim's wife." And so they sent. And so she came with her father and mother and her children' [Daniel 13:29–30]. And after testimony was given, the judges 'condemned her to death' [Daniel 13:41]. But she was freed by liberating truth, and the false witnesses were punished according to the harm 'they had intended to do their neighbour' [Daniel 13:61].[480]

But even the woman 'taken in adultery' [John 8:3], and physically present, was not accused through someone else's testimony or written deposition, [a lack] which ecclesiastical and Roman laws forbid.[481] Her confession is implied, when it was said to her by the Lord '"Hath no man condemned thee?" and she said "No man, Lord"' [John 8:10].[482] Although the Lord was 'seized like a thief and tied up by a band of soldiers, the legitimate order of power was maintained', as Augustine said.[483] Since when the Lord was handed over to Pilate's prefectural responsibility (both through the

477 That is, where they have been told what to write in their confession.

478 This is actually Leo I, *Epistola* 12 to bishops of Mauretania (J 410), c. 12: col. 656 (Feltoe 1895: 16), also cited above, Response 10: 178.

479 That is, a trial *in absentia* or a secret confession does not provide enough information to those making the public judgement.

480 The false witnesses were themselves executed. On Susanna, see above, Response 5: 143.

481 That is, the laws forbid accusations without either witnesses or written evidence. See Böhringer 1992: 174 n. 5.

482 On Hincmar's use of this story, see Introduction, 55. Here, he attempts to fit it anachronistically into a legal framework: Jesus, unlike the scribes and Pharisees, is able to make a judgement on the case without either witnesses or written evidence because of the woman's (implied) confession to him. Hincmar says nothing about whether this should be taken as a secret or public confession, even though that is a key point in his earlier discussion.

483 Augustine, *In Iohannis euangelium tractatus* 112, 2: 634 (Gibb and Innes 1888: 416).

ministers of the Jews, <175> and by Annas to Caiaphas and by Caiaphas to him), Pilate said about the Lord: '"Ye have brought this man unto me"' [Luke 23:14]. Hearing that 'He belonged unto Herod's jurisdiction, he [Pilate] sent Him unto him' [Luke 23:7]. This teaches us that Christian and fair judgements about secular matters are to be expected from secular men, and then we ought to apply ecclesiastical healing ointment, that is judges' medicine, to the infirm.[484] The apostle demonstrates the same thing, when the faithful were still mixing with unbelievers: 'Now therefore, there is utterly a fault among you, because ye are judged by outsiders, and not by the brethren' [1 Corinthians 6:7, adapted]. 'If then ye have judgements of things pertaining to this life' amongst you, 'set them to judge who are the least esteemed in the Church' [1 Corinthians 6:4]. And Gregory says in the Pastoral Rule:[485] 'those unadorned with spiritual gifts should at least serve for earthly matters'. And Augustine in his *Enchiridion* shows that when such judgements must happen, the necessary matters should not be prohibited, but should be judged amongst the faithful.[486] And Ambrose:[487] 'Since there are wise brothers, let some of these whose judgement the world will respect be chosen to judge. It is very shameful if amongst those who are said to know God, none is found who may be able to consider a judgement.'

For how will a repentant murderer be able to claim the peace of the Church before he is pacified with the litigants? How may the discordant person be able to receive forgiveness before he is united by the bond of love? How can the rapacious man, who has cruelly sweated in plundering, perform 'fruits meet for repentance' [Matthew 3:8] before he has made a peace offering by making amends or satisfaction, according to the judgement of David and the example of Zacchaeus?[488] Or how can a marriage be dissolved except by the determination of Christian laws, by which it had been joined by the Lord's authority, or that it should be proven that it had not been entered but rather usurped against Christian laws?[489] And how might this happen in an orderly

484 On this combination of secular judgement and penance, see Introduction, 40.

485 Gregory I, *Regula pastoralis* II 7: I, 220–2 (Barmby 1895: 17).

486 Augustine, *Enchiridion de fide, spe et caritate*, c. 21: 92–3 (Shaw 1887: 263).

487 Ambrosiaster, *Commentarius in Epistolam I ad Corinthios* 6, 5, 2: II, 61 (Bray 2009: 145). Ambrosiaster continued by pointing out that at this time, there was no official leader in the church.

488 Nathan's condemnation of David over Bathsheba [2 Samuel 12:1–6]; Zacchaeus's meeting with Jesus [Luke 19:1–10].

489 On the significance of 'Christian laws', see Introduction, 29. Hincmar shows the possibility of a court deciding that a marriage may be judged invalid rather

way except by laws inspired by him through whom 'establishers of the law decree justice' [Proverbs 9:15]? So St Gelasius wrote to Emperor Anastasius:[490]

> 'If the bishops of religion themselves obey your laws in as much as it pertains to the order of public discipline, recognising your imperial power bestowed upon you by celestial disposition, lest indeed, excluded from secular matters, they might seem to resist your judgement, so, with what emotion, I ask you, is it is fitting and appropriate for you to obey them [the bishops], who are endowed with elevating and venerable mysteries.'

As is written elsewhere, read it again:[491] '"Render therefore under to Caesar the things which are Caesar's, and unto God the things that are God's" [Matthew 22:21]. To Caesar then coins, tribute and money', the honour owed so long as he faithfully honours the Lord, 'and taxes (*vectigal*); <176> to God tithes, first-fruits, offerings and sacrifices, and continual service. Just as He rendered tribute for himself and for Peter, and rendered to God the things which are God's, doing his Father's will.' And St Augustine says in his sixth sermon on the Gospel of John:[492] 'Do not say "What is the king to me?" What are your possessions to you? For possessions are possessed by kings' law.' So questions of secular business are to be sorted out through legal trials – that is, just and Christian ones.

And about the booklet or secret confession, Leo observed:[493] 'to all the bishops in Campania, Samnium and Picenum, greetings. I am moved by great indignation and grieved by much pain, because I learn that some of you have been forgetful of apostolic tradition, and undismayed in the zeal of their error.' And a little later:

> 'About penance indeed, which is demanded from the faithful: rather than making public a profession of every individual sin in a written booklet, let it suffice to indicate [them] to the priests alone, in secret confession

than being dissolved, i.e. that it may never have existed in the first place: see Introduction, 53–4.

490 Gelasius I, Letter to Emperor Anastasius (J 632): 20 (Tierney 1964, 14). On this letter see Preface: 91, Introduction, 71–2.

491 Jerome, *Commentariorum in Matheum* III, 22, 21: 204 (Scheck 2008: 253), with insertions. In particular, Hincmar inserts the phrase 'the honour owed so long as he faithfully honours the Lord', showing how he sees royal authority as dependent on Christian conduct, in a way unforeseen by Jerome.

492 Augustine, *In Iohannis euangelium tractatus* 6, 26: 66–7 (Gibb and Innes 1888: 47–48).

493 Leo I, *Epistola* 168 to the bishops of Campania, Samnium and Picenum (J 545), cc. 1–2: cols 1210–11 (shortened).

> of consciences. Although the plenitude of faith, which on account of the fear of God does not fear to blush before men, is praiseworthy; yet not all sins are of the sort that those requesting penance would not fear to make them known. So let this objectionable custom be removed, lest many should be kept away from the remedies of penance because they are embarrassed, or because they fear to reveal their deeds to their enemies, by whom they could be struck with legal action. Let that confession suffice which is offered first to God, then also to the priest, who goes as an intercessor for the sins of the penitents. For many people will then be able to be called to penance, if the conscience of the one confessing is not made public to the ears of the people.'[494]

If the sacred canons order the excommunication of a bishop for as long as he does not associate with someone whom he says confessed secretly to him,[495] let them also consider whether anyone ought or would dare to submit someone to the laws of public penance on the grounds of a secret confession, whether through a booklet or believed through someone's word.[496] And how much less should a legally initiated marriage be dissolved without certain and evident reason, as the same Leo thundered forth terribly to all the bishops appointed throughout all the provinces, saying:[497]

> 'Our admonition denounces this too: that if any of the brethren shall try to act against these ordinances and dares to allow prohibited things, he should know that he will be removed from his office, and nor will he who does not wish to be a companion in discipline be a future sharer in our communion.'

Question 12

> <177> 'In the fifth chapter, write back to us, on the authority of the Scriptures and the traditions of the Fathers, what the writings say about

494 Hincmar is here again returning to the theme that secret sins should be handled by a secret confession; public confession is only for sins which are already openly known to the community. See Introduction, 40 and 42.

495 This is an adaptation of *Registri ecclesiae Carthaginensis excerpta*, c. 132, already cited at Response 1: 102.

496 Hincmar's argument here is twofold. Firstly, even if details of confessed sins have been written down (and thus are potentially available to be read by all), that does not make them public; the confession remains secret. Secondly, a bishop's general statement that someone has confessed to him does not have value as evidence.

497 Leo I, *Epistola* 4 to bishops of Campania, Picenum, Etruria and all the provinces (J 402), c. 5: col. 614 (Feltoe 1895: 4). Also cited below, Appendix Response 3: 290. Leo's letter does not specifically deal with dissolving marriages, but Hincmar presumably thought it useful for its implied threat to Gunther's position.

debauchery (*stuprum*) and abortion, with the names of the authors and the titles of the books, so that we may know whether a woman can conceive in the way it is said and after an abortion remain a virgin, as is said happened to this woman; and if she be found to have perpetrated these crimes before marriage, whether she ought to or can remain in marriage.'[498]

Response 12

About debauchery (*stuprum*) and abortion, which we have heard has been charged to this often-mentioned woman [Theutberga], let us run back to the pages of the holy Scriptures, lest we may offend the most equitable lord Judge by discerning according to the conjecture of human decisions.[499] The Book of Deuteronomy says:

'If any man take a wife, and go in unto her, and hate her, And give occasions of speech against her, and bring up an evil name upon her, and say, I took this woman, and when I came to her, I found her not a maid: Then shall the father of the damsel, and her mother, take and bring forth the tokens of the damsel's virginity unto the elders of the city in the gate. And the damsel's father shall say unto the elders, I gave my daughter unto this man to wife, and he hateth her. And, lo, he hath given occasions of speech against her, saying, I found not thy daughter a maid; and yet these are the tokens of my daughter's virginity. And they shall spread the cloth before the elders of the city. And the elders of that city shall take that man and chastise him. And they shall amerce him in an hundred shekels of silver, and give them unto the father of the damsel, because he hath brought up an evil name upon a virgin of Israel: and she shall be his wife; he may not put her away all his days. But if this thing be true, and the tokens of virginity be not found for the damsel. Then they shall bring out the damsel to the door of her father's house, and the men of her city shall stone her with stones that she die: because she hath wrought folly in Israel, to play the whore in her father's house: so shalt thou put evil away from among you' [Deuteronomy 22:13–21].[500]

And about incest is written in Leviticus:

'None of you shall approach to any that is near of kin to him, to uncover their nakedness: I am the Lord. The nakedness of thy sister, the

498 Note that it was not just Hincmar who was keen to justify his ideas with reference to precisely cited 'authorities': this was part of the commission.

499 The first section of this response, 192–5 is essentially a disordered list of quotations on sexual sins, to which Hincmar continued to add later.

500 The relevance of this passage is not clear: although by 862, Lothar II's supporters were claiming Theutberga was not a virgin when he married her, this does not seem to have been alleged before then see Introduction, 158.

> daughter of thy father, or daughter of thy mother, whether she be born at home, or born abroad, even their nakedness thou shalt not uncover' [Leviticus 18:6].

And again: 'For every soul which should do any of these abominations, will perish from the people' [Leviticus 18:29]. And again: 'And if a man shall take his sister, his father's daughter, or his mother's daughter, and see her nakedness, and she see his nakedness; it is a wicked thing; and they shall be cut off in the sight of their people: he hath uncovered his sister's nakedness; he shall bear his iniquity' [Leviticus 20:17].[501] Hence, St Augustine:[502]

> 'What does "see" mean in this passage except "know by sleeping with", just as elsewhere in the law it is said "he knew his wife" for "he joined with her". And what does "they will receive their sin" mean, except that He wanted the penalty itself of the sin to be called "sin"?'

And since we are forced by necessity, like the apostle also, who says in one place about certain people, 'What they do in secret it is also shameful to say', but forced by necessity, wrote to the Romans to refute 'men with men working that which is unseemly', and 'women changing the natural use into that which is against nature' [Romans 1:27], whether we want to or not, fearing the condemnation of the Lord saying (just as we set out much earlier) 'whosoever shall be ashamed of me and my words, of him shall the Son of man be ashamed before the angels of God' [Luke 9:26], therefore we set out in this case from the Book of Genesis. Onan, the son of Judah, the son of Jacob the patriarch, went in to the wife of his brother, 'Er, Judah's firstborn, who was wicked in the sight of the Lord, and the Lord slew him' [Genesis 38:7]. Onan spilled his seed on the ground and 'therefore the Lord struck him since he had done a detestable thing' [Genesis 38:10].[503] And it is written in the Book of Leviticus <178>: 'If a man also lie with mankind, as he lieth with a woman, both of them have committed an abomination: they shall surely be put to death' [Leviticus 20:13]. Hence also the laws of the Romans decree in the chapters about debauchers (*stupratores*), which anyone reading will find.[504] And if it is thus decreed about male and

501 On incest, see Introduction, 60–4.

502 Augustine, *Quaestionum in heptateuchum libri septem* III, 75: 224.

503 On the varying interpretations of Onan's sin, see Noonan 1986: 34–6, 101–2, 137–8.

504 This is apparently a reference to the *Mosaicarum et Romanarum legum Collatio*, c. 5: 82–3. This was a rather rare collection of Roman law which systematically compared it to the laws of the Old Testament. Hincmar refers to it again below, 205. On the text, see Introduction, 34.

male, what findings will the laws make about male and brother lying in male sodomitical fashion with a sister?[505]

Nevertheless, St Augustine writes to Count Valerius in the second book of *On Marriage and Concupiscence*:[506]

> 'What the apostle says about the shameless, "leaving the natural use of the woman, burned in their lust one toward another; men with men working that which is unseemly", he did not say "conjugal use", but wanting it to be understood as "natural use" which happens with body parts created for this, so that through them each sex would be able to couple for procreation. And so it follows that when someone with these same body parts couples with a prostitute, the use is natural, yet not commendable but culpable. In truth, if someone also uses his wife in that part of the body which is not instituted for generation, it is against nature and shameful. For the same apostle said earlier about women: "For their women changed natural use into use against nature", then about males: "working shame in males, abandoning natural use of women". Marital intercourse is not praised by that name, that is "natural", but yet the crimes are noted as more unclean and worse than if they used women illicitly, but naturally.'

And again in the book *On the Good of Marriage*:[507] 'When indeed the husband should want to use a woman's body part not intended for that purpose, the wife is more shameful if she permits this to take place with her rather than with other women.'

→ And in the second book of *On Adulterous Marriages*:[508]

> 'But if he does not control himself, let him licitly marry, lest he shamefully procreate, or, more shamefully, not procreate when lying together: since this latter, some licitly married also do. For one can lie together illicitly and shamefully even with a legitimate wife, as Onan the son of Judah did, and the Lord killed him because of this.' ←

Thus also sometimes adultery is committed by the gaze alone, when someone is desired shamefully or the unmarried is desired. As St Gregory says in Book 21 of the *Morals*:[509] 'Generally speaking, this is

505 That is, if both sodomy and incest deserve the death penalty, how much more does Theutberga's alleged combination of offences? On hierarchies of sexual sins, see Introduction, 588.

506 Augustine, *De nuptiis et concupiscentia* II, 20: 289 (Holmes 1887: 297).

507 Augustine, *De bono coniugali* 11: 204 (Wilcox *et al.* 1955: 25). The implication is that this is profanation of something good (marriage), rather than worsening an already bad thing (extramarital intercourse).

508 Augustine, *De adulterinis coniugiis* II, 12: 396 (Wilcox *et al.* 1955: 116–17). On Onan, see above, 193.

509 Gregory I, *Moralia in Iob* XXI, 11, 18: II, 1078 (Bliss 1844: II, 530).

distinguished by the position or order of those desiring, since eager desire defiles the man in holy order, just like the fault of adultery defiles another.' And again, in the letter to Sabinus, the regional sub-deacon:[510] 'Since for the most part, what is a fault in the layman may be a crime in those constituted in holy orders, he who has the zeal of righteousness is not ignorant how much more the shameful crime should be punished in them with particular strictness.' And again in the aforesaid book:[511]

> 'Yet in not dissimilar persons, the same guilt of luxury is differentiated, in whose case the fault of fornication is distinguished from the guilt of adultery, as the tongue of the distinguished preacher [Paul] testifies, saying: Neither fornicators nor those serving idols, nor adulterers will possess the kingdom of God. By separating the guilt in this sentence, he shows how it differs greatly from itself.'

And Augustine in the book *On the Good of Marriage*:[512]

> 'Fornication is evil, adultery is worse – <179> for it is worse to violate someone else's marriage than to cleave to a prostitute, and incest is worse, because it is worse to lie together with one's mother than with another's wife. And always from bad to worse, until one arrives at that, which, just as the apostle says, it is shameful to speak of' [Ephesians 5:12].

→ And St Ambrose in the book *On Abraham*:[513] 'Holy Lot offered the honour of his daughters. For even if that impurity was shameful, yet it was less to couple according to nature than to sin against nature.' And again in the letter to the Corinthians:[514] 'Yet if a man should apostasise or should seek to pervert the use of his wife, neither can the woman marry another nor be returned to him.' ←

These things are collected for the aggregation of the accusation, so that it may be understood here how evil is the incest of brother with sister combined with male sodomitical intercourse, if this is indeed the case: both of which acts, perpetrated on their own, are punished in the Heptateuch by death at the Lord's command.

510 Gregory I, *Registrum* X, 2 to Sabinus, regional sub-deacon (J 1769): II, 827 (Martyn 2004: III, 714).

511 Gregory I, *Moralia in Iob* XXI, 11, 18: II, 1078 (Bliss 1844: II, 530).

512 Augustine, *De bono coniugali* 8: 198 (a somewhat loose quotation) (Wilcox *et al.* 1955: 20).

513 Ambrose, *De Abraham* I, 6, 52: 537.

514 Ambrosiaster, *Commentarius in Epistolam I ad Corinthios* 7, 11, 1: II, 75 (Bray 2009: 151). In the same section, Ambrosiaster stressed the exception for fornication, and permitted men, though not women, to remarry. See Introduction, 53.

→ And may the most evil assertion of those be destroyed, who interpret that it is not a sodomitical wickedness unless one fornicates within the body, that is in the member of the obscene part of the body, that is inside the belly (*aqualicium*), misusing badly and improperly the apostle's testimony, that 'Every sin that a man doeth is without the body; but he that committeth fornication sinneth against his own body' [1 Corinthians 6:18].[515] But pollution of this kind, they say, is such as if someone should rub dirt from his finger with his hand or between his thighs and should wash his hand clean from the same dirt: similarly, also this woman is wholly cleaned from this pollution after a bath.[516] Those who say this should be held not as catholics but Cynics, that is dog-like heretics because of their shamelessness, just as St Jerome demonstrates in the letter to the Ephesians, explaining the statement of the apostle in which he says: 'But fornication, and all uncleanness, or covetousness, let it not be once named among you, as becometh saints' [Ephesians 5:3]. 'For had there not been', Jerome says:[517]

> 'a certain Cynic philosopher, who taught that every titillation of the flesh and flow of seed coming from whatever touch or rub at whatever time was not to be avoided, and some wise men of the world who had consented to this shameful heresy, to be blushed at, the holy apostle writing to the Ephesians would never have joined "uncleanness" to "fornication".[518] "Just as becometh saints" [Ephesians 5:3], he says. Consequently, no one can be called a saint who is found in some uncleanliness and greed of desire in which he delights, beyond fornication. "For this ye know", says the apostle, "that no whoremonger, nor unclean person, nor covetous man, who is an idolater, hath any inheritance in the kingdom of Christ and of God"' [Ephesian 5:5].

And again in book two:[519]

> '"Who, despairing, have given themselves over unto lasciviousness, to work all uncleanliness in avarice" [Ephesians 4:19]. "Despairing", he says, they gave themselves to the error of irrational beasts, immersing themselves in filth and the abyss, working shameless deeds and luxuries, whatever the body should want, the mind should desire, lust should

515 This long addition to the original manuscript to 199 suggests the continued existence of claims that the term 'sodomitical' applied only to anal intercourse and thus possibly not to Theutberga's offence. Hincmar, however, uses 'sodomitical' as a wider category: see Introduction, 50.

516 On terminology and penalties for masturbation in early medieval texts, see Payer 1984: 46–7.

517 Jerome, *Commentum epistolae ad Ephesios* III, 5, 3–4: col. 519 (Heine 2002: 209–10).

518 Branham 1996: 98–101 discusses the Cynic justifications for masturbation in public.

519 Jerome, *Commentum epistolae ad Ephesios* II, 4, 17: col. 504 (Heine 2002: 182).

> suggest. And although they have neglected nothing that might be unclean, <180> they did all this in avarice. Since they are never satiated by luxuriating, nor does their desire have an end, or certainly they go on to things beyond the conceded marriage of a man to a woman, male working shame in male.'

For as the same doctor explains in the third book of the same epistle, an obscenity is 'a secret thought, when the sense is inflamed to lust and the soul, ignited by the titillation of the flesh, is set on fire, and yet is reined in by fear of God and judgement of the mind'.[520] Hence it is agreed that, just as the same apostle says to the Romans, it is uncleanliness when males work shamefulness in males, or women in women, or males in women, or whoever by themselves in whatever way works shamefulness, which separates the person doing it from the kingdom of God and plunges him into the infernal regions, just as the same apostle says: 'No whoremonger nor unclean person hath any inheritance in the kingdom of God' [Ephesians 5:5].[521]

Whence also Isidore in the second book of *Sentences* says:[522] 'Every unclean pollution is called fornication, although each one is dishonoured by the desire of different shames. For varied crimes are born from the delight in fornicating, by which the kingdom of God is closed and man separated from God.' And St Prosper in the book *On Virtues and Vices*:[523]

> 'And so that emission (*fluxus*) of the body which happens without fault in those sleeping, meanwhile may happen to those awake from fault.[524] In the former, the fullness of humours is expelled naturally, in the latter, it is shamefully brought forth by concupiscence. For this concupiscence calls forth this emission in those awake, whose sordid appetite it has aroused through filthy speech.'

Women too have this sordid appetite, as Ambrose says explaining the apostle's 'working shamefulness' [Romans 1:27] in women, who put flesh to flesh not by putting the genital organ of one into the body of the other, since the working of nature prevents this, but changing the natural use of this part of the body into a use which is against nature.[525] They are said to use certain instruments of diabolical work

520 Jerome, *Commentum epistolae ad Ephesios* III, 5, 5: col. 521 (Heine 2002: 214).

521 Hincmar conflates the terms 'fornication', 'uncleanliness' and 'sodomy/sodomitical' in order to find references to the maximum number of disapproving authorities.

522 Isidore of Seville, *Sententiae* II, 39: 175.

523 In fact Julianus Pomerius, *De vita contemplativa* III, 6: col. 482 (Suelzer 1947: 115).

524 On varying early medieval responses to nocturnal emissions, see Leyser 1999.

525 This is probably a reference to Ambrosiaster, *Commentarius in epistulam ad Romanos* 1, 26–7: I, 51–2.

likewise for boiling up desire. And thus fornicating, they sin in their own bodies.[526] Similarly also males working shame in males (that is dispersing the ardour of lust and fulfilling the desire of the flesh, which delights in itself), who are called by the apostle those lying with men and effeminate, who voluptuously succumb to this shamefulness. But he who 'takes the members of Christ makes them the members of an harlot' [1 Corinthians 6:15], in adhering to a harlot, with whom he is made one flesh. And he fornicates who sins shamefully with a woman consecrated to God, or with a relative (*cognata*), or with a woman possessed by a relative, or with the wife of another, or with an animal, or with a woman against nature, or who pollutes himself with his hand or by whatever other means, fulfilling the ardour of lust.[527]

And the more anyone should sin more wickedly in his body against nature, the more damnably he will be tormented and hence with worse punishment, if he should not do worthy penance. Since, as St Augustine and other doctors explain, in the fulfilment of fornication the fleshly mind is wholly absorbed along with the body, so that it is actually then able to think of nothing else. <181> And this sin not so much touches, but rather by polluting possesses body and soul, from which 'when the act passes away, the guilt still remains',[528] so that among the groans of penitence itself, the pricks of the former delight are often miserably excited. And the perpetrators of all such crimes, just as the apostle testifies, will be excluded from the kingdom of God, unless they should take care before they exit the body to wash away the stains of such great crimes through mournful confession and profuse tears and largesse of alms and the worthy fruits of penance, with much affliction of flesh and contrition of spirit.

Therefore, let no one say he has not perpetrated the sodomitical sin, who has worked shamefulness against nature in male or in woman, and deliberately and eagerly is made unclean by rubbing or touching or shameful motion. Such a one, as the apostle teaches, is excluded from the kingdom of heaven, since also other sins against the laws of nature, usurping the reputation of Sodom, are called sodomitical, as the Lord said to the city full of sin through the prophet: 'This was the iniquity

526 Murray 1996: 197–9 and Benkov 2001: 104–6 suggest, with reference to this passage, that medieval writers had difficulties conceptualising sexual activities that did not involve a penis or penis substitute.

527 Intercourse with a nun or other consecrated woman could be considered as incest: see Stone 2012: 255.

528 Augustine, *De nuptiis et concupiscentia* I, 26: 242 (Holmes 1887: 275), also cited below, 202.

of your sister Sodom: leisure, fullness of bread and abundance' [Ezekiel 16:49]. And the Jews sinning before the Lord were called by Isaiah 'princes of Sodom and people of Gomorrah' [Isaiah 1:10], who among other crimes of their iniquity 'hath given a boy for an harlot' [Joel 3:3] and the price of Greek youths into their purses.[529] Effeminates are lords of those who in the place of the Greek youths became eunuchs,[530] as if for the protection of married women, but having been acquired by immodesty and uncleanliness and subjugated by lust (which, as it is said, is accustomed to tame even iron minds), were found to serve and be dominated by the lustful through diabolical innovation.[531] And sins of this kind are not only sacrilege but also idolatry, whose rewards are repaid as the apostle shows, just as is it written about the greedy: 'whose God is their belly'; and about the luxurious: 'And whose glory in their shame, who mind earthly things' [Philippians 3:19]. Indeed the Scripture calls God glory, which says: 'They changed their glory into the image of an ox eating grass' [Psalms 105:20]; and Scripture testifies about avarice, that it is the service of idols. The studious reader will find out about these and other things in the Scriptures. ←

About abortion, indeed, it is said in Exodus: 'If men strive, and hurt a woman with child, so that the child depart from her, not fully-formed, let him be punished, according as the woman's husband will lay upon him; and he shall pay as demanded. But if it [the child] should be formed (*formatum*), then thou shalt give life for life' [Exodus 21:22–23].[532] And it is written in the Gospel about conception: 'For what is born in her', which as Gregory explains without doubt means 'is conceived'.[533] For Joseph then first began to hesitate, since he saw the swelling womb (*uterus*) of his betrothed. Hence let us think over from the law in what way conception may happen according to nature.[534] 'A woman', it says, 'who has received seed gives birth to a male or female' [Leviticus 12:2] and it is written about birth, whether of a formed, or as said above

529 Joel 3:6 refers to Jewish children being sold to Greeks.

530 The Vulgate version of Isaiah 3:5 refers to "effeminates" rather than "babes" as rulers. On Carolingian discourses of effeminacy, see Stone 2012: 319–21.

531 The meaning of this sentence is not clear. It may derive from a biblical commentary, but no source has been traced.

532 This is the Vetus Latina version of these verses; the Vulgate does not distinguish between the developmental stages of the foetus. On abortion, see Introduction, 56–7.

533 Gregory I, *Moralia in Iob* XXIX, 19, 36: III, 1458–9 (Bliss: 1844: III, 327).

534 Hincmar's focus in this section is on the plausibility of the charge, not on possible punishments.

unformed [child], whether of male or female sex: 'everything which throws open the *vulva*' [Exodus 13:2].[535]

→ <182> It is to be noted how Scripture asserts a woman receives seed (*semen*), that is by male coitus emitted through the genital vein into the secret place of the *vulva*, with the womb (*matrix*) carrying it, just as we also learn by the reading of physic;[536] and not, as this invention says, by [the womb] attracting seed to itself or by receiving it elsewhere or emitted in another way.[537] And in the emission of what she conceived from the seed sent in, the same Scripture testifies that the *vulva* is thrown open, namely for the first birth; which also could not preserve the integrity of the enclosure in the first natural intercourse. Let us believe therefore, what we read, and what we do not read, let us believe it wrong to speculate about. ←

For from the beginning it has never been heard, and neither has it been read in Scripture of truth under this heaven, that a woman's *vulva* can receive seed without intercourse and conceive, or with closed womb (*uterus*) and unopened *vulva* or with intact flesh (*caro*) may give birth to either a live or aborted birth, except only singularly the holy and blessed virgin Mary, whose conception was not of nature but grace, as the archangel said to her: 'Hail, full of grace'. The Holy Spirit came over her, and conferred on her the fecundity of offspring from virgin seed and virgin blood without will of the flesh and without will of man, and did not take away her virginity. Mary, just as she conceived with flesh (*caro*) intact and *vulva* not open, that is with closed womb (*uterus*), thus gave birth not with open *vulva*, but closed womb (*uterus*), and at the same time was both mother and remained perpetual and eternal virgin.[538] 'Virginal' (*virgineum*), from which virgins are called who are intact of flesh, is that small part of skin which is broken in them in the first lying together,[539] which nature does not suffer to remain whole

535 Cadden 1993: 64: in the Middle Ages, *vulva* could refer to the vulva, the vagina or women's sexual parts generally; we have therefore left it untranslated.

536 This is probably a reference to Isidore of Seville, *Etymologiae* XI, 1, 136 (Barney 2006: 240). On other possible sources, see Devisse 1975–76: I, 378 n. 77; Garver 2012: 224. Cadden 1993: 13–53 discusses classical medical views on male and female roles in conception.

537 There may have been joking or serious beliefs that women (and men!) could become pregnant through anal or femoral intercourse: see Olsen 2011: 36–7.

538 On the development of the doctrine of the perpetual virginity of Mary, see Hunter 2007: 171–204. By raising the comparison with Mary, Hincmar implicitly suggests that the accusations against Theutberga were blasphemous: see Introduction 57.

539 This may be a reference to the hymen, although Garver 2012: 225 is doubtful.

in the emission of whatever birth; and after that 'virginal' is broken, a woman is not considered as a virgin.[540]

→ But also, in the Scripture of truth we read that Onan, seeking to satiate his lust but not wanting sons to be born, lay with his wife by that diabolical invention which is reported of that woman ⌜Theutberga⌝ and her brother, for which he died, struck by the Lord. Hence we do not believe that this woman had been able to conceive from such lying together. ←[541]

We bishops say these things, not because we wish to reveal the virginal secrets of girls or women (which we do not know by experience) to those who know them or to insinuate them to those who do not, but because it is written: 'The case which I knew not, I investigated very diligently' ⌜Job 29:16⌝. Therefore we recall to our eyes what we read in the Scriptures of teachers of the Church, so that if one caught in this way should come to us from the judgement of just judges seeking penance, we should be able to judge her without error.[542] Therefore we also add that if our lord king found the aforesaid woman a virgin, why does he consent to her being branded as if debauched? If however he did not find her a virgin, why did he keep her so long, or why did he accept the judgement of an examination about her?[543] Truly, those very noble lay married men and very equitable judges, who ought to judge about this, will be more able than us and more quickly to know through themselves and to learn from their wives by marital licence, whether any woman whatever might be able to conceive in such a way as we heard about that woman.[544]

<183> And it is necessary that they investigate this solicitously and carefully, lest perhaps in this judgement of justice and equity they might be able to be caught by some error,[545] which, in a judgement

540 On this section, see Mistry 2015.

541 This addition again suggests that Hubert's alleged offence was not anal sex, but involved ejaculation outside Theutberga's body: see above, 196.

542 On this combination of secular judgement and penance, see Introduction, 40.

543 It is not clear whether this is a reference to the ordeal or whether there was some previous test of Theutberga's virginity. On later claims by Lothar's supporters that Theutberga had not been a virgin when she married, see Introduction, 58.

544 Hincmar at this point suggests on pragmatic rather than legal grounds that the matter be thrown back to the married laity, as better able to decide on these matters than the clergy (as his often unclear previous discussion also suggests). See Introduction, 57.

545 The Latin in the manuscript is 'possint quocumque errore interpendere', a rather obscure phrase. Böhringer suggests correcting *interpendere* to *interprendere*, a rare word meaning 'to undertake', but this does not make the sentence easier to construe.

about people such as this, will come to the attention of many, and which many will take care to take as an example. But we – as inexperienced in this business – say the things we read, and we neither seek to know more about it nor wish to investigate further.[546]

Let, however, the judges of the law see if what is said about the woman should be found true, namely that before betrothal, while she was in her own power or his about whom she is censured [Hubert], she indecently permitted such a thing, and after she was joined to her husband, preserved herself for him alone:[547] whether they decree her to be condemned to death, by Roman law or by their laws or by those to which that woman is subject, or through those they should want to judge her by.[548] For as there are diverse peoples, so are there diverse laws, which the discerning holy Church does not reject, if they are Christian in their commands, and these are just. But just as we know the offence of Bilhah and the punishment of the crime, we flee from the counsel given after the edict of the Lord, so we do not decree that anyone should die, but we want all to be saved, since we desire no one to perish. Nor do we undertake to inflict any violence against the holy and just laws which until now the holy Church and episcopal religion has first accepted, and has then sustained.[549]

But we warn that the royal road in exercising justice should be maintained without any respect of whatever person, just as the magnificent doctor Gregory writes to the metropolitan Domitian:[550]

> 'We advise your Fraternity that you also take care to search for the truth with all subtlety and thus quickly impose an end to the contentions of the parties according to justice, lest each part may complain bitterly that they suffer prejudice in judgement. For just as we do not want anybody to be condemned without judgement, thus for no excuse do we suffer the things that have been decided to be delayed.'

546 The additions to this response suggest Hincmar did investigate further, but presumably he thought simply reading more on the topic was acceptable!

547 Below, 220, Hincmar concludes that Theutberga's conduct before her marriage was relevant.

548 For the plurality of laws in the Carolingian empire, see Introduction, 29. Note that the choice of which kind of law applies is given to the judges and not to Theutberga herself.

549 The sense of these last few sentences is perhaps deliberately obscure, but Hincmar appears to be trying to edge round the question of the death penalty, neither calling for it to be applied nor ruling it out (see Introduction, 55-6). Bilhah was a concubine of Jacob with whom Jacob's son Reuben slept [Genesis 35:22].

550 Gregory I, *Registrum* IX, 4 (J 1528): II, 566 (Martyn 2004: II, 548–9). On the need to avoid 'respect for persons' in judgement, see Introduction, 33: the connection between that and Gregory's letter is not clear.

And he writes to Constantius, the bishop of Milan, in which case everyone knowing and intending rightly will be able to see the similarity, and take from it a not-inappropriate example. <184> For he says:[551]

> 'If there was as much care in the examination as there had been subtlety in discussion, nothing of what is said about our brother [Bishop Pompey] would have been uncertain, but it would have been evident whether it was true or made up. For such a question as is now raised against him was raised against him a little while ago in Sicily before our brother of reverent memory, Bishop Maximian, as we became aware. But since his case was enquired into with subtle investigation, he who had been accused of a crime was found innocent. Now, therefore, since those things which are said against him were not investigated with suitable strictness, and the acts carried out in front of your Fraternity proved adequate neither for condemnation or absolution, it is not a light matter that should be decided incautiously or cursorily. For it is very serious and improper that a definite sentence is given about a doubtful matter.
>
> And indeed these acts could have been suitable for a decision to be made, if confession by the accused were to follow, if only this confession were elicited from hidden matters by subtlety of examination and not extracted by violent pain, which frequently causes this result, that the innocent too are known to confess themselves as guilty.[552] For after the aforesaid brother [the accused], as it said, claimed he was tortured in custody and burned with hunger. If it is thus so, you ought to know whether he is guilty. For if a confession should have been extorted thus, when such cases receive a sentence, and there is an appeal to the Holy See, will the person who is judged not be present, and is the truth not searched for very strictly and from every side, so that then it is decided if a sentence ought to stand or not?[553] And therefore, since both the person is absent and the accounts which you submitted to us do not seem to us to be suitably satisfactory, just as we said above, we neither ought nor are able to decide anything rashly about the person of the brother, lest (may it not happen) we might be found reprehensible in our deeds, to which it is fitting by law to retract the sentences of others.'

551 Gregory I, *Registrum* X, 11 to Constantius, bishop of Milan (J 1779): II, 837–8 (Martyn 2004: III, 720–1). On papal appeals in the ninth century, see Introduction, 75.

552 That is, Gregory allows a confession to be used as evidence against the accused, provided that it has not been obtained by torture.

553 Hincmar discusses this topic further in Appendix Response 2 and 3: 285–7: bishops whose judgements are overturned by a papal appeal may suffer consequences if their judgements had resulted from corruption or negligence.

And he says to Bishop Virgil of Arles:[554] 'Let emendation and punishment strike the culpable and let false rumour not afflict the innocent.' And he writes to Bishop Columbus [of Numidia]:[555] 'For it is proved to be quite perverse and against ecclesiastical opinion that someone whose own fault or action does not evict from the office which he performs is deprived of it in error, for the sake of certain men's wishes.'

Hence therefore let the judges realise that if the woman is accused of debauchery (*stuprum*), that man [Hubert] who imposed force upon her or enticed her to evil should be summoned, and the case should be investigated rather through him, and he himself should be brought in and examined according to the law, and either freed or punished by legal judgement. This is especially the case since, as we heard, he himself handed her over legally to her husband, in the place of a parent.[556] According to the precept of the Lord through Moses, it behoves him, if she was not found a virgin in the first lying together, either to show proofs of certain virginity or to concede these reproaches of debauchery (*stuprum*).[557]

Otherwise, some suspicion may perhaps gnaw those who desire to judge justly, and those who are eager and able to criticise others rather than establishing their own affairs may find a place for disparagement, saying: 'A woman in custody, thoroughly terrified by afflictions and threats, will dare and be able to say nothing other than what is ordered to her.'[558] Let him who is at liberty come, and let him either legally defend himself from the accusation against him and be freed, or, conceding what he is reputed to have done as not only a participant but also author and executor of the crime, let him be legally punished. And in that man's liberation, let her who is in custody and who lied about herself because of fear be legally released, <185> or let her be legally punished in his punishment: just as is ordered in the first book of Roman law, chapter six, 'About debauchers' and in chapter seven 'About incestuous and shameful marriages', and as just judges can read

554 Gregory I, *Registrum* XI, 45 (J 1836): II, 942 (Martyn 2004: III, 791).

555 Gregory I, *Registrum* XII, 3 (J 1854): II, 971 (Martyn 2004: III, 809).

556 Theutberga's parents were dead by the time of her marriage, so she was under the protection of her brother Hubert. Hincmar's comment about what he had heard reminds us that much of his knowledge about the case was based on oral report (see Introduction, 24).

557 A reference to Deuteronomy 22:13–21, quoted above, 192. The relevance is not clear, since in 860, there was no claim that Theutberga had not been a virgin at the time of her marriage: see above, 201.

558 Hincmar again hints that Theutberga's confession was coerced: see Introduction, 42.

in the other things which Christian laws bring forth.[559] For it is unjust for the oppressed woman to be oppressed again and for the oppressor [Hubert] to glory in the liberty of sin, something the very holy Gregory powerfully hated, saying to Guduin, *dux* of Naples:[560]

> 'We marvelled greatly that a very strict punishment has not so far been inflicted on that soldier who by diabolical instigation ruined a handmaiden of God.[561] For it was very suitable to your morals and goodness that [news of] the punishment should have reached us before the iniquity of the perpetrated fault. We urge that without any excuse or limit, you may hasten to emend such a great crime, thus demonstrating by strict example to others your fervour towards the protection of charity.[562] In that way you may make God favourable to you, against whom the man perpetrated this deed, and who by his neglect despised the fear of God. For in no way do we suffer such a great iniquity to remain unpunished.'

And princes of the earth ought not to hear with deaf ear what is said: 'There is an accursed thing (*anathema*) in the midst of thee, O Israel: thou canst not stand before thine enemies' [Joshua 7:13]. And again St Gregory to Bishop Syagrius [of Autun]:[563]

> 'Since it is noxious and pernicious that people be destroyed by imitation of someone acting wickedly, who should have been well fortified by his punishment. In which matter not only is he culpable, but so too is the person who is found not to resist; for he who does not rush in to correct things that should be stopped seems to consent to the one erring.'

And let no one say: 'Such a perverse man [Hubert] should not be called to judgement, but should be condemned, as if already judged.'[564] Let him hear what it is written in the Gospel of John that Nicodemus said to the princes of the Jews about Jesus, whom they had called to be arrested before judgement. For it is written: 'Yet Nicodemus, one of the Pharisees, who had come to the Lord at night, replied to the Jews: For does our law judge a man, unless it should hear from him

559 This is another reference to the *Mosaicarum et Romanorum legum Collatio*, cc. 5–6: 82–93: see above, 193.

560 Gregory I, *Registrum* XIV, 10 (J 1923): II, 1079–80 (Martyn 2004: III, 876).

561 That is, a nun or other consecrated woman. Any intercourse with such a woman was a particular offence to God, since the woman was regarded as a 'bride of Christ'.

562 Chastity is probably meant (*castitas* rather than *caritas*).

563 Gregory I, *Registrum* IX, 224 (J 1752): 797–8 (Martyn 2004: II, 693). On the anathema, see Introduction, 32–3.

564 On judgement *in absentia*, see Introduction, 34.

first and should know what he does?' [John 7:50]. And the Lord: 'Do not judge according to appearances, but judge with just judgement' [John 7:24]. And St Gregory writes to Sabinus the subdeacon, about a priest who was stigmatised by the heinous crime of idolatry and sodomy (*sodomia*):[565]

> 'News has been brought by the report of certain people, that Sisinnius, the priest of the city of Reggio, is a venerator and worshippers of idols, which is excessively intolerable even to hear, indeed that he presumed to place some idol in his home, but also, which is a not dissimilar sin, that he is defiled with the crime of sodomy.[566] And therefore, since the iniquity of such a great crime should be investigated with strict and subtle investigation and punished, we order you by this authority, that you enquire with vigilant zeal and wholly diligent care, <186> and if you should be able to obtain any proof of the charge, then put him in strict custody until you report back to us, so that we may be able to deliberate how such a huge crime ought to be punished and dispelled.'

And if someone should say: 'This perverse man [Hubert] does not dare to come to account',[567] let him hear the advice of St Gregory about the Frontinianist heretics, who were not able to be brought to account otherwise, which he writes to Bishop Maximinius of Salona:[568]

> 'About the Frontinianists, may your Fraternity be altogether solicitous, so that just as you have begun, you may take care about how they may be called back to the bosom of mother Church. But if any should want to come to me and receive a hearing, first let them present and promise an oath that after a judgement they will not persist in their error. And afterwards let your Sanctity promise that they will suffer no violence from me, but that I will give them judgement. Should they recognise the truth, let them receive it, and should they not recognise it, I will send them away unhurt. But if someone from them should want to come to us against you without an oath, let your Fraternity not hold him back, since either coming he will receive reason, or I will ensure that they will not see that land again.'

565 Gregory I, *Registrum* X, 2 to Sabinus, regional sub-deacon (J 1769): 827 (Martyn 2004: III, 714–15). This is the earliest known reference to sodomy (*sodomia*) as an abstract noun, an important moment in the history of sexuality. See Introduction, 59.

566 Romans 1:23–7 links together idolatry and same-sex intercourse.

567 According to Appendix Response 6: 304, Hubert did eventually appear in person before a council, although the details are not known.

568 Gregory I, *Registrum* X, 15 (J 1784): 843–4 (Martyn 2004: III, 725). Frontinian had been deposed as bishop of Salona in 554 over the Three Chapters controversy. See Markus and Sotinel 2007: 267.

→ And it is written in the Council of Carthage:[569] 'It was agreed that the accused, or the accuser who is in the same place as the one who is accused, if he fears violence from the rash multitude, shall choose for himself a place nearby, to where it would not be difficult to bring witnesses, and where the case may be finished.' ←

Perhaps someone might say: 'He cannot be brought to judgement, since supported by the protection of other kings, he maintains rebellion against the king. The king would wish to send him to judgement for this crime and others, if he could; the woman he has, he brings to judgement.'[570] Let our lord kings have before their eyes the truthful statement of the King of kings, who is Truth and the judge of the living and the dead. He says to the king offering assistance against justice: 'You offer help to the impious and you join in friendship with those who hate me. Therefore you merited the wrath indeed of the Lord', that is death, 'but good works were found in you' [2 Chronicles 19:2]. Therefore let the kings be fearful, who unjustly offer protection to such men, by whose defence they might offend God, and the churches and poor of Christ and the humbler men are oppressed and devastated, and just judgements cannot be exercised. Lest perhaps, if these kings do not have such great and good deeds of their own which they could oppose to such great evil, they or the good deeds that they have may perish without any hindrance, and for the sake of another's evil in which they were made participants, although they may be thought safe in body by human judgement, they are lost before the eyes of God.[571]

But so they may not incur the statement of Scripture that 'the just perish for the unjust',[572] and lest anyone should interpret perversely to them the statement of Deuteronomy: 'Thou shalt not deliver unto his lord the servant (*servus*) which is escaped from his lord unto thee: he shall dwell with thee, even among you, in that place which he shall choose in one of thy gates, where it liketh him best: thou shalt not oppress him' [Deuteronomy 23:15–16], <187> let them hear how St Augustine explains that.[573] Augustine says:[574]

569 *Codex Apiarii causae*, c. 30: 110.

570 At some point during 860, Hubert fled to the kingdom of Charles the Bald. On kings' need to promote justice, see Introduction, 70.

571 Hincmar here expresses criticism of Charles the Bald for sheltering Hubert: see Introduction, 15.

572 This quotation is from the Vetus Latina version of the Bible, rather than the more common Vulgate; Hincmar seems to have borrowed it from Pseudo-Gregory, Letter to Felix of Messina (J †1334): see Introduction 60 on this letter.

573 On other 'perverse' interpretations of the Bible, see Introduction, 27.

574 Augustine, *Quaestionum in heptateuchum libri septem* V, 36: 295, also cited above, 103 and 116.

'The Septuagint says you should not hand over the boy (*puer*) to his lord, who is placed with you by his lord: not because his lord placed him, that is commended him, for then it would say "entrusted" (*depositum*), but it says "placed" (*appositum*) by his lord, that is attached, when he departed. It does not therefore prohibit fugitives being received, but rather being returned. Indeed this could be thought unjust, unless we understand this is said to a nation (*gens*) and a people (*populus*), not to one man.[575] So, it prohibited returning a man from one *gens* fleeing from his lord, that is his king, to that *gens* to whom this was addressed. For also King Geth preserved the foreigner when David fled to him from the face of his lord, that is King Saul. But it very clearly explains this when it says about the same refugee: "He shall dwell with thee in that place where it liketh him best"' [Deuteronomy 23:16].

However, this kingdom [Francia] was brought, from the hands of many, into unity in the hand of our kings' ancestors, by the grace of God. And the single kingdom is a single church, which ought in no way to be divided by these kings' divisions, who should be like a single man and a single leader in one rule.[576] Nor should it be said that among our princes someone may flee from one people (*gens*) or one kingdom to another people or kingdom, but rather let them remain in one kingdom, just as befits Christians, and in the unity of mother Church. What protection those fleeing to that church ought to have, St Gregory writes to John, Bishop of Cagliari, saying:[577]

'If some people about whom there is an investigation should perhaps take refuge in the church, the case ought to be disposed so that neither do they suffer violence, nor do those who say they are oppressed sustain losses. Therefore let it be your care that those concerned promise by oath to them [sanctuary seekers] to preserve law and justice, and let these be warned in all ways to come out and to render account for their acts.'

Following this example, our catholic princes ought to obey divine mandates as sons of the catholic Church, remembering what they confirmed with their own hands, with God as witness, namely that they ought not only not to protect men of this kind and defend them against law and reason, but also not receive them, unless for this reason, that they

575 The injustice here to Augustine is that a lord is deprived of his property (the slave)!

576 This is a significant passage, demonstrating the fundamental unity of the Frankish kingdoms in Hincmar's eyes, notwithstanding the formal partition between different kings. See Introduction, 75.

577 Gregory I, *Registrum* X, 17 to Januarius, bishop of Cagliari (J 1786): 846 (Martyn 2004: III, 727). This quotation is repeated in Response 22: 272.

come to render right account.[578] Certain of these kings who affirmed this by the grace of God still live in this body, and one has gone to the Lord.[579] But sons are born for the father, and according to Roman law, which their predecessors, emperors and kings, built and preserved and through which they happily ruled their peoples and corrected them, 'an action begun by a progenitor should be completed by the heirs'.[580] Thus they ought to maintain the statutes of their predecessors in all things, just as they desire that what they constitute be preserved by their successors. And let it not seem trivial for kings or whoever else to infringe that which they take care to confirm with their own hands, <188> since from divine doctrine and apostolic tradition, the confirmation by hand was a very great thing from these first centuries, so that from those vicars of the apostles, these → themselves vicars of the apostles ← decreed about it in addition to celestial authority, that 'who goes against his own subscription in anything, deprives himself of his honour'.[581]

And let kings not say, this is constituted about bishops and not kings.[582] Let them think about it, if they desire to be raised up and honoured in the rulership of the people under Christ the one King and Priest, from the derivation of whose name they are called lords of Christ, and from whose honour, love and fear they are called lords and kings by participation in his great name, although they are men just like the rest, and if they want to have a part in the kingdom of the heavens with those who are anointed with holy chrism, which receives its name from the name of Christ. He anointed priests, prophets, kings and martyrs, and, 'anointed with the oil of gladness above his fellows' [Psalms 44:8], He made them in baptism kings and 'priests for our God and a royal people

578 Hincmar here alludes to one of the agreements in the years following the Treaty of Verdun: he may have in mind the Treaty of Meerssen of 851 (MGH *Capit.* II, no. 205: 72–4). On the significance of royal subscriptions to texts such as these, see Morelle 2004.

579 Charles the Bald, Louis the German and Lothar I all signed the Treaty of Meerssen in 851; of these, Lothar I had died in 855.

580 Theodosian Code I, 2, 10, Int: 32 (Pharr 1952: 14), probably cited, however, via a collection known as the *Epitome Aegidii* (on which see Corcoran 2015: 137–8). Hincmar associates Frankish rulers with the emperors whose decrees were encoded in Roman law: see Introduction, 29.

581 *Codex Apiarii causae*, c. 13: 104. Hincmar stresses here both the binding nature of written agreements and the apostolic nature of episcopal authority.

582 While Hincmar is usually concerned to separate the clerical from the lay order, kings were a special case, as represented by their anointing with chrism (holy oil), which in Hincmar's eyes conferred a special responsibility. They were still however laymen. See Introduction, 28.

and a royal priesthood' [1 Peter 2:9] according to the apostles John and Peter. Let them know and understand that they are deprived of the dignity of the name and office in the eyes of God, although they may usurp that name before the eyes of men and by unstable and earthly power, when they act against the hand of their subscription, if what they confirmed with their hand pleased God.[583] Since, just as just and good kings live within their good and just laws when the guilty are repressed and punished by them and the innocent are lifted up and freed, so apostolic men live within the rules promulgated and confirmed by their hands, by which rules those who act against them are judged, from that day on which they are constituted.

And just as the apostle says about her 'who living is dead' [1 Timothy 5:6], thus also such a transgressor (even if those who now hold the place of the apostles do not judge him, because they do not know or conceal what has been done),[584] if he should not correct himself before the last day, will be judged as among those condemned in judgement for greater transgressions. For 'the law is not made for a righteous man', just as the apostle says, but for transgressors 'and the unholy, murderers of fathers and murderers of mothers, whoremongers' [1 Timothy 1:9–10] and the remaining sinners. For it is read to be written not without reason, that the words of the Ten Commandments are 'written with the finger of God' [Exodus 31:18].[585] Indeed He decreed that law would be valid for ever which He wrote with His finger, that is His Spirit. And the Lord says about the elect in the Gospel: 'Rejoice, because your names are written in heaven' [Luke 10:20]. But the prophet Jeremiah said about the reprobate: 'Withdrawing from you, O Lord, they are written in earth' [Jeremiah 17:13].

> 'But this is not to be understood childishly, as if God for the remedy of forgetfulness wrote the good in the heavens and the bad in the earth, but to be understood beneficially, that someone who has done either heavenly or earthly works, <189> through these, as if marked by letters, will be eternally impressed on the memory of God.'[586]

In this law is demonstrated that what anyone should confirm by his hand justly and rationally, he should preserve inviolably and with persevering justice.

583 Hincmar sees a ruler as losing legitimacy if he breaks his written word, but does not develop any theory justifying deposing him: see Introduction, 72.

584 That is, the bishops neglect their duty in admonishing the king: see Introduction, 73–4.

585 Hincmar gives a long set of mainly biblical examples showing the importance of the written word.

586 Bede, *In Lucae euangelium expositio* III, 10.20.

Nor is it in vain that someone coming for baptism, if he is of age, or the godfather on the boy's behalf, and also the public penitent coming to reconciliation, by Church tradition gives his own name written down, which is placed upon the holy altar among the celebration of the celestial mysteries and commended to the Lord by the priest reciting it at the right moment.[587] And equally, the names of the faithful both living and dead are not frivolously written in the holy diptychs, and those of the unfaithful which have been written are erased from the same diptychs after death by holy judgement.[588]

But perhaps the princes say, as if supported by princely licence: What great evil do I do against God or who will judge me, who stands before all others, if I either infringe or do not heed a diploma (*praeceptum*) or edict confirmed by my hand? First, indeed, let them notice that if they are over others, God is over them. And if they should act wickedly and not correct themselves, they will be judged the more gravely, the more they are loftily placed above others on the royal throne. For kings and priests correct the wicked acts of their subjects, but they ought not to forget that their evils will be judged by the same Lord, nor ought they to hear with deaf ear what is written: 'The mighty shall be mightily tormented, but mercy is granted to the small' [Wisdom 6:7].[589] Therefore let them read the history of holy Abraham who considered a charter of confirmation from the seller of his wife's tomb held before his sons and the people to be so important, that he even 'bowed himself down before the people of the land, even to the children of Heth' [Genesis 23:7] so that he might obtain it of them, having heard their concession, and they [the princes] will be able to find how important they should consider this.

But also they will find enough about this confirmation in the Law, which so flourished before the coming of Christ, that even Pilate, instructed by ancient custom, said to the Jews who were demanding that what he had written in the inscription over Christ should be gainsaid: 'What I have written, I have written' [John 19:22], not wanting what he had done to be unfinished or changed. This was confirmed long before by

587 The insertion of people's names into the liturgy of the mass was common practice in ninth-century Francia, particularly in monastic settings. Documents of a similar kind recording the oblations of monks survive: see de Jong 1996: 100–25.

588 This practice of erasing names from liturgical commemoration, a form of *damnatio memoriae*, is attested at various places, including Rheims, in this period: see Hincmar, *Epistola* 169 to Nicholas I (MGH *Epp.* 8: 159), asking whether Ebbo's name should be removed from the church diptychs.

589 On kings' and bishops' responsibilities, see Introduction, 71–2.

the Lord's stipulations, just as is written above the inscription of the title to the psalm: 'Do not destroy' [Psalms 75:1].[590] And in the Book of Tobit [Tobit 5:2], it is read with how much certain stability and firmness a chirograph (that is something written by hand) ought to be trusted, and this is demonstrated in the Gospel about written bonds [Luke 16:6].

But certain princes (may God make this far from our Christian princes) perhaps do not see that their infirm confirmation (*firmatio*) remains after them,[591] after they have passed away, <190> and just as St Augustine says:[592] 'the act passes and the guilt remains'. What was their own they give to holy places through confirmation, and then usurp for themselves by occupation, so that the poorer folk of the world may not obtain a grant (*praestatio*) by request; they rather take it away for themselves and do not bestow upon the holy places.[593] They perpetrate sacrilege when they ought to have provided a remedy for themselves. And if they perpetrate sacrilege by giving badly what was their own, it should be considered how much danger they create for themselves by taking away things given to God by others, taken away by them [the princes] from God and against Him. Therefore St Gregory in the letter to the subdeacon Sabinus writes:[594] 'It is sacrilege and against the laws if someone wickedly from the desire of his will for profit attempts to retain what is being relinquished to holy places.' And the holy canons:[595]

> 'Let clerics or laymen (*seculares*) who should presume to retain either offerings of relatives or donations or things left by will or who should think to take away that which they themselves donated to churches of monasteries, be excluded from the Church, just as the holy synod states, just like killers of the poor, until they return those things.'

590 This is the rubric to the Psalm.

591 *Firmatio* can mean either 'confirmation' or 'validation': see Morelle 2004: 291.

592 Augustine, *De nuptiis et concupiscentia* I, 26: 242 (Holmes 1887: 275), also cited above, 198. In spite of Hincmar's caution, what follows is clearly a critique of contemporary kings, including presumably Charles the Bald, in their treatment of Church lands.

593 The Latin here is not entirely clear, but Hincmar seems to be complaining about kings making grants to churches that were purely nominal, keeping possession of the land for themselves. This was a common practice, which Hincmar himself had personal experience of: see Mordek 1997 on the disputed villa of Neuilly. This procedure meant that the church could not then grant out the land temporarily (via a precarial grant) to relatively subordinate tenants (the 'poorer of the world').

594 Gregory I, *Registrum* IX, 90 (J 1614): II, 644 (Martyn 2004: II, 598).

595 Council of Agde 506, c. 4: 194. On the early medieval idea of those who removed Church property as 'murderers of the poor', see Moore 2011: 197–9.

Therefore let them know that along with their own sins, they will also be punished in the future judgement for all the sins too of those who gave these things for the redemption of their soul. And let those who perhaps confirm ill-advisedly not disregard what they give to their friends and faithful men, and what they take away [from churches] without judgement, when they bring back to penitent memory what they have given[596] – not noticing that they go from the world when the soul leaves the body, but the land remains in the world, and the charter of royal confirmation of these properties is held by the empty possessor.[597] And while their hearts [of the faithful men] sigh, perhaps the lips (not without the weight of sin) are provoked to cursing, since both should have been foreseen: that a certain king should not give ill-advisedly or take something away from someone without judgement of equity, nor should a charter for what has been taken away remain unbroken after judgement.[598] For it is written: 'The memory of the just is blessed, but the name of the wicked shall rot' [Proverbs 10:7]. Thus it is better and more reasonable that a broken charter may decay through reason, and praise of their equity remain, than that the charter of confirmation remain and the name of praise decay.

But perhaps the princes reading or hearing these things may say: 'The bishops have chastised us well: we will give nothing by diplomas (*praecepta*), lest we are reproved again.' On the contrary, let them hear what the prophet complains of, saying in the voice of those chastising 'We have cured Babylon and she is not healed' [Jeremiah 51:9]. <191> 'Indeed Babylon is cured yet not returned to health, when the mind, confused in wicked action, hears the words of rebuke (*correptio*), receives the whips of rebuke, and yet refuses to go back to the right way of salvation.'[599] And through Wisdom: 'Just as vinegar in natron, thus it is for him who sings songs with a very bad heart' [Proverbs 25:20], 'When vinegar is placed in natron, it bubbles constantly and boils up'[600] and so too very often do the hearts of the powerful, who swell from

596 Hincmar complains elsewhere about rich men who consider how much they have given in alms, but not how much they have stolen: see Stone 2012: 240.

597 Hincmar here uses the Roman law notion of *vacua possessio*: the free and unimpeded possession of property. The implication is that grants or regrants of property originally given by rulers to their followers, often in benefice, are invalid; the Church's full possession takes precedence.

598 For the destruction of charters after a dispute, see Sennis 2013: 157–9.

599 Gregory I, *Regula pastoralis* III, 13: II, 336–8 (Barmby 1895: 36).

600 Adapted from Gregory I, *Homiliae in Hiezechihelem prophetam* I, 9, 32: 140 (Tomkinson 2008: 178).

power and do not humble themselves on account of their humanity (as Abraham said to the Lord, humbling himself from the exultation of his conversation: 'I will speak to my God although I am dust and ashes' [Genesis 18:27]). When they hear the rebuke (*correptio*) of the chastising envoy (*missus*) of the Lord, they erupt into words of contradiction from the tumult of their heart.[601] Bishops have not forbidden giving to holy places or to faithful men, making known to all: 'Vow, and pay unto the Lord your God' [Psalms 75:12] and 'Do all things with counsel and you will not repent afterwards' [Ecclesiasticus 32:24] and 'Ye shall do no unrighteousness in judgement, in righteousness shalt thou judge thy neighbour' [Leviticus 19:15].

Just as a prince does not want what God concedes to him to be taken from him by someone stronger, so too he himself should not take away without judgement of equity from anyone either what he gave or what he did not give, since it is written: 'What you do not want to happen to you, do not do to another.'[602] But rather the bishops again and again have preached: 'Make to yourselves friends of the mammon of unrighteousness, so that when ye fail, they may receive you in everlasting habitations' [Luke 16:9], and 'Whatever your hand findeth to do, do it immediately, since there is neither place nor reason among those below, whither thou goest' [Ecclesiastes 9:10].[603]

And just as the bishops have preached those things which are useful and honest, thus no less they preach that the king may hasten to conceal from himself the shameful mark on the royal name,[604] and as much as he can, wash it away, remembering every day and in every action the statement of Deuteronomy which says:

> 'Thou shalt also have a place without the camp, whither thou shalt go for the requisites of nature, bearing a paddle in your belt, and when you sit down, thou shalt dig a hole and you shall put soil on your excrement, of which you are relieved. For the Lord thy God walketh in the midst of thy camps, to deliver thee and give up thine enemies before thee, therefore shall thy camp be holy and no foulness appear in them, lest he should turn away from you' [Deuteronomy 23:12–14].
>
> 'Indeed encumbered by the weight of corruptible nature, certain overflows of our thoughts, unworthy of our rule, burst out from the womb of our mind' and from the effect of our actions, 'like the burdens of the

601 On the Carolingian vocabulary of correction and rebuke, see de Jong 2009: 118–20.

602 This is the Vetus Latina version of Tobit 4:16.

603 On alms-giving as helping the donor reach heaven, see Stone 2012: 240.

604 On the significance of the 'name of the king', see Introduction, 70.

> belly. And we' who are the leaders of the people 'ought to carry a paddle under our belt, so that always girdled for restraining ourselves, we may have the goad of compunction around us, which incessantly digs the earth of our mind with the sorrow of penance, and conceals what foulness burst out from us. For the excrement of the belly is covered in the ditch in the ground by a paddle, when the overflowing of our mind or the reprehensible foulness of our work, discussed with subtle refutation and corrected by honest work, is concealed before the eyes of God through the sting of its compunction'

and the good act of correction.[605] It is also to be considered that the kings and emperors of old stated in their laws that a charter of confirmation needed to be confirmed by five or seven or ten witnesses, as Ambrose writes.[606] <192> And a conditional regulation is placed by civil law in the writing of charters, about the fine owed to the fisc by anyone who should attempt to break that charter.[607] → And an accuser signing a written accusation may not remove himself from the obligation ⌜that he incurs⌝. ←

They ⌜the kings⌝, however, wrote nothing about their own confirmation, because the hand of the prince, just as we read is said about David in the Book of Kings, is reckoned for 10,000.[608] And a king, constituted by God either by grace or because of the sins of the people, will be crowned by the King of kings himself for his just acts, or will be punished for unjust judgement and wicked actions, judged by an equitable judgement.[609] They also inserted in the same laws:[610]

605 This is mostly a quotation from Gregory I, *Moralia in Iob* XXXI, 27, 54: III, 1589 (Bliss 1844: IV, 467), to which Hincmar has made a few alterations.

606 See above, Response 4: 129; Hincmar also refers here to Roman law: see Corcoran 2015: 130 for possible sources.

607 These clauses are common in private (non-royal) charters. Though less common in royal charters, such a clause does appear in Carolingian charters for Hincmar's old monastery of St-Denis: see D.Lothar I, no. 80 (843), *Die Urkunden Lothars I. und Lothars II.*, ed. T. Schieffer: 201, and D. Charles the Bald, no. 301 (867), *Recueil des actes de Charles II le Chauve, roi de France*, ed. A. Giry, M. Prou and G. Tessier: II, 165; in general, see *Recueil des actes de Charles II le Chauve, roi de France*, ed. A. Giry, M. Prou and G. Tessier: III, 168–70.

608 As Morelle 2004: 308–9 points out, Carolingian royal charters, unlike private ones, did not include witness lists.

609 Note that Hincmar, despite earlier comments on kings losing the name of king for unjust activities, here pulls back, accepting that even unjust kings are constituted by God. See Introduction, 72.

610 Hincmar here cites another collection of Roman law, the so-called *Sententia Pauli* V, 25, 1: 410. On this text and Hincmar's access to it, see Corcoran 2015: 137–8.

'the Lex Cornelia on wills, about those who should knowingly write, suppress, move, devise or destroy a false will or other instrument by fraud: the privileged (*honestiores*) are to be deported to an island, the lowly (*humiliores*) condemned to the mines or raised on the cross, and the slave to undergo capital punishment'.

And as St Augustine reminds in the commentary on the Gospel of John:[611] 'It is the law of the forum that the document obtained by someone who lies to the prince in entreaties should not benefit him, rather he should lose the benefit of the document, in the place to where he had taken it.' But they [the kings] said nothing about confirming their own rescripts, since they held it sinful to infringe what they confirmed, just as is read in the Book of Esther how much force the seal of the king's ring has, and how much caution the voiding of that seal carries: and how much more has the subscription of the royal hand.[612]

And the royal dignity ought not to take as perfunctory what is written in its diplomas (*praecepta*): 'And so that the diploma may obtain fuller strength in the name of God' and 'Given happily in this or that year in the name of God', lest what is happily confirmed in the name of God is unhappily weakened without the judgement of God, that is without the judgement of truth, since it is written: 'Thou shalt not profane the name of thy God' [Leviticus 18:21] and 'Thou shalt not take the name of the Lord thy God in vain' (Exodus 20:7).[613]

Let them also read Paul, and the explainers of that apostle, for how important the sentence is that the same apostle wrote in his letters: 'See how I have written this with mine own hand' [Galatians 6:11]. <193> And again: 'The salutation by the hand of me Paul' [Colossians 4:18].

→ Therefore kings who confirm with the subscription of their hand things given by them or privileges strengthened with anathema by the hands of the saints, and afterwards count it little to preserve these or disparage them, as if they are not held bound by the chain of anathema, let them hear the statement of the blessed Gregory to the patrician Theoctista:[614]

611 Augustine, *In Iohannis euangelium tractatus*, 7, 11: 73 (Gibb and Innes 1888: 52): a loose citation, taking Augustine's original text out of context. Augustine's point was that unlike emperors, God cannot be deceived.

612 On Hincmar's argument that a royal subscription is more significant than a seal, see Morelle 2004: 301–6.

613 Morelle 2004: 306–8: Hincmar here cites formulae similar to those used in royal Carolingian charters; he was familiar with the royal or imperial chancery of his day.

614 Gregory I, *Registrum* XI, 27 (J 1817):II, 912 (Martyn 2004: III, 770–1), adapted. On the anathema, see Introduction, 32; on the connection of the power of

> 'They themselves are witnesses that they are not Christians, who, trying to loosen themselves [from anathema], reckon the bindings of the whole Church as vain. And through this, if they do not reckon its binding as valid, nor do they consider the absolution of the holy Church which it offers to the faithful to be true, and since they believe the truth to deceive, they are therefore truly bound in their sins. But if therefore there are those who under the Christian name dare either to preach this or silently to hold it among themselves, both I and all the catholic bishops and the universal Church anathematise them.'

We say these things so that the princes and kings and rulers of the holy Church may do all things according to reason and the order of law, but also so that the above-mentioned case may be decided with judgement of equity. The same blessed Gregory described, in the letter of instruction to John the *defensor* who was going to Spain, the method of constituting the judgement if Hubert should come to a hearing for this case, not judged by any civil judgement but coming to an ecclesiastical one.[615] Gregory says:[616]

> 'First so that this may happen in an orderly way, when there are some accusers and other witnesses, let the quality of the case be explored there, whether it is worthy of exile or condemnation, so that with him present under oath, testimony may be offered against him or introduced by a written statement of acts, and so that he himself has licence to reply and defend himself. But it also is to be enquired subtly about the persons of the accusers and witnesses, their condition and their reputation, lest they may be destitute or perhaps may have some hostility against him, and whether they give testimony from hearsay or indeed have testified that they know something specific. And let the judgement be in writing and thus let the sentence be recited, and thus all these things may be solemnly confirmed.' ←

For the rest, if the woman is found guilty of crime with her brother before the start of the marriage, we think this should be considered in the fashion of the judgement in the letter of the same Gregory to John, bishop of Palermo about a certain woman, whom some man left before he became a deacon, and a certain man handed her over to a husband after she had changed her clothes.[617] For he said:[618]

'binding and loosing' given to St Peter [Matthew 16:19] with the right of bishops to judge, see Uhalde 2007: 46–8.

615 Hincmar here moves away from his earlier demand for a secular judgement on the case: see Introduction, 50.

616 Gregory I, *Registrum* XIII, 47 (J 1912): I, 1056 (Martyn 2004: III, 862). On assessing the character of accusers and witnesses, see Introduction, 34.

617 That is, become a nun.

618 Gregory I, *Registrum* XIV, 5 (J 1918): I, 1071–2 (Martyn 2004: III, 871).

> <194> 'Since there are faults in which it is a fault to relax the punishment, the truth should always be sought, so that it ought to be inquired whether a crime condemns the accused or whether detected innocence removes him from punishment. Therefore it came to us that Fantinus the *defensor* wished to exercise vengeance on Peter, the bearer of this letter, because, as it is said, at the time he was a tenant he handed over the abandoned wife (*relicta*) of a certain deacon to a husband. But Peter asserts she was not the wife of the deacon, nor did she come to him as a virgin, and finally, that she had not presumed to change to religious clothing after he was promoted into holy orders.[619] He added that before she came to the deacon and afterwards, she had lived with a bad reputation. Therefore with these words we exhort your Fraternity to enquire into this case, with the fear of God as is suitable, and with subtle investigation in all ways. And if the woman concerned was married to the deacon, then let the above-mentioned letter bearer be handed to the above mentioned *defensor* and ruler of the patrimony for punishment in all ways, and let those who have been joined badly[620] be separated (*disiungantur*) with suitable emendation.'

We extract this from the words of St Gregory.

And just as we placed above some words of St Augustine, that in the Church excommunication and separation from the Church does what killing used to do in the old law or even what it now does by the laws of the state (*res publica*);[621] so, if whatever woman, caught by the public laws in crimes of this kind as set out above, should evade the forum's judgement and come to episcopal judgement, then, according to the holy Council of Ancyra:[622]

> 'about those who fornicate irrationally, that is with men or beasts, and about those women who fornicate and kill their offspring or who do things with themselves so that they expel foetuses from their womb (*uterus*), it is commanded, it seems to us, that we should pray amongst those who are imperilled by the unclean spirit',

she will be chastised by a strict ten-year penance. And she will be judged to devote herself to the fruits of worthy penance until the end of her life, with the *viaticum* reserved for her by ecclesiastical piety, if she is menaced by fear of death.[623] And she should be separated not only

619 When a married man entered the diaconate or priesthood, it was normal for him to separate from his wife and for her to enter the religious life.

620 That is, not in a valid marriage.

621 See above, Response 2: 116.

622 Council of Ancyra 314, cc. 15, 16, 20: 93–101, 107–9 (Percival 1900: 70, 73).

623 Penitents were often accepted into communion at the point of death: see Introduction, 39.

from the marriage bed but from all marital consort, according to the decree of the blessed Pope Gregory to Felix, bishop of Sicily. He said:[624]

> 'We decree that someone of those who are faithfully taught and now stand undestroyed, planted with firm roots, should observe his kinship as far as the seventh generation, and as far as they know themselves to be relatives by marriage, he should not form an association of this kind of coupling. Nor indeed is any Christian allowed or will be allowed to take in marriage any woman whom someone from his own kinship had in marriage or has stained with any illicit pollution, since such coupling is incestuous and abominable to God and all humans. Indeed we read that formerly it was constituted by the holy Fathers that incestuous people (*incestuosi*) were not to be reckoned by the name of marriage. Nor also do we omit this, in this part of solicitude, that all the incestuous are to be separated from the thresholds of holy Church until they may be reconciled through satisfaction by the prayers of priests to the same holy catholic Church.'

<195> And in the canonical edict offered before the body of St Peter:[625] 'If anyone should take a wife from his own relatives or she whom a relative had, let him be anathema. And everyone replied three times, Let him be anathema.' And St Ambrose on the first letter to the Corinthians says:[626] 'For a brother or sister [i.e. a Christian] is not subject to service in this way: that is, the reverence of marriage is not owed to him, who appalled the Author of marriage. For that marriage is not established which is without God's devotion.'

→ And St Jerome in the third book of the *Commentary on the Letter of Paul to the Ephesians*:[627]

> 'In the same way as the Church is subjected to Christ, so let the wife be subjected to the husband. Husband and wife are bound by the same order as the pre-eminence (*principatus*) and subjection that Christ and the Church have. For is to be observed that as the joining between Christ and the Church is holy, so should the bond between man and woman be holy. But just as no congregation of heretics can be said to be the Church

624 This is another citation of Pseudo-Gregory, Letter to Felix of Messina (J †1334): 751–2 (shortened). On this forged letter, which Hincmar frequently cites, see Introduction, 60. For the *incestuosos*, see also below, 220; Response 19: 256.

625 Council of Rome 721, c. 9: col. 263.

626 Ambrosiaster, *Commentarius in Epistolam I ad Corinthios* 7, 15, 1–2: II, 77 (Bray 2009: 151), also cited Response 19: 220. Ambrosiaster is actually referring to the case where a Christian has been abandoned by a non-believing spouse: see Hunter 2009: 15.

627 Jerome, *Commentum epistolae ad Ephesios* III, 5, 22–3: cols 530–1 (Heine 2002: 233).

> of Christ, nor is Christ their head, so no marriage (*matrimonium*), in which the wife is not joined to the husband according to the precepts of Christ, can rightly be called marriage (*coniugium*), but rather adultery.'

Hence it is to be noticed intelligently, what the doctor himself said in a letter to the priest Amandus, that:[628] 'as long as the man lives, although he may be an adulterer, although a sodomite, although overwhelmed by all sins and deserted by his wife because of these sins, he is reckoned her husband, and she is not allowed to take another man', he says about him who sins in the marriage itself, after a legitimate marriage is started. In this law (*ius*) man and woman are held by equal sentence. But in this position it is a matter of her or him who, having committed incest before a legitimate marriage is started, takes away from himself/herself the legitimate marriage which he/she had been able to have.[629] ←

And in the Council of Agde:[630] 'We reserve no mercy for incestuous marriages, unless they should be cleansed by the separation of the adulterers. But incestuous people (*incestuosi*) are not to be reckoned by the name of marriage, whom it is deadly even to designate ⌈by the name of marriage⌉.' And St Augustine in the book *On the Good of Marriage*:[631]

> 'It is one thing not to sleep together except only for the wish to beget children, which carries no sin: it is another thing to seek the desire of the flesh by sleeping together, but with the spouse only, which is a venial sin. For even if they do not sleep together for the sake of propagating offspring, the propagation of offspring is not resisted for the sake of this lust, either by evil will or evil act. Those who do resist, although they are called spouses, are not really such. Nor do they retain any truth of marriage, <196> but claim the honest name to veil infamy. Having proceeded so far, they are betrayed into exposing their children, who are born against their will. For they hate to nourish or keep those whom they feared to beget. Thus when this shadowy iniquity rages against those they begot unwillingly, it is dragged into the light by manifest iniquity, and the hidden shameful deed is proven by open cruelty. Sometimes this lustful cruelty or cruel lust goes so far as to procure poisons for sterility, or if that should not be effective, to destroy and eject the conceived foetus in some way from the womb (*intra viscera*), preferring its offspring

628 Jerome, *Epistula* 55, c. 4: I, 493 (Fremantle 1893: 110), cited Response 5: 139.

629 Hincmar clearly suggests that if Theutberga had indeed committed the acts of which she was accused, she would have made herself incapable of marriage; by implication, Lothar II would be free. See Introduction, 62.

630 Council of Epaon 517, c. 30: 31 (identified as Council of Agde 506, c. 61) and also cited in Response 19: 257. On the significance of this (adapted) quotation, see Introduction, 62.

631 Actually Augustine, *De nuptiis et concupiscentia* I, 15: 229–30 (Holmes 1887: 270–1).

to die rather than live, or if it lived in the womb (*uterus*), to kill it before it was born.[632] Well, if both parties are like this, they are not spouses, and if they were such from the beginning, they have not come together by marriage but rather by debauchery (*stuprum*). But if the two are not alike in such sin, I boldly declare that either she is in some way the whore of her husband, or he is an adulterer to his wife.'

Question 13

'And send back word to us in the sixth chapter,[633] if this king [Lothar II], after he heard such things about his aforementioned wife and had suspended carnal business (*carnale commercium*) with her, had perhaps committed adultery with a concubine, and if this came to the notice of many, then by what medicinal judgement should it be healed?[634] And if it should happen to come about that some man obliges himself by oath to try to do something which is criminal, should he fulfil his oath so that he does not commit perjury, or should he make void what he wrongly swore to do, so that he does not allow a crime?[635]

And if it might be true, as many people say, that there are women who by their sorcery (*maleficium*) are able to provoke irreconcilable hatred between man and wife, and to sow an indescribable love between a man and woman? [So that] a man is unable to engage legitimately in marital commerce with his wife yet is able to unite with other women, but that by the same sorcery, the power of sleeping with someone and of love, formerly enjoyed, can be restored by the art of sorceresses (*maleficae*). And tell us the reason for which, it is said, God often allows such things to happen in legitimate marriage. And if such [male] sorcerers (*malefici*) or female magicians (*incantatrices feminae*) should be found, what should be done about them?'[636]

Response 13

We respond: if perhaps, as is said, the king in question carried out the business of sleeping with someone else in carnal union (*commixtio*) after

632 Abortion is here linked to other kinds of sexual sin: see Introduction, 56–7.

633 That is, in response to the sixth of the questions in the list from February/March 860.

634 Lothar's relationship with Waldrada is here implicitly shown to be widely known and hence, if it is a sin, it is a public sin: see Introduction, 40 and 56.

635 The implication is that Lothar has sworn some kind of oath to marry Waldrada and/or to make her queen: on perjury, see Introduction, 35.

636 On love magic, see Introduction, 68.

his marriage was legally initiated, then he cannot deny that he committed adultery; even if the woman he took to wife should perhaps be found guilty of those things as is alleged. For he presumed to do illicit things after a marriage was legally entered into, and before a legal settlement.[637]

→ <197> For the apostle says that a wife is bound by the law of her husband for as long as her husband lives, but when he is dead, she is released from his law [1 Corinthians 7:39; Romans 7:2]. And there is no one who can doubt that she who is legally betrothed, endowed and honoured with a public wedding according to sacred authority, is a wife.[638] And the same sacred authority testifies that there is one rule (*lex*) in the law (*ius*) for both husband and wife.[639] And therefore, before one is released from the other, from 'the heavy yoke upon the sons of Adam from the day they go out of their mother's womb till the day they enter the womb of the mother of all things' [Ecclesiasticus 40:1]; or until it is proven by law by Him 'through whom the founders of law decree just things' [Proverbs 8:15], that what was entered into was not a legitimate marriage:[640] until either of these, whichever one of these two [the spouses] divides one flesh into two by adultery, cannot claim not to have committed adultery. ←

For the great Pope Leo, writing to Nicetas, the bishop of Aquileia, compared the form of secular to ecclesiastical laws, that:[641] 'as [status] is maintained for slaves, fields, even houses and possessions which are taken across the border into captivity and are then returned; so too spouses should be rejoined together, if they have been joined to others'. And we must contribute something from the same laws for an

637 That is, before his marriage was judged illegal or invalid.

638 On this distinction, drawn from Leo I, *Epistola* 167 to Rusticus of Narbonne, see above Response 4: 128; it is also repeated below, Response 21: 262. The imprecise use of 'sacred authority' reflects Hincmar's concern to give all his cited texts the same moral authority.

639 In Response 5: 131, 140–1, Hincmar cites authors arguing that the law applies equally to men and women; here, it is simply stated.

640 Hincmar leaves open the possibility of an 'annulment', leaving space for Lothar II's union with Theutberga to be ended.

641 A loose citation of Leo, *Epistola* 159 to Nicetas of Aquileia (J 536), cc. 2–3: col. 1137 (Feltoe 1895: 103). Leo's letter discusses the procedure when wives whose husbands were captured in war or thought to be dead have remarried and their first husband has subsequently returned. In Roman law the first marriage was dissolved by captivity and the first husband had no automatic claim on his wife; Leo, however, rejected such a view, basing his argument on the Roman law principle of *postliminum*, that automatic rights to property were maintained by a returned captive. See Sessa 2011.

example:[642] that if anyone takes in advance for himself against law (*ius*) what he could strive after for himself by law (*ius*), he is obliged by the law (*lex*) to make legal compensation to the person he despoiled. Therefore if anyone who is legally married should anticipate against the laws of marriage → publicly or secretly ← before a judgement has been made about the accusations, it will be necessary for him to submit to the laws set out for transgressors → secretly or publicly ←.[643] It is decreed for these in the African Council:[644] 'that bishops should discern by their judgement the lengths of penance for penitents, according to the difference in their sins'. And in the Council of Carthage:[645] 'that the priest impose the laws of penance upon him who begs for it, without any acceptance of persons'.[646] And according to the Council of Elvira:[647]

> 'if any of the faithful who has a wife commits adultery not once but often, he is to be addressed at the point of death. And if he promises to stop, communion should be given to him. If thus brought back to life, he commits adultery again, he should be cut off more firmly, so that he may no longer mock the communion of peace.'[648]

And according to the Council of Ancyra:[649] 'an adulterous wife or a husband who commits adultery will achieve the perfection of reconciliation and communion after a penance of seven years'. And again according to the Council of Elvira:[650] <198> 'if anyone who has a wife slips once, he is to be reconciled after five years of penance, though communion should be given to him beforehand if ill health makes it necessary'. Likewise the Council of Toledo decreed:[651] 'Whoever should have both a wife and a concubine is to be separated from the communion of the Church.'

642 Hincmar's source here is unclear: the implication is that he is again citing a Roman law maxim, that even when a valid claim to property exists, the correct legal procedure must be followed before gaining control of the property.

643 That is, whatever the final decision about Theutberga, Lothar is definitely at fault.

644 *Breviarium Hipponense*, c. 30a: 41.

645 *Statuta ecclesiae antiqua*, c. 18: 169. The *Collectio Hispana* cites this as the Fourth Council of Carthage, c. 74.

646 That is, that the priest should not consider the social status of the penitent. On this principle, applied also to secular judgements, see Introduction, 33.

647 Council of Elvira, c. 47: 10 (Laeuchli 1972: 131).

648 On the *viaticum* (communion before death): see Introduction, 39.

649 Council of Ancyra, c. 19: 107 (Percival 1900: 73), also cited above, Response 5: 131.

650 Council of Elvira, c. 69: 13 (Laeuchli 1972: 134).

651 First Council of Toledo, c. 17: 24

In such a separation, or in a reconciliation after a suitable satisfaction, let the pastors of the Church, successors and deputies of the apostles, take the utmost care, since as the blessed Gregory says, they:[652]

> 'take on the authority of binding and loosing when they take on the position of governance.[653] Let them take care lest they follow their own wishes in loosing and binding those subject to them, rather than the merits of the cases: thereby condemning those who do not deserve it, or loosing others while they are bound.[654] And so let them deprive themselves of this power of loosing and binding, if they exercise it according to their own wishes, and not according to the character of those subject to them. Nor should they be affected by hatred or gratitude towards any near relative, for they will not be able to judge those subjected to them worthily if they decide to follow hatred or gratitude in the cases of their subjects. And therefore it is rightly said through the prophet: "they were slaying souls which should not die, and they saved the souls alive that should not live" [Ezekiel 13:19]. Whoever condemns the just is putting to death someone who is not dying, and whoever tries to absolve the guilty from punishment is attempting to bring to life someone not alive.
>
> So the cases should be considered, and then the power of binding and loosing should be exercised. It should be seen what the fault is, or what repentance should follow after the fault, so that the sentence of the pastor absolves those whom the almighty God visits through the grace of compunction. There is true absolution from the one presiding only when it follows the decision of the internal judge [God]. And we should absolve through pastoral authority those whom we recognise our Author has brought alive through his awakening grace. This restoration to life is without doubt indeed recognised in the confession of sin, before any act of righteousness,'[655]

[a confession] which is accustomed to happen not just verbally and barely with the outer lips, but comes from the deepest emotion of the heart, as David said: 'I have sinned against the Lord.' And he deserved to hear: 'The Lord also hath put away thy sin, thou shalt not die' [2 Samuel 12:13].[656] And he again said: 'I have roared by reason of the disquietness of my heart' [Psalms 38:8], and 'For I will declare mine

652 Gregory I, *Homiliae in euangelia* II, 26, 5–6: 222–3, shortened (Hurst 1990: 204–5).

653 On binding and loosing, see above, Response 12: 217.

654 Justice must be impartial and undue mercy is also dangerous: see Introduction, 33.

655 That is, confession itself restores one, even before any meritorious acts done as penance.

656 The reference is to the story of David and Bathsheba, i.e. to that of a royal adulterer.

iniquity and I will be sorry for my sin' [Psalms 38:18]; just as he said in the tribulation which he suffered for the sins he admitted, fleeing from the sight of his son, saying: 'It may be that the Lord will look on mine affliction, and that the Lord will requite me good for his cursing this day' [2 Samuel 16:12]. Through all this it is clear that to those who confess in that way, satisfaction should not be forbidden, nor communion denied.

Yet some dare to take the sacraments of the holy body and precious blood of our Redeemer as a judgement for themselves. Carelessly neither purified nor absolved, they are rather seduced and deceived by the priests of whom the prophet says: 'Woe to those that sew pillows to all armholes, and make kerchiefs upon the head of every stature to hunt souls' [Ezekiel 13:18], that is 'they cherish with alluring flattery the souls falling from their righteousness and reclining amongst the delights of this world, that they may lie softly in error, and not be troubled by the harshness of objections'.[657] Such rectors[658] show themselves lovers to those whom they fear could harm them in their zeal for temporal glory. <199> It is written about these: 'O my people, they that call thee blessed, the same deceive thee, and destroy the way of thy paths' [Isaiah 3:12]. And again: '"Thy prophets have seen vain and foolish things for thee: and they have not discovered thine iniquity, to excite thee to penance" [Lamentations 2:14]: since, when they fear to correct faults, they flatter sinners vainly with the promise of security.'[659] And so, remaining in the state of mind of sin, or usurping divine mysteries[660] prior to a suitable satisfaction, they make God's good gift into their judgement. This is how the holy authors expound the word of the Lord, saying: 'But behold, the hand of him that betrayeth me is with me on the table. But woe to that man by whom he is betrayed' [Luke 22:21–22], as shown by the venerable priest Bede in his commentary on the Gospel of Luke:[661]

> 'They say today also and for ever: Woe to that man who wickedly comes to the Lord's table, who with a plot cultivated in his mind, polluted by some

657 Gregory I, *Regula pastoralis* II, 8: I, 232 (Barmby 1895: 19).

658 Gregory uses the term *rectores* for all those in charge of others: see Markus 1997: 27–31. We have normally translated Hincmar's own use of the term as 'ruler'.

659 Gregory I, *Regula pastoralis* II, 4: I, 188 (Barmby 1895: 11).

660 For example, taking communion.

661 Bede, *In Lucae evangelium expositio* VI, 22, 21: 379–80; part of this is also cited above, Preface: 88. Carolingian moralists frequently use the metaphor of those who are like Judas, because they 'sell the Lord', e.g. by committing perjury. Here Bede uses the analogy in a vaguer sense, for anyone whose concern is with earthly rather than heavenly matters.

> crime, does not fear to participate in the secrets of the mysteries of Christ. And he, like the example of Judas, hands over the Son of Man, not indeed to Jewish sinners, but yet to sinners, that is his limbs, by which he dared to violate that inestimable and inviolable body of the Lord.[662] That one sells the Lord, who, neglecting love and fear of Him, is proven to love and care more for earthly and perishable things, indeed criminal things. Woe, I say, unto that man, about whom Jesus, who is not doubted to be present at the sacred altars among the offerings, ready to consecrate the things placed before him, was obliged to lament to the heavenly ministers standing around Him, "Behold, the hand of him that betrayeth me is with me on the table".'

And Paul said: 'If any man that is called brother be a fornicator or covetous or an idolater or a railer or a drunkard or an extortioner: with such an one no not to eat' [1 Corinthians 5:11], and 'the unrighteous shall not inherit the kingdom of God. Be not deceived: neither fornicators, nor idolaters, nor adulterers, nor effeminate nor abusers of themselves with mankind, nor thieves, nor covetous, nor drunkards, nor revilers, nor extortioners shall inherit the kingdom of God' [1 Corinthians 6:9–10]. And again, 'For fornicators and adulterers God will judge' [Hebrews 13:4] and 'Every sin that a man doeth is without the body: but he that committeth fornication sinneth against his own body' [1 Corinthians 6:18].[663] And Ambrose said:[664]

> 'It shows the sin to be the most serious, since from this the whole body is destroyed, while in other sins a part perishes, but not all. The whole body is the man and wife, since the woman is a part of the man. Whoever commits another sin, sins outside himself, but the fornicator sins within his own flesh (*caro*).'

Although all sins act upon man in the flesh, this is particularly the desire of the flesh, that it should deliver the soul stained with sins together with the body to hell; for the soul, when conquered by the lust of the flesh, is made into flesh, just as the well-governed body is considered as spiritual.[665] It is, however, the mind (*animus*) which either conquered by allurements makes the whole man into flesh, or remaining in the vigour of its

662 Just as Judas handed over the bodily Jesus to the Jews for a wrongful purpose, so the unrepentant sinner who takes communion is wrongfully 'handing over' the elements (understood as the body and blood of Jesus) to himself.

663 On debates about the meaning of sinning 'without the body', see Response 12: 196.

664 Ambrosiaster, *Commentarius in Epistolam I ad Corinthios* 6, 18, 1: II, 67 (Bray 2009: 147).

665 On 'the flesh' used from the time of St Paul as a metaphor for humanity's rebellion against God, see Brown 1988: 47–9.

nature acts upon the flesh, so that it can be called spiritual. Therefore the authors of the canons, with the Holy Spirit speaking through them, decreed that such people should be separated from communion until satisfaction, because those who are alien to the kingdom of God should be separated in every way from the Church, which is and is also called the kingdom of God, until correction and satisfaction. <200> The priests of the Lord should not give holy communion to those with whom it does not suit the disciples of Christ to break bread, as He prohibits in the Gospel: 'Give not that which is holy unto the dogs' [Matthew 7:6], which Peter explains saying: 'as the sow that was washed is returned to her wallowing in the mire, and the dog to his vomit' [2 Peter 2:22], so as Solomon says, the fool 'returneth to his folly' [Proverbs 26:11].

And whoever, while remaining in sin, dares to eat the Lord's supper before correction and satisfaction of his criminal sin, he dares to eat it for his own condemnation, as we said above, and as the apostle attests, saying: 'Whosoever shall eat this bread and drinks this cup of the Lord unworthily, shall be guilty of the body and blood of the Lord' [1 Corinthians 11:27]. And St Ambrose says about this:[666] 'What is it to be guilty of the body and blood of the Lord, except to pay the penalty for the death of the Lord? For He was killed for those who take this benefit in vain.' And Paul says again: 'Let a man examine himself and so let him eat of that bread, and drink of that cup' [1 Corinthians 11:28]. A man should examine himself, that is correct himself from that sin, and reject that sin, and after a worthy satisfaction, 'come to the holy communion, so that the mind (*mens*) should know it owes reverence to Him whose body it comes to take. For this it should consider about itself, that it is the Lord whose body and blood it takes.'[667] And what follows: 'for this cause, many are weak and sickly among you, and many sleep' [1 Corinthians 11:30], to which he [Ambrose] comments:[668] so that 'he may show the image of judgement on those who carelessly take the body of the Lord'. For just as these were weakened in body and dying, so whoever remains in sin or has the disposition (*affectus*) of sinning, and who takes the body and blood of the Lord, brings death upon himself, by unworthily taking that from which he could take life, if he should take the sacraments after a worthy penance with suitable satisfaction.[669]

666 Ambrosiaster, *Commentarius in Epistolam I ad Corinthios* 11, 27: II, 128 (Bray 2009: 175).

667 Ambrosiaster, *Commentarius in Epistolam I ad Corinthios* 11, 29: II, 129 (Bray 2009: 175).

668 Ambrosiaster, *Commentarius in Epistolam I ad Corinthios* 11, 30: II, 129 (Bray 2009: 175).

669 On Hincmar's view of penance, see Introduction, 39–42.

And if anyone asks why those who take it [communion] unworthily even now are not weakened or dying, as they [in the Corinthian church] were then weakened and dying, let him accept that the apostle did not say that all were weakened or died, but 'many are weak and many died'. And in the early Church physical signs were necessary, but now a true faith should suffice.[670] It is different, because as is written, at the end of the world the sun will be like a 'sackcloth of hair' [Revelation 6:12], that is the Church will be in the bitterness of grief without the gleaming of miracles, so that those who are approved may be made apparent. And while some are corrected who take communion in honesty, although like Peter they may sin later, some wickedly taking communion are tolerated like Judas, his own murderer, who showed by a miserable end what the soul now suffers without a body and what it will suffer eternally with the body, since it [the soul] ate and drank the divine mysteries as a judgement upon itself. And what he [Paul] adds: 'For if we would judge ourselves, we should not be judged' [1 Corinthians 11:31]: 'he means if we ourselves should correct our errors, <201> we would not be judged by the Lord',[671] that is condemned.

And therefore the holy canons decreed that sinners should be removed from or reunited to the holy altar by the judgement of the priest, as the Lord said to the lepers, who prefigured the leprosy of sinners now dispersed throughout the Church: 'Go, shew yourselves unto the priests' [Luke 17:14], so that they might consider the appropriate satisfaction according to the magnitude or multitude of sins they saw in the sinners; and so that without acceptance of persons,[672] they should set a length of time for penitence and for their reconciliation. So that they should not take in judgement and condemnation what the Lord gave to believers [communion] for their redemption and their salvation. But if there is a sinner who is slow to comprehend and neglects to repent, confess and do satisfaction for the sin he committed, episcopal care should not advise him to pretend, mindful of the sentence said to it: 'if thou be surety for thy friend, if thou hast stricken thy hand with a stranger' [Proverbs 6:1], that is:[673]

> 'if you receive the soul of a brother at the risk of your way of life, you have bound your mind to anxious care which was not there when you took up pastoral office. "Thou art snared with the words of thy mouth, and thou

670 The motif of the drying up of miracles: see Introduction, 65.

671 Ambrosiaster, *Commentarius in Epistolam I ad Corinthios* 11, 32: II, 130 (Bray 2009: 175).

672 That is, consideration of the social status of the sinner.

673 Mostly based on Bede, *In prouerbia Salomonis* I, 6, 1–5: 52–3.

> art taken with the words of thy mouth" [Proverbs 6:2], for although you are compelled to say good things by preaching to those committed to you, it is first necessary that you yourself keep what you say. "Do, this now, my son, and deliver thyself when thou art come into the hand of thy friend. Run about, make haste, stir up thy friend" [Proverbs 6:3]. Do not just remember to keep guard by living well yourself, but also wean him of whom you are in charge from the sloth of sin by preaching. "Give not sleep to thine eyes, nor slumber to thine eyelids" [Proverbs 6:4]. He gives sleep to his eyes who wholly neglects the care of those subjected to him; he slumbers who recognises indeed their reprehensible deeds, but does not correct them with worthy invective because of a weariness of mind. "Deliver thyself as a deer from the hand of the hunter, and as a bird from the hand of the fowler" [Proverbs 6:5]. As much as a bird tries to escape from the net, or the deer from the hand of the captor, so should you struggle, so that after your listener has been healthily instructed, you will be rendered free from the surety of his life, lest you be stigmatised as a hireling, not a shepherd' [John 10:12].[674]

If you should see anyone being dragged to excess, or inflamed to avarice, raised up in pride or divided through anger, and you remain silent – either making an acceptance of persons, fearing the wealthy lest his hand should angrily take away from you what it enticingly paid out, or in respect of familiarity or for whatever earthly reward – you yourself rejoice in earthly advantages while souls perish, and in the divine view you will be counted not as a shepherd but as a hireling. Instead, 'preach and beseech, pressing every opportunity' [2 Timothy 4:2]. If he will not hear you warning him according to the Gospel, go to the royal power so that he might be restrained. And if you can still not lead the matter to fulfilment, then announce your warning to the Church, according to the divine precept.[675] 'But if he neglect to hear the Church, let him be unto thee as an heathen man and a publican' [Matthew 18:17], lest by dissembling or neglecting to argue (like the sons of the priest Eli, who sinned against God so that they would not be bitter to men) you may perish with him.[676]

674 On the particular responsibility of a bishop for the souls of those committed to him, see Introduction, 72.

675 Matthew 18:16–17, on which this passage was based, follows a warning by one person to a sinner with a warning in front of several other people, and then the matter being taken up by the whole church. Hincmar, in the context of a Christian kingdom, assumes that the king's coercive power is available for use against sinners, but also that this may not be sufficient, especially when, by implication, the sinner is himself a powerful man. On the intertwining of secular and Church actions, see Introduction, 28.

676 References to Eli and his sons (I Samuel 3:13) are frequent in Carolingian texts as a warning to those who neglect rebuking sins (especially those of their sons). See Stone 2012: 208.

And since there should no sparing of any person against God, so we might spare for salvation ourselves and him, to whom we are carefully unsparing according to our measure, as much as the Lord gave to blessed Ambrose, who by not sparing Theodosius, acquired for him merit in heaven in God's presence, <202> and an eternal memory on earth amongst men, so that it should be understood that it was written of him, 'the memory of the just man [is remembered] with praise' [Proverbs 10:7].[677]

Nor should Gregory's sentence to Queen Brunhild be heard perfunctorily by bishops and kings and all those endowed with human power, in which he says:[678]

> 'These things we say should not be neglected, for whoever is able to eradicate sin and neglects to do so, without doubt makes himself a participant in the crime. Look to your soul, therefore, look to your grandchildren, whom you wish to govern happily, look to your provinces, and think very seriously about correcting wicked deeds before the Creator raises His hand to strike, so that He might not strike all the harder, the longer He has been waiting.'

And if perhaps some person disobedient to divine speech is expelled,[679] let him be expelled from the Church by the above-mentioned procedure, so that this expulsion, God willing, will be able to help him to salvation, as St Augustine says in his book *On Rebuke and Grace*:[680]

> 'Therefore, let brethren who are subject be rebuked by those set over them, with rebukes springing from love, varied according to the diversity of faults, whether smaller or greater. Because if God wishes, that very matter that episcopal judgement inflicts that is called condemnation (*damnatio*), than which there is no greater punishment in the Church, can result in and be of advantage for most wholesome correction. For we do not know what may happen on the following day; nor must anyone be despaired of before the end of this life; nor can God be

677 Ambrose's imposition of penance on Emperor Theodosius in 391 was a frequent model for Carolingian reformers: see Introduction, 74. Hincmar also refers to the story in Appendix Response 6: 300 and gives numerous extracts from Ambrose's letters on the topic in Appendix Response 7: 309–14.

678 Gregory I, *Registrum* XI, 46 to Brunhild (J 1837): II, 944 (Martyn 2004: III, 791–2), in which Gregory calls the queen to hold a reforming synod to deal with misbehaving priests. Note that Hincmar saw instructions to a queen as also applicable to kings and bishops.

679 That is, excommunicated.

680 Augustine, *De correptione et gratia*, c. XV: col. 944 (Wallis 1887: 490). Augustine continues by explaining that we cannot know who is amongst the predestined, a controversial topic that Hincmar doubtless preferred not to raise.

> contradicted, that He may not receive and give repentance, and receive the sacrifice of a troubled spirit and a contrite heart, and absolve from the guilt of condemnation, even if it was just, and so Himself not condemn the condemned person. Yet in order that terrible contagions may not crawl through the many, pastoral necessity requires that the diseased sheep should be separated from the healthy ones; perhaps, by that very separation, to be healed by Him to whom nothing is impossible.'

And if perhaps – and may it not happen – someone should rise up who is elated by pride of earthly power and disdains to obey, and snapping the reins of Christianity (*Christianitas*), rushes headlong into the abyss of hell, the bishop, according to the prophet Ezechiel, will have an 'iron pan' [Ezekiel 4:3], that is the glowing zeal of love, to free him.[681] And he should remember the sentence of St Ambrose, who said about the letter to the Corinthians:[682]

> 'St Paul humbled their pride in such things, saying, "ye are puffed up and have not rather mourned, that he that hath done this thing, might be taken away from among you" [1 Corinthians 5:2],[683] not so that he might make them complain, but to make them instead honest – for they were themselves participants, since they allowed someone to come together with them unrebuked for such a great crime – so that all by one accord should cast him out, if he refused to amend himself. If, however, someone who knows that the person is guilty does not have the power to cast him out or cannot prove it, he will be immune. And the judge should not condemn without an accuser, as the Lord did not at all cast out Judas, although he was a thief, because he was not accused.'

<203> And the Holy Spirit said through a worthy and pleasing mouthpiece, that is the blessed Benedict:

> 'and again the free governor (*rector liber*) will be such, that if he have bestowed all diligence on his unquiet and disobedient flock, and employed the utmost care to cure the corrupt actions of the sheep, their pastor shall then be acquitted in the judgement of the Lord, and may say with the prophet: "I have not hid thy righteousness in my heart, I have declared thy faithfulness and thy salvation" [Psalms 40:10], but they have contemptuously despised me. And then finally, death itself shall be inflicted as a punishment upon the disobedient sheep in his care.'[684]

681 On the bishop's responsibility for the souls of kings, see Introduction, 73–4.

682 Ambrosiaster, *Commentarius in Epistolam I ad Corinthios* 5, 2, 1: II, 52 (Bray 2009: 141).

683 The reference is to a Corinthian man who was fornicating with his stepmother.

684 Benedict of Nursia, *Regula Benedicti* 2, 8–10: I, 442 (Clarke 1931: 9–10).

Question 14 and Response 14

Let the words of St Gregory in his book 33 on the *Morals* be read for the question raised about the oath (*sacramentum*). For he says:[685]

> 'Behold someone who seeks friendships of this world, who binds himself by an oath to someone leading a life similar to his, that he will cover over his secrets in total silence; but the one to whom this was sworn is discovered to be committing adultery, and may even try to kill the husband of the adulteress. The man who swore the oath comes back to his senses and is buffeted about by various thoughts: he fears to keep silent about it, lest by keeping silent about the adultery he may also become a participant in the murder; but he trembles also to betray, lest he render himself guilty of perjury. He is tied by the entwined sinews of his testicles, fearing to come down on either side, lest he not be free of the taint of transgression.'[686]

And a little later:

> 'There is, however, a principle which may be useful for eliminating these trickeries, which is that when the mind is compelled between lesser and greater sins, then if there is really no path of escape open without sin, the lesser sins should always be chosen. For he who is enclosed on all sides by a circuit of walls so that he might not escape, jumps off in flight there where the walls are found to be lower.'

And the venerable priest Bede says thus in his homily on the Gospel according to Matthew, in which Herod's foolish oath is described:

> 'How greatly we should avoid the rashness of taking an oath, both the Lord in the Gospel and James in his letter teach, saying "But above all things, my brethren, swear not, neither by the heaven, neither by the earth, neither by any other oath. But let your yea be yea; and your nay, nay, lest ye fall into judgement" [James 5:12]. Clearly this is the judgement to which Herod fell victim, so that he had either to commit perjury, or, fearing to perjure, to carry out another sin. But if it should happen perhaps that we swear incautiously, that is, an oath which if kept would incline to a worse result, then we should openly recognise that the oath can be changed by more healthy counsel. By force of necessity, we shall have to perjure, rather than fall into a more serious crime in order to avoid perjury. For David swore by the Lord to kill Nabal, a foolish and impious man, and to destroy all that belonged to him. But at the first intercession of his [Nabal's] prudent wife Abigail, he revoked his

685 Actually Gregory I, *Moralia in Iob* XXXII, 20, 36 and 39: III, 1656–8 (Bliss 1844: IV, 538–9, 540).

686 The metaphor of testicles comes from a description of Leviathan in Job 40:12, which Gregory also drew on elsewhere.

> threats, sheathed his sword, and did not grieve that he had committed something sinful by such perjury. And Herod swore to give to the dancer whatever she demanded of him, and, lest he be called a perjurer by the banqueters, he defiled the banquet itself with blood, making the death of a prophet into a dancer's reward. Moderation is to be carefully observed not just in swearing, but in all things that we do.
>
> So if perhaps we fall into the traps of the wily enemy, from which we cannot escape without some stain of sin, let us seek to escape it rather by seeking the approach <204> in which we bear less risk. And so, following the example of those shut in by enemy walls, and who, desiring to escape, see all exits forbidden to them: it is necessary that they chose some place from which to jump down, a place where the wall is lower, so they run the least risk in falling.'[687]

And in the Council of Lérida it is decreed:[688]

> 'whoever obliges himself by an oath that he will in no way return to peace with someone with whom he is in contention, he will be separated from the communion of the body and blood of the Lord for one year for his perjury, and let him absolve his guilt with alms, tears and as much as he can, with fasting, and let him hurry to return quickly to love, which "covers a multitude of sins" ⌜1 Peter 4:8⌝'.

And since the questioners wished to ask about an oath of this sort, we thought it not irrelevant to write about such things, which are accustomed to happen to human frailty. We do not target anyone in particular with what we write, but rather in case there is such a person whom this advice would be able to help, mindful of the Scripture saying 'whatsoever thou spendest more, when I come again, I will repay thee' ⌜Luke 10:35⌝. And so, although we were not asked about it, we thought we should include ⌜advice⌝ for someone who must choose between two things and wavers.[689] For no one will easily find, indeed no one is able to find, someone who is holier than David, wiser than Solomon and stronger than Samson. And these, captured by love of a woman, which tames iron wills by lust, and neither shrinks back from the rags of the poor nor fears the royal purple, did things which were not befitting.[690]

687 Bede, *Homiliarum euangelii libri* ii II, 23 (Martin and Hurst 1991: II, 233). Hincmar has already cited this passage extensively in Response 6: 149 and more briefly in Response 1: 111.

688 Council of Lérida 546, c. 7: 57.

689 A reminder that Hincmar did not see himself as entirely bound by the terms of the questions sent to him, but answered with a wider didactic and pastoral purpose in mind.

690 On Samson, see Judges 13–16; on David and Bathsheba, 2 Samuel 11; on Solomon's wives, 1 Kings 11.

And women often come to us complaining that young men made them a pledge of faith (*fidem promiserint*) and then left them, scorned.[691] And it has sometimes been found by us that men have left their legitimate wives and have adhered to adulteresses, in order to keep the faith they promised, to such an extent that they could be separated from these women only with great efforts.[692]

About this business, St Augustine says in his book *On the Good of Marriage*:[693]

> 'There is this further, that in that very debt which married persons pay one to another, even if they demand it with somewhat too great intemperance and incontinence, yet they owe faith (*fides*) one to each other. To this faith the apostle allows so great right as to call it "power" (*potestas*), saying, "The wife hath not power of her own body, but the husband; and likewise also the husband hath not power of his own body, but the wife" [1 Corinthians 7:4]. But a violation in the use of this faith is called adultery, when either by instigation of one's own lust, or by consent to the lust of another, there is sexual intercourse with another man or woman against the marriage compact. And so faith is broken, which is a great good of the soul even in matters that are of the body and low: and therefore it is certain that it ought to be preferred even to the health of the body, in which this life of ours is contained. For, although a little straw in comparison to much gold is almost nothing;[694] yet faith, when it is kept pure in a matter of straw, as in a matter of gold, is not therefore less because it is kept in a lesser matter. But when faith is used to allow sin, it would be amazing that we should call it faith. However, of whatever kind the faith be, if a deed be done against it, it is the worse done; except when faith is abandoned on this account, so that there may be a return to true and lawful faith, that is, that a sin may be amended from perversion by a correct will.
>
> It is as if someone who could not rob a person alone should find a partner in his iniquity, and make an agreement with him to do it together, and to divide the spoil; and, after the crime has been committed, should take off the whole to himself alone. The other man sorrows for himself, and complains that faith has not been kept with him. But in his very complaint he ought to consider that he himself rather should have kept faith with human society in a good life, and not to make unjust spoil

691 Hincmar presumably means that such men promise to marry them and then refuse to.

692 This looks like a not particularly subtle reference to Waldrada, but perhaps suggests a more widespread social practice.

693 Augustine, *De bono coniugali* 4: 191–3 (Wilcox *et al.* 1955: 13–14).

694 That is, the body is worth much less than the soul.

> from a person, <205> if he feels how unjust it was not to preserve it ⌜faith⌝ with himself in the fellowship of sin. The other man, being faithless in both instances, must assuredly be judged as guilty and the more wicked. But if he had been unwilling to divide the spoil with his partner in crime, so that it might be restored to the person from whom it had been taken, not even a faithless man would call him faithless. Thus if a woman, having broken her marriage faith, keeps faith with her adulterer, she is certainly bad: but if she does not keep faith even with her adulterer, worse. Furthermore, if she should repent her of her sin, and returning to marital chastity, should renounce all adulterous compacts and sentiments, I would be surprised if even the adulterer himself will think of her as a violator of faith.'

And this is equally to be understood about an adulterer, that if he renounces an agreement made with an adulteress, that adulteress herself will not be able justly to say that he is a violator of faith.[695]

Question 15

About that which was asked, 'And if it might be true, as many people say, that there are women who by their sorcery (*maleficium*) are able to provoke irreconcilable hatred between man and wife, and to sow an indescribable love between a man and woman', and all the rest which the questioners wanted to bring into investigation.[696]

Response 15

Let them reread the history of the Book of Kings, how after David's sin with Bathsheba, the wife of Uriah, Amnon, the son of the same David, by the devil's prompting fell passionately in love with his sister Tamar, and how on the advice of Jonadab, representing the devil who slew Adam through Eve's encouragement to sin, he slept with this sister.[697] And how before that sleeping together he ⌜Amnon⌝ loved her so much that he was wholly lost in her, and fell sick for her love. But after their sleeping together, 'he hated exceedingly, so that the hatred wherewith he now hated her was greater than the love wherewith he had loved

695 That is, if Lothar proposes to return to Theutberga, he is justified in breaking any promises he made to Waldrada.

696 On magic and the devil, see Introduction, 64–9.

697 On David and Bathsheba, see 2 Samuel 11–12; on Amnon, 2 Samuel 13. In the book of Samuel, this is explicitly shown as rape; for Hincmar, such concerns about consent are obviously irrelevant to this particular question.

her' [2 Samuel 13:15]. And this devilish work ran on through fratricide to other evils, which readers will find there.[698]

→ And St Ambrose explains the verse of Psalms 118, 'Unless thy law had been my delights, I should then have perished in mine affliction' [Psalms 119:92], and speaking about Joseph who suffered what was sent through wicked angels, says 'It is said that the devil said to a certain prophet (many say it was Isaiah held in prison) when a mass of threatening ruin was looming, "Say that you did not speak from the Lord when you said those things, and I will change the minds and opinions of all towards you".'[699] ←

And in a certain diocese (*parrochia*) of ours, what we shall explain took place.[700] A certain young man of noble birth fell passionately in love with a woman of not ignoble ancestry. And seeking her legally from her parents, he won assent from her father, but the girl's mother totally refused his request. But, what rarely happens, the father prevailed in agreeing to the young man's demands.[701] After betrothal, the giving of a dowry and a marriage celebration, the young man led her to a private room, but he was in no way able to sleep with her as is customary. After they had led a life made wearisome by irremediable hatred for two years, the young man went to the bishop, forced by necessity for he could not find advice anywhere else, with words of persuasion, requests and threats: that unless he [the bishop] allowed the marriage to be dissolved, he would take out his sword, through which murder would occur if the marriage could not be dissolved in any other way.[702] <206> But this bishop, sifting through many other such things often done by the devil, brought back to mind what the Lord said through the prophet: 'Son of man, dig now in the wall, and behold the wicked abominations that they do here. And when I had digged in the wall, behold a door' [Ezekiel 8:8] and the rest which

698 Amnon was Tamar's half-brother; her full brother, Absalom, killed Amnon in revenge and later rebelled against David and was killed himself.

699 Ambrose, *Expositio psalmi cxuiii*, c. 12: 270. Ambrose's reference is to the story outlined in chapter 5 of the pseudepigraphical text, 'The Martyrdom of Isaiah' (written in the first centuries AD) in which Manasseh, king of Israel imprisoned and then executed the prophet Isaiah. Hincmar used this section of the text to add in another reference to the devil's power, regardless of its relevance to love magic.

700 For a discussion of this story, see Introduction, 38–9; 68. Here *parrochia* probably means (suffragan) diocese, though elsewhere Hincmar did use it to mean parish: see West 2015a.

701 An interesting indication of the influence of women within Frankish families.

702 On wife-killing, see Introduction, 58.

is read there. And he went from meeting (*placitum*) to meeting,[703] and through many discussions of this sort took the matter from dispute to settlement, until the works of the devil were dissolved by the grace of God, and sexual relations (*concubitus*), which had been possible with enjoyment with a concubine before but impossible with his legally acquired wife, were made possible for the young man with her, after penance and Church medicine. And the devilish hatred was driven off, and the restored conjugal love amongst the spouses has persisted up till now with due affection, and the married couple rejoice in numerous children.

It is shameful to repeat the stories (*fabulae*) known to us, and it takes a long time to reckon the sacrilege which we learn takes place in this sort of matter, with the bones of the dead, ashes and burned coal, and with hairs from the head and from men's and women's genital areas together with threads of many colours, and with various herbs and small snails (*clocleolis*) and snakes, all put together while songs are chanted. Freed and healed from these things, thanks to the blessing of the Church, people have full enjoyment of conjugal favour and the natural debt.[704] Some men were dressed up or covered over by enchanted clothing, others were found to be driven mad by sorcerers[705] by a drink, some by food, some mesmerised by witches (*strigae*) by chants alone, and made almost enfeebled. Some men were debilitated by witches (*lamiae*) or weaving women (*feminae genichiales*), some woman are even found to have suffered sleeping with demons (*dusii*) in the shape of the men for whom they were burning in love.[706] Divine power has restored these men and women alike to health, with devilish fantasies suppressed and cast off by exorcisms and catholic remedies. There are other things which necessity compels us to investigate and to judge, which we do not want to talk about because of the abominable shamefulness. And there are other things of this sort which are wicked and villainous, which we refrain from writing here so that they cannot come to the

703 The reference to *placitum* may imply that these were some public forums for dispute settlement; such *placita* are suggested by Hincmar as necessary for judging Theutberga's case.

704 That is, are able to have intercourse with their wives. In this long section, Hincmar draws on Augustine and Isidore, but possibly adds his own material too.

705 The Latin phrase is 'a sorciariis', which could indicate either men (*sorciarii*) or women (*sorciariae*).

706 Augustine, *De civitate dei* 15, 23: 489 (Dods 1887: 303) describes 'demons, whom the Gauls call Dusii' who attempt to have intercourse with women. The idea is developed by Isidore of Seville, *Etymologiae* VIII, 11, 102–3 (Barney 2006: 190, who also discusses *lamiae*). On *dusii*, see Filotas 2005: 81–2.

attention of wicked people who perhaps might not know them.[707] And moreover we hear about so many monstrous portents of devilish working done by magical art that they exceed what can be believed.

But it is not remarkable if in these last times there come such prefigurings of the coming of the Antichrist, which the Lord and his apostles had described would come.[708] St Paul says about these: 'For the mystery of iniquity doth already work … after the working of Satan with power and signs and lying wonders' [2 Thessalonians 2:7, 9] and again 'Now the Spirit speaketh expressly, that in the latter times some shall depart from the faith, giving heed to seducing spirits, and doctrines of devils' [1 Timothy 4:1].

> 'This vanity of the magic arts, deriving from wicked angels, flourished for many centuries, <207> authored by Zoroaster the king of the Bactrians, whom Ninus the king of the Assyrians killed in battle, and it was propagated by Democritus.[709] And it was practised amongst the Assyrians by many devilish men, of whom some were so proficient in the arts of sorcery that as we said above,[710] they even resisted Moses with similar signs, turning sticks into serpents and water into blood' [Exodus 7:12, 22].[711]

And all these evildoers have one impiety [although] they have a diversity of arts and a diversity of names, just as pagan teachers and even Christians observed.

And omitting many things, let us remind ourselves of some of them:[712]

> 'There are magicians (*magi*), who are popularly called evildoers (*malefici*) because of the magnitude of their crimes. They stir up the elements, they disturb the minds of men and kill without any poisonous drink, by the violence of spells alone. There are necromancers (*necromantii*), by whose chants the dead seem to be brought back to life to make divination, and to respond to questions. There are water-magicians (*hydromantii*), who call up the shades of demons by peering into water, and see images or

707 Note Hincmar's concern not to spread sins inadvertently! See Introduction, 67.

708 Cf. above, 173. On Carolingian apocalyptic thought, especially among Church reformers, see Palmer 2014.

709 Zoroaster, the founder of the religion of Zoroastrianism, was already regarded as a magician in Roman sources, as was the ancient Greek philosopher Democritus.

710 Response 8, 172, referring to Exodus 7.

711 Isidore of Seville, *Etymologiae* VIII, 9, 1–4 (Barney 2006: 181).

712 Isidore of Seville, *Etymologiae* VIII, 9, 9–29 (Barney 2006: 182–3), though Hincmar (or the manuscript he used) has added some material (for instance the reference to animal shoulder-blades, *spatulas*), and altered what he copied. See Introduction, 67–8.

delusions of them, and claim to be able to hear things from them. There are enchanters (*incantatores*), who perform their art with words. There are soothsayers (*harioli*), who utter wicked prayers around the altars of idols, and offer dreadful sacrifices, and from these rituals receive the replies of demons. There are auspicers (*auruspices*), who watch over the times of doing business and working. They gaze upon the bowels of animals, and entrails and shoulder-blades, amongst other things, and from these predict the future. And there are augurs (*augures*), who wait upon the flights and songs of birds, of which one sort concerns vision, that is the flight of birds, the other one hearing, that is birdsong. And there are possessed women (*pythonissae*), otherwise known as ventriloquists. And there are astrologers (*astrologi*), so called because they augur from the stars. And there are some who work on dates of birth, and who track the movement of the stars for those being born, who are popularly called mathematicians (*mathematicii*). And there are horoscopers (*horoscopi*), who speculate from the time of birth with a varied and different fate. And there are interpreters of lots (*sortilogi*), who profess a knowledge of divination through things which they call the lots of the saints, under the name of a fictive devotion, or who guarantee future things by looking at various writings. And there are some who predict something fortunate or sad signified from the movement of limbs, that is the twitching of an eye or a part of some limb.'

And there are illusionists (*praestigatores*), called by another name *obstrigilii*, who hamper or restrict the sight of human eyes, like those who are said to play around with pennies (*denarii*), which is wholly devilish.[713]

And so we read that the devil first brought this forth through Mercury, which is why the inventor of it is called Mercury: and no Christian can allow this devilish work to take place in front of him, or, if he has any power over him who does these things, let him go unpunished, without sin. 'To these also belong the amulets of detestable healings, which the art of the doctors condemns, <208> whether done with chanting, or markings, or hanging things or binding them',[714] or with measuring of certain measures, and what women call in their wool-working and weaving work *superventas*.[715] 'In all these things there is demonic craft, originating from the pestilential association of men and evil angels.

713 Isidore of Seville *Etymologiae* VIII, 9, 33 (Barney 2006: 183) refers to illusionists, but Hincmar (or an intermediate source) has added the reference to coins.

714 Isidore of Seville, *Etymologiae* VIII, 9, 30 (Barney 2006: 183).

715 The meaning of the term is not clear: literally, it would be things that come upon one.

And therefore all these things should be avoided by every Christian, and totally repudiated and condemned with every curse.'[716]

And there are those who say when they go hunting that they should not meet a cleric coming towards them.[717] And there are those who make their dogs bark at a tree-trunk as if it were a beast. And there are those who observe [particular] days for the moving of a journey or the beginning of a house-building.[718] The apostle Paul considered this such a great sin that he said: 'Ye observe days, and months, and times, and years. I am afraid of you, lest I have bestowed upon you labour in vain' [Galatians 4:10]. And the Lord said in the Gospel: 'Likewise also as it was in the days of Lot. They did eat, they drank, they bought, they sold, they planted, they builded' [Luke 17:28].[719]

> 'And apart only from the terrible and unspeakable crime of the Sodomites, He [Jesus] mentioned only those things which they could have thought small or of no significance: so that you might understand what punishments illicit things receive, if licit things and those without which this life could not be led, when done immoderately, are punished by fire and sulphur. Rightly therefore the blessed Augustine, disturbed by a just grief when he saw the alluring habits of harm, exclaimed "Woe to the sins of men! We recoil only from the unaccustomed sins. But often we are forced to tolerate all accustomed sins, for which the blood of God's son was shed to wash away, even though they can be so great that they make the kingdom of heaven to be shut against them; we are forced to tolerate them all by avoiding[720] them, and by tolerating we even practise some of them. O Lord, would that we would not practise all those sins which we are not able to prohibit".'[721]

And it should be known too, as we read in the words of the doctors [of the Church], that there are demons, who as if specialising in looking out for particular sins, though they enjoy all of them, provoke men as if particularly to those over which they have control.[722] Therefore the evangelist Mark mentions that the Lord cast out seven demons

716 Isidore of Seville, *Etymologia* VIII, 9, 31 (Barney 2006: 183).

717 That is, because it is bad luck. On superstition, see Introduction, 65.

718 On beliefs in propitious days, see Filotas 2005: 135–9.

719 The next verse states: 'But the same day that Lot went out of Sodom it rained fire and brimstone from heaven, and destroyed them all.'

720 Augustine's original text read *videndo*, 'by seeing', but in the manuscript it is written as *vitando*. This was probably a simple copying error.

721 Bede, *In Lucae evangelium expositio* V, 17: 318, in turn citing Augustine, *Enchiridion de fide, spe et caritate*, c. 21: 94 (Shaw 1887: 263–4).

722 The source of this reference is not known.

from Mary, who was a sinner in the city,[723] 'so that, where sin had abounded, grace should be shown superabundantly. For the number seven is often placed to stand for everything: so it should be understood that she was cured from seven demons, that is freed from all sins.'[724] And we read, amongst the demons who are masters of the vices, about Mammon, about whom the Lord said: 'Ye cannot serve God and Mammon' [Matthew 6:24; Luke 16:13], 'for, he who serves Mammon, that is riches, assuredly serves him who is placed above these earthly things by the merit of his perversity, and who is said by the Lord to be the leader of this world.'[725] And we read about the type of demon which is released in the heat of wrath, or the voluptuousness of the flesh through enticements, or indeed in the fire of adultery, by which the hearts of the adulterous are set alight;[726] and they send the person they have invaded into the waters which are accustomed to extinguish love: that kind of demon is not able to be cast out except by prayer and fasting. And the ancient enemy [the devil] tempted the first parent of ours [Adam], as is known, 'by greed, vainglory and avarice, and by tempting overcame him, <209> so that he willingly submitted to him. Using the same means by which he laid low the first man, he failed in tempting the second [Jesus]'.[727]

And in the Psalm, we sing about 'the arrow that flieth by day' [Psalms 91:5], 'that is about the speech of heretics and philosophers, who are mouthpieces of the devil and are not able to deceive unless they should promise the light'.[728] And this sort of demon easily corrupts those who

> 'neglect their own actions, and paying attention to the actions of others, wander out of their own proper order (*ordo*), and involve themselves immoderately in external cares. And it leads on the deceived mind of such people through vain hope, so that this mind might hesitate in the intention of penance, showing to it many things spread out far and wide, so that it may receive no good afterwards, since no evils sadden it now, and so that it may then be more fully overwhelmed with punishments, which now even rejoices in its offences.'[729]

723 The references from Mark 16:9, on Mary Magdalene as having had seven demons cast out of her, and Luke 7:37–50, on the woman who washed Jesus' feet, were often combined.

724 Bede, *In Marci euangelium expositio* IV, 16, 9–10: 643.

725 Augustine, *De sermone domini in monte* II, 14, 47: 138 (Findlay 1888: 49).

726 Jerome, *Commentariorum in Matheum* III, 17, 16: 152 (Scheck 2008: 202).

727 Gregory I, *Homiliae in euangelia* 16, 2–3: 111–12 (shortened) (Hurst 1990: 102–3).

728 Pseudo-Jerome, *Breviarium in Psalmos* 90, 6: col. 1098.

729 Gregory I, *Regula pastoralis* III, 29: II, 472 (Barmby 1895: 60), loosely quoted.

[We sing about] 'the troubles that walketh in darkness', that is the preference for denial and lies; 'the attack', that is of headlong haste and fear; and the 'noonday devil' [Psalms 91:6], that is sloth (*accedia*), which makes the fervour of devotion undertaken grow lukewarm, and the heretics blaze with love of pretended right intention and vanity of works of light. About this demon is written: 'He lieth under the shadow, in the covert of the reed, and in moist places' [Job 40:16],

> '"under the shadow", that is in dark consciences; "in the covert of the reed", that which is shining on the outside, but empty within; "in moist places", that is he insinuates pretences into softened and lascivious minds. And this sort of demon, leaving a man at the time of baptism, or after the fruits of penance and the grace of reconciliation, goes and finds seven other spirits worse than he. He comes to the house of the man he left, and finding it "empty, swept and garnished" [Matthew 12:44] – "swept" that is from the initial sins through baptism or penance, "empty" of good actions through negligence, and "garnished" with pretended virtues through hypocrisy – and he and the spirits worse than he whom he brought along enter in and live there. Through the seven evil spirits are signified all vices.[730] For whomsoever heretical wickedness or worldly cupidity seize after baptism, soon he falls into the depths of all vices. And rightly worse spirits are said to enter him, since he will not only have those seven vices which are the opposites to the seven spiritual virtues, but he will also through hypocrisy pretend to have those virtues. And as it is narrated in Isaiah that the seven spirits of virtue descended upon the rod of the root of Jesse and the flower which grew from that root [Isaiah 11:1–3], so in the opposite way the number of vices is consecrated in the devil.'[731]

And there are other types of demons which we read are constituted by their prince for particular vices, which we shall not mention here. We shall take care to mention only those demons who are in charge of fornication, to show how there are even types of demons who delight in fornication so much that they even seek to sleep with humans. We would be able to talk about some things of this sort which happened in our time, except that for the sake of brevity we shall pass over them.[732] And so that what we say can be better believed, let whoever doubts about these things read what St Amphilocius, bishop of Iconium, whom

730 On the early medieval classification of the virtues and the vices (which counted either seven or eight principal vices), see Newhauser 1993.

731 Bede, *In Lucae evangelium expositio* IV, 11, 24: 235–6 (shortened).

732 It is regrettable that Hincmar chose not to give more details, but it is interesting that he does not seem to have thought these incidents particularly important. See Introduction, 67–9.

St Jerome recorded in his book *On Illustrious Men* with appropriate veneration, wrote about the wonderful virtues of Basil, bishop of Caesarea, saying:[733]

> <210> 'Elladius, who saw him ⌜Basil⌝ of most holy memory, who was made by him a minister of perfect miracles, and who was the successor to his see after the death of this apostolic Basil, a marvellous man and decorated with every virtue, told me what follows. A certain faithful senator called Proterius went to the holy and venerable places, wishing to consecrate his daughter there, and to place her in one of the more active monasteries, to offer thereby a sacrifice to God. But at once the murdering devil, jealous of the divine will, moved one of the senator's servants (*servi*) and ignited him with love for the girl.[734] This man, since he was unworthy of this sort of endeavour and did not dare to approach the task, spoke to one of the abominable enchanters (*incantatores*), promising him to pay a great quantity of gold if he could have power over (*dominari*) this girl. The sorcerer (*maleficus*) said to him, "O man, I cannot prevail in this matter, but if you want, I will send you to the devil who is my overseer (*procurator*), and he will carry out your will." He said to him, "Whatever you say to me, I will do." And the sorcerer said to him, "Will you renounce Christ in writing?" And he replied, "Yes." And the worker of iniquity said to him, "If you are prepared for this, I will be your fellow worker." And he said to him, "I am prepared, I shall pursue my only desire."
>
> And the minister of wickedness wrote a letter to the devil and sent it, with this meaning: "Since it behoves me, O Lord and overseer, to hasten to take people away from the devotion of the Christians and to lead them to your will, so that your share may be multiplied, I have sent you this man, who carries these my letters. He burns with desire for a girl, and I request that he may follow through with that deed, so that I may glory in him, and with great alacrity I may gather together those pleasing to you." And giving him the letter, he said, "Go at such a time of night, stand upon the monument of the gentiles, and raise this paper (*charta*) in the air, and there will stand around you those who can take you to

733 Pseudo-Amphilochius of Iconium, *Vita sancti Basilii*, c. 11: 188–97. On this text, see Wortley 1980, suggesting that the Greek text was compiled in Italy around 800 from earlier legends, and that a Latin version of it may already have been circulating north of the Alps in the first half of the ninth century, since Paschasius Radbertus cites a different story from the *Vita*. The story of Proterius's servant was also known to Hrotsvit a of Gandersheim and may have been the origin of the Faust legend (see Wortley 1980: 222, 228).

734 The man is referred to as both a *servus* and a *puer*, suggesting lowly status, but it is not absolutely certain that he was unfree. In ninth-century Francia, marriage of a free woman to an unfree man could threaten her own any children's claim to freedom. In any case, it would have been seen as a shameful relationship: see Hammer 1995.

the devil." He did this eagerly and cast his wretched voice into the air, calling on the devil's assistance. And at once, there were princes of the shadowy power there around him, evil spirits, and taking this erring man with great joy they led him to where the devil was, and they showed to him the devil, sitting on a high seat, and around him were standing wicked spirits. And taking the letters sent from the sorcerer, the devil said to the wretch, "Do you believe in me?" and he said, "I believe." "And do you deny your Christ?" And he replied, "I deny Him." And the devil said to him, "You Christians are treacherous (*perfidi*). When you have something for me to do, you come to me, but when your desire has been achieved, you deny me and you go to your Christ, who is kind and merciful and who accepts you. But make for me a signed attestation (*manuscripta*) of a willing renunciation of your Christ and baptism, and of a willing profession of my things in the world. Then you will be with me in the Day of Judgement, enjoying with me the prepared eternal torments: and I will at once fulfil your desire." And he drew up with his own hand the attestation as he had been asked.

At once the corrupter of souls, the contorted serpent, sent demons who are in charge of fornication, and they inflamed the girl with love for the young man. She threw herself to the ground, <211> and began to cry out "Pity me, pity me, Father, for I am horribly tortured on account of that boy (*puer*) of ours! Pity me from your innards, show to me, your only daughter, your paternal love, and join me to the boy, whom I love! If you do not want to do this, you will soon see me dying a bitter death, and you will account for me on God's judgement day." The father said with tears, "O alas for me, a sinner, what has happened to my wretched daughter? Who has stolen my treasure? Who has mistreated my daughter? Who has put out the sweet light of my eyes? I wanted to marry you to Christ the celestial bridegroom, I was hurrying to make you a fellow dweller with the angels, to sing psalms, hymns and spiritual songs to God, and I hoped to be saved through you. Have you gone mad in a lascivious love? Unless I betroth you to God, just as I want, will you not lead me in my old age to hell with distress, and cover over the nobility of our kin with confusion?" But the girl thought nothing of the things said by her father, and kept on crying out, "O father, do what I want or soon you will see me dying." The father, brought to great weakness and overwhelmed with an immeasurable sadness, believed the advice of his friends encouraging him to defer to her will or to abandon her. He ordered the ardent desire of the girl to be fulfilled, so that she should not give herself over to death. And he brought the boy she sought to his own daughter, and giving them all his wealth, he said to his daughter, "Farewell, truly wretched daughter. Very soon you will wail in repentance, when you have profited nothing."

Once the unjust marriage was carried out and the devil's wicked work completed, and a little time had passed, it was noticed by some that the boy did not enter into church, and did not approach the immortal and life-giving mysteries.[735] And they said to his wretched spouse, "Do you know that the husband you chose is not a Christian, but is a wanderer in faith and a stranger (*alienus*)?" Filled with dark and miserable thoughts, she threw herself to the ground, and began to scratch herself with her nails, and to beat her breast and cry out, "No one was ever saved who did not obey his parents. Who will announce my confusion to my father? O wretched me, that I have fallen to such a depth of perdition! Why was I born, why once born was I not immediately carried off?" Her husband, wholly gone astray, hearing that she was lamenting these things, ran to her, telling her that this was not the truth of things. She was consoled by his persuasive speech, and said to him, "If you wish to satisfy me, and to pity my soul, then tomorrow you and I will go together to church, and you will participate in the uncontaminated mysteries: then I will be satisfied." Then under compulsion, he told her the sentence of his decree. At once she laid aside her womanly infirmity,[736] and giving good advice to him, she ran to Basil the shepherd and disciple of Christ, enemy of impiety, and cried out, "Have pity on wretched me, holy man of God! Pity me, disciple of the Lord, for I have dealt with demons, have pity on wretched me who did not obey my own father." And she told him the story of what had happened.

The holy man of God called the boy and asked him if things were this way. He said tearfully to the saint, "Yes, holy man of God: even if I am silent, my deeds will cry out." And he told to him the wicked work of the devil from the beginning through to the final end. Then the saint said to him, "Do you wish to return to the Lord our God?" To this the boy said, "Certainly I wish it, but I am not able to." And Basil said "Why is that?" The boy replied, "I denied Christ in writing, and professed the devil." Basil said to him, "Do not worry about that. Our God is kind, and he will accept your repentance. He has compassion for our wickedness." And the girl, throwing herself at the feet of the holy evangelist, begged him, "O disciple of Christ our God, help us as much as you can!" And the holy man said to the boy, "Do you believe you are saved?" The boy said, "Lord, I believe, help thou my unbelief" [Mark 9:23]. And Basil at once took his hand, and making the sign of Christ on him and praying, he shut him away in an inner place of the holy enclosure. And giving him a rule (*regula*),[737] he worked with him for three days. <212> After

735 That is, he did not take communion.

736 Female inferiority is not shown as an impermeable barrier: right belief can overcome it.

737 That is, a pattern of behaviour akin to a monastic rule.

this he came to him, and asked "How are you, my son?" And he replied, "I am in great despondency, saint of God: I cannot bear their shouting, their threats and their throwing of stones. They hold my attestation and dispute it with me, telling me 'You came to us, not we to you'." And the holy man said to him, "Do not fear, my son, only believe." And giving him a little food, and again making the sign of Christ over him, and praying, he shut him up again. And after a few days, he visited him and said, "How are you, my son?" And he replied, "Holy father, I hear their shouts and threats from a distance, but I cannot see them." And again giving him food, and praying, he shut the door and went away. And on the fortieth day he returned and said to him, "How are you, brother?" And he replied: "I am well, saint of God. I saw you fighting for me today in a vision, conquering the devil."

Soon afterwards the saint, uttering a prayer according to custom, led him out, and brought him to his dormitory. The next day, he called his holy clergy and the monasteries[738] and the whole people pleasing to Christ, and said to them, "O dearest little sons, all give thanks to God! Behold, the good shepherd must carry the lost sheep on his shoulders and bring him to church. Therefore we also must keep watch at night, and beg his Kindness, that the corruptor of souls may not conquer in this matter." And at once the people, brought together, prayed to God the whole night, with the good shepherd, shouting with tears for him, "Kyrie eleison [Lord, have mercy]." And soon the holy man, with the whole multitude of the people, took the boy, and holding him by the right hand, led him into the holy church of God with psalms and hymns.

And behold! The devil who bewitches the unsaddened (*intristis*) life of all with every destructive strength came and, invisibly holding the boy, tried to take him from the saint's hand. And the boy began to shout, "Saint of God, help me!" And the Wicked One attacked with such force, that he dragged the remarkable man as well as the boy. And the saint turned and said to the devil, "Most wicked corrupter of souls, father of shadows and perdition, is your own perdition not enough for you, which you have brought upon yourself and those who are under you, that you should also tempt the creature of my God?" The devil said to him, "You are being prejudiced towards me, Basil", just as many of us heard the voices of demons saying this while the people shouted "Kyrie eleison." The saint of God said to him, "May the Lord rebuke you, O devil." And he replied saying, "Basil, you are being prejudiced towards me. I did not go to him, but he came to me, and he denied Christ and professed me. And see, I have his attestation, and on the Day of Judgement, I will lead him to the Judge of all." And the saint of God said, "Blessed is the Lord

738 That is, the monks under his control.

> my God; may the people not turn aside their hands from the heights of heaven until you return that attestation." And turning, he said to the people, "Raise your hands to heaven, and shout with tears, 'O Christ, Kyrie eleison'."
>
> And the people stood for a long time, with their hands stretched out to heaven, and behold, the attribution of the boy fell through the air, and was seen by all, and came and was placed into the hands of our memorable father and shepherd.[739] Taking it and thanking God, he was made most joyful, and in the presence of the whole people, he said to the boy, "Do you recognise these little letters, brother?" And he said to him "Yes, saint of God, that is my attestation." And St Basil ripped it up, and led him into church, and made him worthy for the holy ministry and communion of the mysteries and gifts of Christ. And by a great undertaking, he comforted the people, and he led out the boy; and instructing him and giving him a fitting rule, he returned him to his wife, glorifying and praising God with a mouth that could not be silenced. Amen.'

<213> And the venerable priest Bede said in the third book of the commentary on the Gospel of Luke:[740] 'And Jesus asked him, saying: What is thy name? And he said: Legion: because many devils were entered into him' [Luke 8:30].

> 'He did not ask him his name because he did not know it, but so that the virtue of the healer would shine out more gratefully, when the plague that the madman was enduring had confessed. And priests in our times, who know how to cast out demons by the grace of exorcism, often say that patients cannot be cured, unless they openly confess everything they can know that they have suffered from the wicked spirits, in sight, hearing, taste, smell, touch, or in whatever other bodily or spiritual senses, awake or sleeping. And especially in cases when demons which the Gauls call *dusii*[741] appear either to men in female shape or to women in male garb, and seek (through an unspeakable miracle) intercourse of an incorporeal spirit with a human body and claim that they have carried it out, the priests demand that both the name of the demon, by which he said he should be called, and the form of the oaths they swore to each other in a pact of love, should be revealed.
>
> There was a matter very similar to this deceit, but true, indeed, and well known by the attestation of many: a certain priest, a neighbour of mine [Bede], told that he had begun to cure a certain nun from a demon, but as long as the details were hidden, he was not able to get anywhere.

739 One might compare here the tradition of letters from heaven: see Haines 2010.

740 Bede, *In Lucae evangelium expositio* III, 8, 30: 184–5.

741 See above, n. 706.

But when she confessed by what phantom she was being troubled, he soon drove it off with prayers and other types of purification, as was fitting. And he healed the woman's body from the ulcers which she had contracted from the devil's touch with medicinal care, by applying salt which had been blessed. But one of these ulcers, which was deeper in her side, he was not able to close off, but it kept on opening up. And he asked her whom he wanted to cure for advice on how she might be cured.[742] She said, "If you sprinkle the oil consecrated for the sick with the same medicine and anoint me in this fashion, I will be at once restored to health. For I once saw, through the spirit, in a certain city far away which I have never seen with earthly eyes, a certain girl labouring under a similar affliction, who was cured in this way by a priest." And he did as she suggested, and at once the ulcer took the remedy which it had previously refused. I took care to mention this briefly against demonic tricks, so that you may understand that the Lord did not ask the spirit he was about to eject for its name in vain.'

Question 16

About that question which was posed: 'What might be the reason that God, as is said, often allows these things to happen in legitimate marriage?'[743]

Response 16

It should be known that since a good marriage is instituted by God, and 'every sin exists not by its own nature – for evil has no substance, but rather', as we said above, 'strikes root however it can in good nature'[744] – so for the sake of our sins, wickedness happens in the good of marriage by the working of the devil.[745] In the same way, good land belongs to the Lord, since it is created by a good God, and our iniquities are our own, and often through our iniquities we see and feel the land of the Lord wasting away. In anger, He promised that we would have an iron land and a bronze heaven [Deuteronomy 28:23], <214> and when mollified He promised that He would give us 'the first rain and the latter rain of the land' [Deuteronomy 11:14], and that 'the heaven will give

742 As in the story from the *Vita sancti Basilii*, a woman is able to provide good advice to a man.

743 See above, Question 13: 221. Hincmar frequently refers to the question of why God allows actions by evil spirits: see Introduction, 66–7.

744 Gregory I, *Moralia in Iob* XXVI, 37, 68: III, 1317 (Bliss 1844: III, 184).

745 On evil as privation, see above, Response 4: 126.

rain and the earth will bring forth its fruits' [James 5:13]: not so that the nature of created things will be changed, but because according to the difference of merits, when God is angry or pleased, so we feel His vengeance or His grace upon us.

And St Gregory said in his second book on *Morals*:[746] 'By a hidden judgement, permission is given to wicked spirits, that those whom they strangle willingly in a noose of sin, they might drag even unwillingly to the punishment of sin.' And Augustine wrote in the first book of his *On Marriage and Concupiscence*:[747]

> 'Whoever wonders that God's creature is subjected to the devil, should not wonder. For one creature of God is in subjection to another creature of God, the lesser to the greater, that is a human being to an angelic one; and, not owing to nature, but to vice, the unclean to the unclean .... For the devil is himself an unclean spirit: good, indeed, so far as he is a spirit, but evil as being unclean; for by nature he is a spirit, by vice an unclean one. Of these two [qualities], the one is from God, the other from himself. He does not hold humans therefore, whether of an advanced age or in infancy, because they are human, but because they are unclean.'

And in his book *On Grace and Freewill*, he says:[748]

> 'This ought to be fixed and immovable in your heart, that there is no injustice in God. Therefore, whenever you read in the Scriptures of Truth that people are led astray or that their hearts are blunted and hardened by God, never doubt that some evil faults of their own have first occurred, so that they justly suffer these things. Thus you will not run against that proverb of Solomon: "The foolishness of man perverteth his ways, and his heart fretteth against the Lord"' [Proverbs 19:3].

Question 17

About that question which was posed:[749] 'If perhaps these sorcerers (*malefici*) or female enchanters (*incantatrices feminae*) are found, what should be done about it?'[750]

746 Gregory I, *Moralia in Iob* II, 20, 38: I, 83 (Bliss 1844: I, 95).

747 Augustine, *De nuptiis et concupiscentia* I, 23: 238–9 (rearranged) (Holmes 1887: 274).

748 Augustine, *De gratia et libero arbitrio* 21, 43: col. 909 (Holmes 1887: 463).

749 See above, Question 13: 221.

750 See Introduction, 67–9 on magic.

Response 17

St Leo, writing to the bishops throughout the provinces, shows this:[751]

> 'A good many sorcerers (*malefici*),[752] however, who had so deeply involved themselves that no remedy from those helping could assist them, have been subjected to the laws according to the constitutions of the Christian princes, and lest they should pollute the holy flock by their contagion, have been banished into perpetual exile by public judges.'

And a little later:

> 'For we cannot otherwise rule those entrusted to us unless we pursue with the zeal of the Lord's faith those who are both destroyers and destroyed: and with the severity we can bring to bear, cut them off from intercourse with healthy minds, lest this pestilence spread much wider. Wherefore I exhort your Affection, I beseech and warn you to remain alert with that care you ought and are able to employ in tracking them down, lest they find opportunity of concealment anywhere. For as he who diligently carries out what conduces to the salvation of the people committed to him will have a due reward of remuneration from God; so before the Lord's judgement seat no one will be able to excuse himself from a charge of negligence who has not been willing to guard his people against the propagators of a sacrilegious belief.'[753]

<215> And St Gregory wrote to Cyprian the deacon:[754]

> 'The most holy man Maximian our co-bishop desired to purge the Church of God of wicked men, and was praiseworthily concerned about the lives of clerics, as you know. While he was vigilantly watching over their actions with pastoral care, he learned that some had been stained by witchcraft (*maleficium*), popularly called *canterma*, and these he gave to be kept in custody, just as the letter of your Affection informed me. However, because for the sake of our sins he was prevented by death from being able to avenge this crime, it is necessary that your Affection hurry to investigate this with every subtlety, and to take care to punish them according to the enormity of the crime, as the above mentioned bishop from zeal for God's sake for correction and justice would have done in this vengeance, if he were alive. Let your Affection with every virtue and

751 Leo I, *Epistola* 7 to the bishops of Italy (J 405), cc. 1–2: cols 621–2 (shortened) (Feltoe 1895: 6–7).

752 Hincmar changes the Manicheans of Leo's original letter into sorcerers. Presumably Hincmar regards any users of evil forces as equivalent to 'propagators of a sacrilegious belief'.

753 On negligence, see Introduction, 72.

754 Gregory I, *Registrum* V, 32 (J 1347): I, 299–300 (Martyn 2004: II, 344–5). Cyprian was the administrator of the papal patrimony in Sicily.

> every haste take care to show almighty God your zeal in this matter, and to display to his enemies a fitting opposition by the retribution inflicted. So that what is written may be fulfilled: "Do I not hate them, O Lord, that hate thee: and pined away because of thy enemies?" [Psalms 139:21]. If your Affection is set alight with this zeal, let punishment be shown against those who left God and acted against Him with sorcery. But if you cannot follow this through rightly there, then people like this should be sent to us, if however it can be shown here how they can be convicted without difficulty there.[755] But because I think this is impossible, a strict and severe punishment by you ought to happen there.'

And to Januarius, the bishop of Sardinia:[756]

> 'We exhort your Fraternity to keep watch in pastoral care more vigilantly against worshippers of idols and of auspicers (*haruspices*) and soothsayers (*sortilegi*), and publicly to preach to the people against men of this sort, and to call them back by persuasive exhortation from the blemish of such a disastrous sacrilege, the application of divine judgement, and from the danger of this present life. If, however, you find that they are unwilling to amend and reprove themselves in this way, then we want you to seize them with fervent zeal. And if they are slaves, punish them with whipping and tortures, so that they may be able to come to emendation; and if they are free, let them be led to penance by a suitable imprisonment and punishment.[757] So that for those who disdain to listen to salutary words calling them back from peril of death, at least torture of their body will be able to lead them to the desired health of mind.'

And it is written in the canonical edict:[758] 'If anyone pays attention to prophets (*harioli*), soothsayers (*haruspicii*) or enchanters (*incantatorii*), or makes use of their amulets, let him be anathema. And everyone responded thrice: "Let him be anathema".' And in the Council of Ancyra, chapter 23:[759]

> 'Those who seek divinations and follow them in the fashion of the gentiles, or who bring these sort of men into their houses for finding out something by a wicked art or for atoning for something, let them lie

755 Judicial cases from the provinces being dealt with at Rome inevitably brought problems in assembling accusers and witnesses: see Stone 2015: 13 on Hincmar's complaints.

756 Gregory I, *Registrum* IX, 205 (J 1731): II, 764 (Martyn 2004: II, 671). Note the distinction between punishments for the free and unfree, and that Gregory here approves torture, which in other circumstances he worries about (see Response 12: 203).

757 On coercive penance, see Introduction, 40.

758 Council of Rome 721, c. 12: col. 264.

759 Council of Ancyra 314, c. 23: 113 (Percival 1900: 74).

under the rule for a five-year period, according to the established grades of penance.'

And from the Council of Braga, chapter 70:[760] 'If anyone following the customs of the pagans introduces magicians or soothsayers into his home, as if to put an evil outside or to find enchantments, or to perform pagan sacrifices, <216> let them do penance for five years.' And in chapter 71:

> 'Christians are not allowed to observe the traditions of the gentiles, or to honour the elements or the path of the moon or the stars, or the deception of portents for building a house or for planting of crops or trees or the union of marriages. For it is written: "Whatsoever ye do in word or in deed, do all in the name of our Lord Jesus Christ, giving thanks to God"' [Colossians 3:17].

And in chapter 72: 'It is not allowed to pay attention in the collecting of medicinal herbs to any observances or incantations, except those of the holy [Apostles'] Creed and the Lord's prayer, so that only God and the Lord may be honoured.' And in chapter 73: 'Christian women are not allowed to respect any vanity in their wool-working, but let them invoke God as their helper, who gave to them the wisdom of weaving.'[761] And in the Council of Carthage, chapter 89, 'Anyone paying attention to auguries (*augurii*) or enchantments (*incantationes*) must be separated from the society of the Church, like those adhering to Jewish superstitions and celebrations.' → And in the first book of the imperial capitularies:[762] 'That people are not permitted to become magicians (*cauclearii*), sorcerers (*malefici*) and enchanters (*incantatores*), who it is clear are terribly damned, as with Simon Magus.' ← And in the Council of Elvira, chapter 6, 'If anyone kills someone else by witchcraft (*maleficium*), which he could not do without idolatry, he will not receive communion even on his deathbed.'[763]

760 In fact, the four canons following are taken from Martin of Braga, *Canones ex orientalium patrum synodis*: 140–1 (with slightly altered numbering), a translation of Eastern canons. On Martin's interests in pagan customs, see Filotas 2005: 48–9.

761 Cf. the reference to connections between magical practices and weaving women in Response 15: 237 and 239. Note that various practices are acceptable provided it is God who is invoked: see Introduction, 65.

762 Ansegis, *Capitularia* I, c. 21: 451, following the *Admonitio generalis* 789, c. 18 (MGH *Capit.* I, no. 22: 55), which cites the Council of Laodicia, c. 36. For some reason, Hincmar omits the reference to female enchanters (*incantatrices*) in Ansegis's text. On Simon Magus, see Acts 8:9–24.

763 Council of Elvira, c. 6: 3 (Laeuchli 1972: 127).

And it should be known that this severity of punishment by the Council of Elvira towards those who do not come to their senses will have to be observed: but according to the decrees of the blessed Celestine:[764] 'Final penance should not be denied to anyone repenting', and as the great Pope Leo decreed:[765]

> 'neither should satisfaction be forbidden, nor reconciliation and the grace of communion be denied, to those who in a time of necessity and in the pressure of great danger beg for the protection of penance and then reconciliation: even if they have lost their voice, if they can be shown to ask for it through indications of unimpaired understanding. And if they are so burdened by some illness that what they had demanded a little before, they are at that moment no longer able to signify, then the witness of those believers standing around them must profit them, and at once let the benefit of penance and reconciliation follow on – saving, however, the rules of the canons concerning those persons who sin in their forsaking of the Lord's faith.'

'In general, let the giving of the grace of communion not be denied to all those whoever they are on the threshold of death who ask for it',[766] as the Nicene synod defined, 'whose conversion is to be gauged more in their mind than in time',[767] since for God, 'true conversion suffers no delay in mercy.'[768] <217> 'The prophet attests this too, saying "If you are converted and groan out, then you will be saved" ⌈Isaiah 30:15⌉.'[769] And in the Nicene Council:[770] 'And in all things it is fitting to explore the intention and appearance of the penitents, as many show their conversion in thought and with tears, patience and good works, without simulation.' And a little later, 'After this ⌈exploration⌉, the bishop will be allowed to consider these matters more humanely.' And in the Council of Ancyra:[771] 'The bishops testing the form of their conversion will have the power of either acting more humanely towards

764 Celestine I, *Epistola* 4 to the bishops of Vienne and Narbonne (J 369), c. 2: cols 431–2. On this letter, see Firey 2009: 104.

765 Leo I, *Epistola* 108 to Theodore of Fréjus (J 485), c. 5: cols 1013–14 (Feltoe 1895: 80).

766 Council of Nicaea 325, c. 13: 12 (Percival 1900: 29).

767 Celestine I, *Epistola* 4 to the bishops of Vienne and Narbonne (J 369), c. 2: col. 432.

768 Leo I, *Epistola* 108 to Theodore of Fréjus (J 485), c. 4: col. 1013 (Feltoe 1895: 80).

769 Celestine I, *Epistola* 4 to the bishops of Vienne and Narbonne (J 369), c. 2: col. 432. The biblical quotation is here given in the Vetus Latina version, as used by Celestine.

770 Council of Nicaea, c. 12: 12 (Percival 1900: 27).

771 Council of Ancyra 314, c. 4: 69 (*Dionysio-Hadriana* version) (Percival 1900: 64).

them or adding more time.' And the reader will find sufficient material in the fifth chapter of this council and in other councils.

And Pope Innocent wrote to Decentius, bishop of Gubbio:

> 'About penitents, whether they are doing penance for more serious or for slighter offences. If no sickness intervenes, the custom of the Roman Church says that they should be forgiven on the fifth week-day before Easter.[772] But it is for the priest [*sacerdos*] to judge, by estimating the weight of the crimes. He should listen carefully to the confession of the penitent, and his tears and crying as he is set right, and should order him to be released when he has observed a suitable satisfaction. If anyone is struck by illness and comes to despair, alleviation is to be given to him before the period of Easter, so that he will not depart this world without communion.'[773]

Question 18

> 'In the seventh chapter, we ask to be informed as follows. If this often-mentioned woman [Theutberga] again comes to judgement, and is found innocent, would her husband have to return to her, or could he unite with someone else? And if she is found guilty of those crimes which are ascribed to her, tell us whether the king could be joined (*coniungi*) to another woman. And if such matters are also ascribed to the king himself, for which he ought to do public penance, tell us also whether that king could take a legitimate wife following public penance, after she [Theutberga] has been found to be guilty.[774] And tell us whether, if she has been legally rejected, the king could, after penance and if he so wishes, take the concubine [Waldrada] in marriage,[775] whom he kept and with whom he is said to have committed adultery after the marriage [with Theutberga] was initiated.'[776]

Response 18

About what is asked: 'If this often-mentioned woman again comes to judgement, and is found innocent, would her husband have to return

772 That is, on Maundy Thursday (counting Sunday as the first day of the week). On rites of reconciliation, see Meens 2014: 148.

773 Innocent I, Letter to Decentius of Gubbio (J 311): 28–30 (Connell 2010: 44).

774 This question makes explicit an issue already raised in Question 13: 221, that Lothar's adultery should be regarded as a public sin, and hence requires public penance: see Introduction, 41 and 56.

775 Waldrada's name is never mentioned in the text, but it is clear that she is referred to here.

776 One of the key questions thus becomes whether Lothar's marriage to Theutberga has yet ended. If it has not, then even if they are separated, Lothar is still guilty of adultery if he sleeps with Waldrada. See Introduction, 56.

to her, or could he unite with someone else?' It is superfluous to repeat what we have shown above:[777] that if she was innocent before the marriage was legally initiated, and she should be found to have kept faith with her husband once legally married, then according to the Gospel and apostolic truth, the laws of the Church and catholic doctrine, a legitimate marriage may not be separated. And if they are separated, they should either remain unmarried or else be reconciled with each other.

But lest we should leave this repeated question empty: if she should be found innocent of that about which she is accused, <218> the Lord said through Moses in the Book of Deuteronomy: 'If a man find a damsel that is a virgin' and what follows up to 'he may not put her away all his days' [Deuteronomy 22:28–29].[778] And St Augustine says, expounding on this sentence:[779]

> 'It is rightly questioned whether there should be this punishment, that he may not put aside for all time her whom he wrongly and illicitly violated. For if we should wish to understand from that that she cannot, that is should not, be put aside for all time, because she has been made his wife, this runs against the fact that Moses permitted the giving of a booklet of repudiation, and sending [the wife] away [Deuteronomy 24:1]. But for those who corrupt illicitly, he was unwilling to allow this, lest he [the violator] should be seen to make a mockery, and more to have pretended that he has taken her as a wife, than really and acceptably to have taken her. And this was commanded about the woman, whom a husband accused of not being a virgin, about which it was written, as we have said above, "and he shall have her to wife, and he may not put her away all the days of his life"' [Deuteronomy 22:19].

And St Augustine also said about this sentence:[780]

> 'It is sufficiently clear here how far the law wants women to be subjected to men, and wives to be almost servants (*famulae*):[781] that when the husband gives testimony against his wife, by which she should be stoned if this is demonstrated to be true, yet he in turn is not stoned if this is shown to be false, but only castigated and fined, and commanded and ordered to

777 Response 5: 130–140.

778 The passage in question states that a man who has intercourse (whether by force or not) with a virgin who is not betrothed must marry her and cannot subsequently repudiate her. The whole response is used more to demonstrate Hincmar's knowledge of sources than to answer the question again, since neither of the quotations from Augustine is relevant to this particular case.

779 Augustine, *Quaestionum in heptateuchum libri septem* V, 34: 294.

780 Augustine, *Quaestionum in heptateuchum libri septem* V, 33: 293–4.

781 Hincmar sees wives as having a higher status than Augustine does: see Introduction, 51–2.

adhere to her for ever, whom he wanted to be without. But in other matters, he who harms someone by bearing false witness, through which, were it proven, that one would be killed, is to be punished with the same penalty as the other one would have been, had it been true' [Deuteronomy 19:18–19].

Question 19

Concerning what is asked:[782] 'And if she is found guilty of those crimes of which she is accused, tell us whether the same king is able to be joined to another woman': we have already responded to this in part above,[783] but it does not displease me to repeat it now.

Response 19[784]

Clearly if it is found according to Christian laws, that is secular (*forenses*) and ecclesiastical ones, that this union was not a legal one, then let St Gregory's decision to Felix, bishop of Sicily be held, which said:[785] 'We read that formerly it was constituted by the holy Fathers that incestuous people (*incestuosi*) were not to be reckoned by the name of marriage.' And St Ambrose on the first letter to the Corinthians says:[786]

> 'For a brother or sister is not under servitude in such cases. That is, the reverence of marriage is not owed to him who would appal the Author of marriage. A marriage is not valid (*ratum*) which is without devotion to God, and so there is no sin for the person who is abandoned because of God, if he joins himself to someone else. The insult to the Creator dissolves the law (*ius*) of marriage around him who is abandoned, so that if joined to another he should not be accused. But the unfaithful man (*infidelis*)[787] who leaves is understood to sin both against God and against marriage, since he was unwilling to have a marriage under devotion to God. Therefore

782 Question 18: 254.

783 Response 5: 138–44.

784 In the chapter list at the beginning of the treatise (Böhringer 1992: 104), Hincmar summarises this chapter as permitting Lothar's remarriage. 'If it is found that according to Christian laws, civil and ecclesiastical, that the union (*coniunctio*) was not legal, but was rather incest and not worthy of the name of marriage, he will be able to [marry another woman].'

785 Pseudo-Gregory, Letter to Felix of Messina (J †1334): 751, cited above, Response 12: 219. On the significance of this passage, see Introduction, 62.

786 Ambrosiaster, *Commentarius in Epistolam I ad Corinthios* 7, 15: II, 77–8 (Bray 2009: 151–2), also cited above, Response 12: 219. The passage under discussion is St Paul's comment on marriages between Christians and unbelievers: Hincmar's point is that if a marriage has offended God, it may be possible to dissolve it.

787 The Latin term *infidelis* blurs the distinction between 'unbeliever' [in God] and 'unfaithful' [to one's spouse].

there is no need to keep the pledge of marriage to him who left so as not to hear about the Governor of Christians, the God of his spouse. For if Ezra ordered unbelieving wives or husbands to be sent away, so that God might be propitiated, nor angered if they took others from their stock[788] – for it was not ordered to those, that once these had been sent back they might not marry others – how much more, if the unbelieving husband leaves, will she not have free will, if she wishes to marry a man of her law? <219> That should not be reckoned a marriage which was made outside the decree of God; but after he [the husband] recognises and regrets that he has sinned, let him amend himself so that he may deserve mercy. If, however, both believe, their union is confirmed through the recognition of God. For "God has called us to live in peace" [1 Corinthians 7:15]. Truly it is not fitting to take legal action against him who leaves, since he leaves with the hatred of God, and through this is not worthy to be kept.'

→ And here St Augustine in his book to Pollentius:[789] 'Rightly, at the Lord's command, the sons of Israel sent away the wives they had married against His prohibition', for "whatsoever is not of faith is sin" [Romans 14:23].' And the reader will be able to find more things in these books. ←

And in the Council of Agde it is written: 'We reserve absolutely no mercy for those joined together incestuously, unless they heal their adultery with a separation. But incestuous marriages are not to be reckoned by the name of marriage; it is deadly even to designate them [by the name of marriage].'[790] And a little later, 'Indeed, those to whom an illicit union is forbidden have the freedom of entering into a better marriage.'

Question 20

Concerning what is asked:[791] 'And tell us also, if such matters are also ascribed to the king himself, about which he ought to do public penance, whether after she [Theutberga] has been found to be guilty, that king could take a legitimate wife after public penance.'

788 Ezra 10:10–17, in which after the Israelites' return from exile, Ezra orders them to separate from their foreign wives.

789 Augustine, *De adulterinis coniugiis* I, 18: 367 (Wilcox *et al.* 1955: 84). Note that Hincmar continued to add material that might have strengthened Lothar's case.

790 Council of Epaon 517, c. 30: 31 (identified as Council of Agde 506, c. 61), also cited in Response 12: 220. On the significance of this (adapted) quotation, see Introduction, 62.

791 Question 18: 254.

Response 20

St Leo the Pope responded to Rusticus, bishop of Narbonne, saying:[792]

> 'If a young man (*in adolescentia*)[793] under either the fear of death or the dangers of captivity has urgently done penance, and afterwards, fearing to fall into youthful incontinence, has chosen the bond (*copula*) of a wife lest he should be guilty of fornication, he seems to have committed a pardonable act, so long as he has known no woman whatever save his wife. Yet here we do not set out a rule, but weigh what is more tolerable. For according to a true view of the matter, nothing better suits him who has done penance than continued chastity (*castitas*) both of mind and body.'

And in the Council of Toledo, chapter 8:[794]

> 'It is the decision of the old and most holy father Pope Leo, that he who has come to the remedy of penance as a young man (*in etate adolescentiae*) in fear of death, if as a married man he was perhaps incontinent, <220> he should return to his previous marriage, so that he may not afterwards incur the fault of adultery, until he may be able with maturity of age to attain the state of continence.[795] What we decree for men, we decree also for women in the same way, not indeed as a general and legitimate precept, but established by us as an indulgence for human frailty.[796] And only on this condition, that if the person who is not given over to the laws of penance should depart this life first, before returning to their agreed continence, then it is not permitted to the survivor to pass over to the embraces of a wife.[797] If the survivor in this life is the person who did not receive the blessing of penance, then let this person marry if he is not able to contain himself, and enjoy the union of another wife. It is clear that we have decreed the same in equal fashion for both sexes, so that in all these things the regulation of the priest (*sacerdos*) can be expected to distribute the law of absolution or penance according to whether he considers their age suitable for continence.'

792 Leo I, Letter 167 to Rusticus of Narbonne, J 544, c. 13: col. 1207 (Feltoe 1895: 111). On views on the after-effects of penance, see Introduction, 39–41.

793 On the different possible ages included under *adolescentia* by classical and early medieval authors, see James 2004: 13–17: most often for males it extends from puberty to around twenty-five. Lothar II, born around 835, was therefore possibly at the border between *adolescentia* and *iuventus* in 860.

794 Sixth Council of Toledo, c. 8: 239–40.

795 The Council of Toledo here interprets Leo's decision on whether a young man may marry after doing penance as also dealing with the question of whether a young man who is already married when he does penance may continue to have a sexual relationship with his wife afterwards. Their answer is that he can.

796 On fragility as a characteristic of both men and women, see Introduction, 51.

797 That is, a person who has been allowed after penance to return to a marriage on the understanding that intercourse within this marriage will later cease is not then allowed to remarry if they are widowed, as would normally be the case.

Question 21

Concerning what was added at the end of these questions:[798] 'And tell us whether, if this often-mentioned woman had been legally rejected, the king could, after penance and if he so wishes, take the concubine in marriage, whom he kept and with whom he is said to have committed adultery after the marriage was initiated.'

Response 21[799]

Since there is one law for men and for women, as we have shown above from the decisions of the Scriptures and the catholic Fathers,[800] if he [Lothar] is released from the law of marriage, then just as St Paul says about a wife, 'she is at liberty to be married to whom she will; only in the Lord' [1 Corinthians 7:39]. That is, as Ambrose, says:[801] 'let her marry without the suspicion of any shamefulness and to a man of her religion: that is to marry in the Lord'. This dissolution (*solutio*) and licit union (*copulatio*) can be understand and can be done in two ways. That is, in those who either never initiated a legal marriage, or who are released from the law of marriage by the intervention of death,[802] just as St Paul says, 'I say therefore to the unmarried and widows, it is good for them if they abide even as I. But if they cannot contain, let them marry' [1 Corinthians 7:8]. And again, 'Art thou loosed from a wife? seek not a wife. But and if thou marry, thou hast not sinned. And if a virgin marry, he/she [the virgin] hath not sinned' [1 Corinthians 7:27–28]. This is to be understood for both the male and the female: 'virgin' is a common noun, either a man or a woman. And the apostle shows this afterwards, saying, 'such shall have trouble in the flesh' [1 Corinthians 7:28]. Ambrose expounds on this sentence for both man and woman:[803]

798 Question 18: 249.

799 Hincmar, in this Response, strings together a number of cases where the usual rules for what is or is not allowed in marriage are altered in special circumstances. He frames them within a Pauline and patristic framework in which marriage is good (although less good than continence) and all other forms of sexual behaviour are illicit.

800 See Response 5: 131 and 138–9.

801 Ambrosiaster, *Commentarius in Epistolam I ad Corinthios* 7, 39, 2: II, 90 (Bray 2009: 158). It should be noted that Ambrosiaster did *not* believe that there should be one law for men and women: see Introduction, 53.

802 Once again, Hincmar does not permit divorce under any circumstance, but does leave room for a marriage to be declared never to have been legitimate: see Introduction, 53.

803 In fact this quotation seems to come from Gregory I, *Regula pastoralis* III, 27: II, 456 (Barmby 1895: 58), and refers to 1 Corinthians 7:9, 'it is better to marry than to burn'. Gregory's condemnation is for those who have taken a vow of continence and are now going back on it by seeking to marry.

> What is allowed can be made illicit for those 'who have come to marriage without fault and propose to themselves the attainment of a greater good, and make unlawful the less good which before was lawful. For it is written, "No man, having put his hand to the plough, and looking back, is fit for the kingdom of God" [Luke 9:62]. He therefore who has been intent with a more resolute purpose is convicted of looking back, if, leaving the greater good, he reverts to the least.'

And sometimes what was illicit can be allowed by the intervention of a matter which should not be despised, when a marriage which was legally entered into is allowed to be dissolved (*dissolvi*) for the sake of unbelief (*infidelitas*).[804] Whence Paul says: 'If any brother hath a wife that believeth not, and she be pleased to dwell with him, let him not put her away. <221> And the woman which hath an husband that believeth not, and if he be pleased to dwell with her, let her not leave him' [1 Corinthians 7:12–13].[805] And a little later, 'if the unbelieving depart, let him depart' [1 Corinthians 7:15], or if the wife is left because of fornication, about which again Paul says: 'And unto the married I command, yet not I, but the Lord, Let not the wife depart from her husband. But and if she depart, let her remain unmarried or be reconciled to her husband: and let not the husband put away his wife' [1 Corinthians 7:10]. This should be weighed with equal measure, that if he sends her away, he should remain in celibacy (*caelibatus*). And a separation (*disjunctio*) between the faithful after a marriage has been entered into cannot happen, except because of fornication and from the love of continence.[806]

And what was illicit can be allowed through leniency (*indulgentia*), as again the same Paul, once again showing important things through small ones, says: 'But I speak this by permission, and not of commandment' [1 Corinthians 7:6], that when a man and woman are separated because of fornication, let them be reconciled to each other if they are not able to contain themselves. It was illicit that fornicators should return to the union of the flesh which they had joined, because they ought to remain in continence, especially since the Scripture says, 'He that keepeth an adulteress, is foolish and wicked' [Proverbs 18:22].[807] But as St Augustine says in his book *On the Good of Marriage*, often a

804 Again (as in Response 19: 256–7) there is a play on the meaning of faithlessness.

805 On 'mixed marriages' see Reynolds 1994: 366–8.

806 On the 'Matthean exception' which allowed separation (but not necessarily remarriage) if a spouse committed adultery, and on separation to enter the religious life, see Introduction, 48.

807 That is, it is not only permitted, but expected that a man should separate from an adulterous wife.

lesser evil is tolerated instead of a greater ill.[808] For the Lord says that if a man and woman are separated from each other because of fornication, they commit adultery if they join themselves to others, and if they marry others, they are adulterous [Matthew 5:32; 19:9]. → Augustine says this here and in his book on the *Sermon of the Lord on the Mount*, and very clearly in his *Books of Retractions*,[809] and ← Innocent shows the same in his letter to Exsuperius, bishop of Toledo, as we inserted above.[810] It is clear, as again Augustine said:[811]

> 'that adultery is worse than fornication. This does not mean that because adultery is worse, fornication is good, since it is worse to violate another's marriage than to cleave to a prostitute, and nor is adultery good because incest is worse. For it is worse to lie with one's mother than with the wife of another: until we arrive at those things, which, as the apostle says, "it is a shame even to speak of"' [Ephesians 5:12].

And St Gregory says:[812] 'But since, when the sickness of two vices attacks a man, one presses upon him more lightly, and the other perhaps more heavily, it is undoubtedly better to hasten to the aid of that through which there is the more rapid tendency to death.' And between two dangers, let the lesser be carefully sought.[813]

And what is illicit can be allowed through mercy, when, as Leo demonstrated:[814]

> 'a young man (*adolescens*) performing a public penance, fearing to fall into youthful incontinence, has chosen the bond (*copula*) of a wife lest he should be guilty of fornication: he seems to have committed a pardonable act, so long as he has known no woman whatever save his wife. Yet here we do not set out a rule, but weigh what is more tolerable.'

And what is illicit can, almost illicitly (*quasi inlicite*), pass into being allowed, as when it is permitted to pass with the leniency of penance

808 The specific passage of *De bono coniugali* has not been identified, but c. 6 gives the same overall message.

809 Augustine, *De sermone domini in monte* I, 14, 39–I, 16, 50: 41–56 (Findlay 1888: 17–22); *Retractiones* I, 18, 9: 92–3.

810 Innocent I, *Epistola* 6 to Bishop Exsuperius of Toulouse (J 293), c. 6: cols 500–1: see above, response 5: 131.

811 Augustine, *De bono coniugali* 8: 198 (a loose citation) (Wilcox *et al.* 1955: 20). Hincmar has already cited this passage above, Response 12: 195. The implied worst things are 'unnatural' forms of intercourse: see Introduction, 58–60.

812 Gregory I, *Regula pastoralis* III, 38: II, 524–6 (Barmby 1895: 70).

813 See above, Response 14: 232–3.

814 Leo I, *Epistola* 167 to Rusticus of Narbonne, J 544, c. 13: col. 1207 (Feltoe 1895: 111), quoted above, Response 20: 258.

from nefarious incest, of which the Council of Agde talks, to the embraces of a wife.[815]

<222> The same should be said about forms of concubinage, how there is a transition from the not good to the good and honest, from the not good to the good if not exactly honest, and from the bad to the good in parts, but not honest.[816] For it is good and honest for those previously unmarried to seek nuptial union if they are unable to remain in virginity, as we showed above from the apostolic tradition of St Evaristus.[817] And it is good and honest for the celibate, if they are not able to contain themselves, to enter into legal marriage, as St Leo showed above.[818] But it is a transition from the not good to the good and honest to pass from a concubine to a wife, as St Leo demonstrates to Rusticus, bishop of Narbonne, saying:[819]

> 'Not every woman joined to a man is that man's wife, just as not every son is his father's heir. Legitimate bonds of marriage are those between free and equal persons, as the Lord established long before Roman law had its beginnings. A wife is one thing, a concubine another, just as a slave-girl is one thing, and a free girl another. Because of this, the apostle brought evidence for showing the distinction between these persons from Genesis, where it is said to Abraham "Cast out your slave-girl and her son [Hagar and Ishmael], for the son of a slave-girl shall not be an heir with My son Isaac" [Galatians 4:30, citing Genesis 21:10]. Since from the beginning, the fellowship of marriage was so arranged that it should also have in it, beside the union of the sexes, the sacrament of Christ and the Church, so it should not be doubted that the woman in whom there is shown to have been no nuptial mystery does not belong to marriage.'

And again Leo says:[820] 'And to cast out the slave-girl or concubine from the bed, and to take a wife, if she is of proven free status, is not a second marriage, but the progress of honesty', since 'those joined by paternal will to men lack fault if the women these men already have are not married to them, for a married woman is one thing, a concubine another.'

815 On this canon, see above, Response 19, 257. One might note Hincmar's hesitancy here, in the 'quasi inlicite' see Introduction, 64.

816 On concubines, see Introduction, 47–8.

817 See above, Response 4: 127.

818 See above, 261, where Leo is quoted as stating that someone who has completed penance may choose to marry if he is unable to remain continent.

819 Leo I, *Epistola* 167 to Rusticus of Narbonne, J 544, c. 4: cols 1204–5 (Feltoe 1895: 110), see Response 1, 110 with n. 120.

820 Leo I, *Epistola* 167 to Rusticus of Narbonne, J 544, cc. 5–6: col. 1205 (rearranged) (Feltoe 1895: 110).

There is a passing from the not good to the good though not altogether honest, just as the same Leo showed above, when a concubine, perhaps made free if she was previously a slave-girl,[821] is legitimately endowed and honoured by a public ceremony, just as every legally married wife ought after betrothal to be legitimately endowed and honoured with a public ceremony. And to hurry from the wicked to the good in parts but not honest, is tolerable, as Augustine says in his first book *On Marriage and Concupiscence*:[822]

> 'It is certainly not fecundity alone, the fruit of which consists of offspring, nor chastity alone, whose bond is fidelity, but also a certain sacrament (*sacramentum*) of marriage which is recommended to the married faithful. Accordingly the apostle says: "Husbands, love your wives, even as Christ also loved the Church" [Ephesians 5:25]. The substance of this sacrament undoubtedly is this, that the male and the female who are joined together in marriage should remain inseparable as long as they live; nor should it be allowed for one spouse to be parted from the other, except for the cause of fornication. For this is preserved in the case of Christ and the Church; so that living with the living one for ever, it [the sacrament] should not be separated by any divorce (*divortium*).
>
> In the city of our God, on His holy mountain – that is to say, in the Church of Christ – although women marry and men take wives for the purpose of procreating children, it is never permitted to the gathered faithful, who are undoubtedly members of Christ, to leave even an unfruitful (*sterilis*) wife for the sake of having another to bear children. And if whichever man does this, he is held to be guilty of adultery by the law of the Gospel, as is the woman if she marries another; though not guilty by the law of this world,[823] where after a repudiation (*repudium*), joining other marriages with others is conceded without fault – a concession which, the Lord tells us, even the holy Moses allowed to the Israelites, because of the hardness of their hearts [Matthew 19:9]. <223> The rights (*iura*) of marriage endure between those who have contracted them to the extent that while they both live, those who have separated from one another should still be looked on as spouses, rather

821 On the Late Antique distinction between slave concubines and free wives in Leo's letter, see Response 4: 128–9 and Introduction, 47–8. Hincmar here smoothly brings the letter into line with contemporary conditions.

822 Augustine, *De nuptiis et concupiscentia* I, 10: 222–4 (Holmes 1887: 268). Hincmar has lightly altered the passage towards the end, to make it clear that both man and woman are equally bound. The influential edition of *De divortio* by Migne arbitrarily added '[non]' to the phrase 'fieri verum connubium potest cum quo vel cum qua prius adulterium fuit' (a true marriage can now happen with a man or woman that was previously adultery), reversing the meaning of the quotation.

823 That is, Roman law.

than those with whom others have joined.[824] Since surely they [those remarrying] would not be adulterers, unless they remained spouses to one another. When the husband or wife, with whom a true marriage was made, is finally dead, a true marriage can now happen with a man or woman that was previously adultery.'

→ That is, if kinship (*cognatio*), or the religious habit, or the impurity of a dreadful crime or something else of this sort, does not stand in the way.[825] And again Augustine: ←

'Thus there remains between them [the separated pair] something of marriage (*quiddam coniugale*) as long as they live, which neither separation nor union with another can remove. But this remains as the harm of a sin, not as the bond of a covenant.[826] In the same way, the soul of an apostate, which renounces as it were its marriage union with Christ, does not, even though faith is lost, lose the sacrament of its faith, which it received in the washing of regeneration.[827] It would undoubtedly be given back to him if he were to return, although he lost it on his departure from Christ. He who renounced Christ, however, has this sacrament as the increase of his punishment, not as the merit of a reward.'[828]

And in the book *On the Good of Marriage*:[829]

'Therefore the good of marriage throughout all peoples and all men is in the opportunity of begetting, and in the faith of chastity: but, as it pertains to the People of God, also in the sanctity of the sacrament.[830] Because of this, it is unlawful (*nefas*) for one who leaves her husband, even when repudiated, to be married to another so long as her husband lives, even for the sake of bearing children. Even though this may be

824 Augustine thus insists that even separation or repudiation does not break the marriage bond.

825 As part of his additions, Hincmar later inserted this sentence partway through the passage of Augustine. The Council of Meaux-Paris 845–46, c. 69 also allowed a pair of adulterers to remarry after the death of the innocent spouse, provided the spouse had not been murdered and there was no other impediment to the marriage (MGH *Conc.* 3, no. 11: 117). However the Council of Tribur 895, Versio Vulgata, c. 40 (MGH *Conc.* 5, no. 39A: 363) prohibited such a marriage.

826 That is, the marriage bond remains to make the separated pair adulterers, not to benefit them.

827 That is, the sacred sign (*sacramentum*) which it received in baptism. On Augustine's understanding of the term *sacramentum* (normally translated in this text as 'sacrament'), especially as applied to marriage, see Reynolds 1994: 280–311.

828 An apostate was held to be guilty of greater sin than one who had never accepted Christianity, because of the betrayal of God involved.

829 Augustine, *De bono coniugali* 24: 226–7 (Wilcox *et al.* 1955: 47–8).

830 That is, non-Christians have two of the three goods of marriage, Christians also have the third: the sacrament.

the only reason for which marriage takes place, the marriage bond is not dissolved even where that very thing for which it took place does not follow, except by the death of the spouse. Just as if an ordination of clergy took place in order to form a congregation of people, even if the congregation of people did not ensue, there remains in those ordained the sacrament of ordination; and if, for any fault, anyone should be removed from his office, he will not be without the sacrament of the Lord imposed once for all upon him, even though it remains for his judgement.'

And again in the aforementioned book *On Marriage and Concupiscence*:[831]

'But may it not happen that the nuptial bond should be regarded as broken between those who have by mutual consent agreed to observe a perpetual abstinence from the use of carnal desire. Rather it will be firmer, the more they have entered those agreements, which will have to be kept by a special endearment and concord – not by the voluptuous linking of bodies, but by the voluntary affections of souls.'

It is made clear by these testimonies from the Scriptures and the sayings of holy men, how he [Lothar] might be able to join the concubine [Waldrada] with whom he is said to have committed adultery to himself in marriage, should he wish: that is if either the wife who was legally received and found innocent towards him should die in the flesh, or if she should be found so dead in spirit that a bond (*copula*) with her would be legally shown to be incest and 'not to be reckoned by the name of marriage'.[832] However, if he were to take a concubine of this kind as a wife, such a union would not be seen to be without blame or the stain of offence, as St Augustine says in his book *On the Good of Marriage*:[833]

'What, therefore, the apostles order to the married, this is proper to marriage, but what they allow by way of pardon, or what hinders prayers, this marriage does not compel, but endures. Therefore if perhaps – <224> whether it can take place, I do not know; and rather think it cannot take place; but yet, if perhaps – having taken unto himself a concubine for a time, a man should only have sought sons from this same intercourse; that union is not as a result to be preferred to those marriages which are

831 Augustine, *De nuptiis et concupiscientia* I, 11: 224 (Holmes 1887: 268).

832 Council of Epaon 517, c. 30: 31 (identified as Council of Agde 506, c. 61). Once again, and here very explicitly, Hincmar accepts that Theutberga's incest, if proven, could indeed justify Lothar II's marriage to Waldrada: see Introduction, 62.

833 Augustine, *De bono coniugali* 13–15: 208–10 (Wilcox *et al.* 1955: 30–1). Augustine goes on to consider the ancient practice of having a concubine for the sake of children (perhaps a reference to the case of Abraham). Hincmar had already used Augustine's key sentence about sterility in Response 5: 138.

used venially.[834] For we must consider what belongs to marriage, not what belongs to those marrying and using marriage less moderately. For neither if anyone uses lands entered upon unjustly and wrongly, so that out of their fruits he may give generous alms, does he therefore justify plundering: nor if an avaricious man devotes himself to an ancestral estate, or one which he has justly gained, is the rule of civil law to blame, whereby he is made a lawful owner. Nor will the wrongfulness of a tyrannical rebellion deserve praise, if the tyrant treat his subjects with royal clemency: nor will the order of royal power deserve blame, if a king rage with tyrannical cruelty. For it is one thing to wish to use unjust power (*potestas*) justly, and it is another thing to use just power.

Thus neither do concubines who are taken for a time, if they sleep with them for the sake of sons, make their concubinage lawful; nor do married women, if they live wantonly with their husbands, inflict any fault on the order (*ordo*) of marriage. It is clear that marriage (*nuptiae*) can take place well between persons first badly joined, with an honest sentiment following. But a marriage once for all entered upon in the City of our God,[835] where even from the first union of two people marriage bears a certain sacrament, can in no way be dissolved, except by the death of one of them. For the bond of marriage (*vinculum nuptiarum*) remains, even if children, for whom it was entered into, do not follow, because of obvious sterility; so that, when now married persons know that they will not have children, yet they are not allowed to separate and to join themselves unto others, even for the sake of children themselves. And if they shall so do, they commit adultery with those to whom they join themselves.'

For as the holy Fathers agreed about the good of marriage,[836] marriage has what is good, and what is good is not a sin; and through this, whoever acts against a good marriage commits a sin, since he commits adultery. They also decided that a marriage is good and constituted by God and blessed, and which He consecrated by his presence,[837] in which there is 'faith, offspring and sacrament'.[838] Faith is striven for, lest beyond the bond of marriage the spouse sleeps with an adulteress

834 That is, a bad marriage (where sexual intercourse is for pleasure rather than procreation) is still better than sexual relations with a concubine for the 'correct' purpose of procreation. On Augustine's views on marriage, see Introduction, 45.

835 That is, a Christian marriage.

836 Much of the rest of this Response reworks material that Hincmar had already used in his treatise on *raptus*: see Introduction, 24, and Böhringer 1992: 224–6.

837 On the significance of Jesus' attendance at the wedding of Cana in John 2:1–11, see Introduction, 45.

838 Augustine, *De Genesi ad litteram libri duodecim* IX, 7: 275 (Taylor 1982: II, 77–8). The following paragraph is adapted from this passage of Augustine rather than the two other works to which Hincmar refers.

or with another man. Offspring, so that they might be lovingly brought up, kindly nourished, and religiously taught, and let the parents who bear children rejoice only so much as these are reborn in Christ.[839] And the sacrament, so that the marriage shall not be separated; the one or other sent away should not join someone else for the sake of offspring. This is the rule of marriage, by which the fertility of nature is adorned, and the depravity of incontinence is regulated, just as St Augustine shows at length and most eloquently in the book *On the Good of Marriage*, and his book *On Marriage and Concupiscence.*

It should therefore be observed in every way, that the king, about whom the questioners wanted to be advised, should not in any way expect a marital union with a concubine or with any other woman, until by the legal judgement of outstanding men and by priestly decree, the spouse (*coniunx*) whom he legally accepted <225> should be judged unworthy of the name of spouse itself, or she should depart from the body by divine judgement.[840] As is read very clearly in the Book of Esther, when Vashti, queen of the very powerful king Ahasuerus, was deposed from imperial honour after she had offended his spirits with contempt and contumacy not solely by his anger and rage, although he was very fierce, but by public judgement, and the sentence of the princes and judges of the Medes and the Persians ⌈Esther 1:9–21⌉. And after the deposition of this queen through a public judgement had taken place, girls were sought who were 'pleasing to the eye of the king' ⌈Esther 2:4⌉, amongst whom Esther shone out in beauty and elegance as suited a royal bond.[841]

Even the ancient Romans formerly decreed and observed in their laws that this ought to happen only after a legal judgement, not only when already made Christian, but also when they were still pagans, as the law of Antoninus the pagan emperor shows very clearly, which the blessed Augustine → in his book *On Adulterous Marriage* ← recalls in this way and commends, saying:[842]

> 'Those who are displeased that an equal form of modesty (*pudicitia*) should be preserved between husband and wife, and who would rather choose especially in this matter to be subject to the laws of the world than those of Christ, since

839 On the concept of being born again, see John 3:3–8.

840 Hincmar here again indicates that both a secular and an ecclesiastical judgement of some kind are needed in this case: see Introduction, 50–1.

841 Hincmar ignores the fault for which Vashti was divorced (having refused a royal command) and concentrates on the procedure used.

842 Augustine, *De adulterinis coniugiis* II, 8: 389–90 (Wilcox *et al.* 1955: 109–10).

> the secular laws do not seem to them to bind men in the same ties of modesty as they do to women; they should read what the emperor Antoninus, although not at all a Christian, decreed about this matter. That is, that a husband is not permitted to accuse his wife of the crime of adultery, if his own morals did not offer her an example of chastity, so that both would be condemned, if the investigation proved both to be equally immodest. For these are the words of this emperor, which can be read in the *Gregorianus*:[843] "Indeed, my letters will in no way prejudice the case. Nor indeed, if the blame lay with you, so that your marriage were dissolved and your wife Eupasia were to marry according to the Julian Law (*Lex Iulia*),[844] will she be condemned for adultery because of this my rescript, unless it is clear that adultery was committed. [The judges] will have this before their eyes to enquire into, whether you, by your modest life, were also the inspiration for her to cultivate good habits. It would seem to be extremely unfair that the husband should demand a modesty from the wife which he himself does not display. This matter may serve to condemn the husband, but through the balancing of mutual fault, it will not settle the matter between both parties, or remove the cause of the matter." If these things should be observed for the honour of the earthly city, do not the heavenly fatherland and the society of angels seek people even more chaste?'

This is what the blessed Augustine recalls about the laws of the pagan emperor Antoninus. So the kings of the Medes and the Persians, and of the Romans, and the judges of the world, when they were still pagans and idol worshippers, naturally taught what the laws were, ensuring that not cruelty and savagery, but equality and justice ought to be observed, settled and held in marital disputes.

Therefore kings, bishops and judges of this world should fear what is said in the Gospel about the men of Ninevah and the queen of the south, that they 'shall rise up in judgement with this most wicked generation, and shall condemn it' [Matthew 12:41–42]. 'They will indeed condemn it, not by the power of judgement, but by the comparison of what was done better.'[845] If those kings and idolatrous judges thus maintained the order of judgement, should we, under Christ the judge of the living and the dead, deviate from the order of judgement through less consideration than is needed?

> <226>'In the Book of Numbers it is ordered, that if any woman is either guilty of adultery or attacked with false suspicion, and her husband

843 Antoninus Caracalla, Roman emperor (198–217). On the Gregorian Code, which Augustine cites here, see Corcoran 2013. Since the Code does not survive, we do not know the context of the passage Augustine cites.

844 On this law (*Lex Iulia de adulteriis coercendis*) by the Roman emperor Augustus penalising adulterers, see Evans Grubbs 1995: 94–6.

845 Bede, *In Lucae evangelium expositio* IV, 11, 31: 238. Hincmar's point is that concern about correct procedure is not simply a narrow legal matter, but a moral one.

> should have been stirred up by jealousy against her, he shall bring her to the priests and offer her to divine judgement, for condemnation or for liberation [Numbers 5:11–31].[846] And Susanna, when she was falsely accused of the crime of adultery, is read to have been condemned by a public judgement and to have been publicly absolved [Daniel 13].[847] And that woman in the Gospel, who was truly caught in adultery, was first, according to the law, led to the Pharisees, who exercised the power of judging over the people, then for the sake of testing to the Lord, where through His admirable piety, she merited being freed from the punishment of stoning, and from the guilt of her crime' [John 8:3–11].[848]

These are the Christian laws, inspired by the Lord Creator, by which a marriage should be legally entered into. And this is the sanctity of priestly authority, by which the Lord wishes to give his blessing, given by himself in paradise to the first parents [Adam and Eve], in turn to each of those legally joined to each other in marriage. It is given in his stead, by those who are called his mouth,[849] – as the prophet said, 'the mouth of the Lord hath spoken' [Isaiah 1:20], and the Lord himself said: 'if thou take forth the precious from the vile, thou shalt be as my mouth' [Jeremiah 15:19] – and whom he wishes to cure the infirm with the medicine of penitence.[850] And what the Book of Ecclesiasticus says about a slave, how much more about a wife: 'and without judgement, do nothing' [Ecclesiasticus 33:30].

And there is another thing this king should bear in mind, lest he bind himself to a wife, and even more to this same concubine [Waldrada] about whom we are concerned, before he has received a legitimate penance according to the law of the Church, and completed it, and has been reconciled. For King David did not have Bathsheba, with whom he had committed adultery, in marriage without this purging penitence: that his son who was born from that adultery, though David had begged for him with much fasting and weeping, was at once struck by divine judgement and died [2 Samuel 12:13–19]. And he himself [David] afterwards was afflicted and vexed with very serious tribulations and the loss of his kingdom through his son Absalom, and was as if placed in a fiery furnace, burned through and purged, so that he seemed to

846 On the ordeal of bitter water, see Introduction, 37.

847 See above, Response 5: 143.

848 Much of this passage is based on Hincmar's treatise on *raptus* (see Introduction, 24). On the woman caught in adultery, see Introduction, 55.

849 That is, priests, to whom Hincmar applies statements made about the Old Testament prophets.

850 On blessings by priests as part of marriage liturgy, see Reynolds 1994: 362–85, 391–4.

have escaped by divine clemency alone.[851] And then the merciful Lord took away his sin from him, bitterly contrite and repentant in heart and confessing, but since He is just and loves justice, He worthily and very justly punished what the king, appointed by Him to punish wickedness, had himself done wickedly.

Question 22

> 'In the eighth chapter,[852] write back to us, whether it should be followed as some say that some bishops teach, that they should offer the protection of defence to men or women who have confessed to them, lest anyone dare to summon these persons to the judgement of the state (*res publica*) for the crimes about which they had confessed to them, even if they are crimes known to many. And if they wish to separate not by consent for the sake of continence, but because of discord or because of their fragility, and if separated they are unable to contain themselves or are unwilling to be reconciled, these bishops say that by their authority they can give advice. And that since they fled to ecclesiastical piety through a secret confession, like Boso's wife [Engeltrude], <227> about whom we were informed by an appeal (*interpellatio*) at a synod held at Toul, they should not therefore be judged except by the bishops to whom these people confessed.'[853]

Response 22

Anyone who is intelligent, even if he does not know the laws of the Church, will recognise how absurd this is. For, as St Gregory wrote to Leontius the ex-consul:[854]

> 'your Glory ought to have remembered that you have never received my letters for the commendation of anyone, except so that you might confer your protection if justice favours it. For it is shameful to defend what has not first been proven to be just. Indeed I love people because of justice, and I do not put justice second for the sake of people.'

So indeed, as we wrote above that St Ambrose taught, a pact of marriage cannot be confirmed before fewer than ten witnesses,[855] and the

851 On Absalom's seizure of David's kingdom, see 2 Samuel 15.

852 Of the original list of questions sent by the Lotharingian bishops.

853 Engeltrude abandoned her husband Boso and fled with her lover to Lotharingia at the same time as Lothar began efforts to separate from Theutberga.This is the only evidence that her case was considered at the synod of Savonnières, near Toul, in 859. The appeal (*interpellatio*) may have been a letter sent by Pope Nicholas I. On Engeltrude's case, see Introduction, 50.

854 Gregory I, *Registrum* XI, 4 (J 1794):I, 862 (Martyn 2004: III, 738–9).

855 See above, Response 4: 129.

⌈Latin⌉ name for marriage itself (*nuptiae*), which does not have a singular form, shows that the attention of many must be sought. And what is joined in public cannot be separated in a corner. And a marriage joined by Christian and public laws cannot be dissolved from that yoke of marriage by a secret confession, which it is not allowed to make public, nor should such a collusion be said to be a flight to ecclesiastical piety.[856]

And if anyone wants to know what ecclesiastical authority moderately decrees about those fleeing to it as if to a mother's bosom, we suggest that whoever is curious or studious should consider amongst other things the letters of St Gregory, in which several times, indeed as often as the opportunity presented itself, he inserted in letters petitioning emperors and various others on behalf of all those fleeing to him,[857] 'without prejudice to equity', or 'without prejudice to reason', or 'justice standing firm', or 'the matter settled by a judicial meeting, without priestly jealousy', and 'that it is necessary to undergo the judgement of the chosen ⌈judges⌉ with the other side, so that both the truth can be recognised and what the order of equity recommends is able to be established'. And so that 'without further delay every person is to be obliged to go to the judgement of the chosen ⌈judges⌉, and once the truth has been recognised, whatever is decreed by the sacrosanct Gospels is thus to be put fully into execution'. <228> And 'whatever seems advised by justice, let it be determined in writing'; and 'that no one should in any way suffer by being burdened contrary to the law or reason, but justice should be respected towards him in all things, as befits Christianity, and so the one who flees to ecclesiastical piety should ⌈receive⌉ what is promised to him by that piety, and should not be burdened against the order of equity'. And again, 'Wheresoever it is necessary for him to flee, reason, running alongside, will be safeguarded.' And again, 'May he obtain from your Comfort whatever custom demands, subject to justice accompanying this.' And again to Fantinus the *defensor*:[858] 'Give this aforementioned woman protection, without prejudice to equity, and do not allow her to be burdened in any way against the order of reason', and again to Anatolius the deacon of Constantinople:[859]

856 Once again Hincmar returns to one of his central points: Theutberga's confession was secret, and a secret action cannot be brought to bear on a public one. See Introduction, 43.

857 The references that follow are drawn from the widely disseminated collection of Gregory's letters. Many of these phrases recur several times in Gregory's letters: see Böhringer 1992: 227 nn. 8–13, 228 nn. 14–17 for further details. Hincmar has sometimes lightly reworked the phrasing to emphasise the generalising force of the statements.

858 Gregory I, *Registrum* IX, 39 (J 1563): II, 598 (Martyn 2004: II, 569).

859 Gregory I, *Registrum* IX, 237 (J 1764): II, 821 (Martyn 2004: II, 710–11).

'However, we want your Love carefully to look out for this, that you should not allow yourself to be mixed up in any matter where there is a burden for the poor, lest perhaps, under pressure from some people's power, you should be forced to act, to a degree, in a way which could not help your soul. Therefore, deal with everything with the fear of God, and assess carefully in particular the eternal reward.'

And to Sabinus the subdeacon:[860]

'let it be your desire that no one should undergo any expense against reason. And if perhaps someone tries to defend it with some excuse, let the matter be carefully inspected by the mediation of the most holy Gospels,[861] and thus, just as justice and the order of law recommend, it is fitting to settle it, and bring the settlement into effect.'

And to Romanus the *defensor*:[862]

'With regard to ecclesiastical protection of people (whether you have received letters from me, or whether none have been sent to you), you should bestow it with such moderation that, if any have been implicated in public theft, they may not appear to be unjustly defended by us, lest we should in any way transfer to ourselves, by daring indiscreet defence, the reputation of being evildoers: but so far as becomes the Church, by admonishing and applying words of intercession, assist whom you can; so that you may both give them aid, and not stain the reputation of holy Church.'

And he wrote to John, the bishop of the city of Cagliari, about those who flee to the enclosures of churches and even the shrines of saints:[863]

'If anyone being investigated should perhaps flee into a church, the matter should be arranged so that neither may they suffer violence nor may those who say they are oppressed sustain harm (*damna*). Let it be your concern that it shall be promised by an oath by those involved that law and justice will be maintained, and let them be advised in all ways to leave the church, and to render account for their actions.'

→ <229> And in the first book of the capitularies of the emperors Lord Charles and Louis:[864]

860 Gregory I, *Registrum* IX, 90 (J 1614): II, 644 (Martyn 2004: II, 597).

861 This may imply the use of oaths sworn on the Bible.

862 Gregory I, *Registrum* IX, 80 (J 1604): 634 (Martyn 2004: II, 592).

863 Gregory I, *Registrum* X, 17 to bishop Januarius of Cagliari (J 1786): II, 846 (Martyn 2004: III, 727), discussing those accused of oppressing the poor in Sardinia, cited above Response 12: 208.

864 Ansegis, *Capitularia* I, 134: 508, citing *Capitulare legibus additum* 803, c. 3 (MGH *Capit.* I, no. 39: 113). On Carolingian views on church asylum, see Meens 2007.

> 'If anyone makes a flight to a church, let him have peace in the courtyard (*atrium*) of that church, nor should it be necessary for him to enter the church, and let no one presume to drag him from there by force. But it is permitted for him to confess what he did, and from there let him be led forth by the hands of good men to an examination in public.' ←

And in the Council of Orléans, c.1, it is written:[865]

> 'concerning murderers, adulterers and thieves if they should flee to churches, that just as is decreed in the church canons and in the decrees of Roman law, it is not allowed to drag them from the courtyards of the church or from the house of the bishop, but after oaths have been given to them about death, mutilation and all sorts of punishment', lest they suffer violence before legal satisfaction, then let them come out, 'so that the guilty man may make a fitting satisfaction to him who he has offended'.

And in the third chapter:[866] 'if anyone's slave (*servus*) flees to a church for whatever crime, then after an oath that he will not be punished, let him be forced to return to the service of his lord. If after an oath has been given he is unwilling to return, it is allowed for the lord to seize him, even if he is unwilling to leave.' Those who do not keep what they promise are ordered to be cut off from the communion of the Church.

And in the second chapter of this same council it is written:[867]

> 'If any abductor (*raptor*) flees with an abducted woman to a church, and it is clear that this woman was carried off by violence, she should at once be freed from the power of the abductor, and the abductor, with impunity conceded to him regarding death or [physical] punishment, should either be subjected to the condition of slavery (*serviendus*) or will have the free opportunity to redeem himself from this. If she who was abducted has a father, and the girl consented to the abductor, let her be excused and returned to the power of her father.'

And in the Council of Africa, it is written:[868]

> 'That if a cleric of whichever status (*honor*) is condemned by the judgement of bishops for whatever crime, it is not allowed for him to be defended either by the churches of which he was in charge, or by any other person, from the penalty handed down of loss, money and status, for which the promulgators of the law command that neither age nor sex can be an excuse.'

865 Council of Orléans 511, c. 1: 4. Hincmar abbreviates the quotation, and adds his own gloss to the passage cited, which rather changes the implication of the text: now physical punishment is not ruled out completely, only forbidden before judgement.

866 Council of Orléans 511, c. 3: 5–6, again loosely cited.

867 Council of Orléans 511, c. 2: 5. On abduction, see Joye 2015.

868 *Registri ecclesiae Carthaginensis excerpta*, c. 62: 197.

How much less should bishops, the preachers of equity, unjustly defend anyone under the guise of piety, especially when they reread what is written, 'If you have offered aright, but you have not divided aright, you have sinned' [Genesis 4:7] and 'thou shalt follow justly after that which is just' [Deuteronomy 16:20].[869]

And if it seems to anyone that the Council of Orléans sounds somewhat contrary to the decrees of the Apostolic See, since one demands oaths of impunity, the other of preserving equity, it should be known that St Gregory speaks of these people who believe that they can justify themselves in a judgement, but fear violence before the judgement. The Council of Orléans, however, speaks of those who do not hide their injustice, and moreover greatly fear the violence of the equity of judgement;[870] it does not talk about the law of marriage, which the Lord gave in paradise specially, or we might say specifically, to the first parents,[871] and did not change in the Gospel – <230> and even the apostles complained that if this was the law of man and wife, then it would not be expedient to marry [Matthew 19:10]. Nor did Paul, caught up to the third heaven and to Paradise [2 Corinthians 12:2–4], presume to write anything new, or attempt to say anything in defence of this sort of thing.

And it is to be observed by the readers that whenever a council is read to have decreed something because of the quality of the time or the necessity of danger, which diverges from the advice of the apostolic see or the old canons but is not against faith or religion, then according to what is read about that in the Nicene Council, c. 6, that:[872] 'If two or three shall oppose what has been rationally approved by the common decree of all and according to ecclesiastical rule, then let the statement of the majority prevail.' So that as Gelasius wrote:[873] 'it is fitting to keep regularly those ancient rulings maintained from reverence, where no

869 Both these biblical quotations come from the Vetus Latin version of the Bible: Hincmar probably cited them from Gregory the Great. Hincmar frequently warns of the danger of unjust mercy, and returns to them below, 276: see also Introduction, 33.

870 Note Hincmar's concern here to resolve a contradiction in his sources: see Introduction, 26. Hincmar argues that Gregory is talking about those who have not yet been convicted, while the Council of Orléans is dealing with sinners whose 'public' sins (such as murder, abduction or running away from slavery) means that a formal conviction is not needed. The inclusion of references to theft and adultery in the canons suggests that the lines are not clear as Hincmar claims.

871 See Response 3: 124–5.

872 Council of Nicaea, 325, c. 6: 9 (Percival 1900: 15). Also cited below, Appendix Response 3: 288–9.

873 Gelasius I, *Epistola* 14 to the bishops of Lucania, Bruttia and Sicily (J 636), c. 2: 362.

limit of time or place constrains them'. It is discerned that those things are rather to be followed which the Apostolic see decreed should be held unbreakably, or which more councils or those of greater authority decided.[874]

And St Gregory wrote urging the unwilling Venantius, bishop of Luna, to do justice, saying:[875]

> 'Since severity of equity warns that, without prejudice to reason, episcopal comfort should especially be available for the converted,[876] we therefore encourage your Fraternity with these letters, that you should have the already mentioned mother of Adeodata[877] summoned to you, and advise her with calm encouragement, that she should not desist from doing of her free will what she can be compelled to do by legal reason, so that neither should the other [Adeodata] be afflicted, nor should she [the mother] sustain disadvantage. And if, which we do not believe, she wishes to delay following your advice, give protection to the above mentioned nun Adeodata against her, and with your comfort earnestly help her with the judge or in whichever other way custom should demand. And so devote yourself to this cause that she [the mother] might be obliged unwillingly to do by legal reason what she put off doing willingly. Let your Fraternity, without prejudice to equity, keep the bearer of this letter [Adeodata] commended in all things, giving her the protection so that she can, God helping, remain in the habit which she took up, without any other disturbance.'

And to Januarius, the bishop of Sabina:[878] 'We sent Redemptus our *defensor* and the bearer of this letter there, so that he might compel the parties to respect the judgement, and by his own effort bring whatever was judged into effect.' And there are more things of this sort which can be found, and which would take a long time for us to go through.

It is not recognised to pertain to the right (*ius*) of any church or man of the church to strive against this, lest perhaps undue piety be judged

874 Hincmar here distinguishes between different levels of authority attributed to various councils, thus allowing him flexibility in the rulings of which he chooses to accept (cf. <143>). See Introduction, 30–1.

875 Gregory I, *Registrum* IX, 87 (J 1611): II, 641 (Martyn 2004: II, 596).

876 That is, those converting to the religious life.

877 Hincmar incorrectly writes the name of the nun as Deodata; later in the quotation he gives it correctly as Adeodata. The nature of the argument between Adeodata and her mother Fidentia is not clear from Gregory's letter itself. Martyn 2004: II, 596 n. 225 suggests that the demand may have been that Fidentia continued to support her daughter's convent.

878 Gregory I, *Registrum* VIII, 35 (J 1524): II, 561 (Martyn 2004: II, 531).The text reads *Sabinia*, a mistake for the correct location of Januarius's bishopric, Sardinia.

as impiety, just as St Celestine wrote to Nestorius:[879] 'There is often a kind of piety from which impiety is born.' And St Augustine says in the fourth book of *Against Julian*:[880]

> <231> 'Perhaps you will say that a merciful will is good. And this would rightly be said, if mercy were always good, just as the faith of Christ, that is faith which works through love, is always good. But there is a mercy found that is evil, by which the person of the poor man is respected in judgement.[881] Because of this [evil mercy], King Saul deserved finally to be condemned by the Lord, though mercifully, since against His order he had spared the captive king through human affection.[882] Think more carefully, lest perhaps there should be no good mercy unless it be of good faith. Indeed, so that you may understand without doubt, tell me whether you reckon an unfaithful mercy to be good. For if it is a vice to have mercy in an evil way, it is without doubt that it is a vice to have mercy unfaithfully.'

There is no one so merciful that he could be found to be more merciful than God, whom the Psalmist wanted to call mercy, saying 'my God, my mercy' [Psalms 59:18], and who was unwilling to take away a just judgement from just judges concerning the woman caught in adultery and handed over to him [John 8:3–11].[883] In this way St Jerome explains the verse of the Psalm saying 'Because of truth and clemency and justice' [Psalms 45:5]:[884]

> 'Christ himself is the truth, whereby he said to the Jews about that woman, "He that is without sin among you, let him first cast a stone at her" [John 8:7]. Clemency, when he said "Neither do I condemn thee". And justice, when he said, "Go, woman, and sin no more" [John 8:11].'

→ Now, what we read in the above-mentioned volume[885] about this woman of Boso is written as follows:

> 'We summoned her husband with an agreement of safety for his coming, staying and leaving, so that we might examine his wife in his presence.

879 Celestine I, *Epistola* 2 to Nestorius of Constantinople (J 374): 10.

880 Augustine, *Contra Iulianum* IV, 3, 31: col. 754 (Schumacher 1957: 195–6).

881 That is, mercy is shown to the unfortunate without respect to the merits of their case.

882 In 1 Samuel 15, Saul spared Agag, king of the Amalekites, when God had told him to destroy them utterly; God therefore rejected him as king of Israel.

883 On Hincmar's frequent reference to this story, see Introduction, 55.

884 Pseudo-Jerome, *Breviarium in psalmos* 44.5: col. 957.

885 The *Tomus prolixus*, the report of the Second Council of Aachen. See above, Response 1: 107.

> We avoid handing over someone to death who was not examined and who had fled to us, as unjust and cruel, because, when no particular accuser comes forth, although both admonished and questioned, she confesses to nothing else except that she had fled fearing to die from the persecution of Hubert alone.'[886]

The readers must prudently notice whether this is able to suit authority or reason. Authority indeed demands firmness for those fleeing to the Church, for the conservation of equity and justice: and it does not take wholly away the legitimate power (*potestas*) of a husband over his wife, who was legally betrothed, legally endowed and honoured with a public marriage,[887] if he is moved against her by suspicion. For when it is written in the Heptateuch about jealousy, that 'a husband stirred up by jealousy shall take his wife to the priests' [Numbers 5:14] for examination, it is commanded thus since it is the office of the priest, for the ministry imposed on him, to write the exorcisms which will be washed with the water which the woman has to drink.[888] And the sacred canons decreed that secular men (*saeculares*) should neither condemn nor cast off their spouses, before they have told the provincial bishop of the cause for the separation.[889] But otherwise divine authority does not remove legal judgement from husbands about their wives, just as we showed above from the truth of the Gospels.[890]

<232> But let us pay attention more closely to what is contained in this volume mentioned above:[891] 'We avoid handing over someone to death who was not examined and who had fled to us, as unjust and cruel.' We should not hand over those who have been examined to death either, unless they should be living as dead to God through sin.[892] Let us concede, however, that the bishops, keeping in their power that same woman who is said to have fled to them [Engeltrude], should hasten to examine her in the presence of her husband if he accuses her of something improper. What will have to be done, if she is found to be guilty in this

886 Hubert was the brother of both Boso and Theutberga, and thus Engeltrude's brother-in-law. In a letter discussing the case from later in 860, Archbishop Gunther claims that Engeltrude told him that she feared that her husband, Boso, would kill her. On this letter, see Introduction, 9.

887 On this frequent formula of Hincmar's, see Introduction, 48.

888 On the ordeal of bitter water (Numbers 5:11–31), see Introduction, 37.

889 Council of Agde 506, c. 25: 204, cited above, Response 5: 132–3.

890 That is, in the story of the woman taken in adultery. Hincmar had earlier pointed out that this case was taken to the Pharisees: Response 5: 143; Response 21: 269. Presumably he took these to be married men.

891 The *Tomus prolixus*.

892 Hincmar accepts the possibility of capital punishment; see Introduction, 55–6.

episcopal examination?[893] If the bishops want by their authority to remove a legal judgement over her once she has been found guilty, they will be seen to act against Him whose action and speech is known to be perfect authority, as is written, 'all that Jesus began both to do and teach' [Acts 1:1]. For He did not remove judgement from the woman taken in adultery, who ordered through Moses 'that such should be stoned' [John 8:5], but He ordered the legal judgement to take place through just judges, saying 'Let him first cast a stone' [John 8:7]. If indeed the bishops hand her over to be punished, once they have examined her and found her guilty, they will be proven to act against ecclesiastical piety and the head of the Church himself, the fount of piety, who said 'Neither do I condemn thee: go, and sin no more' [John 8:11]. Let us bishops, once we have clearly recognised these things and thought about them extremely carefully, follow the authority of the elders about those fleeing to the piety of the Church, and we shall not be found to be in need of rebuke.[894]

And what is finally written there,[895] that 'when no particular accuser comes forth, although both admonished and questioned, she confesses to nothing else except that she had fled fearing to die from the persecution of Hubert alone'. Then since she was accused by no one, and if the bishops did not find otherwise according to the canons – if perhaps canons were used, which we have not yet read to have been the case – and the Christian and noble laity did not find otherwise according to the laws – which we have by no means learned was the case[896] – what remains to be done other than to return her to her husband, with a promise [from him] to maintain equity, if necessity and reason perhaps demand it for some crime charged to her;[897] in order that she might be protected by the marital defence of her husband as is just, so that she should not be killed by Hubert? And then let the husband exercise legitimate and legal power over her, according to Christian and ecclesiastical law, as a man ought to do concerning his wife.[898] ←

893 On Hincmar's ambiguous view as to whether a convicted adulteress could be judicially executed, see Introduction, 55.

894 Hincmar suggests that the bishops have now foolishly put themselves in an impossible situation, since they should not have attempted to judge a case of adultery themselves.

895 In the *Tomus prolixus*.

896 Hincmar casts aspersions on the method of conduct of the case, without actually stating that it was procedurally incorrect.

897 On the use of oaths to protect wives from their husbands, see Introduction, 55.

898 Hincmar uses the claim recorded in the *Tomus prolixus*, that Engeltrude was threatened only by Hubert, to argue that Boso is therefore not a threat to her, and she should return to him. By the end of 860, however, Engeltrude was claiming that Boso might kill her: see Hincmar, *De uxore Bosonis* (MGH *Epp.* 8: 82).

Question 23

Concerning what it is written that some people said,[899] 'And if a man and a woman wish to separate not by consent for the sake of continence, but because of discord, or because of their fragility, and if separated they are unable to contain themselves or are unwilling to be reconciled, that bishops by their authority can give advice.'

Response 23

Let whoever says this know that in a certain way this was the fourth chapter of the error of those who dared to disparage and contradict the holy Council of Chalcedon, and who were condemned as being in error by the Apostolic See and the unanimity of the bishops of the whole world, as St Leo says many times,[900] and blessed Gregory too in his letter to Theoctista the patrician,[901] <233> writing amongst other things:[902]

> 'For the Truth in person says, "What God hath joined together let not man put asunder" ⌈Mark 10:9⌉. He says also, "It is not lawful for a man to put away his wife saving for the cause of fornication" ⌈Matthew 5:32⌉. Who then may contradict this heavenly legislator? We know how it is written, "Two shall be one flesh" ⌈Genesis 2:24⌉. If, then, a man and wife are one flesh, and a man sends away his wife for the sake of religion, or a woman her husband, while he remains in this world, or perhaps turns aside to unlawful deeds, what is this conversion, in which one and the same flesh in one part passes over to continence and in the other part remains in pollution? If, however, it should suit both to lead a continent life, who may dare to accuse them, since it is certain that almighty God, who has granted what is less, has not forbidden what is greater?[903] And indeed we know of many holy persons who have both previously led continent lives with their spouses, and have afterwards passed over to the rules of holy Church. For holy men are accustomed to abstain even from lawful things in two ways. Sometimes so that they may increase

899 See above, Question 22: 270.

900 On Leo's many letters referring to this council, see Böhringer 1992: 233 n. 3.

901 Theoctista was the sister of the Byzantine emperor Maurice. Gregory's letter discusses four errors he has encountered: on whether a marriage could be dissolved for the sake of religion; on whether baptism removed on sins; the suggestion that three years of penance allowed one to sin subsequently; and the validity of an anathema on someone compelled to do something.

902 Gregory I, *Registrum* XI, 27 (J 1817): II, 909–10 (Martyn 2004: III, 768–9).

903 That is, if God allows the lesser good of a sexually active marriage, he will allow the greater good of a continent marriage.

their merits before almighty God; but sometimes so that they may wipe away the sins of their former life. …

Accordingly, when good spouses desire either to increase merit or to do away with the sins of their former life, it is lawful for them to bind themselves to continence and to strive after a better life. But, if the wife does not follow after the continence which the husband strives after, or the husband refuses that which the wife strives after, it is not lawful for the marriage to be parted (*dividi*), seeing that it is written, "The wife hath not power of her own body, but the husband; and the husband hath not power of his own body, but the wife"' [1 Corinthians 7.4].

→ And in the letter to Hadrian the notary of Panormia, he [Gregory] blames the abbot Urbicus, since he had received the husband of Agathosa against her wishes in his monastery for [monastic] conversion, and he ordered her husband to be returned to her, even if he had already been tonsured, saying:[904]

'unless … you find that the aforesaid woman has committed any crime of fornication, on account of which it is lawful for a man to leave his wife,[905] then, lest his conversion should possibly be an occasion of perdition to the wife left behind in the world, we want you, without any excuse allowed, to restore her husband to her, even though he should be already tonsured. … Since after the husband and wife have been made one body by the uniting of marriage, it cannot be in part converted, and in part remain in the world.' ←

And lest someone grows angry with us, since we have suggested that ecclesiastical judgements should be heard also by laymen,[906] let him read the explanation of the Fathers for this question, why the Lord, who forbade holy things to be given to dogs that bite, or pearls to the irreverent [Matthew 7:6], when asked about the resurrection of the dead with the shameful tale of the woman of seven husbands placed

904 Gregory I, *Registrum* XI, 30 to Hadrian, notary of Palermo (J 1820):II, 919 (Martyn 2004: III, 775), already cited Response 10: 186. Hincmar omits an intervening sentence in which Gregory states that secular law allows an unilateral decision by one spouse to enter a religious life: see above, 186 n. 472. On separation to enter the religious life, see Introduction, 52.

905 That is, the exception given to divorce in Matthew 19:9.

906 The logic of this final section is hard to follow, but Hincmar may have regarded Question 23 as something of a trap (which explains why he did not really answer it). If he says that bishops cannot advise those whose have separated, he undermines his own authority to write *De divortio*; if he says they may give advice, he gives leeway to Gunther to ignore secular judgements in Engeltrude's case. This may be why he reframes the topic as being about bishops telling the truth and admonishing laymen.

before him, opened the secrets of the law to envious infidels and tempters [Luke 20:27–38]. Their explanation is that:

> 'He did not open the secrets of the law to them who were not able to understand, <234> but to those who could and who were also present, whom it was not fitting to neglect because of the uncleanliness of others. And when the tempters questioned him, he responded to them, so they did not have anything with which they could contradict him, although they were wasting away from their own poison more than being filled up with his bread; others however, who were able to understand, usefully heard many things from that opportunity of theirs.'[907]

And he will accept a sufficient explanation from us, such a small half-person (*homullulus*). But let him also receive St Augustine, speaking kindly for us in his book *On the Good of Perseverance*, for he said:[908]

> 'But the reason of keeping silent about the truth is one thing, the necessity of speaking the truth is another. It would be a long business to inquire into or to set down all the reasons for keeping silent about the truth. Of which, nevertheless, here is this one: lest we should make worse those who do not understand, while wishing to make more learned those who do understand; these latter do not become more learned when we are silent[909] about such things, but also do not become worse. When, however, a truth is of such a kind that he who cannot receive it is made worse by our speaking it, and he who can receive it is made worse by our keeping silent about it, what do we think is to be done? Must we not speak the truth, so that he who can receive it may receive it, rather than keep silent, so that not only neither may receive it, but that even he who is more intelligent may himself become worse? For if he should hear and receive it, many might learn also through him. For as he is more capable of learning, so he is the more fitted for teaching others.'

Appendix: introduction

<235> Finally, seven questions follow, which we received for resolution around six months after the ones discussed above, sent by the same people as the first.[910] Just as in the preceding ones, we shall insert the text

907 Bede, *In Lucae evangelium expositio* V, 20, 34: 358–9.

908 Augustine, *De dono perseverantiae*, c. XVI, 40: cols 1017–18 (Wallis 1887: 541–2). The following passage from Augustine concerns predestination.

909 The manuscript actually has *dicentibus* in place of Augustine's *tacentibus*, but this is probably a copying error rather than a deliberate change, and has been corrected here.

910 Hincmar received these in around August or September 860: see Introduction, 16–18.

of these separately before the answers, responding as far as we can, in brief words, as if arranged into a painting box (*buxea*), so that the careful man may understand how he may be able to paint from them more fully; and so that we might not shut up the innards of compassion from the petitions of the brethren, and so that we might offer to the wise man, according to the Scripture, the chance to be made wiser, when he seeks to understand these things, investigating more fully. And in the few little hours which we have extorted rather than borrowed from our multiple and very varied occupations, for we do not have free time for thinking, we have done in every possible way what might suffice and not increase the material for the readers, since the size of the compendium of responses about the questions proposed before almost exceeds the due measure of a volume.

The beginning of these questions is as follows:

> 'We beg of your Love that you will not find it tedious if we importunately persist in asking about things necessary for us to know. For after we recently sent questions to you for resolution, we found out about many things, concerning which we earnestly ask for you to reply, one at a time and individually, from the authority of Scripture and the rules, and from the doctrine of the doctors of the Church.'[911]

Appendix Question 1

> 'Some say that since King Lothar has bishops and noble and faithful laymen in his own kingdom, by whose advice and counsel he settled the matter between himself and his wife, that it does not pertain to the bishops of another kingdom, or to anyone else, to deal again with anything from this.'[912]

Appendix Response 1

<236> To these it should be replied: 'Ye do err, not knowing the Scriptures, nor the power of God' [Matthew 22:29]. When some of the sons of Israel built a heap of witness [Genesis 31:47], the other part aroused by divine zeal rushed to arms, so that the people of the Lord should not be divided, as they were later divided by the calves made in idolatrous crime for Jeroboam [1 Kings 12:26–33]. And now these people want to cut in two the kingdom of the Lord and the catholic

911 Note that Hincmar's questioners shared his emphasis on the use of authority.

912 On this point, see Introduction, 73.

Church, which is one dove and one beloved, as if they do not persuade but rather compel to say what some people said formerly, that you 'have no portion in David, and none inheritance in the son of Jesse: every man to your tents, O Israel' [2 Chronicles 10:16], trying to bring back to our most pestilential age that time when there was neither a king nor a leader (*dux*) over the people, 'but every man did what was right in his own eyes' [Judges 17:6].[913] And would now that the wise and prudent man would do what seems right, and not what is voluptuously pleasing, twisted and wrong. Is there not, as those build up their wickednesses, 'one Lord, one faith, one baptism, one God and Father of all, who is above all, and through all, and in all of us' [Ephesians 4:5], and one kingdom, one dove of Christ, that is holy Church, by the law of one Christianity (*Christianitas*), of one kingdom and one Church, although the helms are guided through many princes of the kingdom and bishops of churches?[914]

And the matter in question is such that is it known to pertain to all those marked by the name of Christian. A reckoning is brought into the presence of all about a king and a queen, a Christian man and a Christian woman, about the law of marriage given by God to our first parents in paradise, and strengthened in the Church, confirmed by divine and human laws through God, and established with a blessing through the sacerdotal ministry, and celebrated in the fashion of no matter who of the faithful.[915] And such a devilish invention stains this most excellent gift, that his operation cannot be doubted whom Scripture predicts will appear, 'that he as God sitteth in the temple of God, shewing himself as if he is God' [2 Thessalonians 2:4] and 'For the mystery of iniquity doth already work' [2 Thessalonians 2:7]; since licit things are illicitly spat out, and illicit things are usurped as if they were licit.[916] Not only those bishops, in whose parishes or diocesan responsibilities, or those of the faithful before whose eyes these things are dared, may be agitated as by things pertaining to them: truly the universal order, and people of every order, are troubled by portentous novelty

913 Hincmar here may be referring specifically to earlier periods of Frankish history or generally to the biblical past.

914 Hincmar's stress on the unity of the Church and the Frankish polity shows the continued power of the theme after twenty years of a divided kingdom: see above, 208 and Introduction, 86.

915 This repeats Hincmar's argument in the Preface: 86, that because the case is about marriage, it is therefore a matter of general concern.

916 Hincmar is more definite than in the first part that the devil is active in the matter: see Introduction, 64–6.

of this sort.[917] And the Roman pope St Celestine, just as we mentioned above,[918] said to Venerius and the other Gallican bishops, 'The universal Church is disturbed by whatever novelty' and to Nestorius, the bishop of Constantinople, 'What is being done should be known by all, whenever the business of all is being dealt with.'

This matter is for all [to see], as if placed on a watchtower.[919] Therefore it is necessary for it to be settled, and when settled to be known by all, since it should be observed by all, as the Lord says 'What I say unto you, I say unto all: watch' [Mark 13:37]. <237> And in the African Council it is defined that 'matters which are not common should be decided in their provinces. But as often as a common matter demands it, let a' general 'synod be gathered',[920] so that the general matter should be settled in it, for as Pope Innocent wrote to Victricius, bishop of Rouen:[921] 'the judgement is sound which is confirmed by the decisions of many'.

Therefore it is necessary that this general matter (*generalis causa*) that pertains generally to all should come to the attention of all, and be settled by a general decision, lest it be said by those who know it less well: 'For every one that doeth evil hateth the light, neither cometh to the light, lest his deeds should be reproved. But he that doth good things cometh to the light, that his deeds may be made manifest, that they are wrought in God' [John 3:20–21]. And as much as concerns the generality, let those things that are said in the shadows be said in the light, and those things which have been whispered into ears in small chambers, let them be preached from the housetops [Matthew 10:27]:[922] so that those may be rebuked by no one, those who, so that they might shine in word and deed to all and be seen by all, are placed like a light on a candlestick and a city that is set on a hill [Matthew 5:14–15], and gazed upon by all.

917 The Latin of this sentence is hard to construe: the text may be corrupted, or Hincmar may have written it hastily.

918 Celestine I, *Epistola* 21 to the bishops of Gaul, and *Epistola* 2 to Nestorius of Constantinople (J 381 and 374), both already cited in Preface: 86.

919 This metaphor of the case as a watchtower may connect to Hincmar's insistence in Appendix Response 7: 310, 321 that the bishop must be a watchman. See Introduction, 71.

920 *Registri ecclesiae Carthaginensis excerpta*, c. 95: 215. Hincmar inserts the word 'general'.

921 Innocent I, *Epistola* 2 (J 286), c. 1: col. 471.

922 That is, there are rumours circulating about the matter that need to be aired: see Response 3: 121.

Appendix Question 2

> 'Some also say that there is neither authority nor reason why this matter which was settled by the judgement of bishops should come back to judgement, because if this were to happen, the bishops who decided it will be as of no authority for other matters, and whatever they decide in the future will not be able to be so firm that it may not be dealt with again.'

Appendix Response 2

It is apparent that this is the voice of the inexperienced and of those who do not know the rules.[923] Read in the Council of Sardica what Pope Zosimus sent through Bishop Faustinus to the Synod of Carthage from the text of the Council of Nicaea, and you will adequately find there that people who say those things are in error.[924] And the Roman pope Leo, and the synod held at Rome, addressed the emperor Theodosius about retracting the Synod of Ephesus, which he seemed dangerously to favour doing:[925]

> 'Behold, O Christian and venerable emperor, I, <238> fulfilling with my fellow bishops the duty of most sincere love towards the reverence of your Clemency, and desiring you in all things to please God, to whom prayers are offered for you by the Church, so that we might not be judged guilty before the Lord's tribunal for our silence – we beseech you in the presence of the Undivided Trinity of the One Godhead, which is injured by such doings, and which is the guardian and the author of your empire, and in the presence of Christ's holy angels, that you order matters to be in the position in which they were before the decision, until a larger number of bishops be assembled from the whole world. Do not suffer yourself to be burdened with the sin of others, because (and we must say it), we fear that He, whose religion is being destroyed, will be provoked to wrath.'

And this is also to be feared not a little in this matter, which is not a small part of faith and religion (*religio*), by all priests (*sacerdotes*), kings and princes, and by all the faithful in general, if it is handled

923 Hincmar himself, however, made a similar point when trying to prevent appeals by clerics to the papacy from the decisions of provincial councils: see de Jong 2015: 273.

924 Council of Serdica, c. 7: 214–17 (Percival 1900: 421–2). This canon, on appeals to Rome by deposed bishops, was wrongly attributed to the Council of Nicaea by Pope Zosimus: see Merdinger 1997: 114–23.

925 Leo I, *Epistola* 44 to Theodosius (J 438) (Feltoe 1895: 52–3), c. 2: col. 829, discussing the Second Council of Ephesus 449.

negligently.[926] And it is clear from the sacred canons that the care of the whole province is in the power of the archbishop and primate, who should know of the judgements of his fellow bishops, from which a complaint might be necessary; and in those cases which the business demands it, he should appoint chosen judges. By all this it is shown that a synod should test or correct the judgement of the provincial bishops, but that a general synod should test or correct the judgements or dissensions of the provinces, as is shown in the African synod, which stated that nothing was to be altered in the Council of Hippo.[927] But the Apostolic See may retract, renew or confirm the judgements of both provincial and general synods, as the letters of Leo and Gelasius and the other Roman pontiffs, and the Synod of Sardica clearly show,[928] so that the authority of the bishops who judge rightly is confirmed, the authority of those who judge otherwise is corrected and authority does not meanwhile perish.

Appendix Question 3

> <239> 'And some say that there are no archbishops, except the pope, of greater authority than those who settled this matter ⌈of Trier and Cologne⌉, and if it were to come back to judgement, and it were found that the matter should not stand as it is, then those bishops who judged it would not be able to remain in the episcopacy any longer.'

Appendix Response 3

On the contrary, St Celestine wrote to Nestorius:[929] 'We want even priests (*sacerdotes*) to be corrected, regarding what is against justice (*fas*).' Let those who say this reread the Acts of the Apostles, and let them see that some people, coming down from Jerusalem to Antioch, raised up dissension against Paul and Barnabas concerning the question of circumcision and the observation of the law, so much so that they determined that they should go up to Jerusalem about this question, with the others who had been sent, to the apostles and priests; and in the same way this question was raised after their arrival by some of the Pharisees in Jerusalem. And let them take note that it was settled by

926 On the overriding importance of divine justice, see Introduction, 33–4.

927 *Registri ecclesiae Carthaginensis excerpta*, c. 34: 183.

928 Council of Serdica, cc. 3, 4, 7: 212–17 (Percival 1900: 416–18, 421–2). Böhringer 1992: 238 n. 9 lists papal letters on this theme.

929 Celestine I, *Epistola* 2 to Nestorius of Constantinople (J 374): 11.

Peter and judged by James differently from how these had judged and settled it, but no one from them [the earlier judges] was condemned [Acts 15:1–29]. Let them also see in the letter of Paul to the Galatians, that Peter was rebuked, reproached and corrected by the same Paul for dissimulation [Galatians 2:11–14],[930] but was not condemned, and that this reproach (*correptio*) was accepted by the first amongst the apostles, so that he honoured with great praise those letters of Paul in which he had read that he was rebuked [2 Peter 3:15–16].

And lest anyone should say that since according to Scripture, 'the less is blessed of the greater' [Hebrews 7:7], so the greater will not be judged by the lesser,[931] let them read the letters of Paul to the Corinthians, and they will found this archbishop and outstanding doctor to have refuted and corrected, but not to have condemned the disobedient bishops who allowed a fornicator to pass time in their midst without suitable criticism. And that he rebuked bishops for an excess of this sort, he makes clear himself, saying 'In the name of our Lord Jesus Christ, when ye are gathered together, and my spirit' [1 Corinthians 5:4], and in the second letter,

> 'Wherefore I beseech you that ye would confirm your love towards him. For to this end also did I write this, that I may know the proof of you, whether ye be obedient in all things. To whom you give any thing, I give also; for if I gave any thing to whom I gave it, for your sakes gave I it in the person of Christ' [2 Corinthians 2:8–11].

'I gave' here means 'I forgave', which for a public crime publicly repudiated pertains to no one but bishops, as those know, who are not unaware of the Church rules.[932] And so it is written in the Council of Carthage:[933]

> 'This also pleased us, that when an appeal goes from whatever ecclesiastical judges to other ecclesiastical judges of greater authority, <240> it shall not be prejudicial against the former if their sentence is dissolved, if they are not convicted of either having judged with hostile intention, or of having been corrupted by some greed or favour.'

930 Peter had concealed the fact that he had been eating with gentiles. On this vocabulary of correction, see above: 213.

931 This was a frequent theme of Pseudo-Isidore, as a way to protect clerics from accusations: see Knox 1991.

932 The typical freedom of Carolingian exegesis is shown here: Paul in 1 and 2 Corinthians makes no mention of bishops. It is also not clear how a claim that the 'archbishop' Paul corrected disobedient bishops contradicts Pseudo-Isidore's statement that the lesser should not judge the greater.

933 *Breviarium Hipponsense*, c. 10a: 36.

Concerning the idea that since 'there are no archbishops of greater authority than those', this matter should again come before them for judgement, we have shown above that what the singular cannot manage, a plurality can achieve, which the authority of Scripture demonstrates, saying 'if two of you shall agree on earth, as touching any thing that they shall ask, it shall be done for them' [Matthew 18:19] and 'For where two or three are gathered together in my name, there am I in the midst of them' [Matthew 18:20].[934] And when the apostles with the rest of the faithful and Mary the mother of Jesus prayed together, the earth moved, and the Holy Spirit appeared in tongues of fire above one hundred and twenty people gathered on the day of Pentecost [Acts 1:14–15; Acts 2:1–4]. And Paul, as we have said, showed this saying 'when ye are gathered together, and my spirit' [1 Corinthians 5:4]. And when the prince of the apostles [Peter],

> 'filled with gifts of grace, and supported by the very great power of miracles, by the admonition of the Spirit went in to Cornelius the Gentile, a question was raised against him by the believers as to why he had gone in among Gentiles and eaten with them, and why he had received them in baptism. He replied to the complaint of the believers, not by power (*potestas*) but by reason, and explained the case to them in order; and he pacified them by giving a reason humbly, and he even produced witnesses for the cause of the censure, saying, "Moreover these six brethren accompanied me" [Acts 11:1–18]. If, then, the pastor of the Church, the prince of the apostles, who gave signs and miracles in an unparalleled way, did not disdain to humbly give a reason in the case when he was blamed, how much more ought we sinners, when we are blamed for anything, to pacify those who blame us by humbly giving a reason',[935]

even if we may be judged of greater authority in some way?

And we say this not to blame our brothers and fellow bishops who judge in some matter according to ecclesiastical rules, but so we might more clearly show what we should do, so that we who are said to be something should not deceive ourselves, 'since we are nothing' [Galatians 6:3], as the apostle said. And if in the matter from which a dispute arises there is something worthy of emendation, let it be changed for the better (without prejudice to love): as Paul realised about not circumcising gentiles and not burdening them with the yoke of the law, and as Peter agreed, and as James helped judge [Acts 15:1–29]. And just as the holy Council

934 These biblical verses, used by Hincmar to argue for a general council, could of course equally have been used to show that there had been sufficient bishops present at the councils of Aachen for their validity.

935 Gregory I, *Registrum* XI, 27 to Theoctista (J 1817): II, 907–8 (Martyn 2004: III, 767).

of Nicaea decreed 'that when all the bishops of the province are assembled together at once, questions of this kind may by them be discussed in common', and once this discussion has taken place, then either what was done should remain, or the decision should be changed for the better; and if, however, two or three bishops, not because of the truth of faith or the sincerity of authority, 'but because of their own disputes, shall oppose the common decree of the rest, it being reasonable and in accordance with the ecclesiastical rules, then let the choice of the majority prevail'.[936]

If the fraternal decision is seen by some to be in need of retraction because of an excess,[937] as often happens, as with the acceptance of the gentiles that we recalled above, and an account is rendered with full faith and authority, let the decision of the Acts of the Apostles be brought out, in which it is said about the gentiles, following Peter:

> 'Forasmuch then as God gave them <241> the like gift as he did unto us, who believed on the Lord Jesus Christ; what was I, that I could withstand God? When they heard these things, they held their peace, and glorified God, saying, Then hath God also to the Gentiles granted repentance unto life' [Acts 11:17–18].

If perhaps a less important question should arise, let the brotherly agitations of the spirit be calmed to keep peace and love, as Gospel authority demonstrates when a question arose amongst the disciples about 'which of them should be accounted the greater' [Luke 22:24]. And should anyone have acted violently and negligently against those subjected to him, or other than he should have done in this sacral ministry, let him be corrected and amended according to the rules promulgated by the Holy Spirit, by those who are present. This is what the Nicene Council did about the excommunicated,[938] and the Sardican Council did about the bishop who was angry, which he ought not to be, and who wanted to drive out his priest or deacon,[939] and what the Chalcedonian Council did about the neglected ordination of bishops,[940] and as other councils and the letters of Leo and Gregory clearly show.

936 Extracts from Council of Nicaea 325, cc. 5–6: 8–9 (Percival 1900: 13, 15); c. 6 is also cited above, Response 22: 274.

937 That is, it goes too far in one direction.

938 Council of Nicaea 325, c. 5: 8 (see above, n. 936) requires checks that bishops have not behaved excessively or ungraciously in excommunicating people.

939 Council of Serdica, c. 17: 222–5 (Percival 1900: 431) originally dealt with bishops who had been wrongly deposed or expelled from their see; it had been altered in later collections to apply to priests and deacons.

940 Council of Chalcedon 451, c. 25: 98–9 (Percival 1900: 285) deals with metropolitans who delay appointing bishops.

If any people whatsoever – and may it not happen – should attempt with rash daring to speak against or trample down faith, or church doctrine, or the statutes of holy authority, let them be warned according to the Lord's precept; and if – and may the Lord spare us from this – they continue to be rebels, and obstinate despisers, it is necessary that they be struck and repressed with suitable rebukes, according to the holy canons and the examples and statutes of the elders, just as St Leo decreed in his letter to all the provinces:[941]

> 'We command that all things which have been promulgated by ecclesiastical orders and the teachings of the canons should be guarded by your Goodwill, so that if anyone acts against them, he will know that henceforth pardon will be denied him. And he who attempts to move against what has been decided, and dares to allow what has been prohibited, should know that he will be removed from his office, and he who did not want to be a sharer in discipline, will not be a companion in our communion.'

And the blessed Gelasius wrote:[942] 'Let those who dare to do this, and also those who noticed it but have so far kept silent, have no doubt that they will undergo the loss of their own honour, if they should not hurry as fast as they can to be cured from their lethal wounds by a suitable medication.' And St Celestine wrote to Nestorius:[943] 'About these we advise, with the foregoing agreement, that if they abuse our health-giving admonition, it is necessary that we confirm the sentence of condemnation against them.' And to Cyril of Alexandria:[944]

> 'We say this lest we should be seen perhaps to desert those wishing to make correction. For <242> if he should add thorns for himself when we are proffering a grape, let the earlier decisions be fulfilled through the fruit of his judgement: let him harvest what he sowed with devilish plough, to perish by his own will, not by our advice.'

Appendix Question 4

> 'They say moreover that if it is not permitted to this king either to take another wife, or the concubine he now has, and that his wife will be judged

941 Leo I, *Epistola* 4 to the bishops of Campania, Picenum, Etruria and all the provinces (J 402), c. 5: col. 614 (Feltoe, 1895: 4), also cited above, Response 11: 191. Hincmar has shortened and changed the order of this quotation.

942 Gelasius I, *Epistola* 14 to the bishops of Lucania, Bruttia and Sicily (J 636), c. 26: 377. 'Honour' here probably also implies office.

943 Celestine I, *Epistola* 2 to Nestorius of Constantinople (J 374): 11

944 Celestine I, *Epistola* 10 to Patriarch Cyril of Alexandria (J 377): 26–7.

to return to him whether he wills it or not, then he will come up with such a plan about her, so that he would be freed of her and would not have to come back to judgement about it again.'[945]

Appendix Response 4

We have not learned about a judgement of this sort from the truth of the Gospels, or apostolic authority or the promulgation of the sacred canons. But as the African synod decided, 'It pleased us that according to the Gospel and apostolic teaching, no one dismissed by his wife or dismissed by her husband shall be joined to another, but let them remain thus or be reconciled to each other.'[946] 'Reconciled' it said, not 'forced', and he who is wise will understand how a reconciliation may happen. And again Paul remembering Him through whom we are reconciled to God and receive the ministry of reconciliation, 'We pray you in Christ's stead, be ye reconciled to God' [2 Corinthians 5:20]. This reconciliation happens by the grace of God who calls, and does not compel, and by free, not forced, human will. And it is written of the just man, 'in the time of wrath he was made a reconciliation' [Ecclesiasticus 44:17], that is so that crimes should not be reckoned. Whoever knows how the words 'I bring together' (*concilio*) and 'I reconcile' (*reconcilio*) are composed cannot be ignorant about the form and order of reconciliation.[947] A diversity of types of illness requires a diversity of treatments by doctors.

And we read in holy authority that some are driven and forced to repentance,[948] some are excommunicated until they return to peace, and some leave in part of their own free will, as we showed above from the letter of St Gregory about the wife of Leo the *cartularius*,[949] who had left him for a while for the crime of fornication, putting on the religious habit. But after an oath had been given, and she recognised the innocence of her husband, she returned to him of her own will: and

945 That is, Theutberga's life may be in danger from Lothar II. On wife-killing, see Introduction, 55.

946 *Registri ecclesiae Carthaginensis excerpta*, c. 102: 218, also cited above, Response 5: 131. Hincmar's claim of the distinction between voluntary and forced reconciliation after separation was not necessarily put into practice: see Introduction 52.

947 That is, a council (or perhaps an individual bishop) should reconcile the couple: for an example, see Response 15: 236–7.

948 On coercive aspects of penance, see Introduction, 40.

949 Gregory I, *Registrum* IX, 3 to Secundinus, bishop of Taormina (J 1527): II, 564–5 (Martyn 2004: II, 547–8). On the case, see above, Response 9: 176–7; Response 10: 187.

Gregory wrote what was to be observed towards her to Secundinus, the bishop of Taormina. For some people, a choice in full liberty is to be awaited, as in this case, since it is conceded that a man and woman may be separated in the case of fornication, and once separated may be reconciled. But it is not conceded but compelled, with free choice completely removed, that a man and woman cannot be separated except in the case of fornication, and once separated should in no way be joined to others.[950] On this account St Augustine says in the second book of his *On Adulterous Marriages*:[951]

> 'We exhort those men who fear to be reconciled to their adulterous spouses who have been healed by penance, to nothing except keeping continent, since the woman is bound. <243> As long as her husband lives, whether as an adulterer or chastely, she commits adultery if she marries another. And the man is bound: as long as his wife lives, whether as an adulteress or chastely, he commits adultery if he marries another. This binding cannot be dissolved even if a spouse is separated from a chaste spouse through repudiation, and so can still less be dissolved if she commits adultery whilst not being separated.[952] And in this way nothing dissolves it, except the death of the husband, not the death of falling in adultery, but of leaving the body.[953] Therefore, if a woman leaves an adulterous man and does not wish to be reconciled to him, let her remain unmarried. And if a husband sends away an adulterous woman and does not want to take her back even after repentance, let him keep continence, even if not for the sake of willingly choosing a greater good,[954] certainly for the necessity of avoiding a destructive evil. And in this way it is this I exhort, even if the wife were in a long and incurable sickness, even if she were bodily separated in a place where the husband could not approach.[955]
>
> And finally I exhort this ⌜continence⌝, even if the woman, wishing to live in continence, modestly sends away her modest (*pudicus*) husband, although this is against the rule, since not done by consent.[956] I think no

950 See Introduction, 52–3.

951 Augustine, *De adulterinis coniugiis* II, 13: 397–8 (Wilcox *et al.* 1955: 118–19).

952 On Augustine's theories of marriage and Hincmar's use of them, see Introduction, 45.

953 This seems to respond to an ingenious potential argument: if adultery made someone spiritually dead, could this be taken as equivalent to them being actually dead, thus allowing the 'widowed' spouse to remarry?

954 For Augustine, continence is always a greater good than a marriage in which sexual activity takes place, though the latter is permissible. See Introduction, 45.

955 That is, in captivity. On the effect of captivity on marriage, see above, Response 4: 129.

956 A vow of continence was supposed only to be taken by mutual consent: see Introduction, 52.

> Christian can deny that he is an adulterer who, while his wife is ill for a long time or she is long absent and wanting to live continently, joins himself to another woman. Thus indeed, if an adulteress is sent away, he [the husband] is an adulterer with an adulteress, since not this man or that one, but rather everyone is an adulterer, who sends away his wife and marries someone else.'

And again in the same book:[957]

> 'We shall deny the grace of baptism and the medicine of penance to those men for as long as they live with adulteresses, if they have repudiated their previous wives for the sake of [their wives'] fornication and married others. Someone perhaps might say that no one can make his wife commit adultery if she is modest (*pudica*). But the Lord says, "But I say to you, that whosoever shall put away his wife, excepting the cause of fornication, maketh her to commit adultery" [Matthew 5:32]. So though she was modest with her husband, once sent away by her previous husband, she is forced through incontinence to join herself to another man while the first is still alive,[958] and that is to commit adultery.[959] And if she does not do this, still he compels her to do it as far as he can, and God will count this as a sin for him, even if she remains chaste.'

And again:[960] 'You will remember that I said this about both sexes.' And again:[961] 'Then there will be those who while their earlier spouses are still alive are joined to adulteresses, not their own spouses. And if they will not be in the kingdom of heaven, then where will they be, except where they will not be saved?'

So it is clear, just as we have shown above[962] by the authority of the Scriptures and the teaching of teachers, that a man and wife cannot be separated except either for continence within marriage, which is better, since they persevere as spiritually joined, or because of fornication, whichever one of them has divided the one body and one flesh. They are able to be separated because of this cause if they want, and if they are unwilling to remain together in worthy penitence or to be reconciled. They should in no way be forced either to remain together or to be reconciled. They should be persuaded if possible, since reconciliation

957 Augustine, *De adulterinis coniugiis* II, 17: 440 (Wilcox *et al.* 1955: 125).

958 The manuscript has in error *viro priore* instead of *vivo priore*.

959 Note Augustine's low opinion of the self-control of (most) women: see Introduction, 51–2.

960 Augustine, *De adulterinis coniugiis* II, 20: 408 (Wilcox *et al.* 1955: 130).

961 Augustine, *De adulterinis coniugiis* II, 18: 406 (Wilcox *et al.* 1955: 128).

962 See Response 5: 130–3.

requires a will, it desires love, which just like faith and pure confession can be encouraged but cannot be extorted, and can be forced only to be pretended. Those who are separated because of fornication must certainly be prohibited from marrying others. And if they disdain this, they must be brought back to repentance.

And since we have touched on pretence: if – and may it not happen – there should be pretence in any man (who because of fornication, can clearly be rejected by his wife, so that he cannot be joined to her again),[963] <244> so that he receives her back through persuasion not force, because while she is alive he will not be able to take anyone else, in the absence of a reason which is not contrary to sacred authority;[964] and if he should consider destroying her in some way: such an undertaking (*firmitas*) should be sought from him, as Gregory ordered should be demanded from certain people in the maintenance of equity for those who flee to the sacred places fearing violent injustice.[965] And if anyone is proven to have broken this undertaking, then he will have to submit to public and Church judgements.[966] And if he should act in secret, so that he cannot legally be convicted, then, warned through sacerdotal persuasion, he will have on his conscience a witness whom he will also have as a Judge. For let perfect episcopal foresight say to him in judgement, what Elijah sought to show to Elisha, 'for that which was my part, I have done to thee' [1 Kings 19:20], and to the Lord, 'I have not hid thy righteousness within my heart; I have declared thy faithfulness and thy salvation' [Psalms 40:11]. And in this and all other things,

> 'sacerdotal authority ought always in its doctrine to observe that apostolic model wherein it is said "Reprove, entreat, rebuke" [2 Timothy 4:2]. That is to say, he ought, mixing threats at some time with compliments at others, to show the severity of a master and the loving affection of a father: those who are undisciplined and restless he must reprove sternly, but he should entreat the obedient, mild and patient, so that they may progress in virtue. But the negligent and the scornful he must severely reprove and rebuke, nor should he shut his eyes to the sins of

963 This implies that Theutberga has the right to reject Lothar II, because he has committed adultery with Waldrada.

964 Hincmar again opens the possibility for an 'annulment'.

965 That is, Lothar should be made to swear an oath not to harm Theutberga: see Introduction, 55–6; on Gregory the Great's discussion of sanctuary, see above, Response 22: 271–2.

966 Note the combination of secular and ecclesiastical judgements here. See Introduction, 28 and 34.

offenders, but, as soon as they begin to arise, as much as he may be able to, root them out utterly.'[967]

Appendix Question 5

'And concerning the wife of Boso, about whom Boso himself complained at Koblenz,[968] and who afterwards came to this king [Lothar II] and stayed under his power.[969] Some people say that he [Lothar] does wrong since he does not return her to her husband when he can do so. And others say that it is not appropriate that he should hand over to death his relative who came to his fidelity, nor is it fitting that he should oppress a Frankish woman (*Franca femina*) and compel her like an unfree woman (*ancilla*), and return her to someone when she did not want to. And others say that if he wishes to return her, she will go to the Vikings (*Nortmanni*), and that it is better that he allows her to live among Christians, and amongst them to save her life, which the other man wants to take from her.'[970]

Appendix Response 5

There are legal capitularies of the emperors and of the kings their predecessors which say what someone should undergo who receives a bandit (*latro*) after he has been outlawed (*post bannum*).[971] And in the chirograph (*cyrographum*) of our kings, it is expressly decreed whose ministry it is to ensure that they are kept, as St Ambrose wrote to Valentinian, <245> 'Let the emperor make laws which he will be the first to keep.'[972] And if he breaks them, it should be feared that he will hear from the apostle, 'Thou therefore which teachest another, teachest thou not thyself? Thou that preachest a man should not steal, dost thou steal? Thou that abhorrest idols, dost thou commit sacrilege?'

967 Adapted from Benedict of Nursia, *Regula Benedicti* 2, 24–26: I, 446–8 (Clarke 1931: 11), where it is applied to the abbot. On the role of bishops in admonishing kings, see Introduction, 71–2.

968 The meeting held between Lothar II, Charles the Bald and Louis the German in June 860: see Introduction, 6.

969 On Engeltrude, see Introduction, 50, and biographical notes.

970 This was not the only marital case in which such a threat was made: see Stone 2007a: 473.

971 See e.g. *Capitulare missorum Silvacense* 853, c. 6 (MGH *Capit.* II, no. 260: 272–3).

972 Ambrose, *Epistula* 75, 9: III, 77 (Beyenka 1954: 54). The text of the *Conventus* from Koblenz in June 860 (MGH *Capit.* II, no. 242: 152–8), repeats an earlier *capitulum* (c. 5: 155) on dealing with those who had been excommunicated and then fled to another kingdom (as Engeltrude had done): such offenders should be returned to the relevant bishop.

[Romans 2:21–22]. Therefore let him hear wholesomely and suitably from the Lord, 'Physician, heal thyself' [Luke 4:23]. Let him fear also what it is written that the Lord said to a certain king, 'Because thou hast let go out of thy hand a man whom I appointed to utter destruction, therefore thy life shall go for his life, and thy people for his people' [1 Kings 20:42], and again 'Shouldest thou help the ungodly, and love them that hate the Lord? therefore is wrath upon thee from before the Lord' [2 Chron. 19:2], and again 'There is an accursed thing in the midst of thee: ... thou canst not stand before thine enemies' [Joshua 1:13], and 'He that toucheth pitch, shall be defiled therewith' [Ecclesiasticus 13:1]. For 'can a man take fire in his bosom, and his clothes not be burned?' [Proverbs 6:27].

And if this is about mercy, let him read and see how Saul offended through impious mercy for an impious man because he spared Agag but did not free him, and he himself lost his kingdom [1 Samuel 15:9]. And St Celestine says:[973] 'There is a piety from which is born impiety.' And if it is about kinship (*propinquitas*),[974] let him read what is written, 'Who said unto his father and to his mother, I do not know you; neither did they acknowledge their brethren for the sake of God: ... they have kept thy covenant, Lord' [Deuteronomy 33:9]. And the Lord said, 'He that loveth father or mother more than me is not worthy of me' [Matthew 10:37] and the rest which follows there. And if it is about freedom (*libertas*), she is known by the judgement of both divine and worldly law to be his [Boso's] who now seeks her, and against whom, as it is said herself a fornicator, she cannot complain of fornication.[975]

If he [Lothar] retains her to save her life, we showed above what firmness ecclesiastical authority demands from him in the maintenance of equity.[976] If, as is said, he retains her so that she might not perish among the Vikings, let the apostle respond to that, 'But if the unbelieving depart, let him depart' [1 Corinthians 7:15] and 'put away from among yourselves that wicked person' [1 Corinthians 5:13], lest one sick sheep should contaminate the whole flock.[977] And this king is not more just than the Lord, who did not forbid the unwilling Judas from going to the Jews or as Peter said, 'to his own place' [Acts 1:25], nor did

973 Celestine I, *Epistola* 2 to Nestorius of Constantinople (J 374): 10, cited above, 276.

974 On Engeltrude's relationship to Lothar see Heidecker 2010: 70–2 and Genealogy 4.

975 On Hincmar's views of wives' status, see Introduction, 51–2.

976 Response 22: 271–6. On the killing of adulteresses, see Introduction, 55–6.

977 Drawing on Benedict of Nursia, *Regula Benedicti* 28, 6: II, 552 (Clarke 1931: 49–50), slightly altered and with order changed.

He forbid Herod to kill the boys through power [Matthew 19:19], nor did He abandon rescuing Peter that very night from the prison from where he was to be led the same day, lest the soldiers should be killed for him [Acts 12:3–11]. And the Lord, who taught to love one's neighbour as oneself, asked no one to sin so that another should be freed from sin, and He who laid down His life, that is the life of His body, for His enemies and preached that it should be laid down for friends [John 15:13], did not teach that anyone should perish in eternity so that another would not perish in eternal damnation.

Anyone who mixes himself in these matters and makes these arguments must take care that he not be thought to be intent on making excuses for sin, for not only those who do such things, but also those who consent to those doing them, are worthy of death [Romans 1:32]. He will not be free from this 'consent' who did not avert evil when he was able to, or who sent off wicked people into their liberty when he was able to suppress them. For the judge, who as it is written 'beareth not a sword in vain' [Romans 13:4], is constituted 'for the punishment of evildoers and for the praise of them that do well' [1 Peter 2:14]. <246> To him in the Book of Deuteronomy the Lord gives the rule of judgement and punishment, saying:

> 'If there be found among you man or woman, that hath wrought wickedness in the sight of the Lord thy God, in transgressing his covenant, and hath gone and served other gods, and worshipped them, either the sun, or moon, or any of the host of heaven, which I have not commanded; and it be told thee, and thou hast heard of it, and enquired diligently, and, behold, it be true, and the thing certain, that such abomination is wrought in Israel: then shalt thou bring forth that man or that woman, which have committed that wicked thing, unto thy gates, even that man or that woman, and shalt stone them with stones, till they die. At the mouth of two witnesses, or three witnesses, shall he that is worthy of death be put to death; but at the mouth of one witness he shall not be put to death. The hands of the witnesses shall be first upon him to put him to death, and afterward the hands of all the people. So thou shalt put the evil away from among you' [Deuteronomy 17:2–7].

And so that no one will say 'This decision does not apply to the wife of Boso, since it is written about idolators', let him read the Scripture which says 'whose God is their belly: and whose glory is in their shame, who mind earthly things' [Phillipians 3:19]. And this decision also applies to that wicked business which it is said is suspected of Hubert and the king's wife, since in the Book of Leviticus, various abominations, listed one by one, are punished with death. And an adulteress is ordered to be crushed by stones by the sound command of the laws, according to those laws established by those who, thanks to God, established the laws, seeing what was right.[978] And so St Augustine in his second book *On Adulterous Marriages*, after the preaching by which he commands that husbands be persuaded that they should abstain from the blood of adulterous wives, says:[979]

> 'Finally I ask of you, whether it is licit for a Christian husband, according either to the old law of God or by Roman laws, to kill an adulteress? Certainly it is better that he should restrain himself from both, that is the permitted punishment for she who has sinned, and from an illicit marriage while she is alive.[980] But if he insists on choosing one, it is better for him to do what is allowed, so that the adulteress may be punished, than to do that which is not allowed, that while she is alive he commits adultery. But if, as is truly said, it is not allowed for a Christian man to kill his adulterous wife, but only to send her away',

it is on this condition, that he may either live in continence or be reconciled to her, since if while she is alive he marries another, he too will without doubt be guilty of adultery.

Appendix Question 6

> 'Some wise men say that this prince is the king, and is subject to the laws (*leges*) and judgements of none except God alone, who constituted him as king in the kingdom which his father left to him. And that if he wishes, he will go to an assembly (*placitum*) or a synod for this or another matter, and that if he should not wish, he will freely and legitimately leave off doing so. And just as he must not be excommunicated by his own bishops, whatever he might do, so he is not able to be judged by other bishops, since he is subjected to the sovereignty of God alone, from whom alone he was able to be constituted in sovereignty. And what he does and how he is in governance is at the command of God, as it is written, "The king's heart is in the hand of the Lord: he turneth it whithersoever he will"' [Proverbs 21:1].[981]

978 Leviticus punished incest, sodomy and adultery by death: see Introduction, 58.

979 Augustine, *De adulterinis coniugiis* II, 15: 400–1 (Wilcox *et al.* 1955: 121). The following sentences, in which Augustine advocates adultery over killing the wife, are omitted by Hincmar, as are the preceding passages in which Augustine condemns husbands' lack of mercy towards adulterous wives.

980 The manuscript reads 'Scilicet melius est', which we have translated as 'Certainly it is better'. Augustine, however, wrote 'Si licet melius est …', i.e. 'If it is allowed'. This may be a copying error, but conveniently removes a tone of doubt from Augustine's words.

981 On this question and what it might reveal about Lotharingian attitudes to kingship, see Introduction, 73.

Appendix Response 6

<247> This is not the voice of a catholic Christian, but of a blasphemer, filled with the devil's spirit. The king and prophet David, rebuked when he sinned by his lesser, Nathan, heard that he was a man of death, and was saved through a very severe penance [2 Samuel 12:1–15]. Saul learned from Samuel that he would be cast down from the kingdom [1 Samuel 15:26]. Rehoboam also learned from the prophet that the kingdom which his father had held well would be torn away his hand.[982] Whenever the kings and sons of Israel sinned, and were given over to the hands of the gentiles, like Manasseh [2 Kings 1:1–18] and Zedekiah [2 Kings 25:1–7], or were fearful of the Lord's gaze like Hezekiah [2 Kings 18–20], either they received the anger of the Lord through the prophets, or they deserved His mercy.

And in Deuteronomy it is written:

> 'If there arise a matter too hard for thee in judgement, between blood and blood, between plea and plea, and between stroke and stroke, being matters of controversy within thy gates: then shalt thou arise, and get thee up into the place which the Lord thy God shall choose; and thou shalt come unto the priests the Levites, and unto the judge that shall be in those days, and enquire; and they shall shew thee the sentence of judgement. And thou shalt do according to the sentence, which they of that place which the Lord shall choose shall shew thee; and thou shalt observe to do according to all that they inform thee: According to the sentence of the law which they shall teach thee, and according to the judgement which they shall tell thee, thou shalt do: thou shalt not decline from the sentence which they shall shew thee, to the right hand, nor to the left. And the man that will do presumptuously, and will not hearken unto the priest that standeth to minister there before the Lord thy God, or unto the judge, even that man shall die: and thou shalt put away the evil from Israel. And all the people shall hear, and fear, and do no more presumptuously' [Deuteronomy 17:8–13].

For the Lord says through priests (*sacerdotes*), 'Be wise now therefore, O ye kings: be instructed, ye judges of the earth. Serve the Lord with fear, and rejoice with trembling. Learn discipline, lest the Lord be angry, and ye perish from the just way' [Psalms 2:10–12, Septuagint version]. And apostolic authority advises that kings too should obey those set over them in the Lord, who watch for their souls, so that they may not do this with grief [Hebrews 13:17]. And blessed Gelasius wrote to

982 Hincmar here conflates 1 Kings 12:1–20 in which King Rehoboam suffers the division of his kingdom, with 1 Kings 11:26–39, in which Ahijah the prophet prophesies to Jeroboam that he will replace Rehoboam as ruler of ten of the twelve tribes.

Anastasius the emperor, that there are two persons:[983] 'by which this world is imperially (*principaliter*) ruled, that is pontifical authority and royal dignity, and the weight of the pontiffs is so much the greater, in as much as they themselves will render account to the Lord for these kings'. And Ambrose separated the emperor Theodosius from the Church, as his sins demanded, and recalled him through penance.[984] And in our time, episcopal unanimity restored by wiser counsel the pious Emperor Louis, who was thrown down from his kingdom, to both Church and kingdom after satisfaction, with the consent of the people (*populus*).[985]

But what is said, 'that the king is subject to the laws and judgements of none except God alone', is true if the king is, as it were, named, since 'king' (*rex*) is so called from 'ruling' (*regendo*).[986] And if he rules himself according to the will of God and guides the good in the right way, but corrects the wicked from the crooked way to the right one, then he is a king and is subject to the laws and judgements of none except God alone.[987] <248> For they ⌈the laws and judgements of others⌉ can be called opinions (*arbitria*), but they are not laws (*leges*) unless they are of God, through whom 'kings reign and the establishers of the law decree justice' ⌈Proverbs 8:15⌉. And whichever king is truly a king, is not subject to the law, since

> 'the law is not made for a righteous man but for the lawless and disobedient, for the ungodly and for sinners, for the unholy and profane, for murderers of fathers and murderers of mothers, for manslayers, for whoremongers, for them that defile themselves with mankind, for

983 Gelasius I, Letter to Emperor Anastasius (J 632): 20 (Tierney 1964: 13) in a free rendition. On this letter, see Preface: 91, Introduction, 71–2.

984 On this penance, performed in 391, see Introduction, 74. In Appendix Response 7: 309–14, Hincmar cites a number of extracts from Ambrose's letters.

985 This formal reconciliation with the Church took place at St-Denis in March 834: see de Jong 2009: 50. Hincmar was a monk of St-Denis before becoming archbishop and thus probably witnessed the event: see Böhringer 1992: 1–2; Stone 2015: 3–4.

986 Augustine, *Enarrationes in psalmos* 44, 17: I, 505, repeated by Isidore, *Etymologiae* IX, 3, 4 (Barney 2006: 200). This etymologically-based statement became a commonplace of Carolingian political thought: see Introduction, 70.

987 Hincmar's argument is hard to follow, since he moves between references to different types of law (*lex*), without distinguishing them. It was easy enough for him to connect together earthly law-making with the law-making role of God in the Old Testament. But what of statements by St Paul that Christians were no longer 'under the law', i.e. the Old Testament law? This section looks like a pre-emptive attempt by Hincmar to cut off a possible argument by Lothar's supporters: a good Christian might indeed not be subject to the law, but Lothar, as an adulterer and someone who 'serves the works of the flesh', is certainly not in that category.

> menstealers, for liars, for perjured persons, and if there be any other thing that is contrary to sound doctrine' [1 Timothy 1:8–10],

and for those who serve the works of the flesh. The apostle says about these,

> 'Now the works of the flesh are manifest, which are these; Adultery, fornication, uncleanness, lasciviousness, idolatry, witchcraft, hatred, variance, emulations, wrath, strife, seditions, heresies, envyings, murders, drunkenness, revellings, and such like: of the which I tell you before, as I have also told you in time past, that they which do such things shall not inherit the kingdom of God' [Galatians 5:19–21].

But he [the true king] rules himself and others according to the fruits of the Spirit, which are 'love, joy, peace, long suffering, patience, goodness, benevolence, meekness, faith, modesty, continence, chastity' [Galatians 5:22–23]; he is not subject to the law, since 'against such there is no law' [Galatians 5:23], but is subject to the judgement of Christ alone, by whom he will be rewarded, and he is Christ's who 'crucified the flesh, with the affections and lusts' [Galatians 5:24]. But in a different way, the adulterer, the murderer, the unjust, the abductor and he who is guilty of whatever other vices, will be judged secretly or publicly by priests (*sacerdotes*), who are the thrones of God, in which God sits and through which He decrees His judgements.[988] The Lord also said to these, through his apostles, whose place priests hold in the Church,

> 'If thy brother shall trespass against thee, go and tell him his fault between thee and him alone: if he shall hear thee, thou hast gained thy brother. But if he will not hear thee, then take with thee one or two more, that in the mouth of two or three witnesses every word may be established. And if he shall neglect to hear them, tell it unto the Church: but if he neglect to hear the Church, let him be unto thee as an heathen man and a publican' [Matthew 18:15–17].

And lest anyone should slight the priest (*sacerdos*) in this, the Lord adds 'Verily I say unto you, Whatsoever ye shall bind on earth shall be bound in heaven: and whatsoever ye shall loose on earth shall be loosed in heaven' [Matthew 18:18]. And again he said, 'He that heareth you heareth me; and he that despiseth you despiseth me' [Luke 10:16].

About what is said, 'that he [Lothar] was able to be constituted in the kingdom which his father left to him, by God alone', let those who say

988 The expression 'thrones of God' for bishops first appears in the Eleventh Council of Toledo, c. 5: see Böhringer 1992: 248 n. 14. On bishops as judging kings, see Introduction, 71–2.

this know that some are constituted by God in princedom, like Moses, Samuel and Josiah, about whom it is written even before he was born, 'Behold a child shall be born unto the house of David, Josiah by name' [1 Kings 13:2] and the rest which follows there. Some are constituted by God through men, like Joshua and David.[989] But some are constituted by men, not without divine permission – for as Augustine says, 'nothing happens except what either He himself does or what He permits to happen',[990] and whatever is done, is done by the ministry of angels and men – like Solomon, by the order of his father David and through Zadok the priest and Nathan the prophet [1 Kings 1:39]. And many kings are constituted or are cast down from their sovereignty (*principatus*) supported by the help of citizens or soldiers, and even saints (*sancti*) like Samuel.[991] Some indeed rule by paternal succession, as is found of all those in the histories and chronicles and even for those who are included in the book which is titled the *Vita Caesarum.*[992] Some indeed obtain their sovereignty by tyrannical usurpation <249> for the fulfilment of their sins, or for punishing the people's sins, about whom it is written, 'They have reigned, but not by me; they have made princes and I knew it not' [Hosea 8:4], and again, 'Who maketh a man that is a hypocrite to reign for the sins of the people' [Job 34:30]. It is necessary that things are this way, so that scandals may come, but 'woe to that man by whom the scandal cometh' [Matthew 18:7]. Since woe is to him, who makes himself by his vice what he must be, so that what pertains to woe may come to pass through him.

Concerning what is said about the kingdom, that his father [Lothar I] left it to him. Rather than boasting in his obtaining of the kingdom by chance, this king ought to dread divine judgements and to feel ashamed about human judgements, if he should not imitate the good habits and holy life and fair and just governance of his father, or if – and may it not be thus – he should choose to follow his wicked habits or unjust life (which we do not say that this man [Lothar I] had), or an unworthy governance.[993] For what family necessity helped the sons of

989 While Moses and Samuel were called directly by God (Exodus 3:1–10; 1 Samuel 3:1–10), Joshua and David were chosen at divine command by Moses and Samuel respectively (Deuteronomy 31:1–7; 1 Samuel 16:1–13).

990 Augustine, *De dono perseverantiae*, c. VI, 12: col. 1000 (Wallis 1887: 540).

991 On Samuel's role in selecting Saul as king and then replacing him, see 1 Samuel 9:15–10:24; I Samuel 16:1–13.

992 Probably a reference to Suetonius, *De vita Caesarum.*

993 On Hincmar's relationship to Lothar I, see Screen 2015. Lothar I himself had a relationship with a concubine, Doda: see Hartmann 2007: 551–2.

Samuel, who were not heirs of his virtue [1 Samuel 8:1–3]? And what paternal care of justice helped the children of Moses, who did not imitate him?[994] And so the power of their father was not carried to them as if from succession, who called him a relative by name alone, and it passed to him who was his son by virtue, not by ancestry (*genus*):[995] which this king too ought to fear. What harm directly is it believed to have done to Timothy that his father was a gentile [Acts 16:1]? And so holy Abraham had an impious father, yet was not made the heir of his impiety.[996] And Hezekiah was the son of the most profane Ahaz, but deserved to be the friend of God [2 Kings 18–20]. Which of his father's varied virtues did Noah's son [Ham] gain, who was made a slave from free status [Genesis 9:22–25]? And Joseph for a while was a slave in the middle of Egypt, but wove for himself the glorious crown of chastity [Genesis 39]. And the three boys and Daniel in Babylon were loftier than princes [Daniel 2:48–49].

Certainly then we see that paternal nobility does not suffice as a favourable support for children. For vices conquer the privileges of nature, and drive the sinner not just from the nobility of the father but even from liberty itself. Was Esau not the son of Isaac, fortified by the great favour of his father? And Isaac tried and wanted to give him a blessing, since he carried out all his father's commands, but since he was of wicked morals, nothing from any of this was of any use to him: but although he was first by the order of nature and more secure in his father's will, yet because he was not pleasing to God, he lost everything which he seemed to have [Genesis 27:1–41]. Every king, including this one, should consider this, and let him not boldly do all things which are pleasing to him, since not all things which are lawful are expedient [1 Corinthians 6:12], and according to the Scriptures, 'Let him bow his head to great men' [Ecclesiasticus 4:7] in honour of the King of kings, whose is the kingdom and through whom kings reign, who says, I will honour those who honour me, and 'those who despise me will be ignoble' [1 Samuel 2:30]. And to his priests He says, 'He that receiveth you receiveth me' [Matthew 10:40], and 'he that heareth you heareth me; and he that despiseth you despiseth me' [Luke 10:16].

994 Moses' sons were Gershom and Eliezer: 1 Chronicles 23:14–24 seems to suggest that they and their descendants held only minor roles in the priestly tribe of Levi. Instead, the leadership was taken over by Joshua, Moses' 'son by virtue'.

995 That is, to Joshua, appointed by Moses as his successor: see above, n. 994.

996 Abraham's father was Terah [Genesis 11:27–32]; he is not specifically said in the Bible to have been 'impious' (*impius*); but presumably, as someone worshipping other gods, Hincmar could consider him to be so.

And finally the example of Scripture, 'The king's heart is in the hand of the Lord: he turneth it whithersoever he will' [Proverbs 21:1] must be demonstrated, for what he does and how he is in the governance of the people might by divine command be turned to evil. In this way the devil mocked the Saviour, 'He gave his angels charge concerning thee' [Matthew 4:6]. Otherwise, the heart of the king is in the hand of the Lord, for as we have shown above, he is truly a king who rules himself and his thoughts, his words and his deeds under divine command.[997] <250> And his heart is in the hand of God, so that risen from this valley of tears, he disposes in his heart, walking from virtue to virtue, until the God of gods shall be seen in Zion, that is in the contemplation of eternal felicity and the divine vision. By contrast, the heart of him who is ruled wickedly by the encamped devil is in his power to the extent that if he hears anything of God's commands, the devil comes and takes the words away from his heart [Luke 8:12], lest believing or persevering in acting on what he had believed, he might be able to be saved. And so 'given up to a reprobate mind, he does those things which are not convenient' [Romans 1:28], since although he recognises God, he does not honour him as God with worthy obedience.

Concerning what is written, that the king if he does not wish to come to a synod, and even if compelled can leave off coming, holy Scripture and the sacred canons show that there should not be an acceptance of persons in judgement, but the quality of the case should be determined.[998] And Hubert, after he was accused of having perpetrated a certain crime against his own sister, and was summoned to the synod by synodal letters, indeed to three synods through letters and legates, came in person (*obtulit presentiam*) to give account only when he was able to come with the assurance that equity would be maintained for him, and the advocate (*causidicus*) and accuser of the crime was as many times absent or denied him the freedom to render account.[999] And Pope Boniface wrote to the Gallican bishops:[1000]

> Those things which were said against someone are proven to be true if he does not want to be present to confound them. And let no one doubt

997 On a king's need to rule himself, see Introduction, 70–1.

998 That is, any synod should ignore the fact that Lothar II is king and consider only the facts of the case.

999 Nothing more is known of these councils, but the First and Second Councils of Aachen could have been among them.

1000 This is the *Collectio Dacheriana* version of Boniface I, *Epistola* III to the bishops of Gaul (J 349): cols 757–8, discussing the case of Bishop Maximus of Valence. The principle that a person had invariably to be present for their own trial was, however, gaining traction in ninth-century Francia: see Introduction, 34.

that the guilty man flees the judgement, just as he who is innocent seeks it so that he might be absolved. Whoever thinks to escape judgement by delay confesses everything. So we command that a synod be gathered, where he will be present if he should wish to be there and he may respond to the accusations, if he has confidence. If he should neglect to be there, let him not gain a delay in sentencing from his absence. It does not matter whether all those things which are said are proven in an examination of him while present, since the absence itself may also as often stand for an enacted confession.'

Appendix Question 7

'And since some wise men say these things, as we said, do bishops and other Christians have any danger who associate (*communicare*) with this adulterer, and if there is a danger, how will they be freed before the Lord from the danger of the association?'

Appendix Response 7

It is written, 'he which converteth the sinner from the error of his way shall save a soul from death, and shall hide a multitude of sins' [James 5:20]. So by contrast, however many are destroyed by someone's wicked example, for so many will he be condemned, unless he repents worthily.[1001] <251> Therefore he does a public penance, repenting in public: not because the Lord does not give indulgence to someone worthily repentant through secret confession and private penitence for his sinful crimes, for even David, rebuking himself in the presence of one person, repented and confessed by the authority of the Lord and deserved the indulgence of his sin, whose punishment he later sustained in public.[1002] But the person who has destroyed many by his wicked example should fortify many for salvation, by the repentance of his humiliation. For as it is said of Paul, they saw him persecuting the Church and later fortifying it, and they glorified the Lord for this [Galatians 1:23–24].

But the person who sins publicly and is unwilling to return to penance is cast out from the society of the Church by public excommunication

1001 On the harsher divine punishment of those who should set a good example, see Introduction, 72.

1002 This is another reference to the story of David's confrontation with the prophet Nathan in 2 Samuel 12:1–14; Nathan tells the king that because of his secret adultery with Bathsheba, another man will commit adultery publicly with David's wives (a prophecy fulfilled by Absalom in 2 Samuel 16:21–22). Hincmar discusses this passage further later in the Response, 312. The suggestion that a secret confession might still receive public punishment does not fit easily with Hincmar's theories elsewhere in the text: see Introduction, 40–1.

by the bishops. This is not so that now excommunicated, he will not be in the presence of Him who promulgated the Church laws speaking through His Spirit: but so that the priests (*sacerdotes*), the successors of the apostles and of apostolic men, carry out their office, lest they be thought by those subject to them to neglect their ministry, and just as the fault of the sinner became known, so let the rebuke of the corrector be known to all.[1003] And he who otherwise does not wish to perceive his sin may return to penitence, either because he is rejected by all and accepted by none, for often good things are offered to the unwilling, or because he is compelled.[1004] His necessity may be changed into piety, and once he has been corrected through humility, he who sinned through pride may deserve to be reincorporated into the Church through a sacerdotal reconciliation.

All kings and princes of the world should take note that the wicked prince and king will be in the damnation of flames for affliction as punishment, underneath as many as he was in charge of in worldly governance (*regimen*). So it is necessary that he incessantly consider his actions, and when he destroys others by his example, let him fear, for he will not die alone who kills very many by the example of his own wickedness, for whom without doubt he will render account to the Lord. And he sins multiple times, not just through himself but also through those who imitated him or who sinned by his example or authority, especially when he himself sinning as though licitly was the kindling for sinning to others. And so speaking of another matter the apostle said, 'But take heed lest by any means this liberty of yours become a stumbling block to them that are weak' [1 Corinthians 8:9]. And again, 'And through thy knowledge shall the weak brother perish, for whom Christ died? But when ye sin so against the brethren, and wound their weak conscience, ye sin against Christ' [1 Corinthians 8:10–12]. And the Lord said, 'But whosoever shall offend one of these little ones which believe in me, it were better for him that a millstone were hanged about his neck, and that he were drowned in the depth of the sea' [Matthew 18:6].

For it would be much better for one of these that he should remain in private life (*vita privata*), than that placed in princedom (*principatus*) he make himself imitable in fault to others, and pay the penalty for as many

1003 Hincmar stresses that excommunication ought not to be a punitive measure, but one imposed for the good of the community (and ultimately of the sinner). See Introduction, 32–3.

1004 That is, excommunication may be effective through social pressure alone or may involve more coercive means.

as those for whom he was a leader into vices and an author of error by his example of sinning as if licitly.[1005] His fault is more serious, his torture will be harsher, the greater was his ability to excel. <252> For no one sins more against the people than those who usurp the order of princedom, acting perversely. For no one presumes to rebuke this sinner, and in his example the blame is very greatly extended, when from reverence for his rule the sinner is honoured. And so that he might give honours and benefices to his flatterers, the sinner is praised in the desires of his soul, and he who does wicked things is blessed, and the dead man is buried by the dead [Luke 9.60] in a very bad death. For it is written, 'When thou sawest a thief, then thou rannest with him, and hast been partaker with adulterers' [Psalms 50:18].

> 'He runs with a thief and is a partaker with him, when anyone joins himself to him in adulterated praises or in the delights that please him, and places the share, which he ought to have had with God and the angels, in hell with him, whose mouth abounded in malice and whose tongue concocted treachery',[1006]

when he praised him acting wickedly and treacherously or gave agreement to his wicked actions. Since not only those who do are worthy of death, but so are those who consent to those who do. And so St Ambrose:[1007]

> 'Since he who does these things sees himself to be honoured by those who are not like him, he grows in evil and perhaps boasts that he is such'. Therefore it is suitable that they should be punished with one penalty. 'And he who judges such things, as the same Paul says, and also does them, will not "escape the judgement of God" [Romans 2:3]. For he will be judged by Him, around whom flattery and the acceptance of persons ceases.'[1008]

→ St Augustine gives us advice on avoiding this sort of danger, saying:[1009]

> 'In two ways a bad person will not defile you; if you do not consent, and if you reprove; that is, do not associate (*communicare*), and do not agree.

1005 This passage (down to 'when from reverence for his rule the sinner is honoured') is adapted from Gregory I, *Regula pastoralis* I, 2: I, 136 (Barmby 1895: 2–3), where the argument is made about priests rather than princes.

1006 Pseudo-Jerome, *Breviarium in psalmos* 49, 18–19: col. 970.

1007 Based on Ambrosiaster, *Commentarius in Epistulam ad Romanos* 1, 32, 3: I, 60 (Bray 2009: 14).

1008 Ambrosiaster, *Commentarius in Epistulam ad Romanos* 2, 3, 1: I, 63 (Bray 2009: 15).

1009 Augustine, *Sermo* 88: 93–4 (MacMullen 1888: 385–6), also cited in Response 12: 161.

For there is an association, when an agreement either of will or of assent is joined to someone's deed. This the apostle reminds us, when he says, "Have no association with the unfruitful works of darkness" [Ephesians 5:11]. And because it was a small matter not to consent, if negligence in discipline followed, he says, "But rather reprove them" [Ephesians 5:11]. See how he included both, "Have no association, but rather reprove them." What is, "Have no association"? Do not consent to them, do not praise them, do not approve them. What is, "But rather reprove them"? Restrain, reproach, repress them .... But then in the reproaching and repressing of other men's sins, a person must beware, lest in reproaching another he exalts himself. Let him who thinks he stands, take heed lest he fall. Let the rebuke sound outwardly in tones of terror, let love of gentleness be maintained within .... So then let us neither consent to evil, so as to approve of it; nor be negligent, so as not to rebuke it; nor proud so, as to rebuke it in a tone of insult.' ←

And St Gregory in his letter to Felix, bishop of Sicily gives advice to all bishops, saying:[1010]

'The wicked should be segregated from the good, the evil from the just, so that at least from shame they may recognise their consciences, and be converted from their wicked deeds. And if they should seem incorrigible, let them be segregated from the faithful until satisfaction, following the sentence of the Lord Saviour, who amongst other things teaching about a brother sinning against oneself, said "But if thy brother shall trespass against thee, go, and tell him his fault between thee and him alone. If he shall hear thee, thou shalt gain thy brother. <253> But if he will not hear thee, take with thee one or two more: that in the mouth of two or three witnesses every word may be established. And if he shall neglect to hear them: tell it unto the Church; but if he neglect to hear the Church, let him be unto thee as an heathen man and a publican" [Matthew 18:15–17].

By these and many other authorities of the holy Fathers, the bad should be segregated from the good, lest the just perish for the unjust, as is written "the just man perishes for the impious". There must always be a distinction between the good and the bad, as there is between sheep and goats. Manifest sins should not be purged with secret correction, but rather things that are openly harmful should be openly rebuked.[1011] So that while they are healed by open chiding, those who offend by imitating them are corrected. For while one is rebuked, many are emended. And it is better that one man should be condemned for the salvation of many, than that through the license of one, many should perish. It

1010 Pseudo-Gregory, Letter to Felix of Messina (J †1334): 752. On this letter, see Introduction, 60. This passage is also cited above, Response 5: 136.

1011 That is, public sins cannot be dealt with by private confession: see Introduction, 50–2.

is no wonder if this notion is observed amongst humans, since we have often known this to happen amongst cattle. Those which are seen to be "scurvy or scabbed" [Leviticus 22:22] are separated from the healthy, lest the rest of them should be damned or perish from their disease. It is indeed better that the wicked should be openly corrected than that the good should perish for them.

So we wish all you bishops to convene together, so that a debate about matters arising may happen and a wholesome discussion about ecclesiastical observance. So that through these, while both preceding things may be corrected and future things may receive a rule, the almighty Lord may be praised by the agreement of the brethren. Know that if you observe this, His presence will be there with you, since it is written "For where two or three are gathered together in my name, there am I in the midst of them" [Matthew 18:20]. If He deigns to be present where there are two or three, how much more will He be not be absent when many priests convene? And indeed it is not unknown that a council should be summoned twice a year, as instituted by the rules of the Fathers,[1012] but lest there should be any excuse, we command it to meet once a year, so that in the expectation of the council, nothing wicked or illicit will be dared. For very many abstain from that which is known to be displeasing to the judgement of all, through fear of examination, if not from love of justice.'

And St Ambrose says in his letter to Theodosius the emperor:[1013]

'I am continually harassed by almost incessant cares, most blessed Emperor, but I have never been in such anxiety as at present, since I see that I must take care that there be nothing concerning the danger of sacrilege that may be ascribed to me. And so I entreat you to listen with patience to what I say. For, if I am unworthy to be heard by you, then I am unworthy to offer for you the vows and prayers with which you have entrusted me. Will you not yourself hear the person, whom you wish to be heard for you? Will you not hear the person pleading for himself, whom you have heard pleading for others? And do you not fear for your own judgement, lest if you should think him unworthy whom you heard, you make him unworthy to be heard for you?[1014]

But it is neither the part of an emperor to refuse liberty of speech, nor of a priest not to say what he thinks.[1015] For there is nothing in you emperors so popular and so worthy of love as to esteem liberty even in those

1012 This is in e.g. Council of Chalcedon 451, c. 19: 96 (Percival 1900: 282).

1013 Ambrose, *Epistula* 74, cc. 1–5: III, 54–8 (Beyenka 1954: 6–9).

1014 On the intercessory role of bishops as making them superior to kings, see Introduction, 73–4.

1015 On *parrhesia* (liberty of speech) in Late Antiquity and the early Middle Ages, see Garrison 2010: 140–51.

who are subject to you by military obedience. For this is the difference between good and bad princes, that the good love liberty, the wicked slavery. And there is nothing in a priest (*sacerdos*) so perilous before God, or so shameful before men, than not freely declaring what he thinks. For it is written: "I will speak of thy testimonies also before kings, and will not be ashamed" [Psalms 119:46]; and in another place: "Son of man, I have made thee a watchman unto the house of Israel" [Ezekiel 3:17], in order, it is said, "that if the righteous man doth turn from his righteousness, and commit iniquity, because thou hast not given him warning" – that is, has not told him what to guard against – "the memory of his righteousness shall not be retained, and I will require his blood at thy hand. <254> Nevertheless if thou warn the righteous man, that the righteous sin not, and he doth not sin, he shall surely live, because he is warned; also thou hast delivered thy soul" [Ezekiel 3:20–21].

I prefer then, O Emperor, to have fellowship with you in good things rather than in evil things, and therefore the silence of the priest (*sacerdos*) ought to displease your Clemency, and his liberty to please you. For you are involved in the risk of my silence, but are aided by the good of my liberty. I am not, then, unsuitably intruding in things where I ought not, nor interfering in the affairs of others, but complying with what is due. I am obeying the commands of God. And I do this first of all out of love for you, gratitude towards you, and desire for preserving your safety. If I am not believed in this, or am forbidden to act, I speak in very truth from fear of offending God. For if my peril would set you free, I would patiently offer myself for you, though not willingly, for I had rather that you might be acceptable to God and glorious, without my peril. But if the fault of my silence and dissimulation both weighs me down and does not set you free, I had rather that you should think me too importunate, than more useless and shameful. Since it is written, as the Holy apostle Paul says, whose teaching you cannot refute: "Be instant, in season, out of season, reprove, exhort, rebuke with all longsuffering and doctrine" [2 Timothy 4:2]. We, then, also have one whom it is even more perilous to displease, especially since even emperors are not displeased when everyone discharges his own function, and you patiently listen to everyone making suggestions in his own sphere, nay, you reproach him if he does not make use of the position of his service (*militiae suae ordo*).

Can this, then, seem offensive to you in priests, which you willingly accept from those who serve you; since we speak not what we wish, but what we are ordered? For you know the passage: "When you shall stand before kings and rulers, take no thought how or what ye shall speak, for it shall be given you in that same hour what ye shall speak. For it is not ye that speak, but the Spirit of your Father which speaketh in you" [Matthew 10:18–20]. And yet if I were speaking in state (*res publica*) cases, although

> justice must be observed even in them, I should not feel such dread if I were not listened to; but in the case of God, whom will you listen to, if you do not listen to the priest, at whose greater peril sin is committed? Who will dare to tell you the truth if the priest should not dare? I know that you are pious, merciful, gentle, and calm, having the faith and fear of the Lord at heart, but often some things deceive us. Some "have a zeal of God, but not according to knowledge" [Romans 10:2]. And I think that we ought to take care lest this also steals upon faithful souls.
>
> I know your piety towards God, your gentleness towards men, I myself am bound by the benefits of your favour. And therefore I fear the more, I am the more anxious; lest you yourself condemn me hereafter by your judgement, because either through my dissembling or my flattery you did not avoid some error. If I were to see you sinning against me, I ought not to keep silent, for it is written: "If your brother should sin against you, reproach him at first, then rebuke him before two or three witnesses. If he will not hear you, tell the Church."[1016] Shall I, then, keep silent in the case of God?'

And in the same letter:[1017] 'I, indeed, have done what could be done more honourably [towards you], that you might rather listen to me in the palace, lest, if it were necessary, you should listen to me in the church.'

And again in another letter to him [Emperor Theodosius], Ambrose says:[1018] 'Should I keep silent? But then my conscience would be bound, my voice snatched away, which would be the most wretched condition of all. And where would be that text? If the priest speak not to him that errs, "he who errs shall die in his iniquity", and the priest shall be liable to the penalty because he warned not the erring' [Ezekiel 3:18].

And again:[1019]

> 'An act has taken place in the city of the Thessalonians, with no precedent within memory, which I was not able to prevent happening; which, indeed, I had before said would be most atrocious when I so often petitioned against it, and which you yourself show, by revoking it after it had happened, that you consider to be grave; such an act I could not extenuate when done.[1020] It was first heard of when the synod had met

1016 Adapted from Matthew 18:15–17.

1017 Ambrose, *Epistula* 74, c. 33: III, 73 (Beyenka 1954: 19): i.e. he is warning Theodosius in advance, rather than publicly shaming him during a service.

1018 Ambrose, *Epistula* 11 *extra collectionem*, c. 3: III, 213 (Beyenka 1954: 21).

1019 Ambrose, *Epistula* 11 *extra collectionem*, cc. 6–7: III, 213–14 (Beyenka 1954: 21–22).

1020 In the year 390, Emperor Theodosius ordered violent reprisals against the city of Thessalonica in the wake of civil disorder, for which he was strongly criticised by prominent churchmen.

> because of the arrival of the Gallican bishops. There was not one who did not lament it, not one who thought lightly of it; your being in fellowship with Ambrose was no excuse for your deed. Rather, blame for what had been done would have been heaped more and more on me, had no one said that your reconciliation to our God was necessary. Are you ashamed, O Emperor, to do that which the royal prophet David, the forefather of Christ, according to the flesh, did? … <255> Recognizing that he himself was being accused in the tale,[1021] he said: "I have sinned against the Lord" [2 Samuel 12:13]. Bear it, then, without impatience, O Emperor, if it be said to you: "You have done this" [2 Samuel 12:7], which was spoken to King David by the prophet. For if you listen carefully to this, and say: "I have sinned against the Lord", if you say also prophetically: "O come let us worship and fall down before Him, and cry aloud before the Lord our God, Who made us" [Psalms 95:6], it shall be said to you also: "Since you repent, the Lord shall put away your sin, and you shall not die"' [2 Samuel 12:13].

And again in the same place:[1022]

> 'And so it repented the Lord, and He commanded the angel to spare the people, and David to offer a sacrifice, for sacrifices were then offered for sins; sacrifices are now those of penitence.[1023] And so by that humbling of himself the king became more acceptable to God, for it is no matter of wonder that a man should sin, but this is reprehensible, if he does not recognize that he has erred, and humble himself before God. Holy Job, himself also powerful in this world, said, "I covered not my sin, but declared it before all the people".'

And again in the same place:[1024]

> 'I have written this not in order to confound you, but that the examples of these kings may stir you up to take away this sin from your kingdom, for you will take it away by humbling your soul before God. You are a man (*homo*), and temptation has come upon you: conquer it. Sin is not taken away except by tears and penitence, neither angel nor archangel can do it. The Lord Himself, Who alone can say, "I am He, who blottest out they transgressions" [Isaiah 43:25] if we should have sinned, does not forgive except those who repent.'

1021 Hincmar here omits the first part of this sentence of Ambrose's letter, referring to the encounter of David with the prophet Nathan [2 Samuel 12: 1–4]: 'To him it was told how the rich man had many flocks seized and killed the poor man's one lamb, because of the arrival of his guest.'

1022 Ambrose, *Epistula* 11 *extra collectionem*, cc. 9–10: III, 215 (Beyenka 1954: 23).

1023 That is, the Christian practice of penitence replaces Old Testament sacrifices.

1024 Ambrose, *Epistula* 11 *extra collectionem*, c. 11: III, 216 (Beyenka 1954: 23–4). Hincmar's version here quotes a verse from Isaiah; other versions of the letter quote Matthew 28:20.

And again:[1025] 'Conquer the devil while you still possess that with which you may conquer. Do not add to sin, so that you usurp what has harmed many to have usurped.'

And a little later:[1026]

> 'I have no reason to be stubborn towards you, but I have cause for fear; I dare not offer the sacrifice [mass] if you wish to be present .... Lastly, I am writing with my own hand what you alone may read. May the Lord deliver me from all troubles, since I have paid attention to what was plainly forbidden to me, not by man, nor through man. For when I was anxious, in the very night in which I was preparing to set out' to you as you had asked,[1027] 'you appeared to me in a dream to have come into the Church, and I was not permitted to offer the sacrifice. I pass over other things, which I could keep silent about, but I bore them for love of you, as I believe. May the Lord cause all things to pass peaceably. He warns us in many ways about these things, by heavenly signs, by the precepts of the prophets; by the visions even of sinners, He wills that we should understand, that we should entreat Him to take away all disturbances, to preserve peace for you emperors, that the faith and peace of the Church, for whose benefit it is that emperors should be Christians and devout, may continue.
>
> You certainly desire to be approved by God. "To everything there is a time" [Ecclesiastes 3:1], as it is written: "It is time for Thee, Lord, to work" [Psalms 119:126]."It is an acceptable time, O Lord" [Psalms 69:13]. Make your offering when you have received the power to sacrifice, when your offering may be acceptable to God.[1028] Would it not wholly delight me to enjoy the favour of the Emperor, to act according to your wish, if the case allowed it? And prayer by itself is a sacrifice, it obtains pardon, when an offering would bring offence, for the one is a sign of humility, the other of contempt. For the voice of God Himself says that He prefers that His commandments be kept, than that sacrifice be brought. God proclaims this, Moses declares it to the people, the apostle Paul preaches it. Do what you understand is better for the time. "I prefer mercy", it is said, "rather than sacrifice" [Hosea 6:6]. Are they, then, who condemn their own sin, not more Christians than those who

1025 Ambrose, *Epistula* 11 *extra collectionem*, c. 12: III, 216 (Beyenka 1954: 24).

1026 Ambrose, *Epistula* 11 *extra collectionem*, cc. 13–16, III, 216–18, shortened (Beyenka 1954: 24–6).

1027 Hincmar adds 'to you as you have asked' to Ambrose's letter, suggesting that he does not know the details of Ambrose's situation; Ambrose was actually trying to avoid meeting Emperor Theodosius, so that he did not have to refuse him communion.

1028 That is, Theodosius can once again take part in the mass when he has done penance.

> think to defend it? The just man is an accuser of himself in the beginning of his words. He who accuses himself when he has sinned is just, not he who praises himself .... You have been anticipated, and I have not shunned that which I did need to fear.[1029] <256> But thanks be to the Lord, Who wills to chastise His young servants (*servuli*), that He may not lose them. This I have in common with the prophets, and you will have it in common with the saints.'

How the same blessed emperor obeyed these warnings, repenting in public, this blessed Ambrose demonstrated amongst other things in his sermon on the fortieth day after Theodosius's death, in the presence of the Emperor Honorius, his son.[1030] How other Christians and the faithful of God may be able to avoid danger in association of this sort, both the Lord in the Gospel shows about him who, reproached for a sin, was unwilling to amend [Matthew 18:17], and Paul says in the letter to Corinthians: 'Be not deceived: neither fornicators, nor idolaters, nor adulterers, nor effeminate, nor abusers of themselves with mankind, nor thieves, nor covetous, nor drunkards, nor revilers, nor extortioners, shall inherit the kingdom of God' [1 Corinthians 6:9]. And again, 'But now I have written unto you not to keep company, if any man that is called a brother be a fornicator, or covetous, or an idolater, or a railer, or a drunkard, or an extortioner; with such an one not to eat .... Therefore put away from among yourselves that wicked person' [1 Corinthians 5:11, 13]. And St John the Evangelist and apostle wrote: 'Even now there are many antichrists' [1 John 2:18], and again:

> 'Whosoever transgresseth, and abideth not in the doctrine of Christ, hath not God. He that abideth in the doctrine of Christ, he hath both the Father and the Son. If there come any unto you, and bring not this doctrine, receive him not into your house, neither bid him God speed: For he that biddeth him God speed is partaker of his evil deeds' [2 John 1:9–11].

And so that no one may say, 'He is the king: how will I be able to remove myself from his association?', let him know that St John the Baptist was crowned with martyrdom because he said to Herod, 'It is not permitted for thee to have her' [Matthew 14:4], that is an adulterous woman.[1031]

1029 Hincmar omits the first part of Ambrose's sentence, 'Remembering that you quickly pardon, and revoke your sentence, as you have often done', before 'you have been anticipated'. A copying error in the manuscript (*debuerat* for *debueram*) has been silently corrected here.

1030 Ambrose, *De obitu Theodosii.*

1031 On the problems of excommunicating the powerful, see Introduction, 33–4. Hincmar here is encouraging the Lotharingian bishops to take a stand even if it involves risk on their part.

And Paul, as we said above, forbade to eat with these sort of people, and he says elsewhere, 'Since ye seek a proof of Christ speaking in me' [2 Corinthians 13:3]. And the Lord in the Gospel exclaimed, 'He that is of God heareth God's words: ye therefore hear them not, because ye are not of God' [John 8:47]. And again, 'If ye love me, keep my commandments' [John 14:15], 'He that loveth me not keepeth not my sayings' [John 14:24]. And the apostle John said 'If a man say, I love God, and does not keep my commandments, he is a liar'.[1032] And the Psalmist says of the Lord, 'Thou shalt destroy them that speak lies' [Psalms 5:6]. And again the apostle John in the Apocalypse, 'There shall in no wise enter into it', that is the heavenly Jerusalem, 'any thing that defileth, neither whatsoever worketh abomination, or maketh a lie' [Revelation 21:27], and again 'But the fearful, and unbelieving, and the abominable, and murderers, and whoremongers, and sorcerers, and idolaters, and all liars, shall have their part in the lake which burneth with fire and brimstone: which is the second death' [Revelation 21:8].

And the terrible reproof of the Gospel weighs against them, they 'who loved the praise of men more than the praise of God' [John 12:43], and who rebuke and pursue those who want to remove themselves from every brother walking out of order.[1033] About these persecutors, it is clearly said in Apocalypse:

> 'Notwithstanding I have a few things against thee, because thou sufferest that woman Jezebel, which calleth herself a prophetess, to teach and to seduce my servants to commit fornication, and to eat things sacrificed unto idols. And I gave her space to repent of her fornication; and she repented not. Behold, I will cast her into a bed, and them that commit adultery with her into great tribulation, except they repent of their deeds. And I will kill her children with death; and all the churches shall know that I am he which searcheth the reins and hearts: and I will give unto every one of you according to your works' [Revelation 2:20–23].

He sweetly consoles those who refute iniquity, since they do not consent to it:

> 'I know thy works, and tribulation, and poverty (but thou art rich), and I know the blasphemy of them which say they are Jews, and are not, but are the synagogue of Satan. Fear none of those things which thou shalt suffer: <257> behold, the devil shall cast some of you into prison, that ye may be tried; and ye shall have tribulation ten days: be thou faithful unto

1032 Adapted from 1 John 4:20.

1033 On the dangers of 'consent' to the sin of others, see Introduction, 72.

> death, and I will give thee a crown of life .... He that overcometh shall not be hurt of the second death' [Revelation 2:9–11].

To those who are not able to resist such a thing with the authority of their order (*ordo*) or the dignity of power, or the fortitude of virtue, divine clemency advises them, saying in the Apocalypse:

> 'But unto you I say, and unto the rest in Thyatira, as many as have not this doctrine, and which have not known the depths of Satan, as they speak; I will put upon you none other burden. But that which ye have already hold fast till I come. And he that overcometh, and keepeth my works unto the end, to him will I give power over the nations. And he shall rule them with a rod of iron; as the vessels of a potter shall they be broken to shivers: even as I received of my Father. And I will give him the morning star' [Revelation 2:24–28].

And St Ambrose says about the letter to the Corinthians:[1034] 'If anyone does not have the power to cast him away or to test him whom he knows is guilty, he is immune. And it is not for the judge to condemn without an accuser, for the Lord did not cast off Judas, although he was a thief, because he had not been accused.'

But priests (*sacerdotes*) and princes and the great men (*primores*) of the world will not have this excuse before God. And the same blessed Ambrose says in the same passage of that letter:[1035]

> '"ye are puffed up and have not rather mourned: that he that hath done this deed might be taken away from among you" [1 Corinthians 5:2]. He [Paul] humiliates their pride so that he makes them not complainants but supplicants – for they were themselves participants, while they allowed someone guilty of such a great crime to come together with them uncorrected – so that all with one agreement would cast him out if he were to refuse to amend himself. For the apostle says that once his work was recognised, he was to be driven out of the gathering of the brotherhood. For all knew his crime and they did not accuse him: publicly, he had a stepmother in the place of a wife. In this matter, there was no need for witnesses, nor could the crime be hidden by turning one's back. "I, verily, as absent in body, but present in spirit" – that is the gaze is absent, but the spirit of authority is present, which is never absent – "I have judged already him that hath so done this deed, as though I were present"' [1 Corinthians 5:3].

1034 Ambrosiaster, *Commentarius in Epistolam I ad Corinthios* 5, 2, 1: II, 52 (Bray 2009: 141).

1035 Ambrosiaster, *Commentarius in Epistolam I ad Corinthios* 5, 2–3: II, 52–3 (rearranged) (Bray 2009: 141 omits certain sentences).

And this is to be noted, that whoever admit criminal sins – whence now judgements are determined by those mouthpieces of Christ, who reign with Him in heaven and gleam with earthly miracles, and before the ashes of those who, dead in nature but alive to God, as demonstrated by the miracles of their merits still live in words and proclamations[1036] – are judged now, and unless they should suffer penance, they are condemned already, although through our inertia we may neglect to follow those things for which we are ordained and constituted, at our peril and at the peril of those committed to us. And so the great Pope Leo speaking to Anatolius, the bishop of Constantinople about the holy Nicene council, which the catholic faith holds is also to be understood about other things, writes:[1037]

> 'These holy and venerable Fathers who in the city of Nicaea, after condemning the sacrilegious Arius with his impiety, laid down laws of Church canons that will last until the end of the world, and they live with us in their constitutions; and, if anyone ever presumes to do other than they established, it is at once invalidated; so that what was generally instituted for perpetual utility can never be modified by any change, nor can the things determined for the common good be diverted to private advantage.'

Weighing up all these things and other authorities of the holy Scriptures and Church rules, which we omit to insert here because it would be very long, and considering also his own danger, let anyone, <258> and also the person who is in question [Lothar], return to his senses. Let him either show that his action is clearly concordant with reason and authority, lest by sinning himself, by which God is seriously offended, as Scripture says about Jeroboam, he also makes others to sin [1 Kings 14:16]; or let him submit himself to wholesome counsel and divine authority, for otherwise he cannot be saved.

And let him consider, since 'youth and pleasure are vain things' [Ecclesiastes 11:10], that he should not give his honour (*honor*)[1038] to others and his years to a cruel one, nor give his flesh so that he should make his soul sin, for a brief and wretched delight, for 'the price of a whore is scarcely that of a single loaf' [Proverbs 6:26].[1039] Nor should

1036 A reference to the cult of the saints. On Hincmar's view of miracles, see Introduction, 65.

1037 Leo I, *Epistola* 106 to Anatolius of Constantinople (J 483), c. 4: col. 105 (Feltoe 1895: 78). Hincmar considered the Council of Nicaea to be binding, more authoritative than other (more recent) councils: see Sieben 1984: 99–100.

1038 Carolingian writers often used *honor* to talk of someone's position and status, and even official position.

1039 Hincmar returns to an emphasis on Lothar's unstable youthfulness.

he yield his members as instruments of unrighteousness unto sin [Romans 6:13], and groan in the last days, when he will consume his flesh and his body, when he will not be able to amend, when the soul will be compelled to render those things which it did through the body. So, considering his paths and turning his feet into the testimony of the Lord, let him do satisfaction through the worthy fruits of penance to the Lord and the Church for the things which he has done wrongly. And for the rest, let him direct his steps according to the eloquence of the Lord through His grace, so that any iniquity may not have dominion over him [Psalms 119:133] and imitating the conversion of Paul, who said of himself, 'And they glorified God in me' [Galatians 1:24], just as the Lord commanded, 'Let your light so shine before men, that they may see your good works, and glorify your Father which is in heaven' [Matthew 5:16].

Finally, we have said as much as we in our mediocrity understand about those matters, which we mentioned came to us in that letter, by the inspiration of the Lord, from the doctrine of the holy Scriptures and catholic Fathers, obliged by truth and the ministry imposed on us, neither prejudging any sound decision, nor dishonouring authority.[1040] As St Cyprian once said:[1041] 'Nor does anyone of us set himself up as bishop of bishops, or by tyrannical terror drive his colleagues to the necessity of obedience, for let every bishop' – reserving in all things the privilege of the holy and apostolic see of Rome, first amongst the whole circle of the world, and of its pontiff the Lord Pope Nicholas,[1042] and the decrees of the holy canons established by the Holy Spirit –

> 'have his own will to the extent of his liberty and power, so he may not be judged by another who cannot himself on his own judge the other. But, as the apostle says, with "every man fully persuaded in his own mind" [Romans 14:5], let us await the judgement of all things, of our Lord Jesus Christ, who one and alone has the power both of promoting us in the governance of his Church, and of judging our action.'[1043]

This alone we warn all the lords and our fellow priests, and us too equally with them, that according to the precept of the great Pope Leo

1040 This final section was initially written as a conclusion to the first part of the treatise. See Introduction, 20.

1041 Cyprian, *Sententiae episcoporum*, Preface: 436, perhaps via Augustine, *De baptismo* 6, 6: 304 (King 1887: 482).

1042 Cyprian's third-century defence of episcopal liberty needed some adaptation to ninth-century realities. On whether Hincmar knew of Nicholas's involvement in the case, see Introduction, 14.

1043 A continuation of the Cyprian quotation from above.

to Rusticus, bishop of Narbonne:[1044] 'In matters', he said, 'which were doubtful or obscure, we thought it best to pursue whatever was found to be neither contrary to the Gospel precepts nor to the decrees of the Holy Fathers.' <259> Indeed, since our Redeemer, who deigned to become equally king to us and priest – priest indeed, so that He might cleanse us from our sins by the sacrifice of his passion, and king so that He might grant to us an eternal kingdom, and make us a kingdom and priests unto God [Revelation 1:6] – and who was the only one able to be made essentially both, that is king and priest in dignity and name, constituted by His providence two [persons], as St Gelasius wrote to Anastasius the emperor, by which this world is imperially (*principaliter*) ruled, that is holy pontifical authority and royal power:[1045] 'in which the weight of the pontiffs is so much the greater, in as much as they themselves will render account to the Lord for these kings of men'.

About these two persons, most excellent in dignity, we thought it suitable to attach to this little work (*opusculum*) the comments of blessed Cyprian the pope and martyr, so that attending to the form of their name, as much as human fragility allows, they might in no way be turned aside from the rule of their dignity given to them by that Priest of priests and King of kings.

For he says in his book *On the Twelve Abuses of the World*, first about the king and then about the bishop, that as much as the rank is higher, so the fall is harder, and as much as the dignity is more spiritual, so the climb is loftier:[1046]

> 'For the ninth grade of abuse is the unjust king (*rex iniquus*). For it is necessary for a king not to be unjust, but to be the corrector of the unjust, so he should preserve the dignity of his name in himself. For the name of king (*rex*) retains this meaning, that he performs the office of a *rector* to all those subject to him. But how will he be able to correct others, who does not correct his own behaviour if it is unjust, since the throne of the king is exalted by justice, and the governance of the people is fortified by truth? The justice of the king is to oppress no one unjustly through power, to judge without acceptance of persons between a man and his neighbour, to be the defender of strangers, orphans and widows,

1044 Leo I, *Epistola* 167 to Rusticus of Narbonne (J 544): col. 1202 (Feltoe 1895: 110). Also cited above, Response 3: 124.

1045 Gelasius I, Letter to Emperor Anastasius (J 632): 20 (Tierney 1964: 13) in a free rendition. On this letter see Preface: 91, Introduction, 71–2.

1046 Pseudo-Cyprian, *De XII abusivis saeculi*, cc. 9–10: 51–6. On this text, see Preface: 90; the long quotation sums up a key theme of Hincmar in *De divortio*: that kings and bishops must fulfil their Christian duties, and that they and the whole kingdom will suffer if they do not.

to restrain theft, to punish adultery, not to exalt the wicked, not to nurture the shameless and actors (*histriones*), to make away with the impious from the land, not to permit parricides and perjurers to live, to defend churches, to nourish the poor with alms, to establish just people over the business of the kingdom, to have old, wise and sober counsellors, not to pay attention to the superstitions of magicians (*magi*), soothsayers (*harioli*) and sorceresses (*pythonessae*), to delay anger, to defend the country (*patria*) bravely and justly against enemies, to live in God in all things, not to lift up his mind in prosperity, to bear all adversities patiently, <260> to have catholic faith in God, not to let his sons act impiously, to devote himself at certain times to prayer, and not to eat food before the appropriate hour.[1047] "Woe to the land, whose king is a child and whose princes eat in the morning" [Ecclesiastes 10:16]. These things make prosperity in the present kingdom, and lead the king to the better heavenly kingdoms.

Who does not arrange things according to this law will surely endure many adversities in his rule. Therefore often the peace of the peoples is broken, and obstacles are raised up even from the kingdom, the fruits of the earth are diminished and the service of the people is hindered, many griefs assault the prosperity of the kingdom, deaths of loved ones and of children bring grief, enemy attacks devastate the provinces everywhere, wild beasts tear to pieces flocks of cattle and sheep, storms of spring and winter inhibit the fertility of the lands and the labours of the sea, and sometimes bolts of lightning burn up crops and the fruit of trees and vine-shoots. Above all these things, the injustice of the king not only darkens the face of the present rule, but also obscures his sons and grandsons, so that they will not hold the inheritance of the kingdom after him. Because of the sin of Solomon, the Lord took the kingdom of the house of Israel from the hands of his sons [1 Kings 11:12]; and because of the justice of King David, he left the oil lamp of his seed for ever in Jerusalem [1 Kings 11:36].[1048]

Behold, how much the justice of the king is worth in the world is clear to those who look: he is the peace of the people (*populus*), the protection of the homeland, the defence (*immunitas*) of the common people (*plebs*), the fortification of the nation (*gens*), the cure of the sick, the joy of men, the moderation of the winds, the serenity of the sea, the fruitfulness of the earth, the solace of the poor, the inheritance of the children, and the hope for himself of future blessedness. But let him know, that just as he is placed first on his throne amongst men, so if he does not do justice, he

1047 That is, to respect fasts.

1048 Hincmar may have seen this section of Pseudo-Cyprian as particularly relevant to Lothar II's case: what good did it do Lothar ensuring he had a legitimate son, if God might remove the kingdom from his lineage for his sins in doing so?

will have the first place in punishments. For he will have in that future as a form of affliction the punishment of all those sinners above him, whom in the present he now has below him.

The tenth grade of abuse is the negligent bishop, who seeks the honour of his rank amongst men, but does not preserve the dignity of his ministry before God, for whom he acts as ambassador. First let it be asked of the bishop what the dignity of his name holds, for bishop (*episcopus*), which is a Greek word, may be interpreted as "one who watches". Why a watcher was appointed and what is required from a watcher, the Lord himself lays bare, when through the person of the prophet Ezekiel he explains the reason for the office of bishop, saying, "Son of man, I have made thee a watchman unto the house of Israel: therefore hear the word at my mouth, and give them warning from me" [Ezekiel 3:17]. But if you see the sword coming and do not proclaim it so that the impious may return to his path, that impious man will die in his impiety, but I will demand his blood from your hand. But if you announce it and he does not return, he will still die in his iniquity, but you have liberated your soul.[1049] It is fitting for the bishop – who is appointed as a watchman for all – to look out for sin diligently, therefore listening and, after he has listened, to correct in word and deed if he can, and if he cannot, to turn aside from the workings of the wicked according to the rule of the Gospel. "If", it says in the Gospel, "thy brother shall trespass against thee, go and tell him his fault between thee and him alone: if he shall hear thee, thou hast gained thy brother. But if he will not hear thee, then take with thee one or two more, that in the mouth of two or three witnesses every word may be established. And if he shall neglect to hear them, tell it unto the Church: but if he neglect to hear the Church, let him be unto thee as an heathen man and a publican" [Matthew 18:15–17].

In this way whoever disdains to adhere to a teacher (*doctor*) or a bishop should be expelled. And who is expelled in this way must not be accepted by any other teacher or bishop. Whoever associates with someone outside communion, although Bacchinal anger does not permit it, withdraws [in communion] from that holy catholic priest, by whom he is ejected from the community of Christians.[1050] For this reason it behoves a bishop to be a bishop for those for whom he is appointed as a watchman. But, for the rest, how indeed he ought to be in himself, it is written in the law about the priest, "Let him not take a widow or a repudiated

1049 This passage is adapted from Ezekiel 33:6–9.

1050 This is Hincmar's attempt to make sense of a passage that had probably become garbled in his source. The original text of Pseudo-Cyprian (c. 10: 55) is: 'Qui ergo excommunicatum a catholico illo non permittente recipit, iura sancti sacerdotis, in quod Christianorum genus electum est, excedit' (Therefore he who receives the

> woman to wife" [Leviticus 21:14]. And the apostle Paul explains that someone coming to the grade of bishop should be sober, prudent, chaste, wise, modest and hospitable, having obedient sons in all chastity, with a good reputation amongst those outside [the Church], proffering conversation faithful in doctrine, <261> not having had more than one wife before the episcopacy, not violent, not duplicitous, not a drunkard, not newly converted, so that in this way he will show first in deed what he teaches others in the word of doctrine.[1051] Let negligent bishops beware of what the Lord complained through the prophet in the time of punishment: "Many shepherds have laid waste my people" [Jeremiah 10:12], and "the shepherds fed not my flock and fed themselves" [Ezekiel 34:8], but let they whom the Lord appointed over his family rather attend in their time to giving them as food a measure of wheat, that is pure and proven doctrine, so that when the Lord comes they might deserve to hear, "Well done, good and faithful servant: thou hast been faithful over a few things, I will place thee over many things. Enter thou into the joy of thy lord"' [Matthew 25:23].

Finally, two other abuses follow on, which cannot be separated from the negligence and danger of the previous two. The common people (*plebs*) without discipline, which pertains to the guilt of the negligent bishop, and the people (*populus*) without law (*lex*), which without doubt pertains to the wickedness of the unjust king.[1052] And the eight which precede these two, that is the wise man and preacher without works, the old man without devotion, the young man (*adolescens*) without obedience, the rich man without alms, the woman without modesty (*pudicitia*), the lord without virtue, the argumentative Christian, the proud poor man: these are known to have regard to these two chapters, 'by whom this world is imperially (*principaliter*) ruled',[1053] whether with praise and glory, or with censure and judgement.

For episcopal authority, by preaching through life and speech, and the royal dignity, through ruling and correcting, must be in charge of and

---

excommunicated man, not permitted by that catholic [the bishop/doctor], goes beyond the laws of the holy priesthood, in which the Christian people is chosen). However, in a number of manuscripts, the sentence is garbled, and appears as: 'Qui ergo excommunicatum a catholico illo non permittente, bacchina ira sancti sacerdotis, in quod Christianorum electus est, excedit'. Hincmar (or an intermediate source) tried to make sense of the text by modifying it to 'Qui ergo communicat non permittente bachina ira non communicati, catholico illo sancte sacerdoti, a quo de Christianorum coetu eiectus est, excedit.'

1051 This passage is freely adapted from 1 Timothy 3:2–7 and Titus 1:6–9.

1052 Pseudo-Cyprian, *De XII abusivis saeculi*, cc. 11–12: 57–60.

1053 Gelasius I, Letter to Emperor Anastasius (J 632): 20 (Tierney 1964: 13). On this letter see Preface: 91; Introduction, 71–2.

benefit[1054] all those who desire to follow and observe discipline, which is the correction that is ordained, and the observation of the rule of the elders who came before us. Those who despise the divine word and the known laws, the bishop should cut off with his medicinal blade from the healthy like a rotten limb, and the king must make away with the impious from the land with his judicial sword. This is so that they, with the sheep and subjects entrusted to them, may deserve to hear from the highest pastor and the King of kings at the future and terrible judgement, that as good and faithful servants in the ministry to which they were appointed, they have been found to be faithful to the Lord who appointed them. 'Come, ye blessed of my Father, receive the kingdom prepared for you from the foundation of the world' [Matthew 25:34], and which God, who does not lie, promised to those loving Him: He who lives and reigns before all and through all and in all, world without end, Amen.

1054 The phrase 'praeesse ac prodesse' is a frequent one in Late Antique and early medieval thought: see Anton 1968: 407.

BIBLIOGRAPHY

Primary sources

Note: where there is a choice of translation, we have generally preferred those that are most widely available, notably those that are freely accessible online in the Nicene and Post-Nicene Fathers (NPNF) series.

Acta conciliorum oecumenicorum. Vol. 1: *Concilium universale Ephesenum*; vol. 2: *Collectio veronensis*, ed. E. Schwartz, R. Schieffer, J. Straub and R. Riedinger (Berlin, 1925–26).

Adventius, *Epistola* 5, in *Epistolae ad divortium Lotharii regis pertinentes* (MGH *Epp.* 6), pp. 215–17, trans. P. E. Dutton, *Carolingian Civilization: A Reader* (Peterborough, Ontario, 2nd edn, 2003), pp. 386–9.

Ambrose, *De Abraham*, ed. C. Shenkl, CSEL 32, 1 (Vienna, 1897), pp. 501–638.

Ambrose, *Epistulae et acta*, ed. O. Faller and M. Zelzer, CSEL 82, 4 vols (Vienna, 1968–96), trans. M. M. Beyenka, *Letters: Saint Ambrose*, FoC 26 (Washington DC, 1954).

Ambrose, *De mysteriis*, ed. O. Faller, CSEL 73 (Vienna, 1955), pp. 89–116, trans. T. Thompson, *St. Ambrose, On the Sacraments and On the Mysteries*, rev. edn (London, 1950).

Ambrose, *De obitu Theodosii*, ed. O. Faller, CSEL 73 (Vienna, 1955), pp. 371–401.

Ambrose, *De sacramentis*, ed. O Faller, CSEL 73 (Vienna, 1955), pp. 15–85, trans. T. Thompson, *St. Ambrose, On the Sacraments and On the Mysteries*, rev. edn (London, 1950).

Ambrose, *Expositio psalmi cxviii*, ed. M. Petschenig, CSEL 62 (Vienna, 1913).

Ambrosiaster, *Ambrosiastri qui dicitur Commentarius in Epistulas Paulinas*, ed. H. J. Vogels, CSEL 81, 3 vols (Vienna, 1966–69), partial trans. G. L. Bray, *Commentaries on Romans and 1–2 Corinthians* (Downers Grove, IL, 2009).

Annales Bertiniani, ed. F. Grat, J. Vielliard, and S. Clemencet (Paris, 1964), trans. J. L. Nelson, *The Annals of St-Bertin* (Manchester, 1991).

Annales Fuldenses, ed. F. Kurze, MGH *SRG* 7 (Hanover, 1891), trans. T. Reuter, *The Annals of Fulda* (Manchester, 1992).

Annales regni Francorum, ed. F. Kurze, MGH *SRG* 6 (Hanover, 1895), trans. B. W. Scholz, *Carolingian Chronicles. Royal Frankish Annals and Nithard's Histories* (Ann Arbor, MI, 1970), pp. 37–125.

Ansegis, *Capitularia*, ed. G. Schmitz, *Die Kapitulariensammlung des Ansegis*, MGH *Capitularia regum Francorum, Nova series* 1 (Hanover, 1996).

Astronomer, *Vita Hludowici imperatoris*, ed. and trans. E. Tremp, *Thegan: Die Taten Kaiser Ludwigs; Astronomus: Das Leben Kaiser Ludwigs*, MGH *SRG* 64 (Hanover, 1995), pp. 280–555.

BIBLIOGRAPHY

Astronomer, trans. T. F. X. Noble, *Charlemagne and Louis the Pious: The Lives by Einhard, Notker, Ermoldus, Thegan, and the Astronomer* (University Park, PA, 2009), pp. 226–302.

Augustine, *Contra Iulianum*, *PL* 44, cols 641–874, trans. M. A. Schumacher, *Against Julian*, FoC 35 (Washington, DC, 1957).

Augustine, *De adulterinis coniugiis*, ed. J. Zycha, CSEL 41 (Vienna, 1900), pp. 347–410, trans. C. T. Wilcox *et al.*, *Treatises on Marriage and Other Subjects*, FoC 27 (Washington, DC, 1955), pp. 9–51

Augustine, *De baptismo*, ed. M. Petschenig, CSEL 51 (Vienna, 1908), pp. 145–375, trans. J. R. King, *The Writings against the Manichaeans and against the Donatists*, NPNF 1, 4 (New York, 1887)

Augustine, *De bono coniugali*, ed. J. Zycha, CSEL 41 (Vienna, 1900), pp. 187–230, trans. C. T. Wilcox *et al.*, *Treatises on Marriage and Other Subjects*, FoC 27 (Washington, DC, 1955), pp. 61–132.

Augustine, *De civitate dei*, ed. B. Dombart and A. Kalb, CCSL 47–8 (Turnhout, 1955), trans. M. Dods, *The City of God; Christine Doctrine*, NPNF 1, 2 (New York, 1887).

Augustine, *De correptione et gratia*, *PL*, 44, cols 915–46, trans. R. E. Wallis, *Anti-Pelagian Writings*, NPNF 1, 5 (New York, 1887).

Augustine, *De doctrina Christiana*, ed. J. Martin, CCSL 32 (Turnhout, 1962), p. 1–167, trans. J. F. Shaw, *The City of God; Christine Doctrine*, NPNF 1, 2 (New York, 1887).

Augustine, *De dono perseverantiae*, *PL* 45, cols 993–1034, trans. R. E. Wallis, *Anti-Pelagian Writings*, NPNF 1, 5 (New York, 1887).

Augustine, *De Genesi ad litteram libri duodecim*, ed J. Zycha, CSEL 28, 1 (Vienna, 1894), pp. 3–435, trans. J. H. Taylor, *The Literal Meaning of Genesis*, ACW 41–2, 2 vols (New York, 1982).

Augustine, *De gratia et libero arbitrio*, *PL* 44, cols 881–912, trans. P. Holmes, *Anti-Pelagian Writings*, NPNF 1, 5 (New York, 1887).

Augustine, *De nuptiis et concupiscentia*, ed. C. F. Vrba and J. Zycha, CSEL 42 (Prague, Vienna, Leipzig, 1902), p. 211–319, trans. P. Holmes, *Anti-Pelagian Writings*, NPNF 1, 5 (Buffalo, NY, 1887).

Augustine, *De sermone domini in monte*, ed. A. Mutzenbecher, CCSL 35 (Turnhout, 1967), trans. W. Findlay, *Sermon on the Mount*, NPNF 1, 6 (New York, 1888).

Augustine, *De trinitate*, ed. W. J. Mountain, CCSL 50–50A, 2 vols (Turnhout, 1968), trans. A. W. Haddan, *On the Holy Trinity*, NPNF 1, 3 (Buffalo, NY, 1887).

Augustine, *Enchiridion de fide, spe et caritate*, ed. E. Evans, CCSL 46 (1969), pp. 49–114, trans. J. F. Shaw, *On the Holy Trinity*, NPNF 1, 3 (Buffalo, NY, 1887).

Augustine, *Enarrationes in psalmos*, ed. E. Dekkers and J. Fraipont, CCSL 38–40 (Turnhout, 1956).

Augustine, *In Iohannis euangelium tractatus*, ed. R. Willems, CCSL 36 (Turnhout, 1954), trans. John Gibb and James Innes, *Homilies*, NPNF 1, 7 (New York, 1888).

Augustine, *Quaestionum in heptateuchum libri septem*, ed. J. Fraipont, CCSL 33 (Turnhout, 1958), pp. 1–377.

Augustine, *Retractionum libri duo*, ed. A. Mutzenbecher, CCSL 57 (Turnhout, 1984).

Augustine, *Sermo* 88, ed. P. Verbraken, 'Le Sermon LXXXVIII de saint Augustin sur la guérison des deux aveugles de Jéricho', *Revue Bénédictine* 84 (1984), pp. 71–101, trans. R. G. MacMullen, *Sermon on the Mount*, NPNF 1, 6 (New York, 1888).

Augustine, *Sermo* 351, *PL* 39, cols 1535–49, trans. E. Hill, *Sermons 341–400 on Various Subjects* (New York, 1995).

Bede, *Homiliarum euangelii libri ii*, ed. D. Hurst, CCSL 122 (Turnhout, 1955), pp. 1–378, trans. L. T. Martin and D. Hurst, *Homilies on the Gospels*, 2 vols (Kalamazoo, MI, 1991).

Bede, *In epistolam I Petri*, ed. D. Hurst, CCSL 121 (Turnhout, 1983), pp. 225–60.

Bede, *In Lucae euangelium expositio*, ed. D. Hurst, CCSL 120 (Turnhout, 1960), pp. 5–425.

Bede, *In Marci euangelium expositio*, ed. D. Hurst, CCSL 120 (Turnhout, 1960), pp. 431–648.

Bede, *In primam partem Samuhelis libri iv*, ed. D. Hurst, CCSL 119 (Turnhout, 1962), pp. 5–287.

Bede, *In prouerbia Salomonis libri iii*, ed. D. Hurst, CCSL 119B (Turnhout, 1983), pp. 23–163.

Benedict III, *Epistola*, ed. A. de Hirsch-Gereuth, MGH *Epp.* 5 (Berlin, 1899), pp. 612–14.

Benedict Levita, ed. G. H. Pertz, MGH *Leges* II (Hanover, 1837), Part 2, pp. 39–158 [a new edition under preparation by G. Schmitz is available at: www.benedictus.mgh.de/haupt.htm (accessed 4 September 2015)].

Benedict of Nursia, *Regula Benedicti*, ed. Adalbert de Vogüé and Jean Neufville, *La règle de Saint Benoît*, Sources chrétiennes 181–6, 6 vols (Paris, 1972), trans. W. K. Lowther Clarke, *The Rule of St Benedict* (London, 1931).

Boniface, *Epistolae*, ed. M. Tangl, *Die Briefe des Heiligen Bonifatius und Lullus*, MGH *Epistolae selectae* 1 (Berlin, 1916), partial trans. E. Emerton, *The Letters of Saint Boniface* (New York, 2000).

Boniface I, *Epistolae*, *PL* 20, cols 749–788.

Bonizo of Sutri, *Liber ad amicum*, ed. E. Dümmler, MGH *Libelli de lite imperatorum et pontificum* 1 (Hanover, 1891), pp. 568–620, trans. I. S. Robinson, *The Papal Reform of the Eleventh Century: Lives of Pope Leo IX and Gregory VII* (Manchester, 2004), pp. 158–261.

Breviarium Hipponense: ed. in *Concilia Africae*, 30–46.

Capitularia regum Francorum, ed. A. Boretius and V. Krause, MGH *Leges*, *Sectio II*, 2 vols (Hanover, 1883–97).

Cassiodorus, *Expositio psalmorum*, ed. M. Adrien, CCSL 97–8, 2 vols (Turnhout, 1958), trans. P. G. Walsh, *Explanation of the Psalms*, 3 vols (New York, 1990–91).

Celestine I, *Epistola* 2 to Nestorius (J 374), ed. in *Acta conciliorum oecumenicorum*, pp. 7–12.

Celestine I, *Epistolae*, *PL* 50, cols 417–558.

Celestine I, *Epistola* 10 to Cyril of Alexandria (J 377), ed. in *Acta conciliorum oecumenicorum*, pp. 26–7.

[Charles the Bald] *Recueil des actes de Charles II le Chauve, roi de France*, ed. A. Giry, M. Prou and G. Tessier, 3 vols (Paris, 1943–55).

Codex Apiarii causae: ed. in *Concilia Africae*, pp. 79–172.

Collaborative Hincmar Project blog, http://hincmar.blogspot.co.uk/ (accessed 21 September 2015).

Conciles gaulois du IVe *siècle*, ed. and trans. C. Munier and J. Gaudemet, Sources chrétiennes 241 (Paris, 1977).

Concilia aevi Karolini [742–842], ed. A. Werminghoff, MGH *Conc.* II, 2 vols (Hanover, 1906–8).

Concilia aevi Karolini, ed. W. Hartmann, I. Schröder and G. Schmitz, *Die Konzilien der karolingischen Teilreiche*, MGH *Conc.* III–V, 3 vols (Hanover, 1984–2012) [III: 843–859, IV: 860–874, V: 875–911].

Concilia Africae a. 345–a. 525, ed. C. Munier, CCSL 149 (Turnhout, 1974).

Concilia Galliae a. 314–a. 506, ed. C. Munier, CCSL 148 (Turnhout, 1963).

Concilia Galliae a. 511–695, ed. C. de Clercq, CCSL 148A (Turnhout, 1963).

Conciliorum oecumenicorum decreta, ed. G. Albeigo *et al.*, 3rd edn (Bologna, 1973).

Concilios visigóticos e hispano-romanos, ed. J. Vives (Barcelona, 1963).

Council of Agde 506, ed. in *Concilia Galliae a. 314–a. 506*, pp. 192–228.

Council of Ancyra 314, ed. in *Ecclesiae Occidentalis monumenta iuris antiquissima*, vol. 2, 1, pp. 1–145, trans. H. R. Percival, *Seven Ecumenical Councils*, NPNF 2, 14 (Oxford, 1900).

Council of Chalcedon 451, ed. in *Conciliorum oecumenicorum decreta*, pp. 75–103, trans. H. R. Percival, *Seven Ecumenical Councils*, NPNF 2, 14 (Oxford, 1900).

Council of Elvira, ed. in *Concilios visigóticos e hispano-romanos*, pp. 1–15, trans. S. Laeuchli, *Power and Sexuality: The Emergence of Canon Law at the Synod of Elvira* (Philadelphia, PA, 1972), pp. 126–35.

Council of Epaon 517, ed. in *Concilia Galliae a. 511–695*, pp. 22–37.

Council of Lérida, ed. in *Concilios visigóticos e hispano-romanos*, pp. 55–60.

Council of Neocaeserea, ed. in *Ecclesiae Occidentalis monumenta iuris antiquissima*, vol. 2, 1, 1–145, trans. H. R. Percival, *Seven Ecumenical Councils*, NPNF 2, 14 (Oxford, 1900).

Council of Nicaea 325, ed. in *Conciliorum oecumenicorum decreta*, pp. 1–19, trans. H. R. Percival, *Seven Ecumenical Councils*, NPNF 2, 14 (Oxford, 1900).

Council of Orléans 511, ed. in *Concilia Galliae a. 511–695*, pp. 4–19.

Council of Rome 721, ed. G. D. Mansi, *Sacrorum conciliorum nova et amplissima collectio*, vol. 12 (Florence, 1746) cols 261–6.

Council of Serdica, ed. and trans. H. Hess, *The Early Development of Canon Law and the Council of Serdica*, rev edn (Oxford, 2002), pp. 211–55, also trans. H. R. Percival, *Seven Ecumenical Councils*, NPNF 2, 14 (Oxford, 1900).

Council of Toledo (First), ed. in *Concilios visigóticos e hispano-romanos*, pp. 19–33.

Council of Toledo (Sixth), ed. in *Concilios visigóticos e hispano-romanos*, pp. 233–48.

Council of Valence 374, ed. in *Concilia Galliae a. 314–a. 506*, pp. 37–45.

Cyprian, *Sententiae episcoporum*, ed. Wilhelm Hartel, *S. Thasci Caecili Cypriani Opera omnia*, CSEL 3, 3 vols (Vienna, 1868–71), vol. 1, pp. 433–61.

Ebbo, *Apologetici Ebonis forma prior*, ed. in Concilium Ingilheimense 840, Appendix 1, MGH *Conc.* II, 2, no. 61, p. 794–9.

Ebbo, *Apologetici Ebonis forma posterior*, ed. in Concilium Ingilheimense 840, Appendix 2, MGH *Conc.* II, 2, no. 61, pp. 799–806.

Ecclesiae Occidentalis monumenta iuris antiquissima: Canorum et conciliorum graecorum interpretationes latinae, ed. C.H. Turner, 2 vols (Oxford, 1899–1939).

Epistolae ad divortium Lotharii regis pertinentes, ed. E. Dümmler, MGH *Epp.* 6 (Berlin, 1925), pp. 207–40.

Flodoard of Rheims, *Historia Remensis ecclesiae*, ed. M. Stratmann, MGH *SS* 36 (Hanover, 1998).

Gelasius I, *Epistolae*, ed. A. Thiel, *Epistolae romanorum pontificum genuinae, et quae ad eos scriptae sunt a S. Hilario usque ad Pelagium II. Tomus I: A S. Hilario usque ad S. Hormisdam: Ann. 461–523* (Braunsberg, 1868), pp. 285–510.

Gelasius I, Letter to Emperor Anastasius, ed. E. Schwartz, *Publizistische sammlungen zum acacianischen schisma* (Munich, 1934), pp. 19–24, partial trans. B. Tierney, *The Crisis of Church and State, 1050–1300* (Englewood Cliffs, NJ, 1964), pp. 13–14.

Gregorian Sacramentary, ed. J. Deshusses, *Le sacramentaire grégorien: ses principales formes d'après les plus anciens manuscrits.* Vol. 1, *Le sacramentaire, le supplement d'Aniane* (Fribourg, 1979).

Gregory I, *Dialogi*, ed. A. de Vogüé, *Grégoire le Grand, Dialogues*, Sources chrétiennes 251, 260, 265, 3 vols (Paris, 1978–80), trans. O. Zimmerman, *Dialogues of Saint Gregory the Great*, FoC 39 (Washington, DC, 1959).

Gregory I, *Homiliae in euangelia*, ed. R. Etaix, CCSL 141 (Turnhout, 1999), partial trans. D. Hurst, *Forty Gospel Homilies* (Kalamazoo, MI, 1990).

Gregory I, *Homiliae in Hiezechihelem prophetam*, ed. M. Adriaen, CCSL 142 (Turnhout, 1971), trans. T. Tomkinson, *Homilies on the Book of the Prophet Ezekiel*, 2nd edn (Etna, CA, 2008).

Gregory I, *Moralia in Iob*, ed. M. Adriaen, CCSL 143–143B, 3 vols (Turnhout, 1979–85), trans. J. Bliss, *Morals on the Book of Job*, 3 vols (Oxford, 1844–50).

Gregory I, *Registrum epistularum*, ed. D. Norberg, CCSL 140–140A, 2 vols (Turnhout, 1982), trans. J.R.C. Martyn, *The Letters of Gregory the Great*, 3 vols (Toronto, 2004).

Gregory I, *Regula pastoralis*, ed. B. Judic, F. Rommel and C. Morel, *Grégoire le Grand, Règle pastorale*, Sources chrétiennes 381–2, 2 vols (Paris, 1992), trans. J. Barmby, *Leo the Great, Gregory the Great*, NPNF 2, 12 (Oxford, 1895).

Gregory II, Letter to Boniface: ed. as Boniface, *Epistola* 26, pp. 44–7.

Hincmar of Rheims, *Capitularia*, ed. R. Pokorny and M. Stratmann, *Capitula episcoporum*, MGH *Capit. Episc.* II (Hanover, 1995), pp. 3–89.

Hincmar of Rheims, *De coercendo et exstirpando raptu viduarum puellarum ac sanctimonalium*, *PL* 125, cols 1017–36, trans. forthcoming on *Collaborative Hincmar Project* blog.

Hincmar of Rheims, *De divortio Lotharii regis et Theutbergae reginae*, ed. L. Bohringer, MGH *Conc.* IV, supplementum 1 (Hanover, 1992), trans. P. Throop, *Hincmar of Rheims on Kingship, Divorce, Virtues and Vices* (Charlotte, VT, 2014).

Hincmar of Rheims, *De ordine palatii*, ed. T. Gross and R. Schieffer, MGH *Fontes iuris* 3 (Hanover, 1980), trans. P. E. Dutton, *Carolingian Civilization: A Reader*. 2nd edn (Peterborough, Ontario, 2003), pp. 516–32.

Hincmar of Rheims, *De uxore Bosonis*, ed. as Hincmar, *Epistola* 135, pp. 81–7, trans. on *Collaborative Hincmar Project* blog.

Hincmar of Rheims, *Epistolae*, ed. E. Perels, MGH *Epp.* 8 (Berlin, 1939).

Hrabanus Maurus, *De institutione clericorum*, ed. D. Zimpel (Frankfurt 1996).

Innocent I, *Epistolae*, *PL* 20, cols 463–624.

Innocent I, letter to Decentius, ed. R. Cabie, *La lettre du pape Innocent I*[er] *à Decentius de Gubbio (19 Mars 416): texte critique, traduction et commentaire* (Louvain, 1973), trans. M. Connell, *Church and Worship in Fifth-Century Rome: The Letter of Innocent I to Decentius of Gubbio: Text with Introduction, Translation and Note* (Cambridge, 2010).

Isidore of Seville, *Etymologiae*, ed. W. M. Lindsay, 2 vols (Oxford, 1911), trans. S. A. Barney *et al.*, *The Etymologies of Isidore of Seville* (Cambridge, 2006).

Isidore of Seville, *Sententiae*, ed. P. Cazier, CCSL 111 (Turnhout, 1998).

Jerome, *Commentariorum in Matheum libri IV*, ed. D. Hurst and M. Adriaen, CCSL 77 (Turnhout, 1969), trans. T. P. Scheck, *Commentary on Matthew*, FoC 117 (Washington, DC, 2008).

Jerome, *Commentariorum in Hiezechielem libri XIV*, ed. F. Glorie, CCSL 75 (Turnhout, 1964), pp. 3–743.

Jerome, *Commentum epistolae ad Ephesios*, *PL* 26, cols 467–590, trans. R. E. Heine, *The Commentaries of Origen and Jerome on St Paul's Epistle to the Ephesians* (Oxford, 2002).

Jerome, *Epistulae*, ed. I. Hilberg, CSEL 54, 55, 56, 3 vols (Vienna, 1910–18), trans. W. H. Fremantle, *Jerome: Letters and Select Works*, NPNF 2, 6 (New York, 1893).

Jerome, *In Hieremiam libri vi*, ed. S. Reiter, CCSL 74 (Turnhout, 1960), trans. M. Graves, *Commentary on Jeremiah* (Downers Grove, IL, 2011).

John Chrysostom, *Homiliae in Epistolam ad Hebraeos*, *PG* 63, cols 9–236, trans. F. Gardiner, *Homilies on the Gospels of St John and the Epistle to the Hebrews*, NPNF 1, 14 (New York, 1890).

John Chrysostom, *Homiliae in Epistolam ad Romanos*, *PG* 60, cols 391–682, trans. J. B. Morris and W. H. Simcox, *Homilies on the Acts of the Apostles and the Epistle to the Romans*, NPNF 1, 11 (New York, 1889).

Julianus Pomerius, *De vita contemplativa*, *PL* 59 cols 415–520 (attributed to Prosper), trans. M. J. Suelzer, *The Contemplative Life*, ACW 4 (Westminster, MD, 1947).

Leo I, *Epistolae*, *PL* 54, cols 581–1218.

Leo I, partial trans. C. L. Feltoe, *Leo the Great, Gregory the Great*, NPNF 2, 12 1895.

[Lothar I and Lothar II] *Die Urkunden Lothars I. und Lothars II.*, ed. T. Schieffer, MGH *Diplomatum Karolinorum* III (Berlin, 1966).

Louis II, *Epistola ad Basilium I*, ed. W. Henze, MGH *Epp.* 7 (Berlin, 1928), pp. 385–94.

Martin of Braga, *Canones ex orientalium patrum synodis*. ed. C. W. Barlow, *Martini Episcopi Bracarensis Opera Omnia* (New Haven, CT, 1950), pp. 123–44.

Mosaicarum et Romanarum legum Collatio, ed. and trans. M. Hyamson (London, 1913).

Nicholas I, *Epistolae*, ed. E. Perels, MGH *Epp.* 6, pp. 257–690, partial trans. D. d'Avray, *Dissolving Royal Marriages: A Documentary History 860–1600.* (Cambridge, 2014), pp. 14–43.

Origen, *In Leuiticum homiliae*, ed. W. A. Baehrens, *Origenes Werke, Band 6, Homilien zum Hexateuch in Rufins Übersetzung. Tome 1, Die Homilien zu Genesis, Exodus und Leviticus*, GCS 29 (Leipzig, 1920), p. 280–507, trans. G.W Barkley, *Homilies on Leviticus*, FoC 83 (Washington, DC, 1990).

Palladius, *Historia Lausiaca*. Latin ed. as *Vitae patrum*, *PL* 74, cols 343–82, trans. R. T. Meyer, Palladius, *The Lausiac history*, ACW 34 (Westminster, MD, 1965).

Paschasius Radbertus, *Epitaphium Arsenii*, *PL* 120, cols 1557–650, trans. A. Cabaniss, *Charlemagne's Cousins: Contemporary Lives of Adalard and Wala* (Syracuse, NY, 1967), pp. 83–204.

Pseudo-Alexander I, Letter to all Christians (J †24), ed. in Pseudo-Isidore, 94–102.

Pseudo-Ambrose, *De lapsu Susannae*, ed. I. Cazzaniga, *De lapsu Susannae (De lapsu virginis consecratae) incerti auctoris* (Turin, 1948).

Pseudo-Amphilochius of Iconium, *Vita sancti Basilii* ed. F. Combefis, *Sanctorum Patrum Amphilochii Iconiensis, Methodii Patarensis et Andreae Cetensis Opera Omnia quae Supersunt* (Paris, 1644), pp. 155–225.

Pseudo-Clement, *Recognitiones*, ed. B. Rehm and F. Paschke, *Die Pseudoklementinen. Band* II, GCS 51 (Leipzig, 1965), trans. T. Smith, *Recognitions of Clement*, ANF 8 (New York, 1886).

Pseudo-Cornelius, Letter to Bishop Rufus (J †115), ed. in Pseudo-Isidore, pp. 172–5.

Pseudo-Cyprian, *De XII abusivis saeculi*, ed. S. Hellmann (Leipzig, 1909).

Pseudo-Damasus, Letter to Bishop Aurelius of Carthage (J †241), ed. in Pseudo-Isidore, p. 21.

Pseudo-Evaristus, Letter to the bishops of Africa (J †20), ed. in Pseudo-Isidore, pp. 87–9.

Pseudo-Fabian, Letter to the Eastern bishops (J †93), ed. in Pseudo-Isidore, pp. 60–6.

Pseudo-Felix I, Letter to Bishop Paternus (J †142), ed. in Pseudo-Isidore, pp. 197–200.

Pseudo-Gregory, Letter to Felix of Messina (J †1334), ed. in Pseudo-Isidore, pp. 749–53.

Pseudo-Isidore, *Decretales pseudo-Isidorianae et Capitula Angilramni*, ed. P. Hinschius (Leipzig, 1863) [a new edition under preparation by K.-G. Schon is available at www.pseudoisidor.mgh.de/, accessed 4 September 2015].

Pseudo-Jerome, *Breviarium in psalmos*, *PL* 26, cols 821–1278.

Regino of Prüm, *Chronicon*, ed. F. Kurze, MGH *SRG* 50 (Hanover, 1890), trans. S. MacLean, *History and Politics in Late Carolingian and Ottonian Europe: The Chronicle of Regino of Prüm and Adalbert of Magdeburg* (Manchester, 2009).

Registri ecclesiae Carthaginensis excerpta, ed. in *Concilia Africae*, pp. 182–232.

Sententia Pauli, ed. J. Baviera, *Fontes iuris Romani antejustiniani* II (Florence, 1968), pp. 319–417.

Siricius, Letter to Himerius, ed. K. Zechiel-Eckes and D. Jasper, *Die erste Dekretale: der Brief Papst Siricius' an Bischof Himerius von Tarragona vom Jahr 385 (JK 255)* (Hanover, 2013).

Statuta ecclesiae antiqua, ed. in *Concilia Galliae a. 314–a. 506*, pp. 164–88.

Tertullian, *De praescriptione haereticorum*, ed. R. F. Refoulé, *Traité de la prescription contre les hérétiques*, Sources chrétiennes 46 (Paris, 1957), trans. T. H. Bindley, *On the Testimony of the Soul and on the 'Prescription' of Heretics* (London, 1914), pp. 35–96.

Theoderic of Cambrai, *Libellus*, Council of Soissons 853, no. 27 Anhang, MGH *Conc.* III (Hanover, 1984), pp. 290–3.

Theodosian Code, ed. T. Mommsen and P. M. Meyer, *Theodosiani libri XVI cum Constitutionibus Sirmondianis et leges novellae ad Theodosianum pertinentes*, 2 vols (Berlin, 1905), trans. C. Pharr, *The Theodosian Code and Novels and the Sirmondian Constitution: A Translation with Commentary, Glossary and Bibliography* (Princeton, NJ, 1952).

Theodulf of Orléans, *Carmina*, ed. Ernst Dümmler, MGH *Poet* I (Berlin, 1881), pp. 445–581, trans. T. M. Andersson, *Theodulf of Orléans: The Verse* (Tempe, AZ, 2014).

Vita s. Deicoli, ed. G. Waitz, MGH *SS* 15, 2 (Hanover, 1888), pp. 674–82.

Secondary literature

Airlie, S. 1998. 'Private Bodies and the Body Politic in the Divorce Case of Lothar II', *Past and Present* 161, pp. 3–38.

Airlie, S. 2006. '"Sad Stories of the Death of Kings": Narrative Patterns and Structures of Authority in Regino of Prüm's *Chronicon*', in E. M. Tyler and R. Balzaretti (eds), *Narrative and History in the Early Medieval West.* Turnhout, pp. 105–31.

Airlie, S. 2011. 'Unreal Kingdom: Francia Media under the Shadow of Lothar II', in M. Gaillard, M. Margue, A. Dierkens and H. Pettiau (eds), *De la mer du Nord à la Méditerranée: Francia Media, une région au coeur de l'Europe (c. 840–c.1050): actes du colloque international (Metz, Luxembourg, Trèves, 8–11 Février 2006).* Luxembourg, pp. 339–56.

Airlie, S., Pohl, W. and Reimitz, H. (eds). 2006. *Staat im frühen Mittelalter.* Vienna.

Anton, H. H. 1968. *Fürstenspiegel und Herrscherethos in der Karolingerzeit.* Bonn.

Anton, H. H. 1982. 'Pseudo-Cyprian, *De duodecim abusivis saeculi* und sein Einfluß auf den Kontinent, inbesondere auf die karolingischen Fürstenspiegel', in H. Löwe (ed.), *Die Iren und Europa im früheren Mittelalter*, Stuttgart, vol. 2, pp. 568–617.

Anton, H. H. 1993. 'Synoden, Teilreichsepiskopat und die Herausbildung Lotharingiens (859–870)', in G. Jenal (ed.), *Herrschaft, Kirche, Kultur: Beiträge zur Geschichte des Mittelalters. Festschrift für Friedrich Prinz zu seinem 65. Geburtstag.* Stuttgart, pp. 83–124.

Bartlett, R. 1986. *Trial by Fire and Water: The Medieval Judicial Ordeal.* Oxford.

Bauer, T. 1994a. 'Die *Ordinatio imperii* von 817, der Vertrag von Verdun 843 und die Herausbildung Lotharingiens', *Rheinische Vierteljahrsblätter* 58, pp. 1–24.

Bauer, T. 1994b. 'Rechtliche Implikationen des Ehestreits Lothars II: eine Fallstudie zu Theorie und Praxis des geltenden Eherechts in der späten Karolingerzeit. Zugleich ein Beitrag zur Geschichte des frühmittelalterlichen Eherechts', *Zeitschrift der Savigny-Stiftung für Rechtsgeschichte, Kanonistische Abteilung* 80, pp. 41–87.

Becher, M. 1993. *Eid und Herrschaft. Untersuchungen zum Herrscherethos Karls des Großen.* Sigmaringen.

Benkov, E. 2001. 'The Erased Lesbian: Sodomy and the Legal Tradition in Medieval Europe', in F. C. Sautman and P. Sheingorn (eds), *Same Sex Love and Desire among Women in the Middle Ages.* New York, pp. 101–22.

Bof, R. and Leyser, C. 2016. 'Divorce and Remarriage between Late Antiquity and the Early Middle Ages: Canon Law and Conflict Resolution', in K. Cooper and C. Leyser (eds), *Making Early Medieval Societies: Conflict and Belonging in the Latin West.* Cambridge, pp. 155–80.

Böhringer, L. 1990. 'Der eherechtliche Traktat im Paris. Lat.12445, einer Arbeitshandschrift Hinkmars von Reims', *Deutsches Archiv für Erforschung des Mittelalters* 46, pp. 18–47.

Böhringer, L. 1992. 'Einleitung', *Hincmar of Rheims, De divortio Lotharii regis et Theutbergae reginae.* Hanover, pp. 1–98.

Böhringer, L. 2007. 'Gewaltverzicht, Gesichtswahrung und Befriedung durch Öffentlichkeit. Beobachtungen zur Entstehung des kirchlichen Eherechts im 9. Jahrhundert am Beispiel Hinkmars von Reims', in S. Esders (ed.), *Rechtsverständnis und Konfliktbewältigung: gerichtliche und aussergerichtliche Strategien im Mittelalter.* Cologne, pp. 255–89.

Böhringer, L. 2011. 'Das Recht im Dienst der Machtpolitik? Anmerkungen zu einer Neuerscheinung über die Scheidungsaffäre König Lothars II.', *Mitteilungen des Instituts für Österreichische Geschichtsforschung* 119, pp. 146–54.

Booker, C. M. 2009. *Past Convictions: The Penance of Louis the Pious and the Decline of the Carolingians.* Philadelphia, PA.

Branham, R. B. 1996. 'Defacing the Currency: Diogenes' Rhetoric and the Invention of Cynicism', in R. B. Branham and M.-O. Goulet-Cazé (eds), *The Cynics: The Cynic Movement in Antiquity and Its Legacy.* Berkeley, CA, pp. 81–104.

Brown, P. 1975. 'Society and the Supernatural: A Medieval Change', *Daedalus* 104, pp. 133–51.

Brown, P. 1988. *The Body and Society: Men, Women, and Sexual Renunciation in Early Christianity*. New York.

Brown, W. 2001. *Unjust Seizure: Conflict, Interest, and Authority in an Early Medieval Society*. Ithaca, NY.

Brühl, C. 1964. 'Hinkmariana II: Hinkmar im Widerstreit von kanonischem Recht und Politik in Ehefragen', *Deutsches Archiv für Erforschung des Mittelalters* 20, pp. 55–77.

Bührer-Thierry, G. 1992. 'La reine adultère', *Cahiers de civilisation médiévale* 35, pp. 299–312.

Bührer-Thierry, G. 2007. 'Reines adultères et empoisonneuses, reines injustement accussées: la confrontation de deux modèles aux VIII–Xe siècles', in C. La Rocca (ed.), *Agire da donna: modelli e pratiche di rapprensentazione (secoli VI–X): atti del convegno (Padova, 18–19 febbraio 2005)*. Turnhout, pp. 151–70.

Cadden, J. 1993. *Meanings of Sex Difference in the Middle Ages: Medicine, Science, and Culture*. Cambridge.

Carey, F. M. 1938. 'The Scriptorium of Reims during the Archbishopric of Hincmar (845–882 A.D.)', in L. W. Jones (ed.), *Classical and Mediaeval Studies in Honor of Edward Kennard Rand*. New York, pp. 41–60.

Collins, R. 2010. *Early Medieval Europe, 300–1000*, 3rd en Basingstoke.

Cooper, K. 1992. 'Insinuations of Womanly Influence: An Aspect of the Christianization of the Roman Aristocracy', *Journal of Roman Studies* 82, pp. 150–64.

Cooper, K. 2007. *The Fall of the Roman Household*. Cambridge.

Corcoran, S. 2013. 'The Gregorianus and Hermogenianus Assembled and Shattered', *Mélanges de l'École française de Rome – Antiquité*, 125(2), http://mefra.revues.org/1772 (accessed 21 August 2015).

Corcoran, S. 2015. 'Hincmar and His Roman Legal Sources', in Stone and West 2015, pp. 129–55.

Costambeys, M., Innes, M. and MacLean, S. 2011. *The Carolingian World*. Cambridge.

Darling, L. T. 2013. 'Mirrors for Princes in Europe and the Middle East: A Case of Historiographical Incommensurability', in A. Classen (ed.), *East Meets West in the Middle Ages and Early Modern Times: Transcultural Experiences in the Premodern World*. Berlin, pp. 223–42.

Daudet, P. 1933. *Études sur l'histoire de la jurisdiction matrimoniale: les origines carolingiennes de la compétence exclusive de l'église (France et Germanie)*. Paris.

Davies, W. and Fouracre, P. (eds). 1986. *The Settlement of Disputes in Early Medieval Europe*. Cambridge.

d'Avray, D. 2005. *Medieval Marriage: Symbolism and Society*. Oxford.

d'Avray, D. 2015. *Papacy, Monarchy and Marriage 860–1600*. Cambridge.

de Jong, M. 1989. 'To the Limits of Kinship: Anti-Incest Legislation in the Early Medieval West (500–900)', in J. Bremmer (ed.), *From Sappho to De Sade: Moments in the History of Sexuality*. London, pp. 36–59.

de Jong, M. 1996. *In Samuel's Image: Child Oblation in the Early Medieval West*. Leiden.

de Jong, M. 1997. 'What Was *Public* about Public Penance? *Paenitentia publica* and Justice in the Carolingian World', in *La Giustizia nell'alto medioevo (secoli IX–XI), 11–17 aprile 1996*, Settimane 44. Spoleto, vol. 2, pp. 863–904.

de Jong, M. 2005. 'Charlemagne's Church', in J. Story (ed.), *Charlemagne: Empire and Society*. Manchester, pp. 103–35.

de Jong, M. 2006. '*Ecclesia* and the Early Medieval Polity', in Airlie, Pohl and Reimitz 2006, pp. 113–32.

de Jong, M. 2009. *The Penitential State: Authority and Atonement in the Age of Louis the Pious, 814–840*. Cambridge.

de Jong, M. 2014. 'Paschasius Radbertus and Pseudo-Isidore: the evidence of the *Epitaphium Arsenii*', in V. L. Garver and O. M. Phelan (eds), *Rome and Religion in the Medieval West: Studies in Honor of Thomas F. X. Noble*. Farnham, pp. 149–77.

de Jong, M. 2015. 'Hincmar, Priests and Pseudo-Isidore: The Case of Trising in Context', in Stone and West 2015, pp. 268–88.

Depreux, P. 2015. '*Hincmar et la loi* Revisited: On Hincmar's Use of Capitularies', in Stone and West 2015, pp. 156–69.

Devisse, J. 1962. *Hincmar et la loi*. Dakar.

Devisse, J. 1968. 'Essai sur l'histoire d'une expression qui a fait fortune: *consilium et auxilium* au IXe siècle', *Le moyen âge* 74, pp. 179–205.

Devisse, J. 1975–76. *Hincmar, archevêque de Reims 845–882*, 3 vols. Geneva.

Dolbeau, F. 2012. 'Ex dono Hincmari. Livres donnés par Hincmar (845–882) à Saint-Remi de Reims', in M. Coumert, M.-C. Isaïa, K. Krönert and S. Shimahara (eds), *Rerum gestarum scriptor: histoire et historiographie au Moyen Âge: mélanges Michel Sot*. Paris, pp. 601–14.

Duby, G. 1978. *Medieval Marriage: Two Models from Twelfth-Century France*. Baltimore, MD.

Elsakkers, M. 2001. 'Genre Hopping: Aristotelian Criteria for Abortion in Germania', in K. E. Olsen, A. Harbus and T. Hofstra (eds), *Germanic Texts and Latin Models: Medieval Reconstructions*. Leuven, pp. 73–92.

Esders, S. and Mierau, H. J. 2000. *Der althochdeutsche Klerikereid: bischöfliche Diözesangewalt, kirchliches Benefizialwesen und volkssprachliche Rechtspraxis im frühmittelalterlichen Baiern*. Hanover.

Esmyol, A. 2002. *Geliebte oder Ehefrau? Konkubinen im frühen Mittelalter*. Cologne.

Evans, G. R. 1999. 'Evil', in A. D. Fitzgerald and J. C. Cavadini (eds), *Augustine through the Ages: An Encyclopedia*. Grand Rapids, MI, pp. 340–4.

Evans Grubbs, J. 1995. *Law and Family in Late Antiquity: The Emperor Constantine's Marriage Legislation*. Oxford.

Faulkner, T. 2016. *Law and Authority in the Early Middle Ages: The Frankish Leges in the Carolingian Period*. Cambridge.

Felten, F. J. 1996. 'Liebe, Lust und Leidenschaft zwischen Politik und Kirchenrecht. Zur Neuedition von Hinkmars Denkschrift über die Scheidungsangelegenheit König Lothars II', *Rheinische Vierteljahrsblätter* 60, pp. 296–302.

Filotas, B. 2005. *Pagan Survivals, Superstitions, and Popular Cultures in Early Medieval Pastoral Literature.* Toronto.

Firey, A. 2009. *A Contrite Heart: Prosecution and Redemption in the Carolingian Empire.* Leiden.

Flint, V. I. J. 1991. *The Rise of Magic in Early Medieval Europe.* Princeton, NJ.

Fouracre, P. 1995. 'Carolingian Justice: The Rhetoric of Improvement and Contexts of Abuse', *La Giustizia nell' alto medioevo (secoli V–VIII), 7–13 aprile 1994*, Settimane 42. Spoleto, vol. 2, pp. 771–803.

Frakes, R. M. 2011. *Compiling the 'Collatio legum Mosaicarum et Romanarum' in Late Antiquity.* Oxford.

Fransen, G. 1983. 'La lettre de Hincmar de Reims au sujet du marriage d'Étienne: une relecture', in R. Lievens, E. Van Mingroot and W. Verbeke (eds), *Pascua Mediaevalia: studies voor Prof. Dr. J. M. De Smet.* Leuven, pp. 133–46.

Fried, J. 1982. 'Der karolingische Herrschaftsverband im 9. Jh. zwischen "Kirche" und "Königshaus"', *Historische Zeitschrift* 235, pp. 1–43.

Fuhrmann, H. 2001. 'The Pseudo-Isidorian Forgeries', in D. Jasper and H. Fuhrmann (eds), *Papal Letters in the Early Middle Ages.* Washington, DC, pp. 135–95.

Gaillard, M. 1995. 'Un évêque et son temps, Advence de Metz (858–875)', in H.-W. Herrman and R. Schneider (eds), *Lotharingia – eine europäische Kernlandschaft um das Jahr 1000.* Saarbrücken, pp. 89–119.

Gaillard, M. 2006. *D'une réforme à l'autre (816–934): les communautés religieuses en Lorraine à l'époque carolingienne.* Paris.

Gaillard, M. 2011. 'Du pouvoir des femmes en *Francia Media*: épouses et filles des souverains (ca. 850–ca. 950)', in M. Gaillard, M. Margue, A. Dierkens and H. Pettiau (eds), *De la mer du Nord à la Méditerranée: Francia Media, une région au cœur de l'Europe (c. 840–c.1050): actes du colloque international (Metz, Luxembourg, Trèves, 8–11 février 2006).* Luxembourg, pp. 301–14.

Ganshof, F.-L. 1965. 'La preuve dans le droit franc', *La preuve. 2e partie: Moyen Âge et temps modernes.* Brussels, pp. 71–98.

Ganshof, F.-L. 1968. *Frankish Institutions under Charlemagne.* Providence, RI.

Garrison, M. 2010. 'An Aspect of Alcuin: "Tuus Albinus" – Peevish Egotist? Or Parrhesiast?', in R. Corradini, M. Gillis, R. McKitterick and I. van Renswoude (eds), *Ego Trouble: Authors and Their Identities in the Early Middle Ages.* Vienna, pp. 137–52.

Garver, V. L. 2012. 'Childbearing and Infancy in the Carolingian World', *Journal of the History of Sexuality* 21, pp. 208–44.

Gaudemet, J. 1980. 'Indissolubilité et consommation du mariage: l'apport d'Hincmar de Reims', *Revue de droit canonique* 30, pp. 28–40.

Gaudemet, J. 1988. '"Separare": équivoque des mots et faiblesse du droit (IIe–XIIIe siècles)', *Revue de droit canonique* 38, pp. 8–25.

Georgi, W. 1995. 'Erzbischof Gunthar von Köln und die Konflikte um das Reich König Lothars II. Überlegungen zum politischen und rechtlichen Konflikt der Absetzung durch Papst Nikolaus I. im Jahre 863', *Jahrbuch des Kölnischen Geschichtsvereins* 66, pp. 1–33.

Gillis, M. B. 2015. 'Heresy in the Flesh: Gottschalk of Orbais and the Predestination Controversy in the Archdiocese of Rheims', in Stone and West 2015, pp. 247–67.

Goldberg, E. J. 2006. *Struggle for Empire: Kingship and Conflict under Louis the German, 817–876.* Ithaca, NY.

Graf, F. 2002. 'Augustine and Magic', in J. N. Bremmer and J. R. Veenstra (eds), *The Metamorphosis of Magic from Late Antiquity to the Early Modern Period.* Leuven, pp. 87–103.

Haines, D. I. 2010. *Sunday Observance and the Sunday Letter in Anglo-Saxon England.* Cambridge.

Hamilton, S. 2001. *The Practice of Penance, 900–1050.* Woodbridge, Suffolk.

Hammer, C. I. 1995. 'The Handmaid's Tale: Morganatic Relationships in Early-Mediaeval Bavaria', *Continuity and Change* 10, pp. 345–68.

Hartmann, M. 2007. 'Concubina vel regina? Zu einigen Ehefrauen und Konkubinen der karolingischen Könige', *Deutsches Archiv für Erforschung des Mittelalters* 63, pp. 545–67.

Heidecker, K. 2010. *The Divorce of Lothar II: Christian Marriage and Political Power in the Carolingian World.* Ithaca, NY.

Heidecker, K. forthcoming. 'Gathering and Recycling Authoritative Texts: The Importance of Marginalia in Hincmar of Reims' Treatise about King Lothar's Divorce', in M. Mostert (ed.), *Organizing the Written Word: Proceedings of the First Utrecht Symposium on Medieval Literacy, Utrecht 5–7 June 1997.* Turnhout.

Herlihy, D. 1990. *Opera muliebria: Women and Work in Medieval Europe.* New York.

Herrick, S.K. 2012. 'Le pouvoir du passe apostolique', in E. Bozóky (ed.), *Hagiographie, idéologie et politique au Moyen Âge en Occident: actes du colloque international du Centre d'études supérieures de civilisation médiévale de Poitiers, 11–14 septembre 2008.* Turnhout, pp. 129–38.

Hincmarus archiepiscopus Remensis, Repertorium 'Geschichtsquellen des deutschen Mittelalters' [2012], www.geschichtsquellen.de/repPers_118551280.html (accessed 21August 2015) [list of Hincmar's works and literature on him].

Hoffmann, H. and Pokorny, R. 2011. 'Ratramnus von Corbie, *De propinquorum coniugiis*: ein zweites Blatt des fragmentarischen Briefgutachtens', *Deutsches Archiv für Erforschung des Mittelalters* 67, pp. 1–18.

Hunter, D. G. 2007. *Marriage, Celibacy, and Heresy in Ancient Christianity: The Jovinianist Controversy.* Oxford.

Hunter, D. G. 2009. 'The Significance of Ambrosiaster', *Journal of Early Christian Studies* 17, pp. 1–26.

Isaïa, M.-C. 2015. 'The Bishop and the Law, According to Hincmar's *Life of Saint Remigius*', in Stone and West 2015, pp. 170–89.

James, E. 2004. 'Childhood and Youth in the Early Middle Ages', in P. J. P. Goldberg and F. Riddy (eds), *Youth in the Middle Ages.* Woodbridge, Suffolk, pp. 11–23.

Jolly, K. L., Raudvere, C. and Peters, E. (eds). 2002. *Witchcraft and Magic in Europe: The Middle Ages.* London.

Jordan, M. D. 1997. *The Invention of Sodomy in Christian Theology.* Chicago.

Joye, S. 2015. 'Family Order and Kingship According to Hincmar', in Stone and West 2015, pp. 190–210.

Karras, R. M. 2006. 'The History of Marriage and the Myth of Friedelehe', *Early Medieval Europe* 14, pp. 119–151.

Karras, R. M. 2012. *Unmarriages: Women, Men, and Sexual Unions in the Middle Ages.* Philadelphia, PA.

Karras, R. M. 2015. 'The Christianization of Medieval Marriage', in D. C. Mengel and L. Wolverton (eds), *Christianity and Culture in the Middle Ages: Essays to Honor John Van Engen.* Notre Dame, IN, pp. 3–24.

Keefe, S. A. 2002. *Water and the Word: Baptism and the Education of the Clergy in the Carolingian Empire.* Notre Dame, IN.

Kéry, L. 1999. *Canonical Collections of the Early Middle Ages (ca. 400–1140): A Bibliographical Guide to the Manuscripts and Literature.* Washington, DC.

Kieckhefer, R. 1989. *Magic in the Middle Ages.* Cambridge.

Kieckhefer, R. 1994. 'The Specific Rationality of Medieval Magic', *American Historical Review* 99, pp. 813–36.

Knox, R. 1991. 'Accusing Higher Up', *Zeitschrift der Savigny-Stiftung für Rechtsgeschichte, Kanonistische Abteilung* 77, pp. 1–31.

Konecny, S. 1976. *Die Frauen des karolingischen Königshauses: Die politische Bedeutung der Ehe und die Stellung der Frau in der fränkischen Herrscherfamilie vom 7. bis zum 10. Jahrhundert.* Vienna.

Kottje, R. 1983. 'Kirchliches Recht und päpstlicher Autoritätsanspruch: zu den Auseinandersetzungen über die Ehe Lothars II', in H. Mordek (ed.), *Aus Kirche und Reich: Studien zu Theologie, Politik und Recht im Mittelalter. Festschrift für Friedrich Kempf zu seinem fünfundsiebzigsten Geburtstag und fünfzigjährigen Doktorjubiläum.* Sigmaringen, pp. 97–103.

Lazzari, T. 2007. 'La rappresentazione dei legami di parentela e il ruolo delle donne nell'alta aristocrazia del Regno italico (secc. IX–X): l'esempio di Berta di Toscana', in C. La Rocca (ed.), *Agire da donna: modelli e pratiche di rapprensentazione (secoli VI–X): atti del convegno (Padova, 18–19 febbraio 2005).* Turnhout, 129–49.

Le Jan, R. 1995. *Famille et pouvoir dans le monde franc (VIIe–Xe siècle): essai d'anthropologie sociale.* Paris.

Lewis, C. and Short, C., *A Latin Dictionary* (Oxford, 1879).

Leyser, C. 1999. 'Masculinity in Flux: Nocturnal Emission and the Limits of Celibacy in the Early Middle Ages', in D. M. Hadley (ed.), *Masculinity in Medieval Europe.* London, pp. 103–20.

MacLean, S. 2003a. *Kingship and Politics in the Late Ninth Century: Charles the Fat and the End of the Carolingian Empire.* Cambridge.

MacLean, S. 2003b. 'Queenship, Nunneries and Royal Widowhood in Carolingian Europe', *Past and Present* 178, pp. 3–38.

MacLean, S. 2013. 'Shadow Kingdom: Lotharingia and the Frankish World, c.850–c.1050', *History Compass* 11, pp. 443–57.

Markus, R. A. 1997. *Gregory the Great and His World.* Cambridge.

Markus, R. A. and Sotinel, C. 2007. 'Epilogue', in C. M. Chazelle and C. Cubitt (eds), *The Crisis of the Oikoumene: The Three Chapters and the Failed Quest for Unity in the Sixth-Century Mediterranean.* Turnhout, pp. 265–78.

Mathisen, R. W. (ed.) 2001. *Law, Society, and Authority in Late Antiquity.* Oxford.

McCarthy, M. J. 2015. 'Hincmar's Influence during Louis the Stammerer's Reign', in Stone and West 2015, pp. 110–28.

McKeon, P. R. 1974. 'Archbishop Ebbo of Reims (816–835): A Study in the Carolingian Empire and Church', *Church History* 43, pp. 437–47.

McKeon, P. R. 1978. *Hincmar of Laon and Carolingian Politics.* Urbana, IL.

McKitterick, R. 1997. 'Perceptions of Justice in Western Europe in the Ninth and Tenth Centuries', *La Giustizia nell' alto medioevo (secoli IX–XI), 11–17 aprile 1996*, Settimane 44. Spoleto, vol. 2, pp. 1075–104.

McKitterick, R. 2008. *Charlemagne: The Formation of a European Identity.* Cambridge.

Meens, R. 1998. 'Politics, Mirrors of Princes and the Bible: Sins, Kings and the Well-Being of the Realm', *Early Medieval Europe* 7, pp. 345–57.

Meens, R. 2007. 'Sanctuary, Penance, and Dispute Settlement under Charlemagne: The Conflict between Alcuin and Theodulf of Orléans over a Sinful Cleric', *Speculum* 82, pp. 277–300.

Meens, R. 2014. *Penance in Medieval Europe, 600–1200.* Cambridge.

Merdinger, J. E. 1997. *Rome and the African Church in the Time of Augustine.* New Haven, CT.

Mistry, Z. 2015. *Abortion in the Early Middle Ages, c.500–900.* York.

Moore, M. E. 2011. *A Sacred Kingdom: Bishops and the Rise of Frankish Kingship, 300–850.* Washington, DC.

Mordek, H. 1997. 'Ein exemplarischer Rechtsstreit: Hinkmar von Reims und das Landgut Neuilly-Saint-Front', *Zeitschrift der Savigny-Stiftung für Rechtsgeschichte, Kanonistische Abteilung* 83, pp. 86–112.

Morelle, L. 2004. 'La main du roi et le nom de Dieu: la validation de l'acte royal selon Hincmar, d'après un passage de son "De Divortio"', in J. Hoareau-Dodinau and P. Texier (eds), *Foi chrétienne et églises dans la société politique de l'occident du haut Moyen Âge: (IV*[e]*–XII*[e] *siècle).* Limoges, pp. 287–318.

Murray, J. 1996. 'Twice Marginal and Twice Invisble: Lesbians in the Middle Ages', in V. L. Bullough and J. A. Brundage (eds), *Handbook of Medieval Sexuality.* New York, pp. 191–222.

Nelson, J. L. 1977. 'Kingship, Law and Liturgy in the Political Thought of Hincmar of Rheims', *English Historical Review* 92, pp. 241–79.

Nelson, J. L. 1985 'Public "Histories" and Private History in the Work of Nithard', *Speculum* 60, pp. 251–93.

Nelson, J. L. 1986. 'Dispute Settlement in Carolingian West Francia', in Davies and Fouracre 1986, pp. 45–64.

Nelson, J. L. 1992. *Charles the Bald.* London.

Nelson, J. L. 1994. 'Kingship and Empire in the Carolingian World', in R. McKitterick (ed.), *Carolingian Culture: Emulation and Innovation.* Cambridge, pp. 52–87.

Nelson, J. L. 1995. 'The Wary Widow', in W. Davies and P. Fouracre (eds), *Property and Power in the Early Middle Ages.* Cambridge, pp. 82–113.

Nelson, J. L. 1998. 'Making a Difference in Eighth-Century Politics: The Daughters of Desiderius', in A. C. Murray (ed.), *After Rome's Fall: Narrators and Sources of Early Medieval History. Essays Presented to Walter Goffart.* Toronto, pp. 171–90.

Nelson, J. L. 2012. '"Hunnish Scenes"/Frankish Scenes: A Case of History That Stands Still?', in J. L. Nelson, S. Reynolds and S. M. Johns (eds), *Gender and Historiography: Studies in the Earlier Middle Ages in Honour of Pauline Stafford.* London, pp. 175–90.

Nelson, J. L. 2015. 'Hincmar's Life in His Historical Writings', in Stone and West 2015, pp. 44–59.

Newhauser, R. 1993. *The Treatise on Vices and Virtues in Latin and the Vernacular.* Turnhout.

Noble, T. F. X. 2009. *Images, Iconoclasm, and the Carolingians.* Philadelphia, PA.

Noonan, J. T. 1986. *Contraception: A History of Its Treatment by the Catholic Theologians and Canonists.* Enlarged ed. Cambridge, MA.

Odegaard, C. E. 1945. 'The Concept of Royal Power in Carolingian Oaths of Fidelity', *Speculum* 20, pp. 279–89.

Olsen, G. W. 2011. *Of Sodomites, Effeminates, Hermaphrodites, and Androgynes: Sodomy in the Age of Peter Damian.* Toronto.

Palmer, J. 2007. 'Defining Paganism in the Carolingian World', *Early Medieval Europe* 15, pp. 402–25.

Palmer, J. T. 2014. *The Apocalypse in the Early Middle Ages.* Cambridge.

Pangerl, D. C. 2011. *Die Metropolitanverfassung des karolingischen Frankenreiches.* Hanover.

Patzold, S. 2008. *Episcopus: Wissen über Bischöfe im Frankenreich des späten 8. bis frühen 10. Jahrhunderts.* Ostfildern.

Patzold, S. 2010. 'Verhandeln über die Ehe des Königs. Das Beispiel Lothars II.', in B. Stollberg-Rilinger and A. Krischer (eds), *Herstellung und Darstellung von Entscheidungen: Verfahren, Verwalten und Verhandeln in der Vormoderne.* Berlin, pp. 391–410.

Payer, P. J. 1984. *Sex and the Penitentials: The Development of a Sexual Code 550–1150.* Toronto.

Peters, E. 1990. 'Wounded Names: The Medieval Concept of Infamy', in E. B. King and S. J. Ridyard (eds), *Law in Mediaeval Life and Thought.* Sewanee, TN, pp. 43–89.

Pohl, W. and Wieser, V. (eds). 2009. *Der frühmittelalterliche Staat: europäische Perspektiven.* Vienna.

Reynolds, P. L. 1994. *Marriage in the Western Church: The Christianisation of Marriage during the Patristic and Early Medieval Periods.* Leiden.

Reynolds, S. 1984. *Kingdoms and Communities in Western Europe, 900–1300.* Oxford.

Riddle, J. M. 1992. *Contraception and Abortion from the Ancient World to the Renaissance.* Cambridge, MA.

Rider, C. 2006. *Magic and Impotence in the Middle Ages.* Oxford.

Sassier, Y. 1988. 'L'utilisation d'un concept romain aux temps carolingiens. La *res publica* aux IXe et Xe siècles', *Médiévales* 15, pp. 17–29.

Sassier, Y. 2005. '*Auctoritas pontificum* et *potestas regia*: faut-il tenir pour négligeable l'influence de la doctrine gélasienne aux temps carolingiens?', in C. Carozzi and H. Taviani-Carozzi (eds), *Le pouvoir au Moyen Âge: idéologies, pratiques, représentations.* Aix-en-Provence, pp. 213–36.

Schmid, K. 1968. 'Ein karolingischer Königseintrag im Gedenkbuch von Remiremont', *Frühmittelalterliche Studien* 2, pp. 96–134.

Schmitz, G. 1979. 'Concilium perfectum. Überlegungen zum Konzilsverständnis Hinkmars von Reims', *Zeitschrift der Savigny-Stiftung für Rechtsgeschichte, Kanonistische Abteilung* 65, pp. 27–54.

Scholz, S. 2006. *Politik – Selbstverständnis – Selbstdarstellung. Die Päpste in karolingischer und ottonischer Zeit.* Stuttgart.

Schröder, I. 2014. 'Was nicht in den Konzilsakten steht', *Deutsches Archiv für Erforschung des Mittelalters* 70, pp. 163–181.

Schrörs, H. 1884. *Hinkmar, Erzbischof von Reims: sein Leben und seine Schriften.* Freiburg im Breisgau.

Screen, E. 2015. 'An Unfortunate Necessity? Hincmar and Lothar I', in Stone and West, 2015, pp. 76–92.

Sennis, A. 2013. 'Destroying Documents in the Early Middle Ages', in J. Jarrett and A. S. McKinley (eds), *Problems and Possibilities of Early Medieval Charters.* Turnhout, pp. 151–69.

Sessa, K. 2011. 'Ursa's Return: Captivity, Remarriage, and the Domestic Authority of Roman Bishops in Fifth-Century Italy', *Journal of Early Christian Studies* 19, pp. 401–32.

Sessa, K. 2012. *The Formation of Papal Authority in Late Antique Italy: Roman Bishops and the Domestic Sphere.* Cambridge.

Shanzer, D. 2002. 'History, Romance, Love and Sex in Gregory of Tours' *Decem libri hist*oriarum', in K. Mitchell and I. Wood (eds), *The World of Gregory of Tours.* Leiden, pp. 395–418.

Sieben, H. J. 1984. *Die Konzilsidee des lateinischen Mittelalters (847–1378).* Paderborn.

Smith, J. M. H. 1998. 'Gender and Ideology in the Early Middle Ages', in R. N. Swanson (ed.), *Gender and Christian Religion. Papers Read at the 1996 Summer Meeting and the 1997 Winter Meeting of the Ecclesiastical History Society.* Woodbridge, Suffolk, pp. 51–73.

Smith, J. M. H. 2003. '"Emending Evil Ways and Praising God's Omnipotence": Einhard and the Uses of Roman Martyrs', in K. Mills and A. Grafton (eds), *Conversion in Late Antiquity and the Early Middle Ages: Seeing and Believing.* Rochester, NY, pp. 189–223.

Sot, M. 1993. *Un historien et son église au Xe siècle: Flodoard de Reims.* Paris.

Stafford, P. 1983. *Queens, Concubines and Dowagers: The King's Wife in the Early Middle Ages*. London.

Staubach, N. 1982. *Das Herrscherbild Karls des Kahlen: Formen und Funktionen monarchischer Repräsentation im früheren Mittelalter*. Münster.

Staubach, N. 1993. *Rex Christianus, Hofkultur und Herrschaftspropaganda im Reich des Karls des Kahlen. Teil II: Die Grundlegung der 'Religion Royale'*. Cologne.

Stone, R. 2007a. '"Bound from Either Side": The Limits of Power in Carolingian Marriage Disputes, 840–870', *Gender and History* 19, pp. 467–82.

Stone, R. 2007b. 'Kings Are Different: Carolingian Mirrors for Princes and Lay Morality', in F. Lachaud and L. Scordia (eds), *Le prince au miroir de la littérature politique de l'Antiquité aux Lumières*. Mont-Saint-Aignan, pp. 69–86.

Stone, R. 2009. 'The Invention of a Theology of Abduction: Hincmar of Rheims on *Raptus*', *Journal of Ecclesiastical History* 60, pp. 433–48.

Stone, R. 2012. *Morality and Masculinity in the Carolingian Empire*. Cambridge.

Stone, R. 2015. 'Introduction: Hincmar's World', in Stone and West 2015, pp. 1–43.

Stone, R. and West, C. (eds). 2015. *Hincmar of Rheims: Life and Work*. Manchester.

Story, J. (ed.). 2005. *Charlemagne: Empire and Society*. Manchester.

Stratmann, M. 1991. *Hinkmar von Reims als Verwalter von Bistum und Kirchenprovinz*. Sigmaringen.

Toubert, P. 1977. 'La théorie du mariage chez les moralistes carolingiens', in *Il Matrimonio nella società altomedievale, 22–28 aprile 1976*, Settimane 24. Spoleto, vol. 1, pp. 233–85.

Toubert, P. 1996. 'The Carolingian Moment (Eighth–Tenth Century)', in A. Burguière, C. Klapisch-Zuber, M. Segalen and F. Zonabend (eds), *A History of the Family*. Vol.1: *Distant Worlds, Ancient Worlds*. Cambridge, pp. 379–406.

Ubl, K. 2008. *Inzestverbot und Gesetzgebung: die Konstruktion eines Verbrechens (300–1100)*. Berlin.

Ubl, K. 2014. 'Bischöfe und Laien auf dem Konzil von Tribur 895. Zur Politisierung der Ehe in der Karolingerzeit', *Deutsches Archiv für Erforschung des Mittelalters* 70, pp. 143–61.

Uhalde, K. 2007. *Expectations of Justice in the Age of Augustine*. Philadelphia, PA.

Vodola, E. 1986. *Excommunication in the Middle Ages*. Berkeley, CA.

Ward, E. 1990. 'Agobard of Lyons and Paschasius Radbertus as Critics of the Empress Judith', in W. J. Sheils and D. Wood (eds), *Women in the Church. Papers Read at the 1989 Summer Meeting and the 1990 Winter Meeting of the Ecclesiastical History Society*. Oxford, pp. 15–25.

Webb, J. R. 2013. 'Notger et Hériger face au passé lointain du diocèse de Tongres-Maastricht-Liège', in A. Wilkin and J.-L. Kupper (eds), *Évêque et prince: Notger et la Basse-Lotharingie aux alentours de l'an Mil*. Liège, pp. 507–24.

West, C. 2015a. 'Hincmar's Parish Priests', in Stone and West 2015, pp. 228–46.

West, C. 2015b. 'Lordship in Ninth-Century Francia: The Case of Bishop Hincmar of Laon and His Followers', *Past and Present* 226, pp. 3–40.

Wood, I. 1986. 'Disputes in Late Fifth- and Sixth-Century Gaul: Some Problems', in Davies and Fouracre 1986, pp. 7–22.

Wood, S. 2006. *The Proprietary Church in the Medieval West.* Oxford.
Wortley, J. 1980. 'The Pseudo-Amphilochian *Vita Basilii*: An Apocryphal Life of Saint Basil the Great', *Florilegium* 2, pp. 217–39.
Zechiel-Eckes, K. 2001. 'Ein Blick in Pseudoisidors Werkstatt: Studien zum Entstehungsprozess der falschen Dekretalen. Mit einem exemplarischen editorischen Anhang (Pseudo-Julius an die orientalischen Bischöfe, JK † 196)', *Francia* 28, pp. 37–90.

INDEX

Notes: 'n.' after a page reference indicates the number of the note on that page. A comprehensive index of Hincmar's sources is given in Böhringer's edition, pp. 265–79